ROME
AND HER
EMPIRE

ROME
AND HER
EMPIRE

David Shotter

An imprint of **Pearson Education**

London · New York · Toronto · Sydney · Tokyo · Singapore · Hong Kong · Cape Town
· Madrid · Paris · Amsterdam · Munich · Milan ·

PEARSON EDUCATION LIMITED

Head Office:
Edinburgh Gate
Harlow CM20 2JE
Tel: +44 (0)1279 623623
Fax: +44 (0)1279 431059

London Office:
128 Long Acre
London WC2E 9AN
Tel: +44 (0)20 7447 2000
Fax: +44 (0)20 7447 2170
Website: www.history-minds.com

_____

First published in Great Britain in 2003

© Pearson Education Limited 2003

The rights of David Shotter to be identified as Author
of this Work has been asserted by him in accordance
with the Copyright, Designs and Patents Act 1988.

ISBN 0 582 32816 0

British Library Cataloguing in Publication Data
A CIP catalogue record for this book can be obtained from the British Library

Library of Congress Cataloging in Publication Data
A CIP catalog record for this book can be obtained from the Library of Congress

10 9 8 7 6 5 4 3 2 1

Typeset by Fakenham Photosetting Limited, Fakenham, Norfolk

Printed and bound by Biddles Ltd, UK

The Publishers' policy is to use paper manufactured from sustainable forests.

Contents

Preface

Interest in the Roman world has grown greatly in recent decades: now access is not restricted to the traditional route of a classical education but is available through a host of popularising books (both fact and fiction), through films and through programmes on radio and television, such as *Chronicle, Time Team*, as well as many on the satellite channels. In turn, such interest may be translated into more formal contact – membership of historical and archaeological societies, tourism and, of course, into extra-mural classes and access to university courses. At a time, therefore, when 'officialdom' appears to view the classical world increasingly as a minority interest, the range of new routes has created among a far wider public than before a great stimulus to learn.

This 'new public' has broader interests, also: no longer is it reasonable to regard 'proper' Roman history as coming to a close in the second century AD, because that is where the 'good' literary sources fail us. The fall, as well as the rise, of great empires excites interest and prompts questions among students of Rome who are all too well aware of the tensions in modern societies. After all, in their own way, the Romans did, in their empire, make 'multi-culturalism' work; there was a degree of religious tolerance; there was some communality of laws and law-making – and there was a 'single currency'.

The present book is, therefore, intended as an introductory taste of the history of Rome and her empire for readers who are approaching the subject along a variety of routes and from a variety of standpoints.

The history of Rome spanned a very long period – more than twelve centuries – which saw changes which were many in number and great in their consequences. The site itself progressed from a collection of villages to a great imperial city; the government changed from monarchy to oligarchy and, at the end of the first century BC, back to a monarchy which became increasingly autocratic. At the same time, Rome moved from the small city-state which had to fight for its continued existence in Italy to being the 'mistress of Italy' and then to being the hub of an empire which spread throughout the Mediterranean, as well as much of Europe and Asia Minor.

This book proceeds, within a broadly chronological framework, to examine the story of these progressions. What were the early village settlements like? Under what influences did Rome become a unified city? Why did she give up her kings in favour of a more broadly based government (the 'Republic'), and why, after nearly half a millennium, did that government revert to monarchy? Why did Rome's territorial interests grow, especially when it is clear that many in Rome did not want this to happen? What were the effects – social, political, cultural and economic – of this expansion, both on Rome herself and on the territories which became 'the Roman Empire'? In days when communication was much slower than it is today, how was the empire's coherence maintained and developed? Finally, what factors brought about the ultimate 'decline', and could they have been avoided?

It is a daunting, as well as an exciting, task to try to provide such a history: exciting both because of the magnitude of Rome's achievement, which was in many ways as stimulating in its decline as in its growth, and because of the vitality which, thanks to classical writers, attaches to so many of the leading figures of all periods; daunting not only for its size and scope but also because it is constantly difficult to do justice to the giant figures of Rome's past who seem so much a part of the ruins which survive in Rome itself, in Italy and in so many other countries which were once provinces of the Roman Empire.

Each chapter will confine itself to a major episode or topic; in the hope that it will prove to be more 'user friendly', lists containing suggestions for further reading, and which are not intended to be exhaustive, will be provided at the end of each chapter. These will consist largely of books rather than periodical literature, access to which is available through the bibliographies of the more special-ised studies which are cited in the reading lists.

I have enjoyed and benefited from the help of many people in the preparation of this history: not least, Heather McCallum and her colleagues at Pearson Education for their advice and encourage-ment at vital times – and for their forbearance. I owe a great debt of gratitude, too, to my wife, Anne, for the sheer hard work that she has put in, 'without any complaint', to produce so lengthy a manuscript and for taking most of the photographs.

Thanks go, too, to those who have facilitated the production of the illustrative material used in the book: authors, publishers and Museum-institutions are acknowledged specifically where appropriate.

David Shotter
September 2002

Acknowledgements

We are grateful to the following for permission to reproduce copyright material:

Figure 1.2 redrawn from *The Etruscan Cities and Rome* by H. H. Scullard, published by Thames and Hudson Ltd, London, reprinted with permission (Scullard, H. H. 1967); Figure 2.1 redrawn from *A History of the Roman World from 753–146 B.C., 4th Edition*, Routledge (Scullard, H. H. 1980); Chapter 2, Appendix 1, and Figure 6.1 from *The Fall of the Roman Republic*, Lancaster Pamphlets, Routledge (Shotter, D. 1994); Figures 5.1, 8.1 and 8.2 redrawn from *Etruscan and Early Roman Architecture*, published and reprinted with permission of Yale University Press, © the Estate of Axell Boethius and J. B. Ward-Perkins (Boethius, A. and Ward-Perkins, J. B. 1970); Figure 5.2 from *Swan's Hellenic Cruise Guide Book*, © Swan Hellenic Cruises 2002, reprinted with permission; Chapter 5, Appendix 2, from *Tiberius Caesar*, Lancaster Pamphlets, Routledge (Shotter, D. 1992).

Plates 5.8, 6.1, 8.13 and 10.4 reproduced with permission of The British Museum, © Copyright The British Museum; Plate 5.12 reproduced with permission of Scala Group SpA; Plate 6.2 reproduced with permission of Colchester Museums.

In some instances we have been unable to trace the owners of copyright material, and we would appreciate any information that would enable us to do so.

Chapter 1

Myth, monarchy and the Republic

Myth and Monarchy

'In its earliest years, Rome was ruled by kings': with these words the Roman historian, Cornelius Tacitus, briefly summarised the beginnings of Rome's history in the opening sentence of his *Annals*. Roman tradition, as enunciated by Varro in the mid-first century BC, dated Rome's foundation to 753 BC and remembered seven kings of Rome between that date and the establishment of the Republic in 509. Archaeological evidence does indeed suggest that such a foundation date coincides approximately with significant developments in the history of the site, although it also indicates that settlement reached back beyond the tenth century. Without doubt, Rome's position on the hills adjacent to the River Tiber – defensible, close to the sea and to deposits of estuarine salt, and with access to the interior – serves to explain its long-standing attraction to so many people.

However, even these introductory sentences demonstrate the nature and magnitude of just some of the problems which face the historian of early Rome and Italy. Classical writers survive who tackled the period – for example, Livy, Dionysius of Halicarnassus, Polybius and Appian – though none of them was close in time to the events which they were attempting to describe. Also, some Italian events were of intrinsic interest to major historians of Greece: thus, Thucydides has left an account of the disastrous Athenian expedition to Syracuse during the Peloponnesian War in the late fifth century. Livy was, however, perfectly honest about the problems inherent in trying to compose an account of early Rome (VI.1): he deals, he says, in his first five books with matters which were obscure because they were deep in the past and because the conditions for contemporary recording did not exist. Further, the traumatic Gallic invasion of Rome in 390 BC destroyed such records as did exist, and these presumably had to be 'reconstructed' in the aftermath. Nonetheless, historians have noted, even in Livy's early books, what they take to be citations from early records. Livy further 'excuses' himself (*Praef.* to Book I): the Romans had achieved so much that they were entitled to some indulgence in glorifying their distant past; nor should we lose sight of the fact that Livy's literary patron, the emperor Augustus, had a vested interest in linking his regime with the heroic deeds of earlier years and in 'proving' an ancient origin for the ancestral custom (*mos maiorum*) which he took as his mission to encourage.

The site of Rome (see Fig. 1.1) lay in that part of Italy known as Latium; here, too, prehistoric settlement went back beyond the tenth century, but expanded notably in scope and wealth in the eighth and seventh centuries, distinguished by very rich tombs and by impressive goods both locally crafted and imported from other parts of Italy and the Mediterranean. It is probably significant that similar advances can be found in other western areas of Italy to both the north and the south of the site of Rome. The implication is clearly the development of wealthy aristocracies, and it is hard to avoid connecting this phenomenon with the arrival of Greeks in southern Italy driven from their home states by a combination of economic hardship and political intolerance; these enterprising people will have required goods and raw materials from the north and will have exchanged them for their

Figure 1.1 Map of Italy, showing principal early sites and peoples. Source: After M. Hadas, A History of Rome (London: G. Bell & Sons Ltd, 1958), p. 21.

own products. The wealthy aristocracies of Latium (and elsewhere) will then have originated with those of their number who were themselves sufficiently enterprising to grasp such opportunities. This period of the eighth to seventh centuries also saw the emergence of defended towns, which again points to wealth accumulation, status and the growth of competition for these.

The pattern of development in Etruria was not dissimilar and was presumably responding to similar stimuli. Although the area to the north of Rome contained people of different origins and cultures (as reflected in tribal names), two cultural names predominate in prehistory – Villanovans (who may have come originally from central Europe) and Etruscans, although the latter name is most widely used. In these areas we see a chronological pattern of development akin to that of Latium, although with different artefactual characteristics. Here, too, defended, 'town-like', centres began to appear in the seventh century, presumably with aristocratic rulers.

The origin of the Etruscans has over the years been a matter of considerable dispute: the written form of their language derives from the same Greek as that used by the colonists of the south, although the nature of the language, unlike Greek, is not Indo-European. This has appeared to lend support to the contention of the Greek historian, Herodotus, that the Etruscans may have originated in Asia Minor; yet, despite the superficial attractiveness of such an idea, archaeological evidence has produced no support for the notion of significant immigration into northern Italy at the relevant time.

However that may be, it does seem that culturally Etruscan influence was spreading in Italy in the sixth century, so that it manifests itself all over the peninsula as far south as Campania – that is, up to the Greek settlements of the south. We should not, however, view the Etruscans as constituting a homogeneous political grouping: they were linked by religion and cultural affinity alone. In their centres ('city-states'), the warlords maintained a fierce independence of one another, which undoubtedly resulted in bitter and frequent strife between neighbours – of the kind that was later evident, for example, between the neighbouring cities of Rome and Veii.

Immigration into the south of Italy by Greeks began in the eighth century, extending from the islands on to the mainland. Some of these city-states, which generally maintained an independence of each other, were founded from already-existing settlements in Italy, while others continued to be founded from city-states in Greece itself. Because of the circumstances which drove such 'colonists' from their homelands, relations between mother-city and colony were poor, often to the point of non-existence.

These Greek city-states in southern Italy and Sicily made up an environment dominated by manufacturing and trade, and evidence of their search for raw materials is ample throughout Italy. Given the importance to them of commerce, the Greek settlements were located principally in the coastal lowlands, where land quality was high – a factor which brought them into conflict with indigenous tribes of the interior, such as the Samnites.

Archaeological evidence suggests that relations between Greeks and Etruscans were often good, leading to the hypothesis of shared participation in some projects. Rectilinear town planning, for example, originated among Greeks in Asia Minor, probably deriving from mathematical principles exemplified in the work of Hippodamus of Miletus. In the sixth century, it made its appearance on an Etruscan site – Marzabotto (near Bologna), prompting the suggestion of involvement by Greek planners, perhaps from southern Italy where land conditions favoured rectilinear town planning, which was said to have been an object of envy among 'northerners'. Similarly, it has been suggested that Greek and Etruscan artists may have worked together on the painted tombs of Tarquinia. Such, then, was the vibrant, cosmopolitan, environment of Italy in which Rome came into being as an urban entity.

An attempt to bring clarity to the early history of Rome itself finds us implicated in a net of myths, legends and pseudo-history, which is occasionally penetrated by the evidence of archaeology and possibly-genuine records. We are faced immediately by an apparent inconsistency: two foundation episodes for Rome were known – that of the Trojan hero, Aeneas, celebrated most fully in the Augustan epic poem, Virgil's *Aeneid*, and that of Romulus and Remus, which figures in the works of several historians.

The story of Aeneas bridges the eastern and western Mediterranean and, by bringing Rome into the 'epic cycle', gives her a place in Greek history and the development of classical civilisation. The Greeks were much interested in Rome; early writers and travellers in the Greek city-states of Italy, especially Cumae, were certainly responsible for the passage of information to the great 'logographers' of Asia Minor of the early fifth century, such as Hecataeus and Hellanikos. In the Greek versions, there is an attempt to connect the aftermath of the Trojan War with the founding of Rome, usually by Trojans (Aeneas, Romé, Romos). Hellanikos certainly said that Aeneas was responsible for the foundation, and named his new site after Romé, one of the Trojan women in his party – that is, in *c.* 1180 BC. Besides the Greek source, this version reappears on Etruscan pottery of the sixth century, suggesting that Aeneas was viewed as a popular founding figure, especially in south Etruria. Another tradition, which ascribed the foundation to an eponymous hero (Romulus), maintained that it took place two generations (that is, approximately seventy years) after Aeneas.

The problem with this was, of course, that a date of around 1100 BC was far too early for Roman writers and tradition; for quite independent reasons, the opening of the consular lists, the dedication of the temple of Jupiter on the Capitoline Hill, the expulsion of the kings and the birth of the Republic had to occur in or around 509 BC. From that point, the traditional line of kings could not possibly stretch back to anywhere near 1100 BC. Roman calculations assumed a generation (approximately thirty-five years) for each king, with a little less for Tarquinius Superbus because he was expelled; various calculations produced dates between 750 and 730, until the encyclopaedic Varro, in the first century BC, came up with his 'refined' date of 21 April 753 BC.

Aeneas was thus left seriously adrift: an ingenious resolution was produced by Livy's Greek contemporary, Dionysius of Halicarnassus, in the form of two foundations. Aeneas left Rome, for the site to be refounded several generations later. For those who were uncomfortable with two foundations and with Aeneas' desertion of the city which he had founded, it was enunciated that Aeneas' son, Ascanius (Iulus), had inaugurated a line of kings to the south at Alba Longa (in the Alban Hills). Iulus, of course, as the son of Aeneas and the grandson of the goddess, Venus, provided a very acceptable eponymous founder of the *gens Iulia*, the family of Julius Caesar and Augustus.

The direct link with the eastern Mediterranean which was upheld in the Aeneas story will have relieved the Romans of having to acknowledge a 'debt of gratitude' to the Etruscans for their transmission of aspects of Greek culture; the pleasure-loving and decadent characteristics of Etruscan leaders, as depicted in some tombs, will have made them poor intermediaries for such matters as close to the heart of the 'Augustan revolution' as Roman religion and the mission of *pius Aeneas* ('god-fearing and dutiful Aeneas'), as Virgil frequently refers to him. Across the years, Rome itself fostered the connection with the eastern Mediterranean; during a 'low' in the Second Punic War it was decided to consult the 'Sibylline Books' which, it was believed, a priestess (or *Sibyl*) could open and from them read a relevant prophecy. On this occasion, the outcome of the consultation was to bring the great Earth-Mother (Cybele) from Pergamum to Rome in an effort to revive Roman fortunes. It is worth noting that it was the emperor, Augustus, who decided that, after two hundred years, Cybele's cult statue, which had been housed in the temple of Victoria on the Palatine Hill, should be given its own 'home' in a new, dedicated, temple.

Thus, the Aeneas legend, which clearly had a perceived value, was refined, presumably in order to give it an air of authenticity for a superstitious people and a sense of consistency with other known stories: when Aeneas arrived in Italy, he was met by Latinus, king of the Aborigines; he married Latinus' daughter, Lavinia, and founded a city named Lavinium. Eventually, he succeeded Latinus, ruling a people now called the Latins. As we have seen, his son founded a new dynasty at Alba Longa, consisting (usually) of twelve kings. Eventually, strife broke out between two brothers, Amulius and Numitor; the latter's daughter was forced to become a Vestal Virgin. She bore twin sons to the god, Mars, namely Romulus and Remus; Amulius exposed them at birth, but they were saved by the she-wolf on the Palatine Hill. Later, Romulus and Remus wished to build a new city on the site of Rome, but could not agree as to whether the Palatine or Aventine Hill should be used. In a quarrel, Remus was killed, leaving Romulus to establish his new city on his preferred hill – the Palatine.

In substance, the story of Romulus and Remus is of Greek origin, although the discovery at Felsina (Bologna) of a gravestone showing a she-wolf suckling a single child indicates that there were Etruscan versions of what was presumably a local Romulus legend. There is no known representation of a she-wolf and twins until a statue was erected in 296 BC; further, an early coin of the mid-third century BC bears the motif, indicating that it had by that time become a symbol of Rome, as it was to remain into the fourth century AD, when it reappeared on the coinage of Constantine I.

What are we then to make of the regal period itself? As we have seen, Livy, in a reference to the material in the first book of his *History of Rome*, complains about a lack of contemporary records. While there may have been early documents concerning legal and religious matters, there presumably never was documentation of the historiographical kind that Livy desired. A study of literary material relating to early Rome does, however, suggest that gaps in the knowledge may have been made up from Greek mythology and early history. For example, as we have seen, aspects of the story of Romulus and Remus appear in Greek versions; Tarquinius Superbus' lopping off of the tallest poppy-heads in a cornfield (Livy I.54) recalls Herodotus' famous story about Periander, tyrant at Corinth, and his anti-aristocratic sentiments. The Athenians expelled their tyrants, Hippias and Hipparchus, in the same year in which the Romans allegedly removed Tarquinius Superbus; it is possible that, by favouring the people over the aristocracy, Superbus may have had a good deal in common with the Greek tyrants. The account of the three hundred members of the Fabii family in the valley of the Cremera during a war with Veii in 477 BC looks very like a Roman equivalent of the deeds of Leonidas and his three hundred Spartans at Thermopylae (Livy II.50). We may wonder, too, whether Coriolanus may be a Roman equivalent of the Athenian leader, Themistocles (Livy II.34ff). It is as if the Thucydidean notion of the repetition of history was taken literally by some.

A further problem arises in the likely source material of writers such as Livy: we discover in Plutarch's *Life of Cato* that Cato wrote a selective history of Rome for his son's education, both to present him with good moral precedents to follow and to provide him with some imposing ancestors whose conduct should be emulated (*mos maiorum*). How many aristocratic Romans had recorded – or even created – ancestral deeds for such a purpose? Families such as the Romilii, the Remmii, the Horatii and others might have had much to gain. Such stories could well have constituted a good resource for historians, such as Livy, who were writing of periods long before their own and for which no genuine historical sources existed.

Yet, there were some brighter aspects of Roman tradition: at various times, Roman writers refer to archaic documents which they had seen, and there survives an inscription from the Forum dating back to 500 BC. Polybius (III.22) refers to a treaty between Rome and Carthage which he had seen and which dated to

507 BC; as recently as 1966, a bilingual document in Etruscan and Punic was recovered from Pyrgi in a chronological context that would support the possibility of this. Other documents are mentioned by Livy: the priests certainly made regular records which resulted in important events being permanently marked on the calendars.

The conservatism of Romans was also a help: many customs – especially of a religious nature – remained virtually unchanged over many centuries; the core of Roman law, the Twelve Tables, was preserved – not only an authentic document, but one which must by implication provide a genuine commentary on social conditions at Rome in the mid-fifth century.

How, then, should we set about interpreting a regal period which, according to tradition, stretched from 753 to 509, with seven rulers featuring within that period? As we have seen, Romulus was associated closely with settlement on the Palatine Hill; clues to the nature of that settlement suggest that it was one principally of Latins whose chief resource was sheep farming. The huts in which they lived are presumably mirrored in the hut urns recovered

*Plate 1.2
Cinerary urn in the
form of a primitive
hut. Source:
Florence, Museo
Archiologico*

from the cemetery area in the Forum valley. The nature of these accords well with a post-hole structure which can still be seen on the Palatine and which was evidently preserved by the emperor, Augustus, as 'The House of Romulus' and which represented a kind of national monument. Such huts would have been timber framed, with walls composed of turves under a thatched roof – probably not very different from the simple dwellings of the rural poor (*tuguria*), which were still to be seen in Latium and elsewhere in the imperial period.

Tradition maintained that there was initially a divided kingship, which left Romulus with the Palatine, but associated the Sabine, Titus Tatius, with the Capitoline and Quirinal Hills (Livy I.11; Dionysius of Halicarnassus II.38–46; Propertius IV.4,9–12). Tacitus, too, maintains (in an oration 'composed' for the emperor, Claudius: *Annals* XI.24) that 'the Forum and the Capitol were added not by Romulus, but by Titus Tatius'; it is possible (and, in the context, appropriate) that Tacitus found such observations in a work known to have been written by Claudius. The references emphasise the strength of Titus Tatius, and the Augustan poet, Propertius, writes of the cliffs of the *Capitolium* trembling to the sound of the 'trumpeter from Cures' (that is, 'the Sabine'). The battle fought between Romulus and

*Plate 1.1 (opposite) Rome, Palatine Hill: the so-called 'House of Romulus';
post-holes cut into the natural rock provided a framework for a primitive hut of
the type shown in Plate 1.2.*

Titus Tatius was bitter and bloody, and Romulus is said to have dedicated a temple to Jupiter Stator, which is recorded as having been built, in fact, in 294. Romulus is said to have felt little distress when Titus Tatius was later murdered.

Although there are obvious confusions in the surviving accounts, there are clear archaeological and literary traces of Sabines in Rome. After Romulus and Titus Tatius, the first king was Numa Pompilius, who came from the Sabine town of Cures; like Titus Tatius, Numa was regarded as a great cult organiser and lived on the Quirinal Hill (see Fig. 1.2) in a house which, according to Plutarch, was still extant in his day (early second century AD). There is a certain amount of evidence suggesting that the Quirinal was a traditional Sabine quarter; Attus Clausus, who migrated to Rome in the late sixth century (505 BC, according to Livy), becoming known in Latin as Appius Claudius, was a Sabine; the house of the Claudii was on the Quirinal and, according to Suetonius, the biographer of the second century AD (*Life of Tiberius* 1,1), the family's tomb was at the foot of the Capitoline Hill.

It may be reasonable to suggest a growth of Sabine influence during the seventh century to a point where they were a force of some consequence among those inhabiting the site of Rome. Indeed, Numa is said to have been followed by two kings with Sabine connections: Tullus Hostilius was married to a Sabine, while Ancus Marcius was the grandson of Numa (Dionysius of Halicarnassus III.1,1; Livy I.32). All three, especially Numa, are credited with significant contributions to the development of Rome: Numa built the *Regia* (the official residence of the Chief Priest – *Pontifex Maximus*), organised Roman religion and perhaps instituted meetings of the *Comitium* (or Popular Assembly). Tullus Hostilius was traditionally regarded as the original builder of the senate house (*Curia Hostilia*), while Ancus Marcius, recorded (impossibly) as the founder of the *colonia* at Ostia on the Tiber estuary, may have presided over an extension of Roman influence to the sea (and the salt deposits). While, as we have

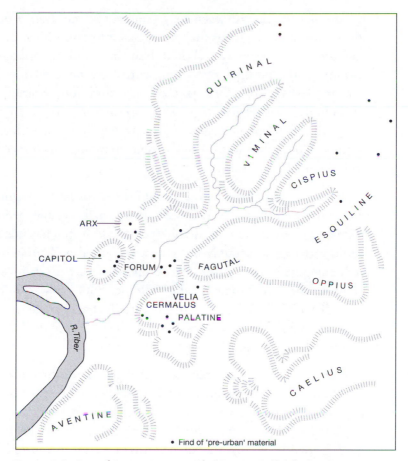

Figure 1.2 Site of Rome. Source: After H. H. Scullard, The Etruscan
Cities and Rome *(London: Thames & Hudson Ltd, 1967), p. 249, Fig. 27.*

seen, we must be alive to the possibility of the invention of
'family-founders/ancestors' of significance – in these cases, by the
Quinctilii (Pompilius), the Hostilii and the Marcii – it is generally recognised that a germ of historicity underlies these stories.

In this way, we may find Sabines among the earliest kings, and a
place for them among the early legends; legend and history are
thus brought together. However, what of the other kings and
their places in chronology and history? In a situation replete with
chronological problems, we should not feel tied inexorably to the

notion of seven kings: seven may represent a 'selection' from a longer line, or seven kings may have related to seven hills. In this connection, however, we should bear in mind the potential fragility of the ground: many appear to have believed that the Roman festival of *Septimontium* (a kind of 'beating of the bounds') was related to the Latin *septem* (or 'seven'). In fact, the word was properly *saeptimontium*, which simply describes its status as a 'boundary festival' and had no etymological connection with the number, *septem*.

Of the last three kings, two (Tarquinius Priscus and Tarquinius Superbus) were certainly Etruscan; as we shall see, the penultimate king, Servius Tullius, despite being held in the legends as a Latin, was almost certainly of Etruscan origin also. The Swedish archaeologist, Einar Gjerstad, has proposed four periods in what he terms the 'pre-Urban epoch' at Rome: 800–750, 750–700, 700–625, 625–575. The first two of these he has characterised by separate, mainly pastoral, settlements of the type described above, on the Palatine, Esquiline and Quirinal Hills.

The second two periods represent change: in the first place, a growth of the inhabited area, and cultural developments, too – a turn to cattle rather than an exclusive concern with sheep; hence, the Latin word for money (*pecunia*) derives from *pecus*, or 'herd'. As well as this, we see the appearance of Etruscan pottery and metalwork, Etruscan imitations of Greek wares and Greek wares themselves. This coincides with a metamorphosis from villages to city; for the people, this had an important implication – evidently, a move from exclusively agricultural occupations to the crafts and trades which are suggested by the artefactual evidence and which are consonant with the growth of cities. Such people required markets for their goods and sought them, without doubt, among southern Italian Greeks and Etruscan city-states; such relationships emphasise the developing significance of Rome's physical situation at the centre of Italy. Nor should we overlook another important 'Roman commodity' – salt, deposited at the Tiber mouth, which emphasises the significance

Plate 1.3 Cerveteri (Caere), Etruscan cemetery: circular tomb.

of the route from the coast, through Rome, into Etruria (which the Romans later called *via Salaria*, or 'salt road').

The 'arrival' of Etruscans in Rome is difficult both to date and to describe; Livy (I.34) has a story concerning Lucumo, the grandson of an exiled Corinthian, who had settled at Tarquinia and subsequently moved to Rome, taking the throne after the death of Ancus Marcius and changing his name to Lucius Tarquinius. While the possible dating of this will be discussed later, two points may be made: first, it is possible that the name, Tarquinius, has led to Tarquinia being claimed as the place of origin; if anywhere, the connections of the Tarquinius family with Caere (Cerveteri) appear stronger, for they took refuge there after their expulsion from Rome (Livy I.60); further, there is in the necropolis at Cerveteri a tomb containing inscriptions of a family named Tarcra.

Secondly, more significant evidence is supplied by paintings in the 'François' tomb at Vulci: these contain a fresco depicting Mastarna rescuing Aulus Vibenna and Caeles Vibenna from one Gaius Tarquinius Romanus. According to the tradition followed by Livy, Tarquinius Priscus was murdered by men in the service

Plate 1.4 Cerveteri (Caere), Etruscan cemetery: interior of 'house-tomb'.

Plate 1.5 Veii, Temple of Apollo: terracotta ridge-statue of Apollo. Source: Villa Giulia Museum, Rome.

of Ancus Marcius; the emperor Claudius, a noted historian of early Rome, said in a speech (*ILS* 212) that Etruscan records identified Mastarna with the 'traditionally Latin' king, Servius Tullius, who succeeded Tarquinius Priscus and who settled on the Caelian Hill in Rome, naming it after his leader, Caeles Vibenna. The most obvious problem with this is, of course, the persistent tradition in Rome that Servius Tullius was a Latin, not an Etruscan.

It is generally reckoned that the arrival of the Etruscans in Rome was a gradual process, which led to the intermingling of peoples at the site. The wide currency of certain gentile names among the Roman aristocracy – for example, Sempronii, Licinii, Larcii –

appears to support this. However, such a hypothesis does not preclude the possibility, given the evident sense of rivalry among Etruscan warlords, that the 'gradual process' was punctuated by violent episodes of the kind depicted in the François tomb. Indeed, as we shall see, the truth of the relationship between Tarquinius Superbus and Lars Porsenna is more likely to lie in rivalry than in alliance.

There does, however, appear to have been a dramatic change in the layout and coherence of Rome early in the sixth century (*c.* 600–575 BC); this bears signs of urbanisation, of centralised buildings and the engineering skills necessary to drain the previously marshy Forum valley and transform it into the 'central square' of a unified city. Religion probably underwent change, too, with the introduction of monumental temples of the kind recognised at a similar period at Veii; with this change probably also came the transformation of a collection of 'nature spirits' and superstitions into an anthropomorphic system akin to those of the Greek city-states alongside such 'sophisticated' Etruscan practices as augury and divination. According to Livy (I.8), the trappings of monarchy – the 'curule chair', attendant lictors, the purple-bordered toga – also derived from Etruscan practices.

Here, however, we encounter a dilemma, as Livy was himself aware: the king to whom tradition assigned all of this was the Sabine, Numa Pompilius, and yet its characteristics were largely Etruscan. On the other hand, the traditional dating scheme has the virtue of allowing such innovation (in *c.* 600 BC) to coincide with kings of undisputed Etruscan origin; for this was approximately the traditional time of the arrival in Rome of Tarquinius Priscus. Gjerstad has proposed a reconciliation of the inconsistencies by dating the whole of the traditional line of kings from *c.* 575 onwards. This has the virtue, with the contemporaneous establishment of settlement on the Capitoline Hill, of providing a place for Titus Tatius, alias Numa Pompilius. Nor is there any difficulty, in a period of great change, in envisaging rivalry not simply amongst warlords of Etruscan origin but also between

Etruscans and others. Later Roman tradition, which held the Etruscans in some contempt, may have been anxious to minimise the Etruscan role, perhaps (to a degree, at least, in this matter) with history on its side.

The proposed re-dating of the traditional kings does, however, create another problem: if we are to retain the traditional date for the establishment of the Republic (510/509 BC), then the monarchic period appears to have become too short. There are, however, events and traditions which, superficially at least, seem to require a rethinking of the Republic's foundation date.

To judge from sophisticated religious practices and a programme of urbanisation, Etruscan influence – in cultural terms, at any rate – in and around Rome in the first half of the sixth century seems to have been strong. Further, the evidence also suggests that in the first half of the fifth century that influence was in decline.

On the traditional scheme of dating, the Etruscan 'dynasty' in Rome lasted from 616 to 510/509, with an intermediate 'reaction' if we assume – although, as we have seen, perhaps wrongly – that Servius Tullius was a non-Etruscan. It could be that Servius Tullius/Mastarna was given a 'Latin identity' because of the crucial role that he is said to have played in the creation of the tribal system of organisation for Roman citizens and of the popular assemblies which derived from it. This was too close to the heart of the Republic's 'sacred institutions' and mode of government to be credited to an Etruscan.

The Roman period of monarchy traditionally came to an end with the expulsion of Tarquinius Superbus in 510/509 BC: his rule had become too much to bear – symbolised by the story of the rape of the Sabine women; this led to his being ousted, and supreme power being vested instead in a pair of officials, called consuls, who were to be elected annually and guided by a senate composed of aristocrats. Tarquinius is said to have taken refuge in Caere (Cerveteri) and to have prevailed on Lars Porsenna, ruler supposedly of Clusium (Chiusi), to aid him in an effort to regain his seat of power in Rome. The tradition followed by Livy makes this attempt unsuccessful: Porsenna was thwarted first by Horatius Cocles' heroic defence of the Tiber bridge and was then so impressed by the courage of one Gaius Mucius Scaevola that he decided to make peace with Rome. He then moved on to the Latin town of Aricia, which he would have captured, had not Greeks from Cumae weighed in and defeated him. Roman tradition, however, was aware of an alternative version (Tacitus, *Histories* III.72) – that Porsenna did in fact take Rome. Thus, the traditional chronology of the end of the monarchy and the establishment of the Republic is called into question, and with it the whole interpretation of the true meaning of this highly important episode in the development of Rome.

The establishment of the Republic

The traditional account of the Republic's foundation and of its early struggles for survival represents them as a period of heroic deeds overcoming treachery, in which the patriotism of the aristocracy saw the fledgling state through to triumph; the evidence regarding a true chronology of the early Republic is ambivalent, but a study of it is instructive regarding the real issues dominating the development of Rome in the late sixth and early fifth centuries.

The essence of the traditional account of the Republic's earliest years appears to mirror the decline of Etruscan power in central Italy during the first half of the fifth century – the loss to them of Latium and the consequent breaking of the links with Campania; the involvement of Cumae, alluded to earlier, is historical, since it was Cumae, together with Syracuse, which, in 474, inflicted a heavy naval defeat on the Etruscans. Perhaps the 'kernel of truth' in this case is of Greek and Latin city-states combining their efforts to drive the Etruscans from Latium and to destroy their power in central and southern Italy. Such a situation may help to explain the involvement of Lars Porsenna in Roman affairs; per-

Plate 1.6 Rome, Capitoline Hill: Temple of Jupiter, as depicted on a denarius of 78 BC.

haps the leader of nearby Veii (rather than of Clusium), Porsenna may possibly have been trying to take advantage of a power vacuum in the Tiber valley rather than, as tradition asserts, acting in support of Tarquinius Superbus. Viewed in the context of the long-term relationship of Rome and Veii, the leader of the latter is much more likely to have been attempting to 'cash in' on his neighbour's misfortunes than he is to have been trying to help him. It was in the longer-term interest of the Republic's leaders to portray the events of the years following the Republic's foundation as a Tarquinian and Etruscan 'plot' to undermine the new state and to rob it of its 'noble independence'; the truth about the Republic's founders was probably a good deal less uplifting.

The site of Rome itself provides some corroborating evidence of Etruscan decline, specifically in the decline in temple building: temples were built to Jupiter (509), Saturn (496), Mercury (495), Ceres, Liber and Libera (493) and the Dioscuri (484). While not all of these deities were Etruscan, the technical and artistic expertise and the wealth required to build this continuing series of temples strongly suggests Etruscan involvement. Beyond this 'flood' of new foundations, only two more are recorded in the remainder of the fifth century – to Dius Fidius (466) and Apollo (431); this appears to point to an economic decline that sits well with the history of the Republic's early years.

In a reconstruction of events, a major difficulty is presented by the Temple of Jupiter on the Capitoline Hill, which was dedicated in 509; such a date must have a reasonable chance of being secure, as it will presumably have derived from pontifical records. Tradition held that Tarquinius Superbus was expelled just prior to the temple's dedication, which thus became one of the first acts of the new Republic. It is hard to avoid the suspicion that this feature of the story – and thus the dating within the period – has been massaged to ensure that the dedication of this temple, which was to be seen as a veritable cornerstone of the spirit of the Republic, was not associated with Etruscan monarchs. Indeed, what could be more dramatically symbolic than the placing of the dedication of the temple to the head of Rome's pantheon and the foundation of the Republic in the same year?

The traditional dating of the temple's dedication gives rise to a further problem: although the record places the dedication in 509, tradition also associates Tarquinius Priscus (traditionally 616–578) with the building; it was he who is said to have brought the sculptor, Vulca, to Rome to work on the temple's terracotta roof decorations. This would appear, therefore, not only to associate Priscus with the building of the temple but also to relate his imput to a late stage in the process. In any case, any association of Tarquinius Priscus with the building of this temple would, on the traditional dating, imply a very lengthy construction process. According to Tacitus (*Histories* III.72), Servius Tullius, too, had a tenuous connection with the project. The name of Tarquinius Superbus has, according to Einar Gjerstad, been associated with the temple only because of Roman insistence on the connection between the dedication of the temple and the removal of Superbus and the inauguration of the Republic.

The perceived awkwardness of the long construction period is apparent in the attempts to obviate the difficulty; perhaps, it is suggested, Priscus vowed the building, while it was Superbus who actually built it, allotting spoils for the purpose. The Elder Pliny, however, citing no less an authority than Varro (*Natural History*

35.157), states categorically that it was Priscus who summoned Vulca from Veii to execute the cult statue and the terracotta *quadrigae* for the roof. If this is so, then it is hard to avoid the connection of the latter stages of construction, the presence of Vulca and the reign of Tarquinius Priscus in the late years of the sixth century.

A further element of Roman tradition linked the temple firmly with the erection of the *Circus Maximus* and the institution of the *Ludi Magni*: a triumphing general held his procession in the *Circus*, made a vow at the temple and then celebrated the *Ludi*. The *Circus* and the *Ludi* are again associated with Tarquinius Priscus; Livy (I.35) further states that the *Circus* and the temple were built from the spoils of Appiolae, which was conquered by Priscus. Another tradition, however, evidently recognised the difficulties implicit in this, and transferred the details of triumphing to Publius Valerius, one of the consuls of 509, supposedly the Republic's inaugural year. We may further ask whether, if the urbanisation of the site of Rome began truly in the early sixth century, a temple on the scale of that on the Capitoline Hill would have been feasible in terms of the available technology of the period traditionally assigned to Priscus. On the other hand, it is clear that both public and domestic architecture in Rome were advancing significantly in the later years of the sixth century.

A simple (although not necessarily the only) way out of the apparent impasse is to say that, while the temple was probably dedicated in 509 BC, it is evident that this was during the reign of Tarquinius Priscus, the last king but two, and that, therefore, the Republic must have been established later than tradition has led us to believe, perhaps by some forty to fifty years (see Appendix 1). Such a 'solution' is the more acceptable in view of the fact that we can see a firm political and sentimental reason for the traducing of the true chronology. The argument may be taken further: Livy (II.19) mentions under 499 BC the capture of Crustumerium, an event which he had earlier (I.38) credited to Tarquinius Priscus. Of course, there could have been two captures of the town, or two different towns could have been meant, or the second mention could be a duplication. On the other hand, it has been suggested that the character of Livy's reference in II.19 suggests its derivation from some official (presumably pontifical) record. In this case, we have another reason to place the reign of Tarquinius Priscus in the late sixth/early fifth centuries rather than in the early sixth.

It is worth taking this part of the investigation a stage further: the dating scheme being suggested here takes the reign of Tarquinius Priscus to, at least, 509 BC, and possibly to beyond 499. Priscus was, according to tradition, succeeded by Servius Tullius; we have already seen that in all probability, and for plausible reasons, he was an Etruscan adventurer (perhaps rather like Lars Porsenna) made to look like a Latin. Tradition assigned to Servius Tullius the institution of one of the Republic's great popular assemblies, the *Comitia Centuriata* (the Assembly of the Centuries), and a new division of the people into tribes. The history of the political organisations of the people had already undergone change; the original, supposedly Romulean, division into ethnic groups or *curiae*, with a popular assembly based on them known as the *Comitia Curiata*, was replaced, presumably under Etruscan influence, by three new tribes (Ramnes, Tities and Luceres), not based on residence or ethnic origin.

Servius Tullius' reorganisation was two-fold: first, the adult male population was assessed into two groups – one which possessed minimum 'hoplite qualifications' (that is, to equip themselves for warfare), the other below that figure. Each group was divided into centuries and from these centuries the army drew its manpower. Livy (I.43) provides a detailed description of this which must be a much later refinement of the original organisation. Clearly, it would be of benefit to know at what point hoplite (or infantry) tactics were introduced, since the reforms depend on this. It is generally assumed that Etruscan cities were adopting hoplite tactics from the Greek city-states from approximately the middle of the sixth century BC – that is, in accord with the *traditional* dating ascribed to Servius Tullius. Cavalry tended to be associated with elitism in society; while this might be seen as offering support for the traditional dating scheme, we should remember that, at the famous battle of Lake Regillus (496 BC; Livy II.19–20), cavalry predominated, and a tangible result of the battle was the dedication of a temple to Castor and Pollux (the *Dioscuri*), the deities of equestrianism.

Contention attaches to the division of the people into tribes; Livy (II.21), under 495 BC, states that in that year twenty-one tribes were created (*Romae tribus una et viginti factae*). Gjerstad has argued for the authenticity of the date, on the ground that it has the appearance of a 'calendar reference'; he also maintains (with some justification) that the reference should indicate the inception of a system of twenty-one tribes – in other words, that Servius Tullius was reigning in 495. Opponents of this view hold that Livy is referring to the raising of the number of tribes to twenty-one from the nineteen that had previously existed; the system was capable of such growth, for it consisted of four urban tribes and a growing number – eventually thirty-one – of rural tribes.

Further supporting points are, first, that the inception of the system of keeping the calendar in order by the occasional insertion of an extra (intercalary) month, credited to Servius Tullius, is dated by Varro to 472. Secondly, Livy (I.44) assigns to Servius Tullius (with modifications by Tarquinius Superbus) the building of a defensive *agger* – the so-called 'Servian' wall – which ran across the Viminal and Esquiline Hills. This was extensively rebuilt following the Gallic invasions of 390 BC. The dating of the earlier work depends on a single sherd of 'red-figure' ware, which would provide a *terminus post quem* of about 520 BC. Thirdly, two temples in the *Forum Boarium* (to Mater Matuta and Fortuna) are thought to date to a period early in the fifth century. However, it cannot be said that the evidence for dating the reign of Servius Tullius to *c.* 495–470 is unequivocal. As for Superbus, we have one reference in Dionysius of Halicarnassus

(IX.60) to a temple built by him and dedicated in 466; it evidently contained a number of objects associated with the Tarquinius family and with events tied by historians to Superbus' reign.

Gjerstad further cites the decline of Etruscan power which, according to Diodorus Siculus (XI.51), came to an end in Campania in 445; Gjerstad questions whether Rome could have expelled the Etruscans while they still held sway further south. Again, the magistrates in Rome after 509, having Etruscan names, fall into two groups, which reflect approximately the periods ascribed by Gjerstad to the two Tarquinii. The problem here is that it is probably not appropriate to equate the expulsion of the Tarquinii with that of the Etruscans; after all, Rome's Etruscans were first of all Romans, not foreign 'imperialists'. It will also be important to consider what the expulsion of Superbus actually represented.

The names of the Republic's early consuls contain many belonging to plebeian families; this is at variance with received Republican practice which, according to tradition, reserved the consulate as a patrician office until 367; on this point, it is not unlikely that the Etruscan kings, perhaps Superbus in particular, behaved in a manner reminiscent of the tyrants of mainland Greece – that is, maintaining their rule with popular support at the expense of the interests of the aristocracy. Plebeians may well by and large have been artisans rather than landowners at the turn of the sixth and fifth centuries and, as such, benefited from the vibrant economy that was evidently characteristic of late-Etruscan Rome but which was clearly 'running down' in the first half of the fifth century. It may be, therefore, that the lot of plebeians deteriorated during this period, leading by the mid-fifth century to the patrician exclusivity and plebeian indebtedness that are regarded as characteristics of the early Republic; in other words, whatever the truth regarding Rome's constitutional position in the first half of the fifth century, economically – and, therefore, politically and socially – there was growing tension between a plebeian order which, as Etruscan influence in central Italy declined, was losing out to an increasingly dominant Latin landowning aristocracy. The period between the 450s and 440s contains much evidence of constitutional upheaval, which has been equated with the establishment of the Republic; equally, however, it could be argued that such tensions derived simply from the growing exclusiveness of the aristocracy after *c.* 475.

Thus, while 'postponing' the inauguration of the Republic by half a century might carry with it some attraction, it is not an essential precondition to explaining events in Rome over the first half of the fifth century; indeed, the turmoil evident in central Italy during the early fifth century may well point to the fact that an opportunist aristocracy at Rome might have chosen almost any moment between 510 and 450 to bring about major constitutional change. There is no virtue, however, in 'cramping' too much the events associated with the early years of the Republic.

The attraction of 510/509 as the Republic's foundation date lay, as we have seen, partly in a desire to ensure that the Capitoline temple was not dedicated by an Etruscan monarch, but probably partly, too, in order to bring together Rome's and Athens' expulsions of their tyrants. Again, the end of the monarchy did not coincide with a 'disappearance' of Etruscans from Rome; indeed, Etruscan features were everywhere to be seen – continuing vibrancy for a time, at least, a dual magistracy, the magistrates' insignia, the *fasces* (which are known also at Vetulonia). Further, religion and practices associated with it remained distinctively of Etruscan character.

There is no real reason to doubt the consular lists in general; while there will always be a suspicion of some interpolations based on the wishful thinking of later generations of Romans, sufficient of the early officers of the Republic came from families which did not play a substantial part in the politics of the later Republic to support their credibility. Nor is there any overwhelming reason why genuine records of such matters should not have survived. Polybius refers to a treaty with the Carthaginians which was dated to 507; he talks of rulers in Rome who are described with the word universally employed by Greek writers of all periods for consuls and praetors ('*hypatoi*'). As we have seen, the discovery in 1966 of the Pyrgi treaty makes the authenticity of Polybius' document a reasonable likelihood.

What should we, then, make of the expulsion of Tarquinius Superbus? The story, as reported by Livy (the 'rape of Lucretia': I.57–60), is thought by many to have the character of a 'Hellenistic Romance'. A possible theory is that Superbus was ousted by Lars Porsenna, perhaps invited by an aristocracy which was tired of Superbus playing the part of a Greek tyrant – that is, favouring the people at the expense of the aristocracy. We have noted the version in the tradition which said that Porsenna did in fact take Rome. R. M. Ogilvie, in his *Commentary on Livy I–V*, has suggested that the introduction of 'hoplite tactics', for which there appears to be evidence from Rome relating to the late sixth/early fifth centuries, probably heightened political awareness among the richer elements in society, just as it had in the Greek city-states. Further, there is little doubt that this was a period of considerable turmoil in central Italy: indeed, Ogilvie has also suggested that the events depicted in the paintings of the François tomb (at Vulci), showing an Etruscan adventurer who took Rome for a time, may have related to this period. It is possible that a Sabine incursion has to be taken into account, also, which is encapsulated in the traditional story of the arrival in Rome in *c.* 505 of the Sabine Claudii. The tribal re-arrangements recorded by Livy in 495 may, in fact, have consisted of an enlargement of the tribal system to accommodate new settlers.

The climax of this insecurity is to be seen in the battle of Lake Regillus (494), when Rome defeated a league of Latin states (Livy II.19–20), which restored Roman supremacy in Latium, recognised by a treaty (II.33). It is also the case that an Etruscan decline towards 475 fits other events recorded by Livy – the wars which Rome fought against the Aequi, the Volsci and the Hernici, as well as the Samnite incursion into Campania. All such movements cohere if we acknowledge that an Etruscan weakening around and to the north of Rome afforded a greater facility for such incursions by hill people into the lowlands of coastal Italy.

Internally, a trend can be traced: the last Etruscan king is portrayed after the manner of a Greek tyrant, championing the ordinary people against the elite. This trend did not change in the immediate post-regal period. The fact that plebeians featured among the early consuls, advanced by Gjerstad as a reason for rejecting them, falls into place, as does the fact that much of the temple building of the early fifth century concerns cults of particular interest to the plebeians.

Yet, at the same time, the early years of the fifth century set the pattern for the internal struggles which characterised the early Republic. It has been pointed out that the difference between rich and poor may matter less in a monarchy. Warfare hit the poor; it used them, it damaged their lands and it probably gave added importance to the rich men favoured by the Centuriate organisation. The nature of the early Republican cults – Ceres (a corn deity), Saturn (a blight deity), Mercury (a trading deity) – perhaps indicates a felt need to invoke heaven in a deteriorating economic situation.

In archaeological terms, Rome in the early fifth century became a less vibrant place: pottery imports decreased, and debt probably became a real problem; with the development of the hoplite organisation, the rich were in a position of dominance. The departure of the Etruscans in *c.* 475 was probably crucial, since it emphasised the fact that the ordinary people were at the mercy of the rich and influential. Here, then, was the origin of the greatest problem of the early phase of the 'Struggle of the Orders' – debt. With this, the early Republic had assumed the characteristic of class struggle, which is the keynote of Livy's account of the period.

What, then, have we discovered? It is probably safe to say that Rome became urbanised under Etruscan influence in the early part of the sixth century, and that in general terms the later regal period corresponds to reality. It is probably equally safe to say that the Tarquinii were expelled in the late sixth century and that our greatest problem – that of the Capitoline temple – may be soluble by a contracting of the last kings' reigns without having to advance the date of Superbus' expulsion to the mid-fifth century. The expulsion made little practical immediate difference in Rome; this came over the next twenty-five years, with the decline of the Etruscans and the rise of an elitist class. With that, the stage was set for what tradition remembered about the early Republic.

Appendix 1

Early Rome: Traditional and Archaeological dates

Traditional	Archaeological (Gjerstad)
2000	**2000**
	?–c. 1600 Neolithic and Chalcolithic
	c. 1600–800 Bronze Age settlement
c. 1180 Landing of Aeneas; kings at Alba Longa	
1000	**1000**
900	**900**
800	**800**
	c. 800 Iron Age settlers on the Tiber hills (four periods):
753 Foundation by Romulus	800–750 I: On the Palatine, Esquiline and Quirinal hills
753–716 Reigns of Romulus and Titus Tatius	750–700 II: On the Palatine, Esquiline and Quirinal hills
715–673 Numa Pompilius	
700	**700**
673–642 Tullus Hostilius	700–625 III: Etruscan culture; scope of villages widens
642–617 Ancus Marcius	
616–579 Tarquinius Priscus	625–575 IV: Increasing evidence of wealth and unity amongst the settlers

600
578–535 Servius Tullius

534–509 Tarquinius Superbus
509 Expulsion of Superbus;
establishment of Republic;
consulship of L.Junius Brutus;
dedication of Temple of Jupiter
on the Capitoline Hill

500

494 Inception of the Tribunate
of the *Plebs*

600
575 Settlement of Capitoline Hill;
unified city; large-scale rebuilding
575–530 Reigns of Numa
Pompilius,Tullus Hostilius and
Ancus Marcius
530–496 Tarquinius Priscus
509 Introduction of twelve–month
calendar; first *recorded*
consuls; dedication of Temple of
Jupiter on the Capitoline Hill

500
499 Priscus wins battle of
Crustumerium

c. 495–470 Servius Tullius
495 New organisation of the
populus

c. 490 Building of the 'Servian'
Wall
483–474 War with Etruscan Veii
c. 475 Building of 'Servian'
temples
474 Etruscans defeated at
Cumae by Hiero of Syracuse
472 Further calendar reform
c. 470–450 Tarquinius Superbus
466 Dedication of temple to
Semo Sancus
c. 450 Expulsion of Superbus;
tribunate (?) of L.Junius Brutus;
establishment of Republic
c. 450–443 Evidence of political
and social upheaval (451,
codification of laws; 445,
plebeian demands for right to
marry patricians; 444, military
tribunate established; 443,
censorship established)
445 Etruscan power broken in
Campania

Further Reading: general

In addition to the bibliographies relating to the subject matter of
this and the ensuing chapters, it is appropriate to cite a number
of publications which span the whole chronological extent of
the present work. The most complete is the *Cambridge Ancient
History*, published by Cambridge University Press, of which a
second and completely revised edition has been appearing in
recent years:

Volume 7   *The Rise of Rome to 220 B.C.* (1989: edited by
F. W. Walbank, A. E. Astin, M. W. Frederiksen,
R. M. Ogilvie and A. Drummond)

Volume 8   *Rome and the Mediterranean to 133 B.C.* (1989:
edited by A. E. Astin, F. W. Walbank, M. W.
Frederiksen and R. M. Ogilvie)

Volume 9   *146–43 B.C.* (1994: edited by J. A. Crook,
A. Lintott and E. Rawson)

Volume 10 *43 B.C.–A.D. 69* (1996: edited by A. K. Bowman,
E. Champlin and A. Lintott)

Volume 11 *A.D. 70–192* (2000: edited by A. K. Bowman,
P. Garnsey and D. Rathbone)

Volume 13 *A.D. 337–425* (1997: edited by A. Cameron and
P. Garnsey)

In addition, a number of multi-volume series cover the period:
(1) *A History of the Roman World* (published by Methuen/
University Paperbacks, London), including

From 753 to 146 B.C.   H. H. Scullard (4th edition, 1980)
From 146 to 30 B.C.   F. B. Marsh (1953)
From 30 B.C. to A.D. 138 E. T. Salmon (1944)
From A.D. 138 to 337   H. M. D. Parker (1925)

(2) some coverage is contained within a series on the history of
the ancient world (published by Fontana Paperbacks, London),
including

Early Rome and the Etruscans	R. M. Ogilvie (1976)
The Roman Republic	M. H. Crawford (1992)
The Roman Empire	C. Wells (2nd edition, 1992)
The Later Roman Empire	A. Cameron (1993)

Over the years, many single-volume histories of Rome have been published; the most accessible are

Cary M., *A History of Rome* (revised by H. H. Scullard) (London, 1976).

Le Glay M., Voisin J. L. and Le Bohec Y., *A History of Rome*, 2nd edition (Oxford: Blackwell, 2001).

Roman coins provide a fascinating source for many aspects of Roman history; the most convenient access to this material is through

Crawford M. H., *Roman Republican Coinage* (Cambridge, 1974).

Mattingly H., *et al.*, *The Roman Imperial Coinage*, Vols 1–10 (London, 1923–1981) (a second edition of Vol. 1 by C. H. V. Sutherland was published in 1984).

An introduction to the historical value of this material is to be found in

Grant M., *Roman History from Coins* (Cambridge, 1956).
Howgego C., *Ancient History from Coins* (London, 1995).
Reece R., *Roman Coins* (London, 1970).

Classical Sources

Of course what survives today represents a small fraction of what was originally produced, both by authors who wrote in Greek and by those who wrote in Latin. A considerable amount of what survives has been translated into English – most accessibly in the Loeb Classical Library Series (Heinemann) and in the Penguin Classics Series. In addition, collections of literary and other documents relevant to specific periods have been produced, for example the following:

Ehrenberg V. and Jones A. H. M., *Documents Illustrating the Reigns of Augustus and Tiberius* (Oxford, 1955).

Lacey W. K. and Wilson B. W. J. G., *Res Publica: Roman Politics and Society According to Cicero* (Bristol, 1978).

McCrum M. and Woodhead A. G., *Select Documents of the Principates of the Flavian Emperors* (Cambridge, 1961).

Smallwood E. M., *Documents Illustrating the Principates of Nerva, Trajan and Hadrian* (Cambridge, 1966).

Smallwood E. M., *Documents Illustrating the Principates of Gaius, Claudius and Nero* (Cambridge, 1967).

Stevenson J., *A New Eusebius* (London, 1957).

Stevenson J., *Creeds, Councils and Controversies* (London, 1966).

Stockton D. L., *From the Gracchi to Sulla: Sources for Roman History, 133–80 B.C.* (London, 1981).

Wiseman T. P. (ed.), *Roman Political Life, 90 B.C.–A.D. 69* (Exeter, 1985).

Further reading: Chapter 1

Alfoldi A., *Early Rome and the Latins* (Ann Arbor, MI, 1965).

Banti L., *The Etruscan Cities and their Culture* (London, 1973).

Barfield L., *Northern Italy Before Rome* (London, 1971).

Barker G. W. W., *Landscape and Society: Prehistoric Central Italy* (London, 1981).

Blake M. E., *Ancient Roman Construction in Italy from the Prehistoric Period to Augustus* (Washington, DC, 1947).

Bloch R., *The Etruscans* (London, 1969).

Boardman J., *The Greeks Overseas* (London, 1980).

Castagnoli F., *Orthogonal Planning in Antiquity* (Cambridge, MA, 1972).

Coarelli F., *Etruscan Cities* (London, 1974).

Cornell T. J., *The Beginnings of Rome* (London, 1995).

Cristofani M., *The Etruscans: A New Investigation* (London, 1979).

Dudley D. R., *Urbs Roma: A Sourcebook of Classical Texts on the City and its Monuments* (London, 1966).

Gjerstad E., *Early Rome* (Lund, 1960–1973).

Gjerstad E., *Legends and Facts of Early Roman History* (Lund, 1962).

Grant M., *The Etruscans* (London, 1980).

Harris W. V., *Rome in Etruria and Umbria* (London, 1971).

Heurgon J., *The Rise of Rome to 264 B.C.* (London, 1973).

Mansuelli G., *Etruria and Early Rome* (London, 1963).

Mitchell R. E., *Patricians and Plebians: The Origin of the Roman State* (New York, 1990).

Ogilvie R. M., *A Commentary on Livy, Books 1–5* (Oxford, 1965).

Ogilvie R. M., *Early Rome and the Etruscans* (London, 1976).

Pallottino M., *The Etruscans* (London, 1975).

Potter T. W., *The Changing Landscape of South Etruria* (London, 1979).

Potter T. W., *Roman Italy* (London, 1987).

Ridgway D. and Ridgway F (eds), *Italy before the Romans* (London, 1979).

Scullard H. H., *The Etruscan Cities and Rome* (London, 1967).

Ward-Perkins J. B., *Cities of Ancient Greece and Italy: Planning in Classical Antiquity* (New York, 1974).

Whatmough J., *The Foundations of Roman Italy* (London, 1937).

Chapter 2

The growth of the *respublica*

The Republic (*respublica*) was supposedly 'the common concern' – a constitution to take the state out of the hands of a single person and place it under the control of the many; as we have seen, however, the Republic actually entailed a shift of power from the one to the few.

In many respects, the governing machinery of the new Republic will not have looked so very different from what had preceded it – apart, of course, from the absence of a king, although even there the title survived in vestigial form in the post of *rex sacrorum* (*'king of sacred duties'*), who took on the religious duties that had resided in the king's office; the *rex sacrorum* enjoyed the privilege of an official residence in the heart of the city – the *Regia*, which was positioned by the *Via Sacra* and adjacent to the *Forum Romanum*, which formed the Republic's political and commercial centre.

What did change, however, was the attitude to monarchy: the whole notion of kingship had become abhorrent, and the new constitutional arrangements were dedicated to the avoidance of kingship (*regnum*) at all costs. This abhorrence remained a cornerstone of the Republic's psyche, so that, in the last century of the Republic, the idea was still sufficiently potent to bring ruin – even death – to politicians suspected of trying to establish a *regnum*; two powerful examples were Tiberius Sempronius Gracchus (133 BC) and Gaius Julius Caesar (44 BC).

Yet, most of the Republic's machinery of government had come about during the regal period. As the Greek historian, Polybius, was to claim in the second century BC, the Republic's government consisted of the interaction of aristocracy, democracy and monarchy, the three basic constitutional types identified by Plato. To Plato, however, these three types were individually unstable, carrying within themselves their own inherent 'agent of destruction'. Thus, the constitutions of Greek city-states were never properly stable, as one form gave way to another in a never-ending cycle. Polybius was able (or, at least, thought he was able) to proclaim that the Roman Republic had brought to an end the quest for a stable form of government, for in 'balancing' in an interaction of powers and needs the three constitutional types –

aristocracy (the senate), democracy (the popular assemblies) and monarchy (the consuls) – Rome had succeeded in providing long-term stability in a 'mixed constitution'. The validity of Polybius' analysis will be examined more closely in a later chapter.

The senate

The aristocratic element was, thus, the senate: this body certainly had its origin in the monarchic period, acting, rather like medieval barons, as the king's advisers; it is to be assumed that this function was exercised both individually and corporately. The king chose his advisers, and the principal criterion of choice appears to have been headship of a household; these heads of households were the *patres* ('fathers'), a term which continued to be used of the senate long after the Republic was dead. It would appear that corporately the senate's *modus operandi* was to meet at the king's calling, to offer him advice when he asked for it, but advice which he was in no way bound to follow. The king may in some circumstances – for example, in the matter of religious ritual surrounding the commencement and conclusion of warfare – have been bound, at least, to seek the advice. The only occasion, however, on which the senate might exceed this position was during the *interregnum* which followed the death of a king. Since the system was not hereditary, the transition from a dead ruler to his successor was managed by the senate effectively choosing, or perhaps even electing, the new king who, subsequently, of course, was not bound by any advice that the senate might offer to him. Thus, from the aristocratic senate's standpoint, its role was for most of the time slight and, in the reigns of domineering monarchs, it was effectively toothless.

Senators were patricians: the origin of the distinction between patricians and plebeians in Roman society is obscure. Some have favoured an 'ethnic' explanation in terms of tribal origins, although this seems difficult to sustain. Others have proposed that the reason was one which inevitably emerges in developing societies – that is,

Plate 2.1 (opposite) Rome, the Forum area: (a) the Forum itself; (b) Basilica of Aemilius Paullus; (c) the senate house; (d) the Arch of Septimius Severus; (e) the Rostra; (f) Temple of Castor and Pollux; (g) Temple of Vesta.

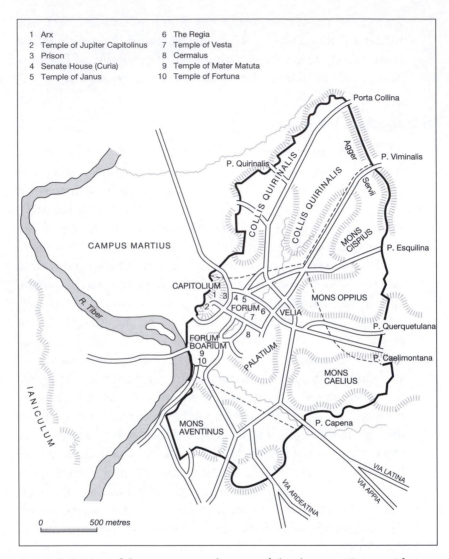

1 Arx
2 Temple of Jupiter Capitolinus
3 Prison
4 Senate House (Curia)
5 Temple of Janus
6 The Regia
7 Temple of Vesta
8 Cermalus
9 Temple of Mater Matuta
10 Temple of Fortuna

Figure 2.1 Map of the city at an early stage of development. Source: After H. H. Scullard, A History of the Roman World from 753 to 146 BC, *4th edition (London: Routledge, 1980), p. 77.*

class distinction based on levels of economic success (or failure). Clearly, some will acquire greater wealth, and thus greater power, than others. In this sense, the patricians were the equivalent to tribal leaders in Celtic society who, like them, appear to have assumed a dominance over and an element of responsibility for less successful fellow citizens – the origin, in fact, of the real stabilising factor in the Roman Republic, namely patronage, an institution akin to feudalism. The patron brought practical help to his client – food, advice, legal and religious support – while the client returned the favour with an obligation to provide political support for his patron. The relationship was, thus, effectively sealed as a set of mutually acknowledged religious obligations, which is encapsulated in one of the most potent of Republican 'virtues' – *pietas*. It should be pointed out that, if the observations of the previous chapter on economic and social decline from the late sixth into the early fifth centuries are valid, then the level and amount of dependence will have been increasing, serving as a consequence to entrench the patricians more securely in power in the early decades of the Republic.

The number of senators in the regal period is hard to assess, although it must have been growing. The Sabine, Attus Clausus, for example, who came to Rome in 505, was on his arrival given land and made a patrician and a senator. Livy, in fact, suggests that, side by side with heads of households, there was another type of senator who was 'co-opted' (*conscriptus*). The historian regards this as the origin of the term invariably used later as a collective address to senators – *patres conscripti*, which he presumably took as abbreviated from *patres et conscripti*. There is, however, no evidence with which either to support or reject this assertion.

In the new Republic, the senate, or corporate aristocracy, had a great opportunity to seize a major role. Whereas the magistrates had limited tenure and the people limited powers, the senate could meet virtually continuously and at will, under the presidency of men who were its own members, debate issues and vote on them, publishing its decisions as decrees (*senatus consulta*). While these were not binding in law, other circumstances, as we shall see, ensured that they became law with little or no difficulty. Further, senators held their positions for life, unless they were removed for disgraceful conduct – presumably by the king during the regal period, and under the Republic by the consuls, whose power over senatorial membership was later devolved to new senior officers called censors; the chief criteria for membership invoked by them were ex-magisterial status and standing in society. From Sulla's time, fulfilment of the office of quaestor gave automatic entry into the senate; thus from then there was an annual inflow into the senate, through an elective process, of new young members.

The Roman Republican system always held in great esteem those who were senior in power and wealth; at first, these men were the sole 'custodians' of political, legal and religious knowledge, and because of this their views were seldom challenged. Thus, a senatorial view which emerged as a *senatus consultum* was almost inevitably led by these men of *auctoritas* ('prestige'/ 'standing'). Indeed, the senate's procedures ensured their precedence; although the system must have been modified as governmental structures became more complex, we can be certain that the 'rules' of senatorial debate in the 'mature' Republic must have reflected the maintenance of principles established long before.

The senate's effective power increased as the senior magistrates devolved more of their powers on to new magistracies, for in this way the magistracy became less coherent than the senate. The senate's procedures also served to highlight the influence of the 'senior men' who were themselves the backbone of the senate's *auctoritas*.

When the senate met, its proceedings were presided over by a senior magistrate, usually one of the consuls. Senators were not permitted to speak as the desire took them, but according to an accepted order of precedence. In the later Republic, following the decision initiated by Cornelius Sulla in the early first century BC to conduct the elections in mid-year for the following year's magistrates, it was normal for the senate's presiding officer to call for senators' opinions in the following order: consuls-designate, ex-consuls (*consulares*; in order of seniority), praetors-designate, ex-praetors (*praetorii*; in order of seniority), tribunes of the plebs-designate, ex-tribunes (in order of seniority). It was not usual for the opinions of men below the rank of tribune to be asked to voice their views. Indeed, this fact was recognised by the application of the term, *pedarii*, to lower ranks of senator; the word signifies that the only function of those junior senators was to 'walk' to cast their votes at the conclusion of debate. It was further entirely at the discretion of the presiding officer to decide how many opinions to call; he could bring an end to this part of the proceedings whenever he wished – that is, whenever he felt that he had secured satisfactory backing for the view that he desired.

It was, in fact, unusual for discussion to be extended as far through the senate's ranks as is described above. On one occasion, however, the debate on the fate of the supporters of Sergius Catilina in 63 BC, the presiding consul, Marcus Cicero, continued down to the rank of tribune before he felt that he had a satisfactory expression – from Marcus Cato, a tribune-designate – of the view that he himself wanted; although the consular ranks had been generally 'sound', this had been weakened by compromising proposals from the praetorian ranks (notably from a praetor-designate for 62 BC, Julius Caesar), and it took the 'hard line' of Cato to restore the senate's resolve. It is worth noting that, despite this expression of the senate's will, it in no way absolved Cicero of personal responsibility for the action that he subsequently took.

Nonetheless, despite the lack of any proper legal competence or responsibility, the senate in its advisory role provided the *de facto* government of the Republic, until it came under increasing pressure, from the mid-second century BC, from individuals and factions from within its own ranks and, more especially, from the deadly combination of generals/magistrates and armies committed to them following Marius' reforms of the army in the last decade of the second century.

The stability praised by Polybius came about because, until the mid-second century, the senate managed to keep at bay the various challenges that it faced. The *auctoritas* of the senate represented an overriding 'standing' in the Republic in the later third and earlier second centuries; it was evidently this that had prompted king Pyrrhus of Epirus to regard the senate as 'an assembly of kings' and Cicero to see the magistrates as the 'servants' of the senate. It was a Republic of this 'Polybian' kind, in which the senate predominated because of its *auctoritas*, that Cicero wished to re-create in his *Concordia Ordinum* from the 60s BC and to which he hoped to re-cruit first Pompey and, later, Caesar as 'sponsors and protectors'. Some even believe that, at the very end of his life, he was attempting to attract the support of the young Octavian, the future emperor, Augustus.

The senate was, thus, the 'key player' in the early and middle Republic: it 'pre-discussed' all proposed legislation and without its approval little happened. Indeed, its principal aim during the earlier part of the Republic was to ensure the continuance of this situation through its manipulation of social and political changes which did take place. A revealing example of this is provided by the way in which the senate reacted to the pressure for change during the 'Struggle of the Orders'. It succeeded in detaching from the plebeian body those plebeians who had the wealth to enable them to undertake a public career; this not only demonstrated the communality of interest that could be forged between patricians and wealthy plebeians, but also succeeded in divesting the plebeian body of those who would otherwise have been its natural leaders.

The magistrates

The magistrates ('state officers') provided the executive arm of the Republic's government, although, for reasons discussed above, they often found themselves acting virtually as the 'agents' of the aristocratic senate.

We associate the magistracy with the inception of the Republic, although the state evidently had 'senior officers' during the period of the monarchy, who may have acted as the kings' deputies, perhaps principally in the role of leading the state's armies into battle. It is thought that they may at that stage have been called praetors, the Latin word, *prae(i)tor,* meaning 'one who goes in front'; the number of these and the conditions of the office in the monarchic period are far from clear. The title, praetor, did not re-emerge in the Republic's magisterial nomenclature until the mid-fourth century BC – possibly in 367, the year in which it was enacted that one of the consuls had to be a plebeian.

The Roman state had a list of consuls which went back to the traditional establishment date of the Republic – that is, 509 BC. According to tradition, the consuls were invested with many of the powers of the monarchs and were the new state's 'chief executives'. The safeguards inherent in the office, which were intended to prevent a maverick attempting to resuscitate monar-chic power, were that it was held on an annual basis and that two men shared the office; it was a principle of Republican office holding that, in a collegial magistracy, the officer who said 'no' prevailed over the one who said 'yes'.

How the two annual consuls split their duties is unclear; some hold that they alternated on a monthly basis with regard to which of the two was the senior, others that the duties were shared on a civilian/military basis – or some combination of the two. At any rate, the consuls, who were elected by the people in the *Comitia Centuriata,* were required at the end of their tenure to render an account to the people of the manner in which they had con-ducted themselves in office. Although this was normally a piece of formal ceremonial, on one occasion – at the end of Cicero's con-sulship in 63 BC – it was used by other politicians to mount serious demonstrations against Cicero.

At first, the range of duties involved in the consulship was very wide: the consuls were the heads of the civilian administration and the commanders-in-chief in wartime (which in the early Republic was frequent and of crucial importance to the Republic's survival). They summoned the senate and presided over its meetings (*ius consulendi*: the right of consulting the senate): although consulting the senate was strictly the consuls' right, in practice it tended to be viewed as an obligation that they should consult the senate prior to taking any kind of action; in this way the corporate senate was exercising a control over the Republic's executive officers, who were of course at the same time its members, which it had no legal right to do. Once the senate had made its recommendation on a matter referred to it through the passing of a *senatus consultum*, it was the consuls' responsibility to refer this to the people (*ius agendi cum populo*: the right of dealing with the people) and to act as 'presidents' of the relevant meetings of a popular assembly (see below), by which normally a senatorial decree was processed into law. That the magistrate's consultation of the senate was only a right, however, is shown by Julius Caesar's ignoring of the senate when, during his consulship in 59 BC, he took a proposal directly to a popular assembly; while this caused outrage, there was nothing that could be done about it. In the late Republic, it became increasingly common for the senate to be bypassed in this way – an indication of the shift of power away from the body.

The consuls had a theoretical right of jurisdiction, although in criminal cases this was generally delegated, civil jurisdiction being largely handled, after the creation of the office in 367 BC, by the *praetor urbanus*. As commanders-in-chief, the consuls had a right of summary jurisdiction on the battlefield, although, following a change in the law in 197 BC, the Roman citizen on campaign could take a consular judgement to an appeal (*provocatio*) to his peers, as was the case in the area of civil jurisdiction. Indeed, the citizen's right of appeal was held to be a cornerstone of the Republic's constitution, supposedly established at the same time as the Republic itself – that is, in 509 BC. It is now generally believed, however, that this date is too early, and that *provocatio* was probably not introduced until the late fourth century. The extension of *provocatio* to the battlefield was to cause considerable difficulty, as non-citizens on campaign enjoyed no comparable privilege.

Consuls (and, later, praetors also) enjoyed *imperium*, the executive authority conferred on them by the *Comitia Curiata* (see below) after their election in the *Comitia Centuriata*; it was this that gave them jurisdiction over a citizen's life and status (*caput*) and ability to command on the battlefield. Later, during the Second Punic War (218–202 BC), it became possible for the senate to extend a consul's and a praetor's *imperium* to enable him to retain battle-field command in an effort to ensure continuity. In such cases, individuals were not retained as consuls or praetors, but as pro-consuls and propraetors: this mechanism, which incidentally had the effect of placing such men under obligation to the senate for granting the extension, was subsequently employed in choosing governors for provinces; immediately prior to the elections which, until Sulla's time, were held at the end of the year, the provinces were assigned by lot to the next year's (as yet unknown) consuls and praetors. It was intended that this would minimise corruption in the distribution of lucrative appointments.

It has to be borne in mind that neither state offices nor member-ship of the senate carried salaries: thus, only men with considerable resources were effectively able to compete for and maintain them-selves in office; the coming of the Republic signalled 'harder times' for those who in commerce and industry had relied upon regal patronage. This fact in itself had, as we shall see, a considerable impact on the 'Struggle of the Orders' and its outcome; Rome was a state in which the wealthy had overwhelming advantages over those less fortunate, and this explains why patronage remained a vital feature of a social and political fabric which was 'tailor made' for exploitation.

Other magistracies were introduced largely with the aim of pro-viding assistance to the senior officers, although it is believed by some that the praetorship was introduced in 367 BC in order to 'compensate' the patricians for their 'loss' in that same year of one of the annual consulships. Quaestors, for example, probably derived their later financial competence from having originally been chosen (later, elected) as 'juniors' to the consuls, with the specific responsibility of assisting the consuls in their management of state funds. The origin of the office is obscure, although it is thought – and the name appears to support it – that the role of the office was investigatory, perhaps in connection with the kings', and then the consuls', criminal jurisdiction. There were at first two quaestors, although this number was raised to four in 421 BC, when the office was also opened to plebeians. Two further assistants to the consuls were the aediles, whose role appears to have been originally one of policing the City, but later extending into such areas as the supervision of public buildings, streets and markets and the laying on of the public games. There were four aediles, two of whom (curule aediles) were magistrates elected by the whole people, while the other two (plebeian aediles) were officers of the plebeians alone. While formally the latter were regarded as assistants of the tribunes of the plebs, their duties came to be virtually the same as those of the curule aediles.

A further delegation of consular power was to the censors; these officers, another dual magistracy, first appeared in 443 BC, and ten years later the duration of their term of office was fixed at eighteen months. How frequently they were elected in the early Republic is unclear, although later it was at five-year intervals. When they were first created, the censors were responsible for registering and assessing the Roman citizen body, to place them in their proper tribes and centuries and to ensure that they were correctly assessed for liability to military service. In the later fourth century, they acquired their tutelage of the senate's membership, and then an oversight of public morals and the leasing out of state contracts. Such weighty duties inevitably endowed the office with an extremely high standing; although the censorship did not carry *imperium*, it was regarded as the summit of a senator's career.

Such then was the range of offices that made up the magistracy, the executive arm of the Republic's government; over the years, apart from the censorship and the aedileship, the numbers of such officials required each year rose in response to the growing complexity of the administration. Eventually, even the number of consuls rose, so that while the consuls who began the year in office (*consules ordinarii*) continued to give their names to the year, by the end of the Republic and regularly during the Principate these would have resigned by mid-year and have been replaced by another pair (*consules suffecti*); the chief reason for this was to bring more men forward to the grade of ex-consul (*consularis*), thus qualifying them for senior administrative posts in the imperial service and, at the same time, gratifying the ambitions of a greater number of 'qualified' men.

In time, these offices were held in a sequence, so that they constituted a career structure for senators (*cursus honorum*): the usual order of offices for a politically ambitious man was quaestor (normally at around the age of 28), aedile or tribune of the plebs, praetor, consul; two-year gaps were normally enforced between offices. Sulla, in the early first century BC, tightened up these sequences, so that a man did not normally hold the quaestorship until about the age of thirty, the praetorship at thirty-nine and the consulship at forty-two. He also enacted that not more than one magistracy could be held at any one time, and that there should normally be a ten-year interval between two tenures of the same office. Further, he weakened the censorship – indeed abolished it for a while – and made fulfilment of the quaestorship the usual route of entry into the senate. Sulla's aim was to weaken the power of the magistracy relative to that of the senate.

In an emergency, the Republic made provision for extraordinary measures: the consuls could agree to resign their office in order to facilitate the appointment of a Dictator. This officer, who usually appointed his own 'deputy', the *magister equitum* ('master of cavalry') was, because he was appointed to deal with an emergency, immune from the veto of the tribunes of the plebs (see below). Dictators were empowered to hold office for six months only, after which they had to resign, although they could be reappointed for a further six months.

It may have been a reaction to the narrowly patrician dominance of the early Republic that the plebeians early on began to elect their own officials – the tribunes of the plebs and the plebeian aediles; the latter acted as assistants to the former. These, then, were not magistrates of the whole people, but officers of the plebeians, elected by the *Concilium Plebis* (see below) and responsible to that body. Nonetheless, there was a growing tendency in the middle and later Republic to treat these officers as if they were regular magistrates.

As we have seen, the plebeian aediles were scarcely distinguishable from their 'curule' colleagues; the tribunate of the plebs, however, was a unique office with special and, as later events were to show, destructive characteristics. At first, these 'tribal officers' of the plebeians who, according to the traditional account, were elected for the first time in 494 BC, were seen as the presiding officers of the plebeian assembly and thus enabled to handle proposals which, when passed, would bind the plebeians alone. They were also, however, the 'champions' and protectors of the plebeians: they had a duty to come to the aid of distressed plebeians *(ius auxilii)* and could, if necessary, physically place their persons between a plebeian and a magistrate trying to cause him harm; this was *intercessio*, which was the origin of the tribunician veto, so often employed to dramatic effect in the politics of the later Republic. In the early days, because the tribunes were unlikely also to be members of the senate, a bench was placed at the door of the senate to enable them to listen to proceedings in case they should need to 'intercede' on a plebeian's behalf. By the conclusion of the 'Struggle of the Orders' (see below), the tribunes were treated as part of the political establishment, and were a part of the bodies in which it might be necessary to use the veto. It was a particular strength of the office that, during tenure, the tribune's person enjoyed *sacrosanctitas*; it was thus a religious obligation on the plebeian citizens to avenge any harm done to a tribune, and this included the treating of his veto with disdain.

The relationships between these magistrates (and non-magistrates) and their relationship with both the senate and the popular assemblies provides the substance of the so-called 'Struggle of the Orders'; to this we shall return in a later section of this chapter.

The people

The composition, voting procedures and duties of Rome's four assemblies are laid out in tabular form as Appendix 1; the purpose of this section is to discuss their relationships with each other and their developing functions in the Republic.

Of the four assemblies, three (*Comitia Curiata, Comitia Centuriata* and *Comitia Tributa*) represented or consisted of the whole people (the *populus*) – that is, of all Roman citizens, no matter where they lived. The fourth (*Concilium Plebis*) was, as its name suggests, an assembly of the plebeians alone – that is, with no patricians present. These assemblies had come into existence at different times and for different reasons.

The oldest of them was the *Comitia Curiata,* which might well have been discarded as a 'fossil' during the Republic, as its duties – the conferring of *imperium* on already-elected magistrates, the formalisation of wills and adoptions – important as these were could easily have been carried out by other bodies. Its continued existence, therefore, bears out the observation of the Elder Cato that the Republic's government developed by evolution, not revolution; indeed, the very complexity implied in a governmental system which contained four assemblies, combined with the intricacies of religion and the law, was one of the chief weapons which allowed the Roman aristocracy to retain control of it for so long.

The antiquity of the *Comitia Curiata* is demonstrated best by its composition; formally, it consisted of ten *curiae* taken from each of the three ancient, so-called 'Romulean', tribes – Ramnes, Tities and Luceres. Little is known about these, and there is much dispute regarding their origins. It is thought that the *curia* was a 'meeting place' – the element recurs, for example, in a number of Romano-British place-names, such as Corbridge which appears to have been known in Roman times as *Corio*. In time, the word was transferred to the group, probably defined by kinship, which met there. This group presumably assembled for a combination of political, religious and military purposes. The origins of such groupings may have gone back to 'pre-urban Rome', although its assembling in the *Comitia Curiata* presumably reflects growing cohesion and strength. Even when it constituted the only assembly of the Roman people – in regal days – it probably was a body more of formalities than of power, perhaps formally marking such events as the succession of kings and the declaration of war. In historical times, the *curia* was represented by one man (a *lictor*) and presided over by a consul or praetor, or occasionally by the Chief Priest; as with all Roman popular assemblies, decisions were formally reached by group voting.

There is much discussion of the timing of reforms affecting the organisation of the Roman people: tradition has linked them with the name of the penultimate king, Servius Tullius, who was (as we have seen) in all probability the Etruscan, Mastarna. Indeed, it has been suggested that this king was 're-invented' with a Latin name, so that Romans would not have to associate a major and long-lasting reform of their organisation with a man of Etruscan origin. Others have, in any case, seen the reforms as more appropriate to the Rome of the fifth, or even the fourth, century; yet others have sought to retain the connection with Servius Tullius and to use it to 're-date' the reign of that king into the fifth century. In fact, there is no pressing reason why a reform, which led to a much tighter military, as well as political, organisation in Rome, should not have been at least adumbrated in the late regal period, but developed over a period of time; certainly changes will have had to take place to accommodate the growing extent of Roman territory (*ager Romanus*) and the developing complexity of the Roman citizen-body over the fifth and fourth centuries – important in a period of relatively vibrant economic activity, when many men of means would have been attracted to Rome, who could not easily be accommodated into a popular system based on kinship groups.

The main thrust of the reform was to secure a registration of property (principally land) belonging to Roman citizens; this would then allow them to be classified with regard to the contribution which they could individually make to Rome's war effort. In a system which married privileges with burdens it was then natural to use this classification in order to arrange the people for voting purposes in an assembly; the resultant assembly, the *Comitia Centuriata*, was thus in effect 'The Nation at Arms'.

To bring about this reform, an essential prerequisite was a major change in the tribal arrangements: the old 'Romulean' tribes were abolished and, in their place, was put a system of urban tribes (in Rome itself) and rural tribes (in the *ager Romanus*). Eventually, by the mid-third century, there were thirty-five tribes – four urban and thirty-one rural – although our sources have various versions, with differing chronologies, of the stages by which those numbers were reached. All citizens were also divided into five classes, according to the amount and type of equipment which they could provide for war; the *classis* literally was a 'call to arms' by a bugler (*classicus*), thus stressing the fundamentally military purpose of these changes. The contributions of the five classes ranged from a full set of armour in the first to nothing but the most basic missiles in the fifth. Although monetary values were later attached to the wealth levels of the five classes, these probably reflected an original equivalent relationship between the different levels of property qualification (at 20:15:10:5:2.5 or 2).

The *classes* were then subdivided into centuries, each *classis* having half of its centuries composed of older men (*seniores*, aged forty-seven to sixty) and half of younger men (*iuniores*, aged seventeen to forty-six). To reflect the differing levels of contribution of the different classes, the centuries in each were of unequal number: thus, there were eighty centuries in the first *classis*, twenty each in the second, third and fourth, and thirty in the fifth; to these were added five centuries of totally unarmed men at the lower end, and eighteen of cavalry at the upper end, making 193 centuries in all. When this body was summoned for political (rather than military) purposes, it did not, when it came to voting, work on the principle of 'one man, one vote' but on the 'group-voting' system; thus, each century established its view by a vote of its members, but a decision of the *populus* was established by a majority of the 193 centuries. If the richest men – that is, the cavalry and the top infantry *classis* – voted together (ninety-eight centuries), they represented a clear majority of the Roman people. In this way, the same men who dominated the senate and the magistracy also dominated the *Comitia Centuriata*; the oligarchy was secure in its control of the mechanisms of government. The *Comitia Centuriata* or, as Cicero once called the body, 'my army of wealthy men', handled the most important electoral, legislative and judicial business of the Republic (see Appendix 1).

The tribal reorganisation, which was the essence of these late-regal/early-Republican reforms, also formed the basis of another assembly of the *populus* which handled the less crucial state business – the *Comitia Tributa*; this used the thirty-five 'Servian' tribes as its basis of organisation. Again, the group-voting system was employed, so that each tribe first determined its vote, and a popular decision was then reached by calculating a simple majority of the thirty-five.

Also employing the reformed tribal system in its organisation was the fourth assembly – the *Concilium Plebis*; as its name indicates, this was not an assembly of the *populus*, but simply a meeting of plebeian citizens, presided over by a tribune of the plebs or by a plebeian aedile, but reaching its decisions (*plebiscita*) by the group-voting system. At first, the *Concilium Plebis* could not pass laws binding the whole people, although a *plebiscitum* could become law if it was subsequently passed through an assembly of the *populus*.

At first sight, it might be thought that the two tribally based assemblies would have represented a shift, even if only slight, in the direction of democracy. However, a combination of circumstances militated against this: first, the group-voting system and the composition of the assemblies themselves ensured that the voice that was heard was not that of the mass of the people. Secondly, the system of patronage, in which the wealthy supported the less fortunate members of the citizen-body, was not in the least altruistic: there was a price to be paid in the form of the political loyalty that was expected of clients towards their patrons; political loyalty was measured principally by the way in which people cast their votes. In a system that did not see the introduction of secrecy in the ballot until the second half of the second century BC, disloyalty (*perfidia*) was easily detectable – and was regarded as a serious failing in the eyes of not simply the patron but also of the whole citizen-body and the state's gods. Further, we should not forget that, until a change in the law in the early years of the second century, although the citizen may have been able to call on his protective rights while in Rome, he was subject to the summary jurisdiction of magistrates while on campaign; the oligarchy's revenge for an act of political disloyalty could thus be swift and decisive. This did not represent fertile ground for the growth of democracy. Indeed, as we shall see, while the 'Struggle of the Orders' may have been nominally concerned with the relationship between patricians and plebeians, its real area of concern was how the governing oligarchy was to stage-manage apparent concessions while not yielding one iota of its control.

It should also be noted that other assembly procedures, besides the voting, undermined independent voices: there was, for example, no right on the citizen's part to speak at a meeting; he could speak only if invited to do so by the presiding magistrate, who would presumably have been determined to allow a hearing only to those who were of similar mind to himself. Further, little or nothing was left to chance in debate: for, prior to a formal meeting of an assembly, at which a motion would be put and voted on, three informal meetings (*contiones*) were held at intervals, at which the presiding officer rehearsed what would eventually be the assembly's formal business. Finally, if the business of an assembly threatened to go seriously awry, then religion could be invoked to bring proceedings to a close. We see an example of an attempt to do this on the part of Marcus Calpurnius Bibulus, Caesar's consular colleague in 59 BC; although Caesar ignored his colleague's 'religious objections' and continued with his business, his 'breaking of the rules' hung over him for the following decade as a matter on which his enemies might prosecute him, if he provided them with an opportunity. The very complexity of the breakdown of relations between Caesar and Pompey in 51–50 BC, which led to the outbreak of civil war at the beginning of 49, was in part caused by the existence of this potential threat.

We shall return to the matter of the relationship between senate, magistrates and people in the final section of this chapter.

The struggle for survival

It is customary to see the wars of early Rome as part of a struggle for survival, distinguished by such heroic acts as the defence of the Tiber bridge by Horatius Cocles. It is certainly reasonable to suppose that the crucial nature of the site of Rome ensured that Rome would have to fight her neighbours for permanent possession of it; for control of the site, giving access to the salt of the Tiber estuary and the grain-lands of Campania, inevitably promised the prospect of dominance within Italy.

It was probably the recognition of the inevitability of conflict against neighbours who were militarily strong that had led to the military reorganisation described in the previous section; for, although we have laid stress on the political use to which these changes were put, their primary intention was surely military. Although much is unclear regarding the very early military organisation, it is thought that each of the three 'Romulean' tribes contributed one thousand infantry (under a *tribunus militum*) and one hundred cavalry (under a *tribunus celerum*). This army thus had a strength of 3,300 men, based on thousands and centuries; the importance of the former is made clear by the fact that the normal Latin word for soldier was *miles* (a 'thousander').

The chief problem with this army is that, like the political organisation which went with it, it was founded in the notion of kinship groups, which made the incorporation of new citizens a difficult matter. The so-called 'Servian' reform had two major advantages: it doubled the size of the army and based its organisation on the centuries; the first three classes provided sixty fighting centuries, and these constituted the 'levy' (or *legio*). The new organisation also broke the influence of the old, and now less relevant, kinship groups. With the coming of the Republic, with its two consuls, the size of the individual centuries was reduced, to provide two consular legions, each of three thousand men, arranged as before in sixty centuries. It should be noted that, although the size of the century changed over time, the principle of a legion consisting of sixty centuries was retained.

Between the mid-fifth century BC and the early third, Rome was at war with various Italian groups virtually continuously; some of these conflicts were extremely serious. Hostilities with Veii dated back probably to the regal period, when rivalries between such neighbouring kings were common within the Etruscan world. Indeed, as we have seen, it is likely that the traditional version of the expulsion of the monarchy from Rome has become intertwined with confused (and misleading) accounts of what was probably an outbreak of warfare between the Roman king (Tarquinius Superbus) and his Veientine neighbour, Lars Porsenna. At the root of the problem were in all probability the issues of control of the Tiber valley and access to Campania. Rome captured the important site of Fidenae in 435, and went on to attack Veii itself, which it also captured after the ten-year siege (406–396) led by the Dictator, Marcus Furius Camillus; the land of Veii was as a result annexed. The growth of the *ager Romanus* was probably not as incidental as is sometimes maintained: one of the effects of the coming of the Republic in Rome and the domination of it by landowning patricians was a sharp rise in land shortage and debt; an obvious way to attempt to alleviate this, and so lessen the threat of agitation in Rome itself, was to make more land available to Roman citizens by warfare and subsequent territorial acquisition. Even while the siege of Veii was still in progress, Rome was engaged in hostilities with other Etruscan neighbours – Volsinii and Tarquinii – which had to be foreclosed because of the Gallic threat from the north.

These Gauls came from the area of Cisalpina, to the north of the Po valley; their movements were a considerable problem in the first half of the fourth century to the people living in northern Italy. The movements themselves indicate a general instability of population in the heart of Europe, and they reached as far west as Britain, where their settlements are generally seen as belonging to the 'La Tène' culture; the penetration of these Gauls in 390 as far south as the city of Rome, as we shall see, was the cause of one of Rome's more traumatic military setbacks, which left a permanent mark on the national consciousness. There are discrepancies in the accounts of these events, and some prefer to place the sack of Rome in the 380s. Although there were further 'Gallic episodes' in the 350s, 340s and 330s, Rome's position in Italy in relation to the Latins, in particular, was becoming stronger; on the last occasion, she was able to impose a thirty-year peace on the Gallic insurgents.

Her domination of Latium left Rome as neighbours of Campania, which was at that time under the control of the Samnite city of Capua; although Rome had signed an agreement with the Samnites in 354, war – the first of three bruising conflicts with the Samnites – broke out probably in 341. During the second war, in 321, two Roman legions were defeated at the Caudine Forks and forced to pass into slavery under the Samnite yoke. This ranked, alongside the Gallic sack of 390 and the defeat of Quinctilius Varus and the loss of three legions in Germany in AD 9, as one of the three most humiliating disasters suffered by Roman armies, all of which were embedded in the Roman memory. The immediate results of these wars were the dissolution of the Latin League and the foundation of *coloniae* in Latium, including Ostia (probably in 335), the integration of Campania into the Roman state, with members of the great Campanian aristocratic families brought into the Roman senate, and closer contact with both the Greek city-states of southern Italy and, of course, the Carthaginians.

Thus, Rome's wars in Italy, which had started as struggles for the survival of the city-state, had brought her to the point where much of Italy, south of the River Po, enjoyed some kind of relationship with Rome, recognising her as the 'mistress of Italy'. Further, this position pointed the way to new relationships in the south of Italy and the beginnings of an overseas empire. That this was not, however, all part of a preconceived 'development plan' is indicated by the fact that, as recently as 348, Rome had signed a treaty with Carthage which was very restrictive of the former's ability to engage with the world outside of Italy; both states evidently recognised that, in the mid-fourth century at least, Rome's interests were essentially based inside Italy.

The 'Struggle of the Orders'

The backcloth to the events described in the previous section was provided by changing political and social relationships within the Republic itself. The 'Struggle of the Orders', which went on intermittently between the foundation of the Republic and the passing of the *Lex Hortensia* of 287 BC and which, according to tradition, included five occasions on which the plebeian section of the community threatened to secede from Rome and military service, has been interpreted by some as a class struggle (between patricians and plebeians) of a type seen widely in more recent world history. In fact, both the aims and, indeed, the outcomes of this struggle were much more limited than is sometimes assumed.

As we have seen, the ending of the Roman monarchy had substantial political, social and economic effects; whereas the monarchy had evidently brought a widespread vitality, which provided work for ordinary people and entrepreneurial opportunity for wealthier plebeians, much narrower attitudes prevailed with the coming of the Republic. Economic vibrancy, and the opportunities which it brought, gave way to the dominance of a patrician landowning clique, who exercised control over government and military command and who were regarded as the only repository of knowledge concerning religion and the law. In such a situation, the remainder of society was totally dependent on the patricians: while they did not extend rights to others in the early days, they did operate a patronage which put others at their mercy and under obligation to them; the patron–client relationship may have been mutually beneficial in many respects, but it afforded a personal protection which was entirely at the discretion of the patron; this could never be construed as social and political justice. Not only this, but, with the passing of the monarchy, the avenues which had led to economic success were now effectively blocked off, and the chief source of prosperity was landowning, of which the patricians had a virtual monopoly. As a result, land shortage and debt afflicted many. In such a situation, it is likely that some at least of the early wars fought by Rome were undertaken in a search for land and with a view to heading off discontent.

Although we cannot vouch for the authenticity of the chronology and the events taken to be part of the 'Struggle of the Orders', it is clear that the overarching thrust of it was a good deal more narrow than has traditionally been assumed. In view of the fact that it was impossible for a man to make political and social headway without money at his disposal, the beneficiaries of any relaxing of the Republic's political constraints had of necessity to be very restricted in extent.

As we have seen, the monarchy had offered opportunities not only to patricians but also to plebeians of means; the latter group will have felt the tightest 'pinch' with the coming of the Republic. It is not surprising, therefore, that on examination the real intended beneficiaries of change were the rich plebeians whose 'class interests' were closest to those of the patricians; we should not be deluded into looking for a genuine social revolution.

Traditionally, the earliest 'concessions' concerned the plebeians' own assembly, the *Concilium Plebis*: when this organisation came into being is not clear, but the patricians evidently tolerated its reaching decisions (*plebiscita*) which were binding on the plebeian section of the community alone. *Plebiscita*, however, could become law, but only if someone could be found to effect their successful passage through an assembly of the *populus*; such a restriction guaranteed that nothing 'radical', which had been approved by the *Concilium*, stood a chance of passage into law. Who, then, benefited from the existence of this body? Clearly, the primary beneficiaries were its leaders, the *tribuni plebis*, who by definition will have been men of some substance; through their 'chairmanship' of the *Concilium* and through their religiously protected powers of acting as champions of the plebeians, holders of this office were potentially men of considerable weight in the Republic. Further, they were given seats at the entrance to the senate house, so that they could carry their protecting role into the heart of the patricians' governmental machinery.

Later in the fifth century, codification of the law, the right of intermarriage between patricians and plebeians, and the admission of plebeians to the senate and to the quaestorship all enhanced the position of wealthy plebeians; indeed, such moves benefited the patricians more than it did the plebeians, for it strengthened the base of a patrician-dominated governing class as well as, of course, depriving the plebeians of the full commitment of their own 'natural leaders'. As far as ordinary plebeians were concerned, the patron–client relationship held them in virtual bondage, adding a 'moral dimension' to that already exercised by the indebtedness and land shortage afflicting many of them: further, we should remember that, although the tribunes and the law could protect them from arbitrary treatment by magistrates at home, they were entirely at the mercy of those same men, as military commanders, when they were on campaign; the frequency of military activity in the early years of the Republic ensured that this was a real constraint. The plebeians as a whole, therefore, had no opportunity to make any headway with a campaign for advancement – even supposing that in the circumstances they had any enthusiasm for such a campaign in any case.

The fourth century saw further 'concessions' on the part of the patricians, such as the introduction of military pay in 396 BC and the opening to plebeians of the dictatorship in 356 and of the censorship (first established in 443) in 351. The Licinian and Sextian laws of 367 had already enacted that one of the annual consulships should go to a plebeian, although there were, in fact, still years in the mid-fourth century which saw two patrician consuls. Further, it is held that the creation in 366 of the praetorship, an office carrying *imperium* and, at first at least, exclusive to patricians, represents a patrician attempt to circumvent the 'plebeian advance' in respect of the consulship.

In any case, the senatorial aristocracy which was now made up of patricians and wealthy plebeians who identified their interests together in the 'governing class' now had other threats on its collective mind; principal among these was the need to protect the senate, as the body of the corporate aristocracy, from encroachment by other bodies and individuals, which was much more concerning to them than any ambitions or complaints on the part of the mass of the plebeians.

The greatest concern of the aristocracy had, by the middle of the fourth century, become the ability of its own members as individuals to 'outflank' it; this was achievable through the right of magistrates to deal directly with the people and without consulting their corporate peers in the senate. The final phase, therefore, of the 'Struggle of the Orders' was concerned less with the completion of popular 'emancipation' than with the determination of the aristocracy to appear conciliatory while, in fact, strengthening the mechanisms of its own control of the Republic.

The architect of a series of reforms which effectively pointed the way to the conclusion of the 'Struggle of the Orders' was Quintus Publilius Philo, consul and Dictator in 339 BC: he enacted that one of the censors had to be a plebeian, thus ending the patrician monopoly of an office, the chief purpose of which had probably been to 'neutralise' the growing power which individual plebeians were able to obtain through access to the magistracies and to membership of the senate. He further enacted that the *plebiscita* (the decisions of the *Concilium Plebis*) should be binding on the whole *populus*, although the equalisation of *plebiscitum* and *lex* appears not to have been fully recognised until the passing of the *Lex Hortensia* in 287.

Publilius Philo's third enactment was in many ways the most important, enjoining that the senate should have the right to hear and discuss a magistrate's proposals prior to their being put to the people. This recognised changes that had taken place during the fifth and fourth centuries: originally, the senate had the right and custom of seeing legislation after it had been passed by the people. Ostensibly, this was intended to obviate any unwitting infringement by the people of legal or religious principle by a body that was regarded as the sole repository of expertise in such matters. In reality, it came to be used as a general check on the popular will on the part of an aristocratic minority. However, the membership and procedures of the popular bodies, including the *Concilium Plebis*, had developed in such a way as to ensure that the patrician/plebeian aristocracy had the means of checking any undesirable trends. The corporate aristocracy's real need in the later fourth century was to be able to protect itself from certain of its own individual members; thus, pre-discussion was a means of controlling not the people but rather those who presided over its deliberations.

Thus, the outcome of the 'Struggle of the Orders' was not the balance of forces in the Republic envisaged by Polybius; rather, despite the fact that magistrates and people had great power invested in them, the aristocracy in the senate was, through a variety of mechanisms, able to control both of them. What should have been a 'struggle' to secure equality of rights and opportunity for all citizens had concluded by entrenching in power the body which represented those who all along had dominated the Republic since its inception; the only concession of significance that the patricians had made was to recognise that in reality wealthy members of the plebeian order had interests and ambitions that were identical to their own. The 'Struggle of the Orders' had thus succeeded in giving birth to an aristocracy of patricians and plebeians – the nobility – who regarded control of the Republic as its birthright. It is little wonder that king Pyrrhus of Epirus saw the Roman senate as an 'Assembly of Kings'.

Polybius saw all of this at a time when its weaknesses were only just beginning to appear: tribunes of the plebs no longer observed the senate's proceedings from chairs set in the doorway of the *Curia*, for they were themselves now members of the senate and their powers were now at the disposal of the senate and of its factions. Further, the Publilian and Hortensian legislation had not destroyed the notion of a magistrate's or a tribune's right to deal directly with his 'constituents'; events were to show that this could still be invoked in personal or factional interest; as long as the aristocracy's 'corporate ethic' predominated, there was little difficulty despite the fact, of course, that the 'Polybian balance' was all the while more apparent than real.

As long as the Republic spent more time at war than it did at peace, the senate's hegemony was unlikely to be seriously challenged. However, as individuals and groups (factions) within the aristocracy awoke to the opportunities for wealth and power that the running of a growing empire could offer them, the 'corporateness' began to dissipate as these factions and individuals set out to exploit the opportunities for aggrandisement that were offered by the Republic's governmental mechanisms. Instead, however, of guaranteeing stability and lawfulness, these came increasingly to point the way to corruption and violence.

Without doubt, the reality of the Roman *respublica* was closer to the views of Plato than of Polybius; the Republic's government did not consist of a series of foolproof checks and balances. Rather, it was an edifice which, like the constitutions of the Greek city-states observed by Socrates and Plato, carried within it the seeds of its own destruction. This ensured a transition, sometimes violent, from monarchy back to monarchy.

Appendix 1

Roman voting assemblies

	Comitia Curiata	Comitia Centuriata	Comitia Tributa	Concilium Plebis
Composition				
Voting units	30 curiae, 10 each from 3 ancient tribes	193 centuries – 18 cavalry, 170 infantry (arranged in the ratio 80, 20, 20, 20, 30, according to five property classes), 5 of unarmed (i.e. unpropertied) citizens	35 tribes	35 tribes
Citizens attending	Each curia represented by one man (a lictor)	All citizens	All citizens	Plebeians only
Presiding officer	Consul or praetor or (for religious purposes) Chief Priest	Consul or praetor	Consul or praetor or curule aedile	Tribune of the plebs or plebeian aedile
Duties				
Elections		Consuls, praetors, censors	Curule aediles, quaestors, lower officers, special commissioners	Tribunes and aediles of the plebs
Legislative	Confirmed *imperium* of magistrates; confirmed adoptions and wills	(Until about 218 BC, chief law-making body); subsequently used for declaration of war, confirmation of powers of censors	All types except those restricted to *Comitia Centuriata*	All types except those restricted to *Comitia Centuriata*; decisions (known as *plebiscita*) had force of law after 287 BC
Judicial		Capital charges (increasingly after 150 BC limited to treason charges)	All crimes against the state which were punishable by fine (after the time of the Gracchi, these duties increasingly lost to the other courts)	

Source: D. Shotter, *The Fall of the Roman Republic*, Lancaster Pamphlets (London: Routledge, 1994), p. 101.

Appendix 2

The passage of legislation in the Roman Republic

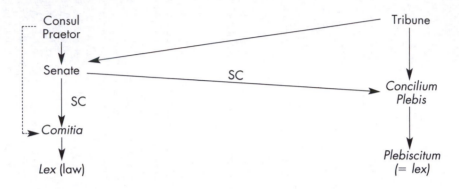

SC: *senatus consulto* ('by decree of the senate')

Further reading

Astin A. E., *Cato the Censor* (Oxford, 1978).

Boethius A. and Ward-Perkins J. B., *Etruscan and Roman Architecture* (Harmondsworth, 1970).

Broughton T. R. S., *The Magistrates of the Roman Republic* (New York, 1951–1952).

Brunt P. A., *Italian Manpower, 225 B.C. – A.D. 14* (Oxford, 1971).

Chilver G. E. F., *Cisalpine Gaul* (Oxford, 1941).

D'Arms J. H., *Commerce and Social Standing in Ancient Rome* (Cambridge, MA, 1981).

Finley M. I., *The Ancient Economy* (London, 1985).

Frank T., *Rome and Italy of the Republic: An Economic Survey of Ancient Rome*, Vol. I (Baltimore, MD, 1933).

Frayn J. M., *Subsistence Farming in Roman Italy* (London, 1979).

Frederiksen M. W., *Campania* (London, 1984).

Gabba E., *Republican Rome: The Army and the Allies* (Oxford, 1977).

Meiggs R., *Roman Ostia* (Oxford, 1973).

Nicolet C., *The World of the Citizen in Republican Rome* (London, 1980).

Ogilvie R. M., *The Romans and their Gods* (London, 1969).

Salmon E. T., *Samnium and the Samnites* (Cambridge, 1967).

Salmon E. T., *Roman Colonisation Under the Republic* (London, 1969).

Salmon E. T., *The Making of Roman Italy* (London, 1982).

Scullard H. H., *Scipio Africanus: Soldier and Politician* (London, 1970).

Scullard H. H., *Roman Politics, 220–150 B.C.* (Oxford, 1973).

Scullard H. H., *Festivals and Ceremonies of the Roman Republic* (London, 1981).

Starr C. G., *The Beginnings of Imperial Rome* (Ann Arbor, MI, 1980).

Staveley E. S., *Greek and Roman Voting and Elections* (London, 1972).

Taylor L. R., *Roman Voting Assemblies* (Ann Arbor, MI, 1966).

Toynbee J. M. C., *Death and Burial in the Roman World* (London, 1971).

von Fritz K., *The Theory of the Mixed Constitution in Antiquity* (New York, 1954).

White K. D., *Roman Farming* (London, 1970).

Chapter 3

The birth of an empire

Expansion in Italy

There was little hint in the nature of Rome's early expansion to suggest that she would eventually become the centre of the largest, most highly organised, collection of territories that the world had seen. We have noted that Rome's earliest military endeavours, shrouded in myth though many of them are, represented a fight for survival on the part of the fledgling city-state. This fight for survival was part of a much greater confusion as Etruscan warlords attacked each other to win seats of wealth and power. The legends concerned with the end of the monarchy and the birth of the Republic probably conceal a series of power struggles, of which that between Tarquinius Superbus and Lars Porsenna represents but one example; this, in its turn, may have been a part of Rome's long struggle with her near neighbour, Veii, which came to its climax at the beginning of the fourth century.

Eventually, Rome emerged – a monarchy no longer, but the Republic; in all of this, it had kept its territory intact. However, such was the sensitivity attaching to Rome's physical location that it was bound to continue to be a target for jealous and land-hungry neighbours; for Rome, it was a question of 'kill or be killed'. Over the next two hundred years, until the middle of the third century BC, Rome fought wars against various Italian neighbours which were designed to secure the integrity of Roman territory. However, such wars eventually took Roman territory to the banks of the River Po and to the toe of Italy. We should probably not, however, view all of these activities as purely defensive; the Roman Republic was initially short of the land necessary for her population to survive and prosper. Thus, territorial acquisition provided a motive for expansion alongside the search for peaceful neighbours.

In the course of this, lessons had to be learned quickly; it was undoubtedly a combination of fear and jealousy of the growing state which induced the Gauls from the north to attack the city of Rome in 390 BC. Although, as an 'event', this was probably of little consequence and recovery evidently took place rapidly with the building of new walls by 378, the 'sack of Rome', as we have seen, took its place as one of those traumatic episodes which left a profound impression; the story of it had not 'dimmed' when recounted by the Augustan historian, Livy, nearly four centuries later. Romans had not succumbed, but had successfully defended the integrity of 'Jupiter's city'. Rome's mission was thus demonstrated for all time as divinely inspired.

No thought was presumably given to the reasons that had driven the Gauls from *Cisalpina* to behave as they had: their action and that of their Italian allies will have been put down to jealousy, which on the part of some Italians it probably was; the kind of population instability that had driven the action and which was to drive many more such episodes until the sack of Rome in the fifth century AD was a 'closed book'.

A Roman 'sphere of influence' was developing: by the mid-fourth century, it extended to Capua in the south, and took in Etruscans and others to the north. Not all were equally happy about this, and the Latin communities tried unsuccessfully to revolt from

Rome (341–338 BC), but the fact that Rome had a leadership role in Italy was, according to Polybius, recognised by the Carthaginians in a treaty which respected Rome's hegemony in her sphere of influence.

The background to Rome's success was multi-faceted: to the Etruscan oligarchies to the north she seemed not only to be a means of defence against outsiders, such as Gauls, but was for the aristocrats themselves a 'kindred spirit' in their difficulties with their own peasant communities. The Greeks of southern Italy, for their part, mostly saw Rome as civilised – almost Greek, in fact – and, therefore, a source of support against their own barbarian enemies, principally the Samnites of central southern Italy. Here was a shared concern, for the Samnites were for Rome, too, a dangerous presence set adjacent to her own recently acquired interests in Campania. The cities of *Magna Graecia* inherited a characteristic from the 'motherland', namely a fierce sense of their independence. Thus, allying with one was bound to create difficulties for Rome with others; because Rome chose to ally herself with the wealthiest of them, Naples (*Neapolis*), she made enemies elsewhere – for example, Tarentum. However, if Rome was to safeguard her own interests and do justice to the protection which her hegemony obviously implied, it made sense to choose Naples as a source of resources for the wars against the Samnites.

Such an arrangement was, however, bound to involve change for Rome; her traditions and way of life were very different from those of a Greek city-state, such as Naples – the simple morality traditionally associated with an agricultural economy on the one hand, and the economic sophistication derived from commercialism on the other. In short, for Rome to be able to acquire from Naples the resources which she needed to fight the Samnites, she had to leave behind some of the protective isolationism with which she had shielded her institutions and traditions and to start talking the same economic language as the Greek city-state; it was an experience which not all in Rome will have found equally palatable. One obvious consequence was the development of a coinage – not perhaps initially, at least, a true Roman coinage, but a Greek coinage for Rome to use in her dealings with Greek city-states. Not surprisingly, fears will have been raised about the effects on 'national integrity'. Inevitably, too, new relationships will have given new opportunities to new groups of people in Rome, contributing to a softening of the exclusiveness of Rome's governing class.

However, even though Rome may have found some aspects of such advances difficult, in other aspects of her new 'imperial' role she showed herself to be extraordinarily enlightened and far-sighted – as the emperor, Claudius, was later to remind his contemporaries (Tacitus, *Annals* XI.23–24); as Rome's territorial responsibilities grew, so she had to devise forms of relationship with new friends, erstwhile enemies and subjects. The methods employed were hierarchical, suiting a state that thought in terms of hierarchies – and these proved to be durable, also; it was essentially these same features which were, much later, to dominate and guide the relationships between Rome and her overseas provinces, including Britain.

It may seem to be an indication of surprising generosity, especially when contrasted with the attitudes of the Greek city-states in their heydays, that at the centre of the whole scheme lay something as precious as Roman citizenship. This consisted essentially of five 'rights' (*iura*): *suffragium* and *honores* were the rights of voting and holding office in Rome; *coniubium* and *commercium* concerned the ability to test the legitimacy of offspring and of contracts in a Roman court of law; finally, *provocatio* was every citizen's right to an appeal to his peers in cases involving his *caput* – his status as a citizen or even his very life. Together, the second two constituted 'half-citizenship' (*civitas sine suffragio*), which enabled their holders to relate to Rome socially and commercially, although carrying the assumption that they retained some measure of control over their own political and administrative affairs. In this way, Rome avoided the Greek concept of *isopoliteia* (or reciprocal citizenship of two states). Some holders of 'half-citizenship' – those with 'Latin rights' – also had *migratio*, which allowed them access to Rome and full citizenship. In any case, voting, office bearing and appeal could be exercised only in Rome, and office bearing carried the additional 'qualification' that, in the absence of a salary for holders of public office, candidates had to be sufficiently wealthy to be able not only to seek office but also to maintain themselves in that office, if successful at the polls. Thus, the apparent generosity in the making of citizenship grants was in practice sharply reined in with respect to the real ability of holders to affect issues of consequence.

Citizenship or half-citizenship could, of course, be awarded on an individual basis, but the real importance of the grants was their application to communities. At the top of this hierarchy were the *coloniae*: these initially were 'transplantations' of groups of citizens from Rome to found new cities in freshly conquered territory; as such, they represented a 'military reserve', and took responsibility (their *munus*, or 'duty') for defending and administering an area around them (or 'showing the flag'). Colonists were awarded plots of land both inside and outside the new town; in many cases, they were 'downgraded' to half-citizenship, although this was only a device to leave in their hands some measure of local control in their new environments. Later, *coloniae* could be created by adding a group of colonists on to an existing settlement, which might be done either to strengthen the military 'backbone' in the area or to honour the town in question.

Municipia were existing communities to which citizenship awards were made – usually, again, of the half-citizenship type. As can be seen, these awards were generally made in urban contexts; however, the majority of those who lived in conquered territory were left 'free', notionally, at least. *Civitates liberae ac foederatae* had, as the title suggests, no citizenship privileges, but rather a treaty with Rome which enjoined the principle that such states could have only a foreign policy which Rome accepted, although in return they could rely on Roman help if they were attacked. This, then, was the range of legal relationships which Rome created originally to bind the Italian peoples to her and then proceeded to use in the expanded empire of future years.

There was then the question of land: although Rome did not generally remove all the land from conquered peoples, some – presumably the land of better quality – would be taken over and declared to be public property (*ager publicus*). On this, *coloniae* might be planted, or it might be let out to smallholders. Conceivably, the original owners might be left on it, although now, of course, as tenants of the Roman state. The importance of this was that those who owned land or who farmed *ager publicus* (*adsidui*) were eligible for service in the legions of the Roman army (if they were citizens) and might be called on to serve in an emergency. Others (non-citizens) could be enrolled into the allied contingents (*socii*) to serve alongside the legions; indeed, Rome did not exact tribute from her Italian allies, only military manpower – again, not falling victim to the mistake made by the Athenians of the fifth century BC of making their allies in the Delian League contribute money (tribute) to the common cause. It was obviously crucial that resources of manpower should be kept up to strength; in the early days, while campaigning was in Italy and of relatively short duration each year, there appears to have been no great difficulty in combining farming with military service. Later, as the seats of warfare became more distant, as we shall see, real problems arose which came to threaten the very fabric of the Republic.

Thus, Rome 'wove' her Italian neighbours into a kind of 'confederacy', all acknowledging Rome's hegemony and all co-operating and sharing in the common defence of the homeland. This straightforward formula, not surprisingly, came under developing strain, as Roman military interests came increasingly to embrace a wide overseas stage.

This initially came about as a direct result of Rome's new commitments in Italy, particularly her relationships with the Greek city-states of the south. As we have seen, while Rome had formed alliances with some such Greek city-states, not all such states had viewed the development with equanimity. Tarentum (Taranto), for example, 'flirted' with Carthage and with the leaders of states of the Greek mainland, partly because of Rome's involvement with some of her 'neighbours', but largely because of her own fears of those who lived inland of her. Indeed, Rome's victory over Pyrrhus of Epirus (275 BC) marked her first success over an overseas power – and one that, in a sense, carried with it all the traditions of Greece and Macedon.

The overseas empire

It is often argued that Rome was a reluctant imperialist, interested only in acquiring sound neighbours in Italy. Certainly, it is true that some in Rome will have been apprehensive of what effects foreign influences might have had on Roman traditions, as is clearly demonstrated in the surviving *senatus consultum* of 186 BC concerning the worship of the Greek god, Dionysus. However, despite the fear of widening the bounds of Roman society, of having to share privileges more widely and of undermining the simple form of life that they could traditionally control, there is evidence which suggests very clearly that other people's land and wealth were of interest to Rome's governing class; the well-publicised reluctance might have been, at least in part, a temporary 'spin'. It is, however, true that those in Rome who were responsible for making decisions were not first and foremost commercially minded, whereas many of those with whom Rome came into contact in the wider world were – especially the Greek city-states and the Carthaginians.

Rome's relationship with the 'great power' on the opposite side of the Mediterranean (founded in 814 BC) went back a long way; treaties are recorded (for example, in Polybius III.24,3) which set out to define the spheres of influence of the two states. Fundamentally, Rome and Carthage were possessed of two very different preoccupations: Rome was driven largely by considerations of security and land – hence her notion of wars as 'just' – while the chief interest of the Carthaginians lay in the creation of commercial opportunities. Contrary to what is often asserted, therefore, Carthage was not a crudely expansionist and militaristic power; her wars were fought, chiefly with mercenary troops, to win and protect 'markets'. Not surprisingly, initially at least, this led to potential clashes of interests with Greek city-states rather than with Rome herself.

Sicily had long been within the sphere of Carthaginian commercial interest and influence; this of itself did not seem to be of great moment to Rome, until her involvement with certain Greek city-states lent to the Carthaginian presence on Sicily an 'Italian dimension'. Particularly sensitive was the Carthaginian desire to expand her commercial activities into southern Italy, a 'project' in which she felt encouraged by the divisions amongst the Greek city-states. In this way, Rome's pride and the integrity of her hegemony in Italy came into question; there was also, of course, a question of security involved. Polybius' account (I.10–11) makes it clear that Rome's real problem lay with the illogicality of the actual *casus belli* – that is, helping a group of Italian mercenaries who, to the Roman mind, did not have right on their side. According to Polybius, the reluctance – for this reason and no other – of the senatorial aristocracy was overruled by the people who were persuaded that glory and booty were there to be had. In other words, the often-cited senatorial insularity was probably not the issue.

The First Punic War (265–241 BC) was for a time a rather desultory affair, with the Romans effectively dominating Sicily, while the Carthaginians, not surprisingly, ruled the seas around; Rome did not possess a navy at this time. Despite Rome's undoubted stance as a 'militaristic nation', there were other problems in making the transition from the kind of warfare to which she had become accustomed in Italy; the notion of seasonal campaigning was hardly suited to a war which plainly required a continuous commitment. Equally problematic was the Roman command

Plate 3.1 (opposite) S. Maria di Falerii Novi: town gateway.

structure: since military power was vested in Rome's political leaders, it automatically followed that military commands had to change hands, along with civilian office, at the turn of each year. It is a major sign, however, of Rome's adaptability that she equipped herself *ab initio* with a navy, using a wrecked Carthaginian ship as a model.

Victory in the First Punic War in 241 BC was a mark as much as anything of Roman persistence, but it was important for more than that: it brought Rome her first overseas possession (province) – in the form of the island of Sicily – which required, therefore, the introduction of some form of organisation and administration. Secondly, there are signs of a new and harsher attitude emerging in Rome – a mark, perhaps, of the real cost of the victory; the war-indemnities imposed were harsh, and regarded by Carthage as unreasonably so – to the extent that the

bad feeling so caused was to fester to the point of further warfare between the two cities before the third century was over. Shortly after the conclusion of the First Punic War (in 238), Rome, without any apparent justification, seized the islands of Sardinia and Corsica which, like Sicily, had long been recognised as being within the Carthaginian sphere of interest. Thirdly, the recent experience of war seems to have highlighted in Rome a sharper sense of her responsibilities as 'leader of Italy' and, with it, the loyalty which she felt that she was entitled to expect from Italian communities, if she (Rome) took their security on to her own shoulders. This was demonstrated dramatically in 241 BC by Rome's handling of the albeit ill-conceived revolt of the Faliscans, her near neighbours to the north, a people who were regarded culturally as Etruscan, but who were, in fact, Latin speakers. Their chief town (Falerii Veteres / Civitacastellana) was demolished and its inhabitants removed to the new, less defensible site of Falerii Novi (S. Maria di Falerii Novi). This was the sharpest

indication yet that Rome was coming already to regard her 'allies' as her 'subjects'.

The major wars of the third century, therefore (against Pyrrhus and against Carthage), had launched Rome as an undoubted power in the Mediterranean world, a development of major importance for Rome herself as well as for others. In fact, the seeds of further conflict were already laid: Carthage was smarting under what she regarded as treatment at the hands of Rome which was both unjust and humiliating. This in itself led to a pressing desire among some – particularly the Barcid family, of which Hannibal was a member – to seek redress. As pressing, however, for the Carthaginian leadership was the need to replace the 'markets' which she had lost with the recent Roman acquisitions of Sicily, Sardinia and Corsica; Africa itself, because of the activities of nomadic Numidian tribesmen, provided little secure scope for this. Thus, Hannibal was sent to Spain to develop existing markets and to open new ones, which were situated at a safe distance from Rome; no doubt, too, the Carthaginian authorities were not sorry that they had the opportunity to put a considerable distance between themselves and the 'firebrand', Hannibal.

For Hannibal himself, the new markets were of smaller importance than the opportunity in virtual seclusion to raise and train the army which he planned to deploy against Rome in a great crusade of vengeance. The *casus belli* in the case of the Second Punic War was the Spanish city of Saguntum, which in 220 BC was attacked by Hannibal and promptly appealed to Rome for help. In terms of legality, since Saguntum was situated in that part of Spain which lay within a Carthaginian sphere of influence acknowledged by Rome, the Romans had no business to become involved. After a delay of two years, they did become involved, although the delay did nothing to enhance the righteousness of the Roman cause.

Hannibal's performance was spectacular, at first at least; he inflicted a series of morale-damaging defeats on Roman armies and a succession of commanders in Italy itself – although his

Plate 3.2 (opposite) Faliscan territory (Ager Faliscus): road and bridge of the Republican period.

famous elephants probably caused more pandemonium on his own side than they did among the Romans. At the same time, Hannibal was being drawn further into Italy and stretching his supply lines, while the real victory eluded him: the defeats which he inflicted failed to have the intended effects; the people in Rome, although they caused some political embarrassment to their oligarchic 'masters', did not revolt from them. Further, although twelve Latin *coloniae* (including Capua), largely because of exhaustion, went over to Hannibal (and were severely punished later), Hannibal's Italian successes did not precipitate a general desertion amongst Rome's Italian allies. Further, Hannibal omitted the *coup de grâce* which would have been an attack on Rome itself – probably because he waited too long to reinforce the desertion of Capua, in the hope of causing more panic on the Roman side.

The other factor which undermined Hannibal's cause was the emergence on the Roman side of a leader whose charisma was at least the equal of that of Hannibal – namely, Publius Cornelius Scipio. Initially Rome's commander in Spain, he may well have shared with Hannibal a distrust on the part of his governing colleagues who were happy to put some distance between themselves and him; like Hannibal, too, he took the opportunity to train an army which was to become devoted to him personally, regarding him as virtually godlike. Rome had rarely seen a leader of this order, since it was normal aristocratic practice to subordinate the individual, however talented, to the corporate interests of the oligarchy. Although Scipio did not seriously disrupt the oligarchy during the course of the war itself, subsequently his became a divisive figure whose actions and eventual fate made a decisive impact on factional politics in Rome. For the moment, however, he was Scipio Africanus who had finally, in 202 BC, overthrown Hannibal on African soil. Rome had thus weathered another storm, and gained more territory – this time in Spain; politically, the control of the aristocracy in the senate was at its zenith.

Throughout the period of Rome's first two conflicts with Carthage, there was in addition a sometimes-tense relationship with various leaders on the Greek mainland, who sought to bolster the credibility of their own positions by 'raising a national flag' over Rome's dealings with – and increasing dominance of – Greek city-states in Italy and by attempting to take advantage of Rome's preoccupations in other theatres.

It seems clear that, at least until the last years of the third century, Rome's purpose, not surprisingly, was to avoid unnecessary involvement in the affairs of the Greek peoples, whose cultural influence spread a great deal further than the Greek mainland itself. Since the time of Alexander the Great, who had carried 'Greek imperialism' as far east as the borders of modern-day India, the Greek world had consisted essentially of three major groupings – the kingdom of Macedon, the Seleucid Empire (Asia Minor) and the Ptolemaic Empire (Egypt). To these should be added the kingdom of Pergamum which, in the third century, detached itself from the Seleucid Empire, and the so-called 'free' leagues and city-states.

Rome's decision, almost immediately following the conclusion of the war with Hannibal, to engage with mainland Greece, requires some explanation, particularly in view of the fact that the people of Rome, worn out by the effort maintained during the recent war, were clearly not anxious to fight again so soon. It is certainly true that Philip V of Macedon had been unhelpful to Rome, thus possibly inviting some measure of punitive action, and was perhaps seen to threaten danger because of his behaviour towards other Greeks. Further, Rome, because of piracy mounted from the eastern Adriatic coast, saw a legitimate role for herself in the region, and may have feared that this might in its turn prompt Philip to interfere on Rome's side of the Adriatic.

While the Roman people's initial reluctance to fight was both real and perfectly intelligible, the views of the governing aristocracy have proved harder to unravel: that they were touched by altruism towards those who had suffered at Philip's hands or by a sentimental attachment to the 'glory days' of the Greek city-states seems unlikely, particularly at such a juncture. Nor does it seem likely that an onset of aggressive expansionism provides an answer. The Greek world would, in any case, have been a dangerous place in which to indulge such notions; indeed, there were, if they were required, easier 'killings' in the west. Commercial ambitions can similarly be discounted; even though the planned effects of the embargo on commercial ship owning by senators, introduced in 218, can be ignored (because of the loopholes in such legislation), there is in fact little evidence that commerce in the east was a sufficiently large issue to precipitate warfare to secure it. On the other hand, we should not disregard the possibility that aristocratic posturing on the issue could have been intended to appeal to those to whom commercial opportunism was of significance – namely, groups within the so-called Equestrian Order; equestrians, who made up the second order of Roman society, were free of the constraints which kept senators out of commercial enterprises and were thus in a good position to take advantage of the new opportunities that were brought with a growth of empire. We may, therefore, be witnessing in this matter that subordination of common sense and statesmanship on the part of aristocratic elements in the interests of clientage and power. The growth of individual ambition was, over the next two centuries, to become a formidable element in the Republic's political process – and, indeed, in its eventual decline.

A further motive, which emerged rather more clearly from the conclusion of the Second Macedonian War than from its causes, has been dubbed 'defensive imperialism' – or, put in a slightly different way, the search for 'good neighbours'. While there was an understandable desire on the part of Rome's Greek allies to see Philip of Macedon humiliated, that thinking was not shared by Rome: she wanted Philip weakened, but not broken. The reasons for this were probably, in part, a fear of a new threat from the Balkans, if Macedon was destroyed – a fear which much later events in the region showed to have been not without foundation

– and, in part also, a reluctance to offer an opportunity of a power vacuum which could be filled by the aggressive and dangerous Antiochus III of Syria. In 195, the proconsul, Titus Flamininus, formalised a peace treaty and declared the liberation of the Greeks, in which the free Greeks would police the peace under a Roman protectorate – but one which would not be guaranteed by the leaving in Greece of Roman troops.

It was not long before the Greeks began to realise that their liberation was less complete than they had supposed. Disturbances were caused first by the Aetolian League, whose leadership after a short time (in 192) persuaded Antiochus to join them in re-asserting the freedom of Hellas. The initial Roman objective, which was achieved with relative ease, was evidently to restore equilibrium by driving Antiochus from the Greek mainland. This done, however, the view of Scipio and his political allies in Rome prevailed that Antiochus should be treated in the same way as Hannibal had been in 202 – defeated and thus 'cut down to size' in his own homeland. The opportunity to impose a settlement was provided by the defeat of Antiochus at Magnesia in 189. There was, however, to be no question of Rome remaining in Asia Minor: instead, the dominant powers left in the region were Rome's allies, Pergamum and Rhodes; once again, the Greeks, who had just been freed, were left to use their 'privilege' as they wished.

Although many Greeks may not have seen it so, they had during the 190s and early 180s, when Roman politics were dominated by the Scipios and their allies, 'benefited' from what might be seen as a relatively philhellenic and outgoing attitude in Rome, coupled with a desire to avoid permanent military engagement with the Greeks. As the Scipios lost favour, however, in the later 180s, harder counsels began to prevail.

Rome's relations with the Greeks of the mainland and of Asia Minor in the ensuing years of the mid-second century increasingly demonstrated the impracticability of leaving them to themselves and hoping for the best: Rome could not, by the nature of things, avoid the consequences of events. For example, the decline of Rhodian naval power left a vacuum in the control of maritime piracy which Rome was herself unable to fill. Eventually, therefore, the old policy of disengagement was abandoned and, in 148, Macedon was declared a province of the Roman Empire; two years later came the total sacking of the city of Corinth, which coincided with the meting out of a similar fate to the old enemy, Carthage, at the conclusion of the strange and rather desultory Third Punic War (150–146). Indeed, these two acts of imperialism, committed at opposite ends of the Mediterranean in the same year (146), appear to herald a turning point in Rome's relations with others; as events were to show, it would by no means be an exaggeration to assert that it was a turning point for Rome and its empire, marked by the realisation that an imperial power had to control directly and with the stamp of authority.

The consequences of expansion

By 146, there were seven overseas provinces – Sicily, Sardinia, Corsica, Tarraconensis and Baetica (in Spain), Africa and Macedonia. Yet, Rome's political institutions were hardly suited to the governing of an ever-widening overseas empire and, as we shall see, the strains imposed by the new responsibilities on the system itself and on those who ran it were instrumental in leading the Republic and its aristocratic government back in the direction of monarchy.

The growth of a formal empire affected all of Rome's citizens – the senatorial class, the Equestrian Order, and the ordinary people, also. In the first place, there were no ready-made institutions or mechanisms for coping with the governing, administration and taxing of overseas territories. The first province (*provincia*) was Sicily which, as we have seen, came to Rome by right of conquest after the First Punic War, although its acquisition had never been an objective on Rome's part: to provide a governor for the new province, Rome arranged to elect an extra praetor each year who would hold office, like other magistrates, for a year. In this way, Sicily was treated effectively as an extension of Italy. A major problem, however, which was implicit in this 'solution', was a widening of the Roman governmental power base: if extended indefinitely, an increasing number of annual praetors would mean an enlargement of the number of those qualified to compete for the two annual consulships. This had obvious implications for the future conduct of the elections and, perhaps more importantly, for the ability of the aristocracy to control the outcome of those elections. It would obviously become less reasonable to expect individuals to be prepared to subordinate their ambitions to the perceived needs of the corporate aristocracy.

In another context, however, a different solution came to hand during the Second Punic War: conduct of the war was seen to require continuity of command, which was not possible in a system which gave military commands to the annually elected consuls and praetors. A natural adaptation was to prolong 'tours of duty' (*provinciae*), but not by *electing* men to extended consulships and praetorships; this was a widening of an older device whereby, after the expiry of their terms of office, men could be retained to undertake a variety of necessary tasks. In such capacities, they were 'retitled' proconsuls and propraetors, and could be retained as long as feasible – although, of course, purely at the senate's discretion. This mechanism had been employed to provide continuity in military commands, and it was capable, too, of being adapted to provide for provincial governorships: a man could be elected to an annual consulship or praetorship, and then be chosen/required to spend a year (or more) as a proconsul or propraetor in charge of a province. In time, a system was devised whereby, prior to the relevant elections each year, lots were drawn to determine the provinces to which the successful candidates would be sent after the completion of their consulships and praetorships. Importantly, such men were not seen as powerful in the 'executive sense' of consuls and praetors, but were seen as obliged to the senate for the prorogation of their *imperium*. Further, it was now necessary only for the combined total of consuls and praetors elected each year to equal the number of provinces requiring governors.

However, the problems which attended the arrangement soon became apparent: the authority which, as a proconsul, a Roman senator could wield in his province might be very different from that which, as consul in Rome, he could exercise under the constant scrutiny of his peers. In some places, he might even be treated as 'godlike', particularly in those parts of the empire which were used to seeing their rulers in such a light. It was understandably a hard task for some, once ambitions had been fired, to return to Rome and semi-anonymity. Further, a period as a provincial governor provided opportunities for a Roman senator to acquire wealth on a large scale and the backing of wealthy locals (including even kings and chieftains) as clients. As we have seen, wealth and clientage provided the routes to power in Rome: the growth of empire greatly sharpened the rivalry over the acquisition of these. In other words, great damage was done to the former 'class-corporateness' of the Roman aristocracy, as it gave way to rivalries played out on an individual, although more frequently factional, basis. The fact that some provincial governorships involved the command of troops served only to heighten the tension and rivalry as well as the opportunities (as will be shown later).

Economic and fiscal matters in the provinces provided a no less bumpy road: on the face of things, the burden of taxation imposed on the provinces was not excessive. Whereas Rome's Italian allies were required to contribute manpower to the army, provinces were asked either for a percentage of their harvested crop or for a fixed sum of money (*stipendium*). In addition, some provinces provided revenues from the exploitation of their natural resources. The system was not, however, intended for abuse, since the senate appreciated that provincial discontent might lead to a need for an armed response, which would itself prove expensive.

However, in some cases, governors and tax collectors showed that they could resist anything except temptation. A governor, whose need for money (in the form of cash or saleable items) has already been emphasised, might see his province as a 'soft source': such 'easy money' might offer the means to pay off debts and to finance future election campaigns. While the governor, along with his financial 'agent' (*quaestor*), managed the collection of direct taxes, the collection of indirect taxes and revenues from a province's natural assets was left in the hands of businessmen of the Equestrian Order who formed themselves into companies (*societates publicanorum*) for the purpose. The taxes which they collected were fixed in Rome by a crude 'auction process' among the companies and thus often failed to reflect people's ability to pay. In these circumstances, the companies might 're-invent' themselves as money lenders, inflicting exorbitant rates of interest on those who were forced into their clutches in order to pay their dues. A governor would usually be reluctant to intervene, because the equestrians who made up the companies might either at the time or later constitute his creditors over the matter of loans to cover previously incurred election expenses. For a similar reason, governors would often be reluctant to keep too close an eye on the commercial activities of equestrians.

Evidence from a variety of sources suggests that the mishandling of financial matters could wreak havoc in a province and that Polybius' insistence (VI.56) on the strong moral sense shared by Roman officials was over-optimistic. The reality is highlighted by a number of *causes célèbres*, especially after 146, and by the need to establish in 149 an 'extortion court' (*quaestio de repetundis*). Even then, justice and fair-dealing were severely hampered by the sheer weight of difficulty experienced by provincials in trying to bring cases to court in Rome, especially over the matter of securing the services of an advocate, and by the corruption which was frequently gross in a court in which a senator was judged by a group of his peers.

It is clear that the problems outlined above sprang from a desire on the part of the Roman aristocracy that the acquisition of an empire should impinge as little as possible on their ability to pursue power and on the traditional manner of running the Republic. However, these very traditions were threatened in other ways, too, by the growth of empire.

Wars inevitably meant prisoners of war, who in their turn meant slaves. Although slavery was by no means a new phenomenon in Rome caused by the growth of the empire, its growth was now greatly accelerated; such growth, of course, undermined the employment of free citizens, especially on the land. As we shall see, the consequential decline in the free property-owning citizenry posed major problems for recruitment to the Roman army; many were forced into 'state charity', which could easily prove to be an extension of individual patronage and which was certainly to prove to be disruptive to good order – especially in Rome itself.

Slaves also took over many functions inside family households, which had previously prided themselves on their self-sufficiency in matters such as the education of the children and household management. The weakening of the family as the bedrock of the Republic's social fabric was, as the emperor, Augustus, was later to show, of great consequence. Slaves also provided for mass entertainment which, many have argued, served to 'brutalise' their audiences, despite the serious origins which many of the forms of entertainment may have had. More importantly, perhaps, the provision of such arena entertainment as animal hunting and gladiatorial contests became another 'arm' of the patronage by means of which the rich 'bought' the poor. Indeed, the influx of money itself became a feature of patronage – and not simply through the crude mechanism of electoral corruption: mass entertainment, for example, required venues; these and other public buildings provided work, which had to be paid for. In all, therefore, the field of mass entertainment and recreation provided extensive opportunities for patronage, which naturally served to bring the 'donors' (patrons) to the forefront of public notice.

A further disruptive consequence of imperial growth can be identified in the field of religion; the state cults of Rome were, as we have seen, regarded as central both to the Republic's well-being and to the continued ability of the aristocracy, in their roles as priests, to exercise a dominant control over the Republic. Roman traditionalists feared the moral damage that might be done to the Roman people by the influx of cults – especially from the east – which were established on principles very different from those of traditional Roman paganism and which were often orgiastic in their conduct. There was, however, a much more important matter at stake in this than the dangers that were imagined to threaten the moral fibre of the Roman people.

A greater danger was that, on the whole, the incoming cults were personal religions, whose tenets were often secret to initiates; worship took place 'behind closed doors' and was orchestrated by priests, most of whom, in Roman eyes, were of little consequence socially – and so politically also. Such cults were concerned not with the welfare and prosperity of the Roman state – the principal concerns, according to Cicero, of Jupiter Optimus Maximus – but with the spiritual salvation of individual initiates. This seemed to smack of the same kind of individualism that was raising its head among the governing class, as we have seen, for other reasons. Thus, foreign cults were not just immoral and dangerous – they were subversive, too.

Traditional Roman paganism was centred not on individuals, but on the Roman state, and was essentially materialistic. Its ceremonial was often complex, and its language archaic and obfuscated; very few will have understood what it was about. Its purpose was the interpretation of signs sent by the gods and their correct translation into the actions required. There was little room here for individual participation: the temple was 'the house of the god' where the priest 'communed' with the god, while ordinary people were spectators who waited outside to hear the priest's interpretation of what the god wanted. Not only was this totally unsatisfying to individuals, particularly as the 'certainties of life' appeared to be becoming less certain, but it gave – as was intended – great influence to the priests who were, by and large, drawn from members of the ruling aristocracy. Thus, traditional religion became one of the mechanisms by which the aristocracy controlled the mass of the people; the introduction of alternative cults carried the clear implication that this control might be weakened. It is significant that the same fear linked the senate's decree of 186 BC which aimed to curtail the sometimes-riotous worship of the Greek god, Dionysus, and the action taken in AD 19 by the emperor, Tiberius, against the practice of Jewish and Egyptian rites in Rome. Looking forward, it stands to the great credit of the statesmanship of the emperor, Constantine I, that he was able, in the fourth century AD, to graft Christianity (itself, of course, an eastern cult) onto the Roman state and to use it in the fashion of a traditional state cult.

Thus, it can be seen that the growth of empire, which was largely unplanned, carried both advantages and disadvantages for the traditional system of government. In the short term, the advantages will have been seen by many to outweigh the advantages. At the very least, the governing aristocracy was forced to face up to the implications of the changes that took place. Their reluctance to do this, preferring to revel in a self-destructive manner in the short-term advantages to them, ensured that the process of change would be both painful and turbulent.

Further reading

Adcock F. E., *The Roman Art of War Under the Republic* (Cambridge, MA, 1940).

Badian E., *Foreign Clientelae* (Oxford, 1958).

Caven B., *The Punic Wars* (London, 1980).

Chevallier R., *Roman Roads* (London, 1976).

Connolly P. (ed.), *Greece and Rome at War* (London, 1981).

Curchin L. A., *Roman Spain: Conquest and Assimilation* (London, 1991).

D'Arms J. H. and Kopff E. C. (eds), *The Seaborne Commerce of Ancient Rome* (Rome, 1980).

David J. M., *The Roman Conquest of Italy* (Oxford, 1996).

de Beer G., *Hannibal: The Struggle for Power in the Mediterranean* (London, 1969).

Duncan-Jones R. P., *The Economy of the Roman Empire* (Cambridge, 1982).

Garnsey P. D. A., Hopkins K. and Whittaker C. R. (eds), *Trade in the Ancient Economy* (London, 1983).

Goldsworthy A. K., *The Roman Army at War* (Oxford, 1996).

Harris W. V., *War and Imperialism in Republican Rome 327–70 B.C.* (Oxford, 1979).

Harris W. V. (ed.), *The Imperialism of Mid-Republican Rome* (Rome, 1984).

Hopkins K., *Conquerors and Slaves* (Cambridge, 1978).

Keay S., *Roman Spain* (London, 1988).

Keppie L. J. F., *The Making of the Roman Army* (London, 1984).

Lazenby J. F., *Hannibal's War: A Military History of the Second Punic War* (Warminster, 1978).

Lazenby J. F., *The First Punic War: A Military History* (London, 1996).

Mommsen T., *The Provinces of the Roman Empire* (ed. T. R. S. Broughton) (Chicago, IL, 1968).

Richardson J., *Roman Provincial Administration 227 B.C.–A.D. 117* (Bristol, 1984).

Rosenstein N. S., *Imperatores Victi: Military Defeat and Aristocratic Competition in the Middle and Late Republic* (Berkeley, CA, 1990).

Roth J. P., *The Logistics of the Roman Army at War (264 B.C. –A.D. 235)* (Leiden, 1999).

Salmon E. T., *Roman Colonisation Under the Republic* (New York, 1970).

Salmon E. T., *The Making of Roman Italy* (New York, 1982).

Sherwin-White A. N., *The Roman Citizenship* (Oxford, 1973).

Smith R. E., *Service in the Post-Marian Army* (Manchester, 1958).

Sterpos D., *The Roman Road in Italy* (Rome, n.d.).

Stevenson G. H., *Roman Provincial Administration* (Oxford, 1939).

Suolahti J., *The Junior Officers of the Roman Army in the Republican Period* (Helsinki, 1955).

Toynbee A. J., *Hannibal's Legacy* (Oxford, 1965).

Van Deman E. B., *The Building of the Roman Aqueducts* (Washington, DC, 1934).

Walbank F. W., *Polybius* (Berkeley, CA, 1972).

Wardman A. E., *Rome's Debt to Greece* (London, 1976).

Westermann W. L., *The Slave Systems of Greek and Roman Antiquity* (Philadelphia, PA, 1955).

Chapter 4

The disintegration of the Republic

The crossroads

The victory at Actium in 31 BC of Octavian and Agrippa over Marcus Antonius and Cleopatra marked the end of what later Roman writers referred to as *vetus respublica* ('the Old Republic'); Rome once more had the single dominant figure that the Republic's foundation had been intended to prevent. Although writers continued to refer to the state under the emperors as *respublica,* it was in essence very different from its 'old' predecessor. What, then, served to bring about the disintegration of a system of government which a little more than a century previously had won the plaudits of the Greek historian, Polybius, for its stability?

In one sense, the question itself is unreal: we have seen that, steeped as he was in the thinking of Plato and Aristotle, Polybius was attempting to force a 'Greek model' on to his observations on the Roman Republic. The balance which he claimed to see between the magistrates, the senate and the people was not genuine; he failed to grasp the real domination of the aristocracy over the other elements; nor did he allow for the powerful and pervasive effects of patronage. The Republic did, indeed, appear stable,

Plate 4.1 (opposite) Rome, the Forum: circular temple of Vesta, the 'hearth goddess'; the tending of the flame of Vesta, which burned in the temple, was the sacred duty of the Vestal Virgins.

but not for the reasons adduced by Polybius. As the grip of a corporate aristocracy began to loosen, so too did the apparent stability begin to evaporate.

We have seen that the removal of the monarchy in the sixth/fifth centuries BC was presented as a blow struck for *libertas* ('freedom'), a fine-sounding word with elevated associations: the Roman state should never again become subject to the *dominatio* ('domination') of one man. The reality was a little less principled; the patrician aristocracy wished to prevent their corporate and individual interests from being dominated by one of their own number winning power for himself, and maintaining himself through the support of the people against his fellow aristocrats. 'Freedom', therefore, was the returning to the aristocracy of its corporate ability to dominate the Roman state unhindered.

The history of the early Republic revolved around the manoeuvrings of that aristocracy to prevent change only in so far as it did not damage that corporate domination. Thus, wealthy plebeians were 'allowed' to join the patrician 'club' because their interests were totally in keeping with those of the patricians. In these circumstances, magistracies could be opened to plebeians, because only the wealthy members of that class would be able to maintain themselves in office. Concessions could be granted on the issue of popular sovereignty, because all of the popular assemblies came under the domination of this 'new nobility'. Further, the 'loose cannon' of the tribunate was itself in this way brought into aristocratic control; the significant powers that this office bestowed on relatively junior figures made it a ready target for manipulation by unscrupulous politicians in furthering their own ends. So, the aristocracy came to dominate the magistracies, the senate and the popular assemblies. This was the real source of stability in the Republic, and it survived as long as the aristocracy remained essentially corporate and as long as the ability of individuals or groups within it to dominate the rest was limited.

It was the growth of the Roman Empire that changed this by bringing to the aristocracy new obligations and new opportunities and by bringing to a governmental system that had evolved to suit a small city-state a need to adapt to a new role as an imperial power. The consequences in terms of the acquisition of power and wealth and the enhancement of lifestyles went a long way towards destroying the corporateness of the aristocracy and introducing in its place a new competitive edge. Thus, institutions and practices which had previously guaranteed the dominance of the Republic by the aristocracy now provided those same aristocratic families with the means to outdo one another. So high were the stakes that the corruption of the Republic in the search for the wealth that could be used to acquire power was both inevitable and serious; at the end of the day, the members of the aristocracy were still competing for the same two consulships each year, and these remained the summit of ambition. It is little wonder that 'outsiders' (novi homines) stood little chance of breaking in except with the help of the wealth and influence which were at the disposal of the most powerful figures – the faction leaders.

Obviously, the political leaders should have been deploying their resources and energies in helping the Republic to adapt to its new situation and to cope with the problems that arose. Instead, they were exclusively devoted to outdoing one another. Nothing demonstrates this more clearly than the handling of the military problems which arose in the wake of imperial growth. It was through attitudes taken specifically to the matter of military recruitment that the corporateness of the aristocracy and, with it, the stability of the Roman Republic were fatally undermined.

In essence, the problem which reared its head in the second century BC was simple in nature: how to adapt to the new imperial situation the structures of the army and the method of recruitment to it, since both of these represented responses to earlier and simpler situations. Rome relied on the concept of the 'farmer-soldier' – a man who made his living on the land, but who answered the call to serve in the army as the need arose. This arrangement, which was based on the simple self-sufficiency which was characteristic of Rome's traditional way of life, was seen to have a number of specific advantages: first, the 'stake' in the land of a farmer-soldier was thought to guarantee that a man would 'give his all' to defend it; secondly, the attitude of mind generated by proximity to the land was assumed to provide the proper 'mental equipment' for a soldier. Thirdly, perhaps, the state would not be required to become involved in complex financial responsibility in the case of a man who had his own property and livelihood to which to return at the completion of a spell of soldiering.

However, these advantages related most closely to warfare which was based in mainland Italy itself – which, of course, was the case until the first half of the third century BC. In these circumstances, a man might be absent from his family farm during the campaigning season, but he would still find time to devote to the needs of his farm when campaigning was over for the year. Clearly, campaigns fought at a greater distance from home would impose greater constraints on the efficacy of this simple pattern; further, the nature of post-war situations with increasing frequency called for the implementation of some kind of garrison policy in newly won territory. Under these circumstances, far from being away for a single campaigning season, a man could be absent from home for up to seven years, only to return then to find his livelihood gone and perhaps his family dispersed: the physical and financial difficulties involved in trying to keep a farm operating during the prolonged absence of the head of the household should in no way be underestimated, for they could lead to the effective enslavement for debt of free persons. It would not be in the least surprising if such a man should be brought to the point of asking himself whether he had the stomach to start all over again, or whether he would be better off in a town (probably Rome itself), where without responsibilities he could benefit from patronal handouts, superior facilities and regular entertainment.

Because of the readiness of members of the governing class to invest some of their newly acquired wealth in such enterprises, the towns had taken on a new 'magnetic' attraction, where life in them seemed infinitely preferable to the thankless burdens of scratching a living in the countryside: the latter was a far cry from the utopian idealism with which traditional thinking set out to invest it. Once he became propertyless, the former farmer was no longer eligible for the military levy; thus, at a time when the number and difficulty of Rome's military commitments were rising, the size of the pool of recruits was falling. Alongside this, we must place the fact that the pool was further damaged by deaths on campaign and by deaths from disease during campaigns. Although quantifying such factors would be a hard task, recent parallels (such as the Crimean and Boer Wars) would suggest that the numbers involved would not have been inconsiderable. There can be no doubt that recruitment to the army was, by the second half of the second century BC, in a state of deep crisis; it is little wonder that Quintus Metellus Macedonicus, the censor of 131 BC, made his famous speech exhorting Roman citizens to increase the birth rate.

This growing crisis was not restricted to Roman citizens and recruitment to the Roman legions; the 'allies' (*socii*), consisting of those who were 'half-citizens' and non-citizens, and who fought alongside the legions, were under similar pressures – the more so, since legislation in the early years of the second century BC had reduced the allies' share of the booty won on campaign to the level of fifty per cent of what was offered to legionaries. This was demeaning to the 'allies', as well as making the economic stringencies facing them even greater, but as much damage was done to the principle of shared dangers between citizens and allies when legionaries were given an extension of the citizens' right of *provocatio* on to the battlefield, thus affording to them protection from summary punishment meted out by officers/magistrates that was not available to the allies. It is sometimes suggested that this hardening of attitudes among the Republic's governing class was a consequence of the desertion to Hannibal during the Second Punic War on the part of a few of Rome's Italian allies.

The solution for many of those who were suffering such indignities was to 'migrate' into Rome; those with 'Latin rights' appear to have enjoyed the right to do this, and so to become full citizens (provided only that they left their eldest son on the family farm). For others, however, the legality of 'migration' was far more questionable, although many no doubt slipped through the net because of the difficulty of distinguishing between those among the Italian allies who had 'Latin rights' and those who did not. On at least two occasions – in 187 and 177 – such 'immigrants' into Rome were expelled and forced to return to their homes in order to resume their eligibility for military service: in the minds of Rome's governing class, this motive was probably (to be fair to them) more powerful than the xenophobia and racism that is sometimes alleged. However it was, the matter served to heighten problems in the army, as well – an important development for the future – as souring relations between Rome and her Italian allies; the outcome of this was the so-called 'Italian question' and the bitterly divisive Social War of 91–89 BC.

An effort to deal with the problem of military recruitment was made in the 140s – the precise date is not clear – by a powerful senatorial faction under the leadership of Publius Cornelius Scipio Aemilianus, also known as Africanus after his adoptive grandfather, the conqueror of Hannibal; the stock of Aemilianus was high following the successful completion, under his leadership, of the Third Punic War. Lowering the property qualification for military service and reducing the size of the legion, which were intended to have the effect, at least, of 'papering over the cracks', had, unsurprisingly, not worked to improve the situation. Thus, Scipio and his associates (notably Gaius Laelius Sapiens) proposed a programme of resettling landless citizens on public land (*ager publicus*) and thus restoring to them their qualification for military service; it is to be imagined that such a bill had more of a 'popularist' wrapping than the mere recital of its chief provision would suggest. It was, however, evidently opposed by Scipio's main rival in the senate, the *princeps senatus* ('leader of the senate'), Appius Claudius Pulcher. The reasons for the opposition are not stated, but are likely to have stemmed from Claudius' fear of the political and patronal advantage that might accrue to Scipio, if the measure were successfully carried; opposition on principle is hardly likely, since this same Claudius, a decade later, was the faction leader behind virtually identical legislation proposed in 133 BC by the tribune, Tiberius Sempronius Gracchus. Thus, we see a very clear demonstration of the new competitiveness between factions of the senatorial nobility obstructing a necessary reform; just how necessary was soon shown by the poor performance of Roman legions in the Numantine War in Spain in the early 130s – a war in which the Roman commander was Scipio Aemilianus.

If the issue of military recruitment had already proved disruptive, this was nothing in comparison with the events of 133 BC, a year that has been described as a 'crossroads' in the life of the Roman Republic. In that year, one of the plebeian tribunes was Tiberius Sempronius Gracchus, elder son of the Tiberius Gracchus, who had been consul in 177 and 163 and censor in 169, and Cornelia, daughter of Scipio Africanus (see stemma in Appendix 1). The elder Gracchus linked two formidable senatorial factions – the Scipiones and the Claudii. Tiberius Gracchus had held his first consulship and his censorship with Gaius Claudius Pulcher as his colleague; Gaius' son, Appius Claudius, was the leader of the so-called 'Gracchan faction' of 133.

Presumably under the influence of his mother, the younger Tiberius Gracchus was 'apprenticed' to Scipio Aemilianus during the Numantine War. However, in 137, following a policy disagreement during that war, Gracchus, capitalising on clientage in Spain that he had inherited from his father, had tried to 'upstage' Aemilianus – only to be peremptorily put down by his patron. Gracchus broke his tie with Aemilianus – or, in the words of Cicero who entertained an uncritical admiration for Aemilianus, 'became a revolutionary'. It is clear that this 'revolutionary' element in Gracchus' behaviour had nothing to do with what we would regard as 'principles of policy'; rather, it was his ambitious self-interest that prompted him to change factional allegiance, effectively deserting his mother's family in favour of his father's political friends. It must have been at this point, too, that Gracchus sent out a clear 'signal' of his intentions by marrying Claudia, the daughter of Appius Claudius.

The remainder of Gracchus' short career, until his death in 133, was devoted to the humiliation of his erstwhile patron, recalling not dissimilar behaviour which his father had shown towards Aemilianus' adoptive grandfather in the late 180s. That there was a personal element in all this cannot be doubted, but it should also be seen as a part of a drive for factional primacy which he shared with his faction leader and father-in-law (and Aemilianus' chief rival in the senate), Appius Claudius. The events of 133 surrounding Gracchus' agrarian legislation amply demonstrate the degree to which individual and factional self-interest now dominated government. The issue which lay behind Gracchus' legislation was that of military recruitment: indeed, the bill which he brought forward was probably a re-run of that which had been proposed a decade earlier by Aemilianus and his friends and which had been scuppered by the Claudian faction. In a similar fashion, Aemilianus and his faction now opposed Gracchus.

This behaviour on separate occasions by each of these factions was not the product of stupidity or awkwardness; for them something far greater was at stake than simply being upstaged in a piece of legislation. Gracchus' conduct, which was driven more by personal and factional ambition than it was by principle, was single minded and ruthless – his ignoring of the senate in taking his bill straight to the Plebeian Assembly, his overturning of the veto and effective dismissal of his fellow tribune, Octavius, as well as his interference in the senate's traditional role of looking after the financial resources involved. All of these moves highlight not just Gracchus' determination to see his bill passed but also his desire to utilise constitutional mechanisms which would achieve not simply the defeat of his opponents but, more importantly, their long-term marginalisation. This would have been secured both through the voting support which the adoption of his measures would have brought – Tiberius Gracchus presenting himself as the people's champion – but also (and more insidiously) by the fact that he was shifting the focus of governmental business from the senate to an assembly which Gracchus evidently expected that he and his supporters would be able to control – by fair means or foul. His stated intention of seeking a second term as tribune is indicative of this, and it was evidently this that 'warned' his opponents of the seriousness of the political danger that was facing them. It was at this point that opposition to Gracchus became not just overt but violent, too.

For the first time, 'street violence' became part of the political process in Rome: Tiberius Gracchus was murdered by Aemilianus' cousin, the Chief Priest (*Pontifex Maximus*), Publius Cornelius Scipio Nasica; the description of the act indicates that cynically Nasica's stance was that he was acting 'in an official capacity' – conducting a sacrifice, albeit a human one, to ward off disaster. That it was portrayed as a religious sacrifice to save the Republic becomes clear in a verbal exchange that ensued between Aemilianus and the Gracchan, Gaius Papirius Carbo; when asked by Carbo whether it had been right to murder Gracchus, Aemilianus replied that it was if Gracchus had been trying to establish a 'kingship' *(regnum)*. In other words, Aemilianus regarded Gracchus' marginalising of his faction and the 'poaching' through the legislation itself of his voting support as tantamount to *dominatio* on the part of the Claudian–Gracchan faction – that is, the denial of the *libertas* of their opponents. Checking that was more important than the carnage that was involved in doing it; thus far had the corporateness of the senatorial nobility been dissipated in little more than half a century.

Gracchus was on the point of achieving what was the goal of most Roman politicians – glory for himself, his family and his faction with a piece of necessary legislation – *patria et gloria* ('patriotism and family glory'); Gracchus had acted in keeping with that vital yardstick, ancestral custom (*mos maiorum*).

In actual fact, 'solving' the recruitment crisis by confiscating areas of public land (*ager publicus*) and settling landless citizens upon it was at best a temporary expedient; nor should we forget that the cost was high – the introduction of violence into the conduct of the Republic's government and the further alienation of Italians who were probably the principal victims of the programme of land confiscation. This sense of alienation was twice to flare into rebellion on their part (in 125 and in 91–89), before eventually Italians received the citizenship which gave them legal equality with other Roman citizens and protection from arbitrary treatment.

The Gracchan type of solution to the military recruitment problem, although not all of Tiberius' methods, was tried again by his younger brother, Gaius, in 123 and 122, and continued to be used until its last-known re-enactment in 111 BC (the *Lex Thoria*). It is likely that by that time there was no more *ager publicus* that could reasonably be repossessed. Renewed problems in recruitment, however, could not have come at a worse moment, since Rome was at that time deeply embroiled in a long-running guerrilla encounter with Jugurtha, a local leader in north Africa.

The background to this conflict lay partly in the desire of senators to protect themselves from the type of political threat that had been posed by Gaius Gracchus during his two tribunates in 123 and 122; the younger Gracchus had, as we shall see, tried to bolster the plebeian support sought by his elder brother with the specific support of the wealthiest part of the plebeian section of the citizenry – the members of the Equestrian Order. In a bid, therefore, to be seen as protective of the business interests of equestrians in north Africa, and thus to 'outbid' any repetition of Gaius Gracchus' tactics, the senate had been persuaded to enter into a war that was intended to prevent the harassment of those interests by Jugurtha. It was, of course, of crucial importance to be able to deliver on this objective. However, before long, corruption in the higher echelons of command and the unsuitability of the legion for confronting guerrilla tactics pointed strongly to the need for a 'shake-up'. Accordingly, in 109, a new commander, Quintus Caecilius Metellus (Numidicus), was sent out: his virtue lay in the fact that his family had had a long history of patronising equestrians; he would thus provide the proof that the senate was truly serious in bringing the war to a successful conclusion.

On Metellus' staff was a protégé from an Italian equestrian family – Gaius Marius. He, the first member of his family to compete for a senatorial career, had reached the praetorship and, at the age of fifty, was now contemplating seeking the office of consul; as a 'new man' (*novus homo*) he was by no means certain, or even likely, to win election. Marius, however, played what he regarded as his 'trump card' – a promise to do what was necessary finally to bring the African war to a successful conclusion. He won his consulship – for 107 BC – and persuaded the Plebeian Assembly to vote the African command to him, thus ousting his patron. To finish the war, he set in train two major reforms – a complete overhaul of legionary organisation and tactics and the introduction of a new method of recruitment. This involved revoking the property qualification for legionary service and opening up military service to all who wanted it.

The reform was successful in helping Marius to deliver his promised victory, followed by further victories over two Germanic tribes, the Cimbri and the Teutones, who had caused great consternation by threatening the territorial integrity of Italy itself. It soon became clear, however, that the price for this was to be extremely high: landless soldiers had no homes, no livelihoods to which to return after their campaigns; they were, therefore, dependent on what they could make out of their campaigns and on a grant of land on which they could settle when they returned.

The Republic, inexplicably, made no automatic provision for this by the establishment of a 'pool' of land from which such grants could easily be made as the need arose. Instead, the initiative lay with the troops' commander to arrange for the carrying through on each occasion that an army returned the legislation necessary to provide the land for 'discharge payments'. Thus, the interests of men and generals were inextricably intertwined while they were on campaign, because success brought wealth to both. Similarly, their interests were intertwined on their return to Italy: because men were still recruited on a campaign basis, they and their generals effectively left military service together; they needed him to secure their demobilisation settlement, while he might decide that he could make use of them to strengthen his political 'clout'. The Roman army had become the clients of its generals; in this way, what has been called the 'vicious nexus' had been forged – with the Republic at its mercy.

Thus, the events which flowed in the second half of the second century from Rome's developing military role had transformed the Republic from its apparent stability to a cauldron of chaos in which factions and individuals sought their own interests with no regard to the good of the Republic – or what Cicero and others were to call *cura reipublicae*; the crossroads had been passed.

The Equestrian Order

The Equestrian Order constituted the second rung of Roman society in terms of status: in the later Republic, it consisted of often-wealthy members of society who were not members of the senate; they were joined by the sons of the senatorial nobility prior to their achieving senatorial status. The order was thus a disparate group, not as in the earlier days of the Republic, held together by commonly shared ambitions and interests. Geographically, too, they were disparate, as the most influential amongst them were the local 'magnates' in Italian towns – families like those of Marius or Cicero, or the Octavii (the antecedents of the emperor, Augustus).

As individuals, the equestrians were members of the popular assemblies, perhaps in the clientage of notable senators, but their direct political influence was slight. The growth of the Roman Empire in the later third and the second centuries changed this because, standing as they did outside the senate, they could take on a range of activities, largely in the commercial and financial sectors, for which senators, because of the *Lex Claudia* of 218 BC, were substantially ineligible. In short, the growth of the empire changed the equestrians from a disparate collection of individuals to a group with definable, coherent and influential interests.

The Republic lacked what we would identify as a civil service; thus, the collection of taxes and the running of state assets (such as mines) were taken on by companies of equestrians who expected to make a profit from such enterprises; the family of Gaius Marius had, for example, over succeeding generations made a great deal of money from the organisation of mining in Spain. Control was exercised by the state through the censors and the senate utilising such practices as limiting the size of work-forces or the number of days in a year on which mining could take place.

The collection of taxes was another profitable enterprise for equestrians: forming themselves into companies (*societates publicanorum*), they would bid for the right to collect a tax in a province; the successful bid then became the tax assessment, and the company had to remit that amount to the treasury and (of course) collect money besides, which constituted the company's profit. From a province's point of view this 'assessment' was extremely crude, bearing little or no relationship to the principle of ability to pay. As we have seen, those who could not meet their tax demands found themselves forced into the hands of equestrian money lenders.

Many equestrians went into business in the provinces, such as those who opened up agriculture on the coastal strip of north Africa, and for whom the senate, as we saw, involved Rome in the war against Jugurtha. There was profitable business, too, in shipping a wide variety of goods around the empire, especially such vital commodities as grain and precious metals. Some of the 'offices' of such companies can still be identified in the Forum of the Corporations at Rome's port of Ostia.

Occasionally, equestrian companies became too greedy and ambitious, as when, in 61 BC, a group which had contracted to collect taxes in Asia found that they had been too optimistic and sought a contract revision. The letting of state contracts was properly the business of the censors who held office for an eighteen-month period in every quinquennium; when censors were not in office, the matter became the business of the senate. On the occasion in question, equestrian difficulties arose out of the after-effects of the war against Mithridates of Pontus, which had been punishing for the region, and because of the fact that, in order to embarrass Pompey (Gnaeus Pompeius Magnus), the senate was refusing to regularise his peacetime arrangements in the area. In this instance, further difficulty arose out of the anger of some senators, notably the cantankerous Marcus Porcius Cato and his friends, over the corruption, probably at the instigation of Marcus Licinius Crassus, of the jury of equestrians at the sacrilege trial of Publius Clodius, who in 62 BC had invaded the ceremonies of the Vestal Virgins dressed as a woman. Relations between senators and equestrians could at times come under severe strain, something which, as we shall see, Marcus Tullius Cicero sought to obviate by his ideas on the 'Harmony of the Orders' (*Concordia Ordinum*).

It was inevitable that the coherence which the Equestrian Order had gained as a result of the expansion of the empire should bring it more sharply into the political arena. The effect of this was usually disruptive of stability, although it should be emphasised that this was not because equestrians in general wished to be more directly involved in the government. Indeed, in one notable example – the uncle of Cicero's friend and correspondent, Titus Pomponius Atticus – Cicero asked why such a rich and influential man did not seek the accolade of a public (that is, senatorial) career; the response was that Atticus' uncle was happy as he was, making money.

The real problem was that the newly discovered coherence of the order and the great wealth of many of its members brought it more closely into the patronage–clientage arrangements of senators. By tradition, senators constituted a landed aristocracy and, as for many landed aristocracies, 'cash-flow problems' were not uncommon. Equestrians were thus drawn by members of the senatorial aristocracy to act as 'bankers' in the cut-throat business of career building and electioneering. In other words, their money greatly enhanced the level of bribery and corruption which increasingly, during the second and first centuries BC, threatened to engulf the integrity of the Republic. Laws were frequently passed in an attempt to keep the level of bribery (*ambitus*) under control – and just as frequently ignored. Indeed, it emerges in a 'pamphlet' (the *Commentariolum Petitionis*), supposedly written by Quintus Cicero as advice to his brother, Marcus, in the latter's consular candidature in 65–64 BC, just how organised and cynical the business of electoral corruption had become. It was common practice for candidates for public office to borrow large sums of money from equestrians in the expectation that they could be easily paid back as a result of the 'pillage' to which the successful candidate would be able to subject his province in the year following his city magistracy. It was, in part at least, to break this cycle of corruption and resultant violence that, in 52 BC, Pompeius (then sole consul) introduced a change in the law which interposed an interval of five years between a city magistracy and a provincial post. Presumably, it was hoped that creditors would not be prepared to wait so long for the settlement of such debts.

Obviously, not all equestrians were as oblivious as Atticus' uncle to the benefits of a public career; indeed, some senatorial faction leaders saw great advantage in acquiring a solid block of equestrian clientage both inside and outside the senate. Thus, Gaius

Sempronius Gracchus tried to strengthen his faction within the senate by proposing the translation of some three hundred members of the Equestrian Order into that body. When this failed, he offered two inducements to ensure himself of equestrian support in the popular assemblies. The first was the right of equestrians to bid for the contract to collect taxes in the newly formed province of Asia (the former kingdom of Pergamum which had been willed to Rome by its late king, Attalus III). It is a significant development that in different ways both of the Gracchus brothers had tried to make use of inherited foreign clientage to advance their positions in Rome: Tiberius Gracchus had twice done this – first, using Spanish clientage won by his father as a lever against Scipio Aemilianus during the Numantine War and, secondly, when he tried to use part of the bequest of Attalus III, a client of his father's, to finance his land resettlement programme.

Gaius Gracchus' second inducement to the Equestrian Order was to give it the exclusive right to supply, from its own members, the juries which manned the 'extortion court' (*Quaestio de Repetundis*), which tried senators on charges of malpractice (mostly financial) arising from their terms as provincial governors. This court, while manned by juries made up of senators, had been a notorious source of 'mutual favours'; it is less likely, however, that Gracchus was trying to extinguish corruption than to ensure that senators who had tried to obtain illicit funds in the provinces would ultimately find their cases judged by Gracchus' friends. It is also worth adding that equestrians appreciated this role, because it provided them with a 'threat' which they could hold over senators who might try, for whatever reason, to interfere in the equestrians' own money-making ventures. The manning of the juries on this court, and on other permanent courts (*quaestiones*) which were subsequently introduced, became a kind of 'political football', with the constitution of the juries changing according to whichever faction or individual dominated the government at the time.

Others who brought substantial numbers of equestrians into the senate were the dictators, Lucius Cornelius Sulla (in the late 80s) and Julius Caesar (in the 40s). Sulla's motives have been frequently questioned – whether he hoped thereby to introduce some degree of harmony between the Orders, or whether he wished to deprive the Equestrian Order of its leading members, and thus to emasculate it. Harmony may have been on Caesar's mind, although he was widely accused of the motive of crowding the senate with his 'cronies' and, indeed, of debasing the senate's importance and thus of weakening the influence of the old aristocracy, many of whom were opposed to him, by raising the senate's numbers to what was seen as the outlandish figure of nine hundred members.

That equestrians had become influential and important in the late Republic cannot be denied, nor is it open to objection that this development, together with their relationships with the aristocratic factions, made them a disruptive factor. It is not surprising, therefore, that in his reorganisation of the Republic the emperor, Augustus, sought to bring under greater control and regularity the Order itself, its activities in a variety of fields and its relationship with the Senatorial Order. His reforms, as we shall see, linked both of the Orders in the provision of the civil service facilities that the increasingly complex Republic so obviously required.

The 'Italian question'

As we have seen, Rome's progress through Italy resulted in a variety of arrangements of a political and social nature to regularise relations with her Italian neighbours. These appeared to work well enough until the expansion of warfare and empire introduced greater pressures and clearly an increasingly arrogant attitude on the part of the Romans themselves; there was evidently a growing tendency to treat Italians as akin to conquered subjects elsewhere. As the rewards of imperial growth began to be felt, there was a more jealous guarding of privileges on the part of those who thought themselves to be entitled to the 'lion's share'.

An important moment in this deterioration was the example of the twelve Latin *coloniae* which defected to Hannibal during the Second Punic War. Although their true motive was probably exhaustion and despair, their behaviour was seen by some in Rome as treacherous, and it evidently helped to exacerbate a feeling of exclusiveness on the part of the imperial power.

Militarily, as well as politically and socially, the harmony between Italians and Romans was important, as the legions of Roman citizens and the 'allied' contingents served alongside each other, sharing the same dangers and winning the same rewards. This sense of partnership evaporated in the years following Hannibal's defeat in 202 BC; rewards after campaigns were skewed so that citizens began to receive twice as much as others. Also, as we have seen, the citizen received a better deal on campaign itself when *provocatio* was extended on to the battlefield.

As farmers, Italians were undoubtedly subject to the same pressures that affected citizen small farmers, and their reaction was similar – a desire to leave a lifestyle that had become a 'losing battle' and find a better life in the towns. Legally, the positions of Italians were obscure and confusing; some undoubtedly enjoyed the *ius migrationis* – the right to do what they were now attempting to do – while others did not. The Roman reaction was indiscriminate – to send such people back whence they had come; so-called 'aliens acts' were passed (for example, in 187 and 177) to achieve this. However, the real motive may not have been solely (or even at all) the arrogance and even 'racism' that have sometimes been suggested. Rather, against a background of failing recruitment and rising commitments, the Romans needed such people at home, qualified and ready to fulfil their military commitments. As the second century wore on, the agricultural conditions that precipitated the 'migrations' did not improve, but were made worse by greater military demands and greater arrogance on the part of Roman officials. The disruption caused by the banditry which resulted from slave rebellions will have served further to exacerbate the difficulties.

As already stated, a decisive deterioration may well have come with the *Lex Agraria* of Tiberius Gracchus in 133 BC. It is tolerably clear that the principal losers as a result of the land confiscations were not the great senatorial landlords but smaller people, and especially non-citizens who farmed *ager publicus* without title. Such people were subject to the confiscations but without entitlement to any compensation. We are told that an event of some significance in 133 was the arrival in Rome of considerable numbers of dispossessed Italians to agitate against the bill. In the absence of a 'champion', the cause of these people was taken up by Gracchus' opponent, Scipio Aemilianus, perhaps seeing in them an opportunity to salvage something from the clientage losses to which Gracchus' bill had subjected him. Significantly, in 129, Aemilianus either died or was murdered before any kind of 'Italian programme' took shape. If any doubt existed about the strength of Italian resentment, it was made clear by the brief, but bitter, rebellion of the town of Fregellae (Monte Cassino) in 125. This was in part a response to an 'aliens act' passed in 126; in some degree, however, the rebellion was probably precipitated by attempts to marginalise Fulvius Flaccus and Gaius Gracchus who, since the death of Aemilianus, had emerged as the chief proponents of an improvement in the Italians' position; indeed, Flaccus had himself proposed, but not won, a modest franchise bill in 125.

Gaius Gracchus' two years as tribune of the plebs (123–122 BC) brought the first real attempt to make progress through legislation on the issue of the Italians; Gracchus proposed a modest improvement – that half-citizens should receive full citizenship, while non-citizens would become half-citizens. It was probably the moderation of this proposal, and its consequent likely success, that drove the opponents of the change to attack not by demolition but by appearing to offer even more. Marcus Livius Drusus (the father or, more likely, uncle of the tribune of 91 BC) proposed a more 'radical' measure – full citizenship for all Italians. In all probability, this was cynically proposed in the expectation that its radical appearance would ensure its rejection by those who did not wish to share their privileges so widely. That it was intended to cut the ground from beneath Gaius Gracchus seems clear from the fact that his attempt at further re-election (for 121) failed. Gracchus' ultimate removal was brought about by the passage of the *Senatus Consultum Ultimum* ('Senatorial Decree of National Emergency'). This was an 'empowering' decree, by which the senate 'authorised' the consuls to 'see to it that the Republic came to no harm'. In reality, it was a method of encompassing the deaths of individuals with a high nuisance value, with little practical likelihood of comeback on the perpetrators. In the highly charged atmosphere in which this decree was usually passed, it was not expected that actions would be scrutinised too closely. However, despite its high-sounding verbiage, it was lynch law; the senate was not a sovereign body, and thus enjoyed no right to interfere with the capital status (*caput*) of Roman citizens; such was the people's business.

Also, as was to emerge after 63 BC, when Cicero (as consul) acted on such a decree to bring about the ruin of Catilina's friends, a consul who so acted could not claim immunity; despite the senate's *auctoritas* the consul remained answerable for his actions. Julius Caesar, in 63 BC, had set out to demonstrate this point in the trial of Rabirius who, as a private citizen, had nearly forty years previously helped Marius, as consul, destroy Saturninus and Glaucia.

The outbreak of the Jugurthine War probably helped to relegate the 'Italian question' into the background again, but the final solution of the war through the efforts, as we have seen, of Gaius Marius served to raise expectations anew: the fact that Marius was himself an Italian was thought to guarantee his support for relieving the plight of his fellow Italians. It was a false assumption, for despite the appearance of populist behaviour and radical ideas in Marius, it was evidently his greatest desire to find acceptance among the traditionalist Establishment in Rome. In warfare he had demonstrated clearly enough that his countrymen needed him, and he them; in peacetime it was a different matter. As a 'new man' in politics Marius had no ready place in the factional power politics, nor did he have access to large (and reliable) blocks of clientage. Because he had no obvious niche in senatorial politics, he found himself forced into the hands of two unscrupulous and demagogic politicians – Lucius Appuleius Saturninus and Gaius Servilius Glaucia, who were more intent on using Marius for their own ends than they were on helping and supporting him. Marius needed them, however, to secure a demobilisation settlement for his soldiers (his future political clients) and, in a sinister anticipation of future events, this was achieved only by Saturninus' threat to use the 'muscle' represented by Marius' soldiers.

Marius' political downfall came with the passage in 100 BC of a *Senatus Consultum Ultimum* against Saturninus and Glaucia: this placed Marius in a 'career-destroying' dilemma; as consul, he was called on by the terms of the decree to act against his friends (seen as *perfidia* – 'betrayal'), whereas, if he ignored that call, then he would forfeit the support of the Establishment, which was his earnest desire. Marius sided with the Establishment, but went into eclipse, nonetheless.

There was certainly no mood in Rome now to do anything for Italians; indeed, the *Lex Licinia-Mucia* of 95 BC instituted a process whereby the citizenship claim of each and every Italian would be put to the test, with the exclusion from the citizen roll of all those who could not prove their claims. The Italians' discovery of this regression in their fortunes brought them to Rome to exert pressure just at the time when the younger Marcus Livius Drusus, in 91, was proposing his new citizenship law. It remains unclear what Drusus intended; if he was repeating the tactic employed by his father (or uncle) against Gaius Gracchus, it was in these circumstances a highly rash and dangerous thing to do. On the other hand, in view of the fact that his measure fell because of its infringement of the *Lex Caecilia-Didia*, a law of 98 BC which had been passed in order to outlaw 'omnibus' legislation, it is hard to believe that he would have failed to anticipate this. In either case, Drusus' sincerity appears questionable.

Nonetheless, the Italians evidently regarded Drusus as their last hope; his murder, therefore, was the 'last straw' and precipitated the outbreak of revolt at Asculum in 91. A demand for citizenship was made – and refused; the Italian response to this was the declaration of an independent state (Italica), based at Corfinium, with a complete repudiation of Roman sovereignty. The 'Social War' which followed proved the military mastery of Rome, but left all parties physically and financially exhausted – particularly dangerous at a time when Rome was involved in intermittent hostilities against the wily Mithridates, king of Pontus. A series of enactments, most notably the *Lex Plautia-Papiria*, conceded the principle of full citizenship to all who resided south of the River Po, while the *Lex Pompeia* (of Pompeius Magnus' father) extended half-citizenship to those who lived between the River Po and the Alps (Cisalpine Gaul).

Plate 4.3 Rome, Forum Boarium: *circular temple, perhaps of the late second century* BC *(the present roof of the building is post-Roman).*

For Rome, without doubt, the leading figure in this sorry episode was Lucius Cornelius Sulla, who had been elected to a consulship for 88 BC. He organised a 'rearguard' action to restrict the significance of the new Italian voters by constraining them within eight of the thirty-five tribes, and insisting that they vote last; it was a way of limiting the usefulness of their vote – and humiliatingly so. It created an issue – and unnecessarily, for it was never likely that ordinary Italians would be frequently able in large numbers to make the journey to Rome to vote and join in assembly business. Indeed, the tenor of the Republic's politics remained much as it had before, with the factions of the nobility jockeying for position. In the longer term, however, what had happened was of

Plate 4.2 (opposite) Rome, Forum Boarium: Republican-period temple *(c. 40 BC) to* Fortuna Virilis, *decorated in the Greek Ionic Order.*

Plate 4.4 Rome, Forum of Julius Caesar. The three tall columns to the rear belong to the temple which 'crowned' the Forum and which was dedicated to Venus Genetrix, the legendary founding deity of the family of Caesar and Augustus. The Forum was planned by Caesar but brought to completion by the emperor, Augustus, as an act of pietas.

considerable importance: Rome was now less of an independent city-state than an administrative centre for Italy.

Optimates, populares – and kings

As we have seen, the bruising conflict between Romans and Italians, fought out at great cost to all, gave to Italians concessions of which they had at one time felt no need, but which recently had become vital to their protection and self-respect. For all this, however, the conduct of government remained firmly seated in Rome, with only the wealthiest Italians able to make any practical contribution to it. In practice, therefore, the nature of Roman politics and government remained unchanged; the Italian conflict may have been an interlude in it, but the reasons for the conflict themselves lay in the blinkered and self-serving attitudes of the senatorial nobility, which had been bringing the Republic to its destruction, and which now in the aftermath of the Social War could (and did) continue to do so.

The Republic had come to its crossroads in the events which culminated in the street violence of 133; that year had been a watershed in politics and government and had found the senatorial nobility broadly divided into two large factional 'umbrella groups', grouped at that time around Scipio Aemilianus and Appius Claudius. These were not, however, groups of men linked by a similarity of policy aims. Indeed, the aims of all remained centred around the preservation and enhancement of individual family reputations. The two groups were, therefore, in no sense internally coherent; they were not political parties, as they have sometimes been portrayed, on either side of a central divide. The application to them of such modern concepts as left/right, socialists/conservatives, progressives/reactionaries is a totally inappropriate and misleading exercise, based on a false analogy.

Although the terms *optimates* ('the best men') and *populares* ('mob panderers') were not actually used of those involved in the events of 133 BC, the conduct of the chief participants looks forward to the conduct of Roman politics and government in the first century BC. Then, the terms had clear application: the characteristic of *optimates* was their determination that their domination of the Republic should rest on the senate's continued primacy in the governmental process, dominating both magistrates and assemblies. In practice, this was the situation which the senatorial nobility had engineered for itself in the middle years of the Republic: they saw themselves as the true patriots, and they evidently coined the pejorative use of *populares* for their opponents to reflect what was seen as the hallmark of their activities – demogogic control of the assemblies by relevant magistrates/officers. The events of 133 BC looked forward to this through the tribune's attempt to control the *Concilium Plebis*, although it might equally well, as with Julius Caesar in 59 BC, be the consul's control of the *Comitia*. In such a situation, the senate's position in government was reduced – even marginalised. It could be said that constitutional rectitude was on the side of the *populares* in recognising the principle of popular sovereignty: tradition and practice, however, favoured the *optimates*.

Conflicts between these groups and, indeed, within each of them dominated the politics of the final century of the Republic, as groups or individuals strove for dominance. Each would habitually accuse the other of constituting a threat to *libertas*, of *dominatio*, of trying to establish kingship (*regnum*). The weapons used in these disputes were the manipulation of clientage arrangements, street violence, military threats, religious manipulation or straightforward bribery and corruption. For the *nobiles*, the stakes were high and the ends always justified the means. Those ends were not about improving the lot of Roman citizens by the development of policies that were socially aware; they were about the acquisition of power and dominance. In short, the Republic's greatest problem came to reside in the suicidal self-interest of its governing class. As Ronald Syme put it in *The Roman Revolution*, they might call it the defence of liberty and the laws; in reality, it was the maintenance of their privileges and vested interests.

Marius' army reforms in the last decade of the second century raised the stakes higher by making the Roman army effectively part of the clientage of the nobility, thus guaranteeing its use in factional infighting. Thus, from the types of violence witnessed in the Gracchan episodes, which could be described as 'murder made to look respectable', there was now a real chance that the nobility would plunge the Republic into civil war to protect its interests.

The first clear sign of this came in the wake of the Social War in 88 BC, when Lucius Cornelius Sulla was one of the consuls and Publius Sulpicius was one of the Tribunes of the Plebs: Sulla, a patrician and an optimate, had emerged from the Social War as something of a military hero. The consulship of 88 was his reward and, more important, it was the stepping-stone to an eastern military command to deal with king Mithridates of Pontus who, in 88, was putting into action a plan, long cherished, to drive the Romans out of Asia Minor.

We have already seen that, despite the bitterness that had precipitated and characterised the Social War, and despite the fact that in the end wiser counsels had prevailed in the granting to the Italians of the concessions which they needed, Sulla and his optimate associates had, by 'gerrymandering' the allocation of the new citizens to the voting tribes, tried to minimise their effectiveness – or, put more realistically, their ability to interfere in the 'closed shop' of the nobility's factional infighting. Sulpicius has usually been seen as the champion of justice in reversing this and seeking a fair distribution of the new citizens among the tribes. However, one might wonder why, if this was his aim, he also raised a private army and used it to drive Sulla, the consul, out of Rome; why also did he seek the transference of the Mithridatic command, by irregular means, from Sulla to the now-ageing Gaius Marius?

All of this resembles the 'sledge-hammer to crack a nut', unless his real aim was not justice and fair play for Italians, but a bid for factional dominance either in his own interest or perhaps in that of Marius who was in any case desperate to regain the pedestal from which he had fallen in 100. Sulpicius, indeed, comes to resemble Tiberius Gracchus – a *popularis*, using the weapons at his disposal to maximise his voting strength and to marginalise/destroy his optimate opponents. If Tiberius Gracchus could be accused of seeking to establish a *regnum*, the charge applies no less appropriately to Sulpicius.

The difference in this case was the optimate response: not the manipulation of religion or the passing of the 'Ultimate Decree', but Sulla's illegal use of the army, which was designated for his Mithridatic campaigns, to attack Rome with military force, killing Sulpicius in the process, and thus restore the factional equilibrium in favour of himself and his optimate friends. It is, therefore, in no way surprising that he used the opportunity of his military victory in 88 to alter the constitution to suit his own factional interests.

A package of measures was introduced, and subsequently reinforced after his second march on Rome in 82, to make a '*popularis* onslaught' of the type mounted by Sulpicius virtually impossible. The question which has, over the years, exercised historians is whether Sulla did this to ensure a factional dominance or whether these were actions of Sulla (the statesman and 'last Republican') to restore sanity and order to the Republic's government: ironically, the optimate in him would probably have argued that there was essentially no difference between the two propositions.

In two periods of reform – during his consulship in 88 and, again, following his return from the Mithridatic War – Sulla set out to re-orientate governmental practice with the purpose of setting the senate firmly in control. The nature of this exercise was essentially of a negative character: Sulla identified the sources of danger to the senate's pre-eminence that had emerged over the previous fifty years or so and determined to neutralise them. This demonstrated to him that the senate required protection from the activities of magistrates and tribunes, of promagistrates and their armies and of the people's assemblies. He set out to provide this protection within a framework of law. He evidently failed to grasp the fact that, in the Republic's earlier days, the senate's *auctoritas* and its ability to command a general respect as the *de facto* government derived precisely from the fact that it had then had no need of such a 'fence' of protective legislation. However, the structural weakness of his approach was that it addressed symptoms rather than causes.

In brief, the thrusts of Sulla's changes were as follows: first, enforcing age limits for the holding of particular magistracies and intervals between successive tenures of the same office; secondly, rendering the Tribunate of the Plebs a 'dead-end' office (by restricting its holders proceeding to further office), and restricting the scope of its veto; thirdly, encompassing the conduct of pro-magistrates within a framework of rules, which were intended to weaken their relationship with the troops under their command. Further, by raising the number of annual praetorships to eight, he ensured that there would be a regular availability of ten senior promagistrates for the number of provinces which at that time stood at ten: fourthly, restricting the freedom of both magistrates and popular assemblies by insisting on the tradition of senatorial 'pre-discussion' of all assembly business; fifthly, abolishing the censorship, making fulfilment of the quaestorship the route of entry into the senate and raising the annual number of quaestor-ships to twenty. The senate was also to be immediately enhanced to a membership of six hundred by the addition of three hundred members of the Equestrian Order.

It is not difficult to identify the episodes from the recent past which had prompted each of these measures. In a sense, however, the most disturbing was the last, which ensured not a strong senate but one which was totally dependent on Sulla himself. The Dictator was pointing the way to the organisation of the govern-mental machinery which was to characterise the Principate. Perhaps, however, the most valuable – and certainly the most enduring – element of Sulla's reforms was his institution of permanent courts (*quaestiones*) to handle named offences. This, effectively, all but removed the administration of justice from the popular assemblies.

Accompanying these reforms was the introduction of a harsh programme of proscriptions, whereby named individuals could be legally murdered and their property forfeit to the Republic; Sulla needed a mechanism by which to remove his enemies, and he required money to pay, reward – and bribe. The removal of enemies also satisfied the desire for vengeance on the part of Sulla's support-ers, many of whom had themselves suffered harshly at the hands of Cinna and Marius in the course of their bloody and brutal march on Rome in 87, which led to Marius' seventh and final consulship in 86. It may also be surmised that, in the short term at least, Sulla appreciated the value of a programme of institutionalised intimidation and violence. He also ensured that all slaves belonging to the proscribed were freed and granted the franchise, taking Sulla's gentile name; the estimated ten thousand new Cornelii were valuable voting support for Sulla in the popular assemblies.

It is no easy task to assess the view that Sulla took of his own position in the Republic. He held the office of Dictator, but it was one in which the normal rules of tenure did not apply, but were in essence 're-written' by Sulla to suit himself. His tenure was also unlimited in time. Indeed, the Dictatorship of Sulla had less to do with the existence or otherwise of an emergency than with the means which it provided for the permanent supervision of the Republic. In effect, therefore, Sulla had outlawed earlier routes to kingship in order that he might become 'king' himself. The office was accompanied by other trappings of monarchy: for example, Sulla was attended in public by twenty-four lictors (attendants) rather than by the normal twelve. An image of an equestrian statue of him appeared on the coinage with an accompanying legend, and he backed himself and his role with the title *Felix* (or 'Fortunate'), which suggested that he was the man picked out by destiny and protected by the gods; the title had a particular association with the goddess, Venus, whose place in Rome's foundation legends was crucial. This may also have been aimed at the Marian *populares*, whose dead hero had been married to Julius Caesar's aunt, Julia; the *gens Iulia* looked specifically to Venus as its legendary foundress. The chief difficulty in the assessment of Sulla's role, however, lies in his sudden resignation of his office in 79; it will always remain an open question whether he resigned because he thought that he had done enough, or because he was already a dying man. According to the later satirist, Juvenal, the question continued to intrigue Romans for years to come; Julius Caesar, who evidently came to Sulla's notice as a notable youthful opponent and who later held the Dictatorship himself, is on record as having observed that Sulla, by his resignation, demonstrated his political ineptitude. We may assume that, perhaps like Sulla, Caesar also came to recognise the need for some kind of permanent supervision to guarantee the stability of the Roman Republic.

Ultimately, therefore, Sulla's perception of his role remains enigmatic. What, however, is in no sense enigmatic is that his conduct in the 80s guaranteed the continuation of civil violence: he had shown a route to power for ambitious men, and the restrictiveness of his measures ensured that a reaction was inevitable. If nothing else, the desire for vengeance provoked by his brutality guaranteed that. Further, and perhaps most importantly, despite the protective 'fence' that Sulla had erected around the senate, that body soon demonstrated that it lacked the ability to withstand armed adventurers: as Cicero was later to observe of a different episode, 'faced with force of arms, the laws fall silent'. The extraordinary and illegal rise to power of Gnaeus Pompeius Magnus (Pompey) during the 70s demonstrates in abundance the truth of that.

In the decade that followed Sulla, Pompey invoked or threatened the use of force to which he had no legal entitlement – to put down the 'rebellion' of Lepidus in 78–77 (which he himself had been largely responsible for instigating), to go to Spain to 'help' the proconsul, Metellus Pius, put down the Marian remnants based there under the inspirational leadership of Quintus Sertorius and finally, after 'helping' Marcus Licinius Crassus deal with the remnants of the gladiatorial uprising in Italy under Spartacus, to join with Crassus to demand the two consulships of 70 BC. It had been a decade of illegality and violence which saw Pompey rise to an office for which he had fulfilled none of the required qualifications: by 70, indeed, Pompey was not even a member of the senate, and he had demonstrated himself to be a master of political deception and disloyalty; he had been optimate and *popularis* to suit his changing needs; a politician, in short, of considerable talent, but no principles – even by Roman standards. For this he would find that, before long, he had a price to pay.

The temporary coalition (*amicitia*: 'friendship') between Pompey and Crassus was a peculiarly Roman phenomenon: there was ordinarily little affection between these two former associates of Sulla. While Pompey's route to power had been unorthodox and based originally on privately raised legions which he had 'inherited' from his father (Pompeius Strabo; consul in 89), Crassus had pursued a more normal path which had been facilitated by the large amount of money which he was alleged to have made out of Sulla's proscription programme. In 70, Crassus wanted and was eligible for the consulship, whereas the unqualified Pompey wanted it for the opportunity that it would provide to build his role as a *consularis* (ex-consul).

The conjunction of clientage of the two men in 71 proved unstoppable – their two armies, together with the anti-Sullans, and particularly those who wanted a relaxation of the stiff constraints that Sulla had placed on the tenure of the Tribunate of the Plebs. Although it is often asserted that the joint consulship of 70 saw to the dismantling of Sulla's constitution, this is something of an exaggeration; in essence, the significant changes were the 'unmuzzling' of the Tribunate and the return to the Equestrian Order of some measure of influence on the juries of the *quaestiones* – the permanent courts established by Sulla. This amounted to keeping faith with clients and, in Pompey's case, it opened the way to two major commands which he 'won' by votes in the Plebeian Assembly on tribunician bills in 67 and 66 – respectively, the military commands against the Mediterranean pirates and against Mithridates of Pontus, which were to provide the chief base of Pompey's power in the 60s. Such was the surge of support behind Pompey among, particularly, equestrians and plebs that little could be done by his optimate opponents to stop him. Further, the fact that Pompey delivered success on both enterprises, where success for others had proved so elusive, meant, as he himself used to boast, that no Roman politician had ever had a clientage to match his for size. Clientage was essentially the measure of success for Pompey, the *princeps* ('preeminent citizen'); other politicians attached themselves to him, because his support promised them success as well. Pompey's 'network' in the mid-60s was impressive, although he still had some dangerous enemies among former supporters of Sulla – the price of perfidy.

Among those who supported Pompey was the orator, Marcus Tullius Cicero (from Arpinum), a *novus homo* ('new man') who had made his name by attacking forensically men who had made themselves rich from Sulla's proscriptions; Cicero crowned this part of his career by taking on the prosecution, on behalf of clients in Sicily, of the island's notorious praetor, Gaius Verres. Verres enshrined in his governorship of Sicily all that was regarded as most corrupt and degraded in the oligarchy that had gathered around Sulla.

It was never an easy task for a 'new man' to win the consulship; not content with the fruits of his own reputation and Pompey's support, Cicero enhanced these with 'projects' of his own, which on occasion caused embarrassment and anger among his princi-pal supporters, notably Pompey. For example, he supported the claim for a triumph made on behalf of Lucius Licinius Lucullus, Pompey's predecessor in the 'eastern theatre' and bitter opponent; Lucullus had once referred to Pompey as a 'carrion bird' who fed on the leftovers of others – an allusion to the alle-gation that Pompey's successes were largely 'mopping-up' opera-tions in the wake of the real successes achieved by others. Without doubt, the optimate Lucullus had fought Mithridates in the king's prime, and deserved much of the credit for breaking him; the Mithridates who committed suicide while Pompey was east-ern commander was a pale shadow of his former self. Pompey would not have relished Cicero's 'courting' of Lucullus, but then Lucullus 'opened the door' to influential optimate support for Cicero's consular candidature. Cicero also launched a pretty unprincipled attack on his chief competitor for the consulship, Lucius Sergius Catilina, who appears to have been associated in some way with Pompey and who had declined Cicero's overtures for an electoral alliance. The centre-piece of this character assassination was a piece of fiction which is, thanks to Cicero, known to history as 'The First Catilinarian Conspiracy' (of 66–65 BC). Such matters demonstrate that, when the stakes were high, Cicero was as unprincipled as any of the leading figures of the late Republic.

If Pompey was upset by these activities, he was probably still more alienated by Cicero's conscientious attempt to defeat the land bill proposed by one of the tribunes of 63, Servilius Rullus. Cicero assumed (or affected to assume) that this land bill was master-minded by Crassus with the intention of making Pompey dependent on him for land on which to settle his troops, when the time came to discharge them from service. Cicero, who dis-liked the inclusion in this bill of 'general welfare measures' and would have attacked it for this reason in any case, may or may not have realised that the true identity of its ultimate author was probably Pompey himself.

The major event of Cicero's consular year (63 BC) was the Conspiracy of Catilina, which Cicero eventually constrained with the help of a passing of the 'Ultimate Decree'. Once again, Cicero probably provoked this former supporter of Pompey into desper-ate measures. It is, in any case, evident from a letter which Cicero wrote to Pompey in 62 that the great *imperator* was by that time decidedly cool towards Cicero – presumably because of the cumulative effect of episodes such as those described above; nor is there any doubt that Cicero, perhaps largely unwittingly, had managed to put some dents in Pompey's reputation.

There was, in fact, a fundamental conflict between the two men, the nature of which Cicero probably did not fully appreciate. Pompey was a man of immense arrogance – as is witnessed by his decision to disband his eastern army on his return from the east – and probably saw nothing standing in the way of his being the man of unquestioned dominance in the light of his cumulative achievements; he was, in his own eyes, 'king' of Rome in all but name. Cicero's perspective was different: he acknowledged Pompey's dominance of the political scene, but wished to place it in a rather more structured Republic, in which he himself would have a place as the voice of reason and moderation alongside the great general; Cicero may indeed have made the mistake that many have subsequently – of seeing Pompey as a military genius, but a political novice.

Cicero's 'Union of the Orders' (*Concordia Ordinum*) originated in the events of his own election campaign in 65–64; he was the friend of the good and the implacable foe of the bad. He believed that his own election victory demonstrated that his vision of Rome was shared by all 'right-minded' people; this vision was of a Rome where the senate dominated by its *auctoritas*, which was accepted by all reasonable men, whether they were senators, equestrians or ordinary Italians. Pompey's role, in Cicero's mind, was to act as the 'guardian' of senatorial dominance and of the coalition which supported it. Cicero saw Pompey as an 'almost-Platonic' facilitator of a governmental stability, which existed independently of him, whereas Pompey evidently believed that, without him, there was no Republic.

In fact, Cicero's dream was founded on a series of false premises – that the coalition which had secured his election as consul represented a discernible 'national movement', that he had marshalled this 'national movement' into action in the defeat of Catilina and that Pompey enthusiastically adhered to this coalition; this was not the only time in his life that Cicero convinced himself that he knew best what was best for Pompeius Magnus. Cicero was obsessed with the events of 63 – 'O happy the Rome that was born in the year of my consulship' is the translation of a line of Cicero's verse account of his consulship, as quoted by the satirist, Juvenal (*Satire* X.122); ironically, the same year saw the birth of the man who was to rule the Roman world as Augustus Caesar. Unfortunately for Cicero, Pompey and the contemporary nobility were much more concerned with the acquisition and retention of personal power and influence than they were with the visions of an 'outsider' whom they could barely bring themselves to recognise as one of their own 'club'. Also, Pompey could not realise his aspirations with the ease that he expected: his ruthless path to power had left him with too many enemies. Although he remained the single most powerful individual for most of the rest of his life, his ultimate weakness was demonstrated by his need in 60 BC to enter into an alliance – the so-called first triumvirate – with Crassus and Caesar to secure goals that should have proved straightforward for one in his position. Instead, it was Caesar, during a turbulent consulship in 59, who set in motion the legislation necessary to secure what his two partners needed – for Pompey the ratification of his eastern command and the provision of land for his veterans, for Crassus the revision of the eastern tax contract. Indeed, the struggle between optimates and *populares* was, in the final analysis, greater than both Cicero and Pompey and was becoming steadily more anarchic and increasingly divorced from the Republic's real needs.

Cicero, during the 50s, found himself ever-more marginal to the power conflicts that were being acted out between Pompey, Crassus and Caesar, their friends and their enemies; as he realised increasingly in the wake of the renewal at Lucca in 56 of the triumviral *amicitia*, the self-indulgence of the three was beyond belief. Throughout the 50s, the streets of Rome were dominated by the gang warfare organised by Publius Clodius and others, nominally in the interests of patrons, but in reality in the interests of the organisers themselves. The annual elections, a touchstone of a stable state, became an orgy of corruption and violence. The deaths of Crassus and Clodius in 53 and 52 respectively removed players from the scene, although this simply served to sharpen the conflict between Pompey and Caesar. Cicero's letters of the late 50s cannot disguise his sense of disillusion: there was nothing to choose between Pompey and Caesar, because 'both wanted to be king'. When he returned from a year (51–50) of provincial government in Cilicia, he wrote, 'I was too late; I had entered a madhouse of men lusting for war'.

It was a fair comment to make: Marcus Cato, a man once described by Cicero as 'our hero', formulated a plan whereby, he hoped, the Republic would be able to rid itself of both Pompey and Caesar, and which entailed forcing the two into war; his hatred of both men evidently blinded him to the most likely outcome of a civil war – the supremacy of one. As the final senate vote before the outbreak of civil war at the beginning of 49 demonstrated, men such as Cato were able to inflict their views on others despite their minority appeal and despite the efforts of a few, such as the Caesarian tribune, Gaius Scribonius Curio, to effect a compromise between Caesar and Pompey; 370 senators voted against civil war, while only twenty-two supported Cato's plan to destroy the dynasts. Yet the twenty-two could secure their aims by means of tribunician vetos. The civil war was fought to serve the narrow sectional interests of the twenty-two, not to bring any benefit to the Republic; just how high minded these men were is made clear by their alleged preoccupation with the mansions that would come on to the market once their owners had fallen in the civil war. Such a scenario amply justifies Syme's contention that 'liberty' and 'the laws' were high-sounding euphemisms for 'privilege' and 'vested interests'. 'This was what they wanted' was Julius Caesar's alleged observation as he gazed on the optimate dead after Pharsalus in 48.

Thus, that stage of the struggle for dominance was settled in favour of Gaius Julius Caesar; Caesar's thinking both about Rome and about the empire's relationship with Rome was probably more radical than that of any of his contemporaries. Suetonius quotes him as observing that 'the Republic is a mere name, without form or substance'; the remark sounds disparaging, but was not intended to be. It was, after all, little more than the truth: the term, *respublica*, was broad and vague, and certainly did not imply, except as traditionally interpreted, any specific mode of government.

Caesar, in power, experienced real difficulties; never the most patient of men and despite the fact that his military victory was clear cut, he had to deal with considerable numbers of optimate opponents, most of whom were no more prepared to accept him in 48 than they had been two years earlier. Further, their cause lived on in a number of theatres around the Mediterranean, notably in Spain and North Africa. Thus, the great luminaries of the Republic had not supported Caesar in 50, and wished to continue to oppose, even fight, him now. Nor is there any doubt that the absence of these luminaries from his *popularis* faction made Caesar look all the more monarchic, as he stood head and shoulders above those who adhered to him. Caesar's own supporters were not that impressive; even without some refugees from the defeated faction, there were divisions among his own supporters. Caesar thus had problems developing all around him, as men anxiously looked to see whether they could continue pursuing their own self-interested agendas and whether Caesar's handling of the peace would be effective in restoring an acceptable stability to the Republic.

Perhaps because of this divisiveness, perhaps because it in any case reflected his own nature and perhaps because he genuinely recognised that the Republic and the empire needed firm government, Caesar proceeded to stamp a far more authoritarian character on the government than had previously been the case. His remark about the foolishness of Sulla's resignation indicates clearly the direction which he intended to take. If people were afraid of this, then those fears will have seemed confirmed by the way in which he treated the senate, raising its membership to nearly one thousand by filling it with his supporters, and then using it as a 'rubber stamp'; his treatment of elections and the magistracies was equally cavalier. Even his treatment of the provinces – instituting more accountable government and fairer methods of tax collection, as well as seeking to raise the status of 'worthy' provincials – will have counted against him in the eyes of many who will have interpreted such measures as a diminution of their own privileges.

The real crisis in Caesar's period of dominance came in 46–45; until then, some at least – for example, Cicero and others who, like Brutus, accepted office under him – were prepared to give Caesar a chance. However, at about that point, his grip on power appeared to be becoming stronger, leaving little hope to those who had accepted Caesar's Dictatorship as a necessary, but temporary, phase to put the Republic back on its feet. In 46, he moved from the traditional six-month terms as Dictator to a ten-year term, albeit with the proviso of annual renewals, and thus a form of accountability; in 44, however, he became *dictator perpetuus* which, although it may not have implied that Caesar intended to be Dictator for ever, nonetheless removed the specific points of accountability, which had always been a fundamental principle of power holding in the Roman Republic. It is clear that it was at this time that Cicero shifted from readiness to think of Caesar as the possible *moderator* ('guardian') of a Ciceronian Republic to a conviction that Caesar was, in fact, bent on destroying the Republic.

Cato's suicide in 46, and its clear indication that he could no longer stomach Caesar's Republic, shook the Dictator because it showed clearly that Caesar was now viewed by traditionalists as *dominus* ('a master of slaves') or, even worse, as *rex*; this state of affairs could not be tolerated. To Cassius, Caesar was *clemens dominus*: even his attempt to compromise with defeated enemies (*clementia*) was seen as unacceptable or, even worse, as an instrument of despotism; for *clementia* was a despot's gift, not a citizen's right. It made no difference that Caesar protested – 'I am not king, but Caesar' – or that he was still the admired patron of many ordinary people (for whom he had provided work and food through his extensive programme of public building), of the army, of equestrians and even of some senators. Caesar's behaviour and the disenchantment of Cato and others demonstrated that Caesarism and the Republic were viewed as incompatible; some probably, with a short-sightedness that had long been typical of the Roman nobility, had convinced themselves, against all that recent history had shown them, that once the despot/king was removed, the Republic would by that act alone be restored.

The futility of Caesar's murder on the Ides (15th) of March in 44 BC became immediately apparent: it was not the conspirators who took the initiative to shape the future; they had evidently made few plans beyond killing Caesar. The initiative very rapidly passed to Caesar's own associates, principally Marcus Antonius (Marc Antony), who ensured that 'Caesarism' did not die with Julius Caesar. In any case, talk of that peculiarly senatorial 'virtue' of *libertas* made little impression on those who were feeling the benefits of the Dictator's patronage. The Republic retained a vocal spokesman in Cicero, but the political conflict that mattered was not that between 'Caesarism' and the Republic (*populares* against *optimates*) but that which was soon to develop between factions within Caesar's own 'party'.

The nature of this conflict was momentous, for it was between a faction's senior members (men such as Antonius and Lepidus) and the young man (Gaius Julius Caesar Octavianus), who believed that his blood tie with Caesar and the fact that he had been adopted as the Dictator's heir transcended traditional views regarding the importance of seniority. This was perhaps the first real indication that 'Caesarism' was transforming the Republic back into a hereditary monarchy.

For the moment, however, little attention was paid to the eighteen-year-old Octavian as he tried to court the interest of his father's most trusted friends and of senior members of the republican faction opposed to Antonius. For their part, the republicans clearly saw Antonius as their most dangerous opponent, and Cicero appears to have re-invented Cato's 'battle plan' of the late 50s – that was to use Pompey to destroy Caesar and thus to leave Pompey marginalised. Now, Octavian was to be used to destroy Antonius – and then discarded. It was a bad error of judgement (as it had been in the late 50s), and it overlooked the forces that, temporarily at least, kept Antonius and Octavian together. Cicero was too obsessed with his battle with Antonius to see this; for him, as he rather tastelessly put it, the banquet of the Ides of March had been 'one course short'.

In his own eyes, Cicero now reached the apex of his career, achieving a prominence that had not been his since the year of his consulship and the destruction of Catilina. Sadly, Cicero was as blinkered in 44–43 as he had been in 64–63, and his obsession removed from him any comprehension of the real world. Indeed, the cause on which he was expending (literally) the last reserves of his energy was now irrelevant except to a very few. Undeterred, Cicero, having lambasted Antonius throughout the autumn of 44 in a series of scurrilous orations (the *Philippics*), set out to destroy him politically and militarily. On 1 January 43, Antonius was entitled to take up his proconsulship of *Gallia Cisalpina*, although he had first to secure the 'retirement' of his predecessor, Decimus Brutus.

Cicero, appealing to some higher authority, argued that Decimus Brutus should ignore the requirements of the law and retain his province and that, because Marcus Brutus and Cassius had in the east bribed some of Antonius' troops to desert, Antonius could no longer be regarded as a 'proper proconsul'; the reasoning was as dextrous as it was flawed. Cicero further proposed that Decimus Brutus should be supported in his illegal retention of his province by an army raised for the purpose by the Republic and led into the field by the two consuls, Hirtius and Pansa. He added that Octavian should be given the status of an ex-praetor so that he, too, could join the Republic's command structure.

That there was collusion between Antonius, Lepidus and Octavian seems in little doubt despite the fact that Octavian did not enjoy a good relationship with his two faction leaders, who regarded him as an 'upstart'. The result of the military action which took place around Mutina (modern Modena) was that Decimus Brutus survived intact, while the deaths in action of the two consuls left Octavian in charge of all of the Republic's armies. Antonius was allowed to escape to Gaul. When Cicero demanded that Octavian should hand over his troops to Decimus Brutus, Caesar's heir, with a cynicism well beyond his years, announced that he could not be expected to co-operate with a man who had been involved in his father's assassination – and refused to heed the instruction of Cicero and the senate.

Showing again the vulnerability of the Republic in the face of a faction leader backed by troops, Octavian marched his army on Rome and demanded (and was given) a consulship while still twenty-three years under age. He then promptly returned north where he met with Antonius and Lepidus; together they formed the pact known to history as the second triumvirate. This was a very different arrangement from the informal *amicitia* formed in 60 between Pompey, Crassus and Caesar. The pact of 43 was sanctioned in law as an office of state for the 'ordering of the Republic'; the three members were given consular authority for a five-year period, with the power to appoint magistrates and divide the territory of the empire between them. Further, to remove enemies and acquire funds, like Sulla they instituted a programme of proscriptions; unsurprisingly, the list was headed by the name of Marcus Tullius Cicero.

Thus, the Dictatorship of Caesar had given way to the dictatorship of the three leading exponents of 'Caesarism'; as with any trio in power, however, it was only a matter of time before one of the three emerged as dominant. The last twelve years of the old Republic (43–31 BC), therefore, were taken up with this final struggle for dominance, complicated briefly by the intervention of a fourth figure in the person of Pompey's son, Sextus, who had based himself on the island of Sicily, backed by 'republican diehards'; from here he hoped to bargain based on his ability to interfere by sea with Italy's vital supplies. He announced his mastery of the sea by styling himself 'son of Neptune'.

In the initial division of territory between the *triumviri*, Antonius took the eastern lands, remembering perhaps Pompey's strength in this region, while Octavian and Lepidus divided the west between them; Octavian's share included Italy. Their initial task, however, was the avenging of Caesar's murder; this act was formally completed with the victory at Philippi in Greece, in which

Brutus and Cassius were both killed. In return for the victory, Octavian, now to be noted for his *pietas,* vowed a temple to Mars the Avenger, which was finally to open in very different circumstances forty years later as the 'crowning glory' of Augustus' Forum in Rome.

The mastermind behind the territorial division was clearly that of Antonius: his own share (the east), although to become infamous for his relationship with Cleopatra, contained both great wealth, much of Italy's grain supply and sources of manpower which had originally come into the Roman domain through Pompey's clientage arrangements of the 60s. In Antonius' eyes, Italy was something of a poisoned chalice because of the disruption that was expected to be caused there, as Octavian confiscated land to facilitate the settlement of large numbers of demobilised triumviral troops. In the hope of ensuring that Octavian would be 'buried' beneath this, Antonius' wife (Fulvia) and brother (Lucius) were deputed to stir matters up further.

However, Antonius' plans for the next decade went badly wrong, partly at least because of the political maturity which Octavian would display: he deflected and turned to his own advantage traps that were laid for him, and made use of every opportunity offered him by the errors and bad judgement of Antonius. He managed with no great difficulty the land settlement in Italy and dealt effectively (and with a certain magnanimity) with Fulvia and Lucius Antonius. The threat of disruption posed by Sextus Pompeius was solved, temporarily at least, by an agreement which allowed back into Italy those republicans who had taken refuge with Pompey's son. In no way did this cause difficulty for Octavian: on the contrary, the return of the great luminaries of the Republic put them under obligation to him and helped Octavian, by the accumulation of great names around him, to avoid the appearance of monarchy which had so distorted the cause of Caesar. Not only that, but Octavian linked himself to this group when he married Livia Drusilla, the wife of the ex-Caesarian, but now very republican, Tiberius Claudius Nero. The marriage to Livia brought Octavian a much-needed political respectability; it also brought him two stepsons, of whom the elder was the future emperor, Tiberius Caesar.

Octavian was thus able to identify himself with the interests of the Republic – indeed to stand as its defender. Since Julius Caesar's deification in 42, Octavian was now 'Son of God' (*Divi filius*), and his relationship with the gods enhanced that very important republican 'virtue' of *pietas*. Overall, he was a dispenser of patronage, taking on the image of the great dynasts of the past. When the rapprochement with Sextus Pompeius broke down, he was able to secure a military victory through his friend, Marcus Agrippa, who was prepared to ascribe his victory to the 'overarching generalship' of Octavian (*Imperator Caesar*). Further, Octavian was able to turn to his own advantage the desperate attempt by Lepidus in 36 to win Sicily for himself; Octavian had only to display the patronal 'pulling power' of the name, Caesar, to destroy Lepidus as a credible political rival. This one-time ally of Julius Caesar had to be content to see out the rest of his days (until his death in 12 BC) in Africa with the post of *pontifex maximus*.

Antonius' mistakes, too, were turned to Octavian's advantage: at the renewal of the triumvirate – a year late, in 37 BC – Antonius divorced Fulvia and married Octavian's sister, Octavia, in her place. Henceforth, as a consequence, Octavian could not only point out the 'un-Romanness' of Antonius' liaison with the queen of Egypt, but also deal with it, in a traditional fashion, as the head of an injured household: Antonius' relationship with Cleopatra brought dishonour to Octavian's sister; Octavian's propaganda machine could be deployed on that error of judgement, as it could also on the loss in 36 (under Decidius Saxa) of a further legionary eagle to the Parthians – that is, in addition to those lost by Crassus at Carrhae. The publication of Antonius' (supposed) will – the 'Donations of Alexandria' of 34 BC – with its bequests of money and territory to Cleopatra and her children, presented another unmissable propaganda opportunity.

Indeed, the military victory at Actium in 31, which was orchestrated by Agrippa, was the only real hurdle remaining; the political victories had all been won in the 30s. Thus, Octavian emerged as the victor of Actium; the deaths of Antonius and Cleopatra in 30 left him without rivals. The 'old Republic' was finally dead, but in its death throes it had produced a leader with the now-proven capability to raise the phoenix from the ashes and create the Republic's continuation. The wheel had turned full circle: the old Republic had come into being with the death of a monarchy; it had given way in its turn to a new monarchy (the Principate) which would have as a primary objective the stressing of its continuity with the traditions of the past and the developing of mechanisms which were to prevent that monarchy, in the short term at least, from moving too far away from the tenets of the old Republic.

Octavian's victory at Actium brought the 'old Republic' to an end after four-and-a-half centuries; the 'old Republic' had been born as the Roman nobility sought to rid itself of a monarchy which favoured the ordinary people above the aristocracy. It ended as one member of the nobility triumphed over his fellow aristocrats to establish a personal hegemony that was supported by the mass of the people. Early in the second century BC – that is, when the Republic was on the brink of the changes described in this chapter – the Elder Cato observed that the Republic developed by evolution, not by revolution. In other words, a form of government designed to restrict power to the aristocracy changed just enough to allow the descendants of that aristocracy to retain that hold on power. Cato was praising the Republic for continuing to live in the past; ancestral custom (*mos maiorum*) – the practice of traditional virtues in public and private life – continued to win plaudits and provide the models for future success.

However, the growth of the empire proved to be an irresistible force in the pressures which it created; there were new problems to solve and new opportunities to grasp, which encouraged a much fiercer competitive sense within that aristocracy. They became concerned not just to maintain a corporate control over the Republic, but how to outdo and dominate each other; they were fighting 'power games' which largely ignored the issues of the day. The self-indulgence of that aristocracy was almost beyond belief, particularly in the way in which, from the late second century, it was prepared to add armies to its clientage and plunge the Republic into civil war to satisfy personal and factional ambition.

If such conditions were driving the Republic back to monarchy, a few came to see that the growing volume and complexity of government were beckoning in the same direction. In a bizarre way, the interests of Rome and of its aristocratic grandees were in a sense coinciding to urge the desirability of a centralised control which at one time many had regarded as unthinkable. The last century of the Republic demonstrated a number of different ways in which that centralised authority might be provided. When it came in 31, it was entirely typical that it was provided in the most conservative way possible – not a break with the past to establish a kingship, but an evolution from the 'old Republic' to a 'restored Republic'. The Augustan Principate was founded on principles which were thoroughly traditional and demonstrated that the spirit of the Republic's founding fathers lived on. As we shall see in the next chapter, the most succinct 'prospectus' for the Augustan Republic is to be found in the so-called 'Roman Odes' of the poet, Horace (*Odes* III.1–6). Those odes are not concerned with change and revolution; they provide the justification for tradition and restoration. In literature, that was provided by the *pietas* of the Trojan hero, Aeneas; in reality, it was provided by the prestige and standing, the *auctoritas* of Octavian, the son of god – Augustus Caesar.

Appendix 1

Stemma of the Claudii and the Scipiones

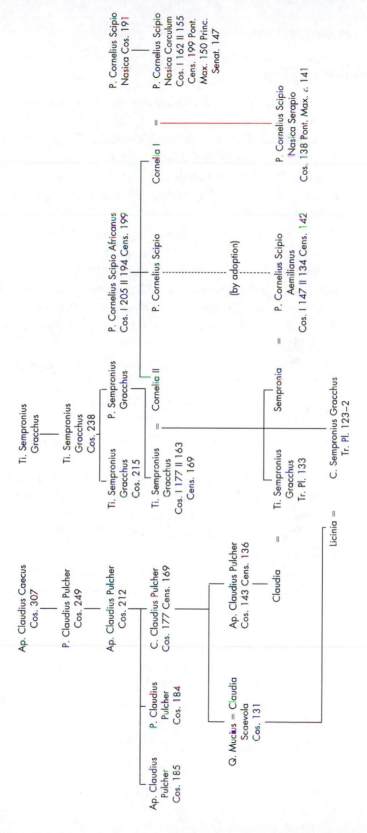

Further reading

Adcock F. E., *Roman Political Ideas and Practice* (Ann Arbor, MI, 1959).

Adcock F. E., *Marcus Crassus: Millionaire* (Cambridge, 1966).

Astin A. E., *Scipio Aemilianus* (Oxford, 1967).

Astin A. E., *Cato the Censor* (Oxford, 1978).

Badian E., *Roman Imperialism in the Late Republic* (Oxford, 1968).

Badian E., *Publicans and Sinners* (London, 1983).

Bauman R. A., *Crimen Maiestatis in the Late Republic and Augustan Principate* (Johannesburg, 1967).

Beard M. and Crawford M. H., *Rome in the Late Republic: Problems and Interpretations* (New York, 1985).

Beard M., North J. and Price S., *Religions in Rome* (Cambridge, 1998).

Broughton T. R. S., *The Magistrates of the Roman Republic* (New York, 1951–2).

Brunt P. A., *Social Conflicts in the Roman Republic* (London, 1971).

Brunt P. A., *The Fall of the Roman Republic and Related Essays* (Oxford, 1988).

Carney T. F., *A Biography of Gaius Marius* (Chicago, IL, 1970).

Clarke M. L., *The Noblest Roman: Marcus Brutus and his Reputation* (London, 1981).

Crawford M. H., *Coinage and Money Under the Roman Republic* (London, 1985).

Crawford M. H., *The Roman Republic* (London, 1992).

Earl D. C., *The Political Thought of Sallust* (Cambridge, 1967).

Earl D. C., *Tiberius Gracchus: A Study in Politics* (Brussels, 1963).

Gelzer M., *Caesar: Politician and Statesman,* (Oxford, 1968).

Greenhalgh P., *Pompey* (London, 1980).

Gruen E. S., *Roman Politics and the Criminal Courts, 149–78 B.C.* (Cambridge, MA, 1968).

Gruen E. S., *The Last Generation of the Roman Republic* (Berkeley, CA, 1974).

Hill H., *The Roman Middle Class in the Republican Period* (Oxford, 1952).

Huzar E. G., *Marc Antony* (Minneapolis, MN, 1978).

Keaveney A., *Sulla: The Last Republican* (London, 1982).

Keaveney A., *Rome and the Unification of Italy* (New York, 1987).

Keaveney A., *Lucullus: A Life* (London, 1992).

Kelly J. M., *Roman Litigation* (Oxford, 1966).

Lacey W. K., *Cicero and the End of the Roman Republic* (London, 1978).

Leach J., *Pompey the Great* (London, 1978).

Lintott A. W., *Violence in Republican Rome* (Oxford, 1968).

McDonald A. H., *Republican Rome* (London, 1966).

Meier C., *Caesar* (London, 1996).

Michels A., *The Calendar of the Roman Republic* (Princeton, NJ, 1967).

Mitchell T. N., *Cicero: The Ascending Years* (New Haven, CT, 1979).

Mouritsen H., *Plebs and Politics in the Late Roman Republic* (Cambridge, 2001).

Rickman G., *The Corn Supply of Ancient Rome* (Oxford, 1980).

Riddle J. M. (ed.), *Tiberius Gracchus* (Boston, MA, 1970).

Sabben-Clare J., *Caesar and Roman Politics, 60–50 B.C.* (Oxford, 1971).

Seager R., *Pompey: A Political Biography* (Oxford 1979).

Shatzman I., *Senatorial Wealth and Roman Politics* (Brussels, 1975).

Shotter D. C. A., *The Fall of the Roman Republic* (London, 1994).

Smith R. E., *The Failure of the Roman Republic* (Cambridge, 1955).

Smith R. E., *Cicero the Statesman,* (Cambridge, 1966).

Stockton D., *Cicero: A Political Biography* (Oxford, 1971).

Stockton D., *The Gracchi* (Oxford, 1979).

Syme R., *The Roman Revolution* (Oxford, 1939).

Syme R., *Sallust* (Berkeley, CA, 1964).

Taylor L. R., *Party Politics in the Age of Caesar* (Berkeley, CA, 1949).

Taylor L. R., *The Voting Districts of the Roman Republic* (Rome, 1960).

Taylor L. R., *Roman Voting Assemblies* (Ann Arbor, MI, 1966).

Treggiari S., *Roman Freedmen During the Late Republic* (Oxford, 1969).

Ward A. M., *Marcus Crassus and the Late Roman Republic* (London, 1977).

Weigel R. D., *Lepidus: The Tarnished Triumvir* (London, 1992).

Weinstock S., *Divus Julius* (Oxford, 1971).

Wirszubski Ch., *Libertas as a Political Idea at Rome* (Cambridge, 1950).

Wiseman T. P., *New Men in the Roman Senate, 139 B.C.–A.D. 14* (Oxford, 1971).

Yavetz Z., *Julius Caesar and his Public Image* (Ithaca, NY, 1983).

Chapter 5

The Augustan peace

The constitution

Civil strife had made the Republic increasingly ungovernable for at least a century before the battle of Actium; the victory of Octavian and Agrippa, however, over Antonius and Cleopatra effectively brought it to an end. Presented by Octavian's propaganda as a titanic struggle between the forces of civilisation and barbarism, the issue which was in reality settled by the battle was that of primacy within Caesar's faction, which had been a matter of dispute since the Dictator's death thirteen years before. As Tacitus succinctly put it, the faction now had no leader but Caesar.

The victory brought great prestige to Caesar's heir – the more so since he made out that he had won it in the name of Roman tradition, and with the blessing of the gods, especially Apollo. The death of Cleopatra also brought him Egypt and all of its wealth, which had been seen by Roman politicians since the 60s as a prize of inestimable value. Although a part now of the Roman Empire, Egypt was treated as Octavian's own domain, and its wealth was therefore available to him to facilitate patronage on a scale scarcely conceivable before. Thus, this successful and wealthy faction leader had the means to dominate; more than that, however, as he used it, he had to learn lessons from the past – particularly Caesar's Dictatorship – and transform himself from a faction leader to a national leader without precipitating the sense of alienation that had so disastrously tainted those around Julius Caesar.

The last century of the Republic's history had been punctuated by struggles for dominance among faction leaders, followed by attempts by the victors at self-assertion. Some achieved temporary success, although most were eventually consumed in accusations of regnal ambitions and the nobility's phobia of *dominatio* and loss of *libertas*. A few, however, were beginning to think the unthinkable – that the Republic needed the supervision of an individual who, through wealth, prestige and patronage (the 'ingredients' of *auctoritas*), would be heeded. Such a man was not a 'king' and, indeed, might not enjoy an office at all, but would provide unity and stability through his *auctoritas*. The closest to this 'model' was the role envisaged by Cicero for Pompey: some, indeed, have argued (wrongly) that, in old age, Cicero rather presciently had Octavian in his mind; events, however, as we have seen, showed that Cicero's role for Octavian was rather more cynically conceived.

None of this means that overnight Romans abandoned their fear of kingship; Caesar's abrupt end shows that clearly enough. Also, Actium will not have appeared at the time to have been quite the watershed imagined by many modern historians. Rather, it was expected that the victor of Actium would bring the stability which the Republic had for so long lacked and a resumption of the opportunities which enabled the Roman nobility to live in a manner worthy of their ancestors.

Some advantages Octavian had: Caesar, usually adept at wrong-footing his opponents, had himself been seriously wrong-footed in being 'forced' to cross the Rubicon; by contrast, Octavian controlled Rome following the successful conclusion of a 'national crusade'. Caesar was still, after his victory, surrounded by his enemies, the great luminaries of the Republic's nobility; Octavian had come to terms with the descendants of most of them years before (in 39–38 BC), and many of those who remained obstinately opposed to Caesar's heir had joined Antonius before Actium and had paid the ultimate price. Thus, Octavian had no credible rivals within or without the Caesarian faction. He was thus surrounded by men who were dependants and supporters, or who were ready to be lured by his patronage. Further, Caesar's legacy was the awful example of what to avoid.

At first, Octavian was careful to consolidate and celebrate, allowing people to realise that they now enjoyed peace and that he was the source and guarantor of it. In 28–27, however, came the first momentous change, which he himself recorded thus (*Res Gestae Divi Augusti* 34,1):

> In my sixth and seventh consulships, after I had extinguished the civil wars, and at a time when, with universal consent, I was in complete control of affairs, I transferred the Republic from my own power to the dominion of the senate and people of Rome.

This has been seen as a dramatic gesture of resignation – 'back me or sack me'. Of course, it was intended to galvanise support, but its real object was at once more subtle and more important. In the first place, the emphasis on 'universal consent' not only reminded people of the 'crusade to defend traditional standards' but also served to demonstrate the gulf which separated Octavian's position in 27 from Caesar's two decades previously. The move also had the serious propagandist purposes of 'drawing a line' under the less-than-salubrious activities of the second triumvirate and firmly establishing (or re-establishing) senate and people as the ultimate sources of sovereignty in the Republic. The gesture, therefore, amply demonstrated the 'return to normality' and signalled the fact that legally Octavian was in the hands of senate and people; this represented an important underlining of *libertas*.

Various 'rewards' followed, of which the most significant was undoubtedly the acquisition of his new name, Augustus; the name was redolent of traditional virtues. It connected its holder with the 'august augury' that had marked the foundation of Rome; etymologically, it stressed his *auctoritas* ('prestige'), a quality to which he himself attached major importance and which linked him with the prestigious figures of Rome's past (the *principes*). Also, through its verbal root – the Latin verb, *augere*, it demonstrated that he was a man who was enhanced by his peers' view of him and who enhanced the Republic by his involvement in it.

The virtue of the *principes* had been the decisiveness of their influence, whether they were in or out of office; Augustus Caesar, however, wanted office to provide him with both security and the levers of control. He avoided the title of dictator, an office inevitably connected with emergencies, and specifically now with men such as Sulla and Caesar; this was not an emergency, nor was he about to emulate his dictatorial predecessors. Instead, he relied on two means of control, both of which, although extraordinary when held in conjunction, had individually something of a traditional ring to them, echoing the position occupied in the late 50s by the man whose propaganda enshrined him as the defender of the Republic against Caesar – namely, Gnaeus Pompeius Magnus; descendants of *optimates* might be expected to react well to that. Thus, he used annual tenures of the consulship to preside over Rome and a grant of proconsular *imperium* over the provinces of Gaul, Spain and Syria (the three provinces distributed at the Lucca meeting in 56 between the members of the first triumvirate): the latter ensured his proximity to the bulk of the Republic's armed forces, which had been cut from the seventy legions under arms after Actium to twenty-eight; this figure was evidently regarded as politically and economically supportable, and adequate to do the jobs required. Above all, the 'choice' of powers distinguished him from his adoptive father in another important way: he was accountable for his tenures, so that there were fixed points at which he would need to render his accounts and at which (presumably) further tenures could be withheld.

Caesar's infringing of this cardinal principle of the Republic with the title, *dictator perpetuus*, had probably made a major contribution to his downfall.

Of course, Augustus could not govern his three provinces (as well as Egypt) directly and personally; so he employed the Pompeian principle of delegating his authority to senatorial *legati* (or an equestrian *praefectus* in the case of Egypt). Such men were obviously chosen for seniority, proven efficiency and loyalty; as we shall see later, this represented a step that was significant in making the old and highly regarded senatorial career structure (*cursus honorum*), together with a newly created *cursus* for equestrians, into what was effectively to become the 'civil service' that the Republic had always lacked.

This so-called 'first settlement of the Principate' in a real sense, therefore, provided Augustus with the means to control, but not in a way that put him beyond the law and the need to account; he was thus subject to a sovereignty which lay elsewhere in the system. He was not dictator, and certainly not *rex*, but could with some justification argue that he was *princeps*, or (loosely translated) 'first among equals'. As he put it himself (*RGDA* 34,3):

> I excelled all in *auctoritas*, but of actual power I possessed no more than those who were my colleagues in the several magistracies.

The claim was, of course, specious: it was the importance of *auctoritas* that saw to that, for it justified the position he held in practice.

For much of the mid-20s Augustus was away from Rome with his armies – a significant acknowledgement of his perception of the true root of his power. The fact that he felt able to leave Rome testifies to the reality of his security and the freedom of manoeuvre which it gave him: he did not need to dominate in person; his patronage was as effective when exercised from a distance.

However, events which are now hard to reconstruct led, in 24–23, to a re-appraisal of his position, producing the 'second settlement'. It is generally held that, if taken at face value, a crucial cause was the behaviour of Marcus Primus, proconsul of the province of Macedonia, one of the few armed provinces that had remained outside Augustus' direct control. Whatever happened in Macedonia – and Augustus seems to have ensured that the facts would not be known – it appears to have indicated the need for an adjustment of powers on Augustus' part. So, too, did what appears to have been a plot against him in 23, in which the 'ringleaders' seem to have been Varro Murena (a senior senator who was dangerously close to Augustus' 'inner circle') and Fannius Caepio. A serious illness suffered by Augustus at this time may have contributed to uncertainty. It is less clear that there were any objections, either in theory or practice, to Augustus' iterated consulships. It is possible that, behind these events, lay a jockeying for position between three more significant individuals – Augustus himself, his wife, Livia, and Marcus Agrippa; this possibility will be explored more fully in the section on Augustus' dynastic policies.

Augustus had, therefore, dispensed with the use of the consular power; his management of the government at home was now to be based on an 'honorary power' which he had been given by the plebs in 36 BC, the *tribunicia potestas* (a kind of honorary tribunate). This, of course, emphasised his patronage of the plebs (an important continuation of a role which had been mutually valued in the period of Caesar's Dictatorship), and it harked back to those senators who, in the century before Actium, had tried to base a personal or factional hegemony on the office of Tribune of the Plebs – men like the Gracchi, Sulpicius and Publius Clodius, the notable *populares* of the late Republic. Apart from the matter of precedence, which was specifically addressed, this power gave Augustus all the opportunities which he had enjoyed in the consulship, together with the specific benefits of the tribunate, such as the power of veto.

For public consumption, the tenure of *tribunicia potestas* was trumpeted; its use on the coinage, for example, made it effectively

Plate 5.1 Augustus as Pontifex Maximus.
Source: National Museum of Rome.

the chief indicator of the passage of regnal years. Augustus' other power, however, was given less publicity, but was no less real and significant: his *imperium proconsulare* was made to override that of other proconsuls (*maius*), and his provincial 'portfolio' widened to include all those which from time to time might require a military presence. The other – peaceful/non-military – provinces were left to be governed in the traditional way by proconsuls and propraetors (all of whom were now called 'proconsuls'). Although, of course, Augustus would not have been so crude as to intervene excessively in 'senatorial' provinces, he now had the means to do it (and used it when he thought it to be necessary, as in Cyrene in 7 BC); his status was now, of course, legally superior to that of all other provincial governors. Above all, his control of the army was now secure; it was commanded by men whose careers had developed through his patronage, and it swore an annual oath of allegiance to him as its *imperator* (general).

Traditionally, proconsuls had not been able to enter the gates of Rome; Augustus was given the concession that he could do so

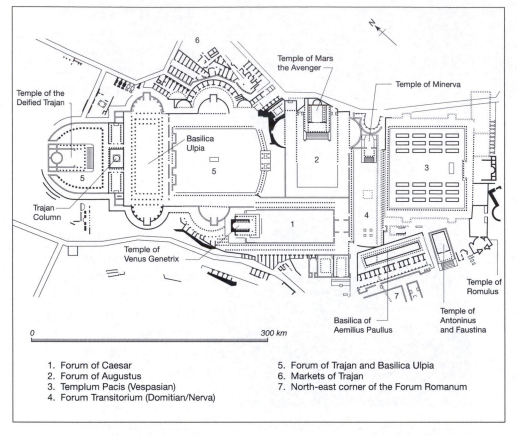

Figure 5.1 Rome, the Imperial Fora. Source: After A. Boethius and J. B. Ward-Perkins, Etruscan and Early Roman Architecture (London: Yale University Press, 1970), p. 189, Fig. 84.

without surrendering his *imperium*. This was important and may have been the source of the mistaken statement of Dio Cassius about a grant to Augustus in 19 BC of a life-consulship: Augustus was a holder of *imperium*, but he was not consul; there was no inherent difference of nature between consular and proconsular *imperium*, except for their areas of application. The concession which he held in his *imperium* not lapsing when he entered Rome, therefore, meant that inside Rome he remained a holder of *imperium*, but one which could be used only if this was specifically designated. It is thought, for example, that he may have undertaken some censorial duties, as in conducting reviews of the senate's membership (*lectiones senatus*), by having his *imperium* temporarily redefined for the purpose. This may help to explain the authority by which he undertook certain operations in Italy.

Some positions and honours, such as *pontifex maximus* ('Chief Priest') and *pater patriae* ('father of the nation') came later, but the 'second settlement' of 23 essentially laid down the constitutional basis of the Principate as it was to remain into the third century AD.

Augustus and the *Respublica*

The biographer, Suetonius, says (*Life of the Deified Augustus* 28) that Augustus twice thought of 'restoring the republic' but did not do so. Evidently, the biographer was referring to occasions when Augustus was thought to be seriously contemplating withdrawal from public life. Although he did not restore the Republic in that particular way, nonetheless a great deal was done to restore and revitalise the traditional way of life; to a Roman, *respublica* did not imply a narrow concept limited to institutions, but something a great deal broader, embracing the fabric of society, religion and morality.

Many Romans believed (or affected to believe) that the long period of civil strife that had characterised the late Republic was a punishment visited on them by gods who were angry at the neglect which they had suffered and the degree of departure from the traditional norms of Roman behaviour. The victory at Actium provided not just an opportunity to attend to such matters but an obligation to do so; such an obligation is made very clear by Augustus' friend, the poet, Horace, in the 'Roman Odes'. Similarly, that Augustus' very mission represented an obligation is implicit in Aeneas' mission as depicted in Virgil's epic poem, *Aeneid*. This essentially was the nature of Aeneas' (and Augustus') *pietas* – a recognition of a traditional sense of duty to gods, family and the Republic.

Plate 5.2 Rome, Forum of Augustus: Temple of Mars the Avenger. The temple was opened in 2 BC in fulfilment of a vow which Augustus had made forty years previously in return for success at the battle of Philippi against Brutus and Cassius, the conspirators against Julius Caesar.

Augustus did not become head of the state religion of Rome (*pontifex maximus*) until the death of his former triumviral colleague, Marcus Aemilius Lepidus, in 12 BC. From then on, he (and his successors until the time of Gratian in the late fourth century AD) had an institutional responsibility for the upkeep of the state religion, reflecting the widely held supposition that Rome's well-being was dependent on the continued favour of Jupiter, Juno and their Olympian 'colleagues'. Long before he became *pontifex maximus*, Augustus was busily responding to the obligation placed on him by Horace (especially in *Odes* III.6); large numbers of temples were built or rebuilt (*RGDA* 19–20), some of which serve to demonstrate the high political profile of Roman religion.

For example, temples such as those of Saturn, of Castor and Pollux and of Vesta had connections with the earliest beginnings of the city, while the completion of the temple to Venus Genetrix (in the Forum of Caesar) celebrated not only an important deity but one who was the mythical creator of the *gens Iulia* (Caesar's and Augustus' family). Again, strongly centred on Augustus himself were the temples of Apollo (his guardian at Actium) and of Mars the Avenger, the latter of which was the thank-offering for the avenging of Julius Caesar's murder.

Of course, it was not sentiment alone (or even principally) that led to Augustus' activity in this field; he well understood the potential for political manipulation that traditionally rested with Roman religion and its political priesthoods. Thus, such restoration work was providing an important weapon in his own political armoury. Further, the work itself that was provided by the rebuilding was an important feature of his patronage of ordinary Romans; it was in no way accidental that the emperor, Vespasian (AD 69–79), was later to observe that part of the object of building work was to give the people bread (Suetonius, *Life of the Deified Vespasian* 18).

The disintegration of family life and lax morality of the late Republic were viewed with a similar concern and also addressed by Horace in the 'Roman Odes'. Traditionally, the integrity of family life was seen as fundamental to Rome's well-being and was symbolised in the cult of the hearth goddess, Vesta, whose temple in the *Forum Romanum* was one of those restored during the Augustan period. The traditional Roman view of the family was somewhat idealised in its simplicity, and the ostentatious frugality of Augustus' own lifestyle was intended to demonstrate his faith in it. He looked to stability in marriage to provide a sound basis for the upbringing of children, and he encouraged this in the senatorial class by offering acceleration in office-bearing for those who complied. Traditionally, sound family life was also associated with the notion of self-sufficiency and life on the land. Romans had long espoused the virtues of the rural life, and Augustus'

Plate 5.3 Rome, Altar of Augustan Peace: outer enclosure wall.

enormous programme of military discharges after Actium provided an opportunity for settling large numbers of former soldiers back on the land. In practical terms, of course, land ownership had long since ceased to be a qualification for military service, although the 'repopulation' of Italy was bound to increase the reservoir of recruits; this, like many other 'messages' that emanated from Augustus' propaganda machine, found its way on to the *Ara Pacis Augustae*, which was erected on the Campus Martius in 13 BC. Further, the wholesomeness traditionally associated with rural life was close to the simple morality which had been regarded as a cardinal virtue of the Republic's earlier days. The theme was a frequent feature of Roman fresco painting and was taken up by the court poets – in this case, Virgil in his *Georgics* and *Eclogues*.

As part of the family programme, Augustus also strengthened the laws on divorce and adultery, giving much more sweeping powers to aggrieved husbands and fathers. Ironically, he was himself forced to put this into effect when, in 2 BC, his only daughter, Julia, was revealed at the centre of a scandal involving a number

Plate 5.4 Rome, Altar of Augustan Peace: the 'Earth-Goddess' (Tellus) suckling children; this is probably symbolic of Augustus' revival of Italian agriculture.

of young aristocrats, including Iullus Antonius, the son of Augustus' defeated rival. Julia was banished to a 'comfortless' island and never released from custody, although she was evidently allowed back to the mainland of Italy.

In his celebration and revitalising of tradition, Augustus was offering no 'soft options'; if Rome was to survive, he made it clear that there were difficult choices to be made, and the distant past offered some better examples to follow than did the more recent past. Like *pius Aeneas*, Augustus was engaged on a mission in which he called for the rest of society, and certainly its upper classes, to join him. Virgil wrote of how great a task it had been to found the city of Rome; Virgil's imperial patron showed that the re-foundation was no less challenging.

Libertas, patronage and the senate

Inextricably intertwined in Roman literature with the *respublica* is the concept of *libertas* ('liberty'). The word had many shades of meaning, but without doubt the most powerful of these related to the senatorial order. The aristocratic senators of the Republic had regarded that Republic as their own; even first-generation senators, no matter how eminent personally, were to some extent excluded from this 'inheritance'. Typically, Cato, in his struggle with Julius Caesar, had questioned Cicero's adherence to a Republican cause that 'was not his'. Centuries before, Pyrrhus, the king of Epirus in Greece, had dubbed the senate an 'assembly of kings', while Cicero had without question viewed the consuls as the senate's 'servants'. It is such aristocratic arrogance as this that is subsumed within the concept of *libertas*.

Particularly, *libertas* related to two matters, one of which concerned senators corporately, the other as individuals. The senate as a body had dominated the government of the Republic despite having no legal title to do so; it managed to achieve this by a variety of means which together constituted its *auctoritas* ('prestige'). Ironically, its *libertas* was thus its freedom to dominate other parts of the governmental machinery – the magistrates and the popular assemblies. The senate's custom (treated as a 'right') to pre-discuss all matters which magistrates wished to put to the people provided one of the means by which this domination was achieved.

For senators as individuals, *libertas* was the freedom to climb the career ladder (*cursus honorum*) as of right and without undue hindrance from others. In this way, they fulfilled their highest ambition – that of acting in a 'manner worthy of their ancestors'. Interference with this freedom was again *dominatio*; Caesar's use of the senate as a 'rubber stamp' for his decisions and his manipulation of the *cursus honorum* constituted the *dominatio* for which he was assassinated. We have already noticed Cassius' observations to Cicero that Caesar's *dominatio* could not be ameliorated by his decent treatment of individuals; for this was *clementia* ('clemency'), which was a 'virtue' of a tyrant, and was a matter of arbitrary whim rather than constitutional entitlement. Nero's *clementia*, much vaunted by his tutor, Seneca, was similarly unacceptable.

Augustus knew that, to govern the Republic and prevent it from falling into another bout of civil war, he had to reach an accommodation with the senatorial order; Caesar's example lay before him to indicate paths to avoid. Of course, Augustus' position did differ from that of Caesar; his decisive victory at Actium was, thanks to his propaganda and political acumen, seen in a light quite different from that of Caesar at Pharsalus. Further, as Tacitus implies, the senatorial order with which Augustus had to deal was very different from that which confronted Caesar, dominated as it had been by the imposing figures of the late Republic, whom essentially he needed to curb. 'Who was left', wrote Tacitus of Augustus' situation, 'who had seen the old Republic?'

Not only were Augustus' situation and circumstances different, but he also had the wealth of Egypt to help him persuade: such was his *auctoritas* that he could afford to treat 'trouble-makers' as 'privileged nuisances' (as Ronald Syme describes the late Republican senator, orator and historian, Asinius Pollio). As a body, the senate was recognised as in need of reconstitution; deaths and political disgrace left gaps in its membership, which Augustus and Agrippa set about sorting out by means of a *lectio senatus* ('review of the senate's membership') in 28 BC. Augustus made it clear, however, that he did not wish to exercise this kind of dominance over the senate's membership on a permanent or regular basis and tried (unsuccessfully) in 22 to revive the office of censor. Clearly, those whom he persuaded to take on this office soon felt themselves to be undermined by his power and *auctoritas*; within days they had resigned. Thereafter, Augustus did undertake *lectiones*, although, superficially at least, with reluctance. Reluctantly or not, however, he was able to use such opportunities to introduce new members under his own patronage. Thus, control of the senate's membership was exercised, although unobtrusively, and Augustus did not pre-empt the practice of some of his successors – of holding censorial power on a permanent basis.

Augustus may have pre-discussed business with his chosen advisers (the *consilium principis*), but formally he put it before the senate and encouraged magisterial colleagues to do the same. Thus, much legislation followed a traditional procedure, and such was the withering of 'popular power' that the *senatus consultum* came virtually to constitute law. In provincial government and the direction of finance (including the minting of coinage) – two crucial areas which originally in the Republic the senate had 'usurped' from the people – it now shared responsibility with Augustus; here, however, his powers and *auctoritas* left no doubt as to who was the senior partner. Under Augustus, too, the senate became a court of law, with the privilege of trying those of its own members who were caught up in the judicial process. At the very end of his life, Augustus also entrusted to the senate the previously popular process of magisterial elections, although it was evidently Tiberius who enacted this for the first time (Tacitus, *Annals* I.14–15).

Thus, with a deft political hand, Augustus could in his dealings with the senate present himself as a 'giver' rather than a 'remover' of status. For those who wanted peace with honour the reality evidently mattered less than the appearance. Indeed, the processional scenes depicted on the *Ara Pacis Augustae* (13–9 BC) well symbolised the harmony that Augustus had achieved with the *nobiles*.

For the *princeps*, the management of the *cursus honorum* was even more crucial, for the men who rose through its stages were to be his colleagues and *legati* ('deputies'). It was here, if anywhere, that a clash of interests and with tradition might have been expected, particularly with regard to the future of the post that he himself held, although, of course, his careful insistence on accountability left it in the hands of senate and people, notionally at least, whether the post was to continue. Although, as we shall see, Augustus was clearly preoccupied with a dynastic policy for the future, we are informed by Tacitus (*Annals* I.13) that the *princeps* did at least consider the possibility of his succession by a senator who was not a part of the Julian and Claudian families.

Although information for the Augustan and Julio-Claudian periods is by no means as ample as it is for the later first and second centuries, it is clear that Augustus 'interfered' with the process of elections in order to secure candidates of his choice. He was careful, however, not to 'swamp' the process. Tacitus, for example, in describing Tiberius' practice with regard to the praetorship elections at the beginning of his reign, indicates that Tiberius took over Augustus' practices. It appears that, numerically at least, the *princeps* placed restrictions on himself, and that because the required number of praetors varied from year to year, this left a variable degree of freedom in the election process. It appears from what Tacitus says about the consular elections under Tiberius (*Annals* I.81) that two lists of nominations were drawn up – one by the *princeps*, the other by the presiding officer (presumably one of the consuls); the list of the *princeps* contained twelve names of whose candidature the *princeps* approved. However, others were still enabled to present themselves on the other list. Of his twelve nominations, the emperor insisted on the election of four, who were *commendati* or *candidati Caesaris*.

This evidently represented a formalising of earlier and more traditional procedures, when the emperor, following the practice of the nobility in the Republic, actively canvassed for the candidates whom he supported; those 'nominated' and those 'commended' were then receiving different levels of imperial support. Augustus, as he grew older, had given up this strenuous activity in favour of posting a list which presumably made his feelings and wishes known. It is evident, again from Tacitus' observations regarding Tiberian practice (*Annals* I.81), that the procedures employed in the consular elections were less formal and that the emperor continued to pursue a policy of personal, although more covert, support for his favoured candidates.

Thus, we can see that Augustus for a good deal of his long reign continued essentially with Republican practices, and that his patronage and *auctoritas* secured his ends – that is, the unimpeded progress along the *cursus honorum* of those candidates in whose reliability and efficiency he had confidence. In this way, he could be sure to secure the advancement of his candidates to key appointments. Thus, he put the old *cursus honorum* to use without risking being accused, as Caesar had been, of treating it with contempt and so destroying *libertas*.

In time, as new senatorial families gradually became a majority in the Order, such 'subtle' practices gave way to more direct intervention, as Pliny indicates in the case of Trajan (*Panegyric of Trajan* 69–71); senatorial career inscriptions from the later first century show clearly that manipulation of the *cursus honorum* for political and administrative reasons became more open and acceptable. Indeed, the senatorial attitude to relations with the *princeps*, as enunciated by Tacitus in his *Life of Agricola*, makes such a development wholly understandable. The senatorial *cursus honorum* was thus gradually transformed from the means by

Plate 5.6 Denarius *issued by Augustus in 2* BC *in honour of his adopted sons, Gaius and Lucius Caesar.*

which the nobility dominated the Republic into a process for providing the senatorial 'branch' of the emperors' service. *Libertas* was modified, but not in a way that pointed glaringly towards *dominatio*; Augustus thus learned from Caesar's impulsive (and costly) error, and his conduct points the way to Galba's compromise (Tacitus, *Histories* I.15–16: see Appendix 1) of ruling a state that could take neither total servitude nor total liberty.

Dynastic succession

It is clear from Tacitus' observations that the greatest perceived inconsistency with *libertas* in the Augustan Principate was the insistence of the *princeps* on pursuing a succession policy based on his and Livia's families; it is this that led the historian to refer to the existence of a *domus regnatrix* ('royal family'), which militated against what he elsewhere (*Life of Agricola* 3) calls the 'harmonisation of *Principatus* and *Libertas*, two concepts that had been poles apart' – that is, until the reigns of Nerva and Trajan at the turn of the first and second centuries. After a century dominated by dynasties – the Julio-Claudian and the Flavian – Rome was embracing a policy, adumbrated by Galba in AD 69, of serving the interests of *libertas* by choosing as *princeps* the best man available.

Plate 5.5 (opposite) Rome, Palatine Hill: house of Augustus and Livia; detail of wall decoration, employing traditional classical design of heavy garlands between columns.

The existence of dynasties made Rome an 'heirloom' and, in any case, did not secure good government, because 'to be born of emperors was a matter of pure chance'. The eventual solution was a true compromise because, while an emperor chose as his successor the man picked out by some form of senatorial consensus as the best available, the process was formalised through an adoption of the intended successor as a son of the *princeps*. Thus, the availability of the 'top job' was restored to all senators, and the post of *princeps* placed at the apex of the *cursus honorum*, just as the consulship had been during the old Republic.

As noted, however, Augustus paid no more than lip service to such ideas; for him, both the security of what he had achieved and the traditional glory of his family demanded a dynastic succession. This did not necessarily represent a great lurch away from the practices of the old Republic, for the progression of the family factions of the *optimates* and *populares* through the generations

was certainly not without a dynastic element. Augustus' dynastic intentions did not become obvious until the mid-20s; before that, there were two clear focal points within the Caesarian faction – the family (of which, of course, Augustus was the head) and the 'rank and file' (of which Agrippa was obviously a principal figure). In the aftermath of Caesar's assassination, a similar bipolarity had existed between Octavian and Antonius. An added complication, however, in the early Augustan years was the position and role of Livia. It has been suggested that an 'alliance' between Agrippa and Livia acted as a political counterbalance to Augustus; such an alliance would help to explain the readiness of Livia to see her elder son, the future emperor, Tiberius, married to Agrippa's daughter, Vipsania Agrippina. If such rivalry did exist, then it is possible that a number of events of the mid-20s, including Agrippa's 'withdrawal' to the east and the 'plotting' of 24–23 (noted above), were related to it.

The marriage in 25 BC between Julia and the nephew of the *princeps*, Gaius Claudius Marcellus, may have been a plan on Augustus' part to win the initiative from the other two, and thus to 'marginalise' Agrippa politically: the general's withdrawal to the east appears to offer some support for this. At the same time, the marriage will have strengthened the heart of the *princeps'* family by drawing into it a young man who was not only related to the *princeps*, but was also a son of a consul of 50 BC and whose 'optimate credentials' were thus impeccable; this will not have enhanced the ambitions of Livia. In all, then, Augustus had played a strong dynastic card and established his dominance over his two 'factional rivals'; he was not to be tested again in such a fashion until the problems of AD 4. The episode, however, also serves to show how far the politics of the early Principate represented a continuation of the well-tried practices of the Republic.

Marcellus died in 23, but the marriage had probably achieved its principal objective: Augustus was now in a position to impose a settlement on his own terms. Agrippa returned to Rome;

Plate 5.7 (opposite) Rome, Theatre of Marcellus; outer wall of cavea.

Augustus' reaction, now from a position of strength, was to arrange a second marriage for his daughter – this time to Marcus Agrippa. This was intended to draw together the two parts of the Caesarian faction, marginalising Livia and looking forward to a dynastic future; for Augustus adopted as his sons the two elder children of this marriage, known to us from this point as Gaius and Lucius Julius Caesar. That these young boys were regarded as heirs to factional leadership, and thus to the Principate, can hardly be doubted; Agrippa himself was tied closer to the family as the boys' natural father and guardian.

How this 'package' was received at the time can only be surmised; in any case, its implications will have seemed far distant. Livia's sons, Tiberius Nero and Nero Drusus, were for the moment among the 'workers' who supported the *princeps*. It is possible that their own distinguished lineage allowed them to be viewed as potential rallying points for the descendants of the *optimates*, although there is little sign that this was a powerful lobby in the middle years of Augustus' Principate.

Strains began to show again with the premature death of Agrippa in 12 BC; the naming of Tiberius Nero as Julia's third husband was probably intended to provide continued supervision and guardian-ship for Augustus' adopted sons, although it may also reflect Livia's wish to see her elder son closer to the heart of Augustan politics. The marriage was not successful; further, in 6 BC, Augustus secured for Tiberius a grant of *tribunicia potestas*, although it is the impli-cation of Cassius Dio that this was not done to elevate him so much as to act as a warning to Gaius and Lucius that heredity was not the only criterion by which they would be judged. At any rate, Tiberius evidently saw it all as an affront to his *dignitas*, and with-drew into a voluntary retirement on Rhodes, which soon became a virtual exile; there seems to have been a strong coincidence between the fates of Tiberius and his former father-in-law.

The family of Augustus was severely shaken over the next decade, first by the 'Julia scandal' (2 BC) and then by the deaths of Lucius

(AD 2) and Gaius (AD 4). Rumour implicated Livia in the last two of these events, but evidence is lacking. In any event, Augustus was required to 'reconstruct the future' all over again. His 'package' on this occasion was more varied and may have been, in part at least, the result of pressure exerted by Livia and a group of *nobiles* centred around Gnaeus Cornelius Cinna Magnus, a descendant of Pompey's. Augustus now named as his sons Tiberius and Agrippa Postumus, the surviving son of Agrippa and Julia. Tiberius was further required to adopt his nephew, Germanicus, who despite his lineage was seen as close to the family of Augustus, through his marriage to Agrippina, the granddaughter of the *princeps*; later events were to show how seriously she took the matter of her descent from Augustus, even to the point of expecting to rule herself as 'queen empress'. Apart from some evident skirmishing within the family in AD 7, of which details are extremely scarce, the 'package' of AD 4 remained essentially intact, and Tiberius Julius Caesar duly succeeded on his adoptive father's death in AD 14.

The 'struggle' between Augustus' 'Julians' and Livia's 'Claudians' looks murderous – and at times it undoubtedly was; however, it did yield one obvious advantage for the Principate: both factions were determined on a continuation of the Principate in preference to a return to the old Republic. This allowed true factional skirmishing of a traditional kind to be practised within the system – in a sense inheriting the mantle of the *optimates* and *populares* of the late Republic. Because of this, those few who genuinely did seek a return to the old ways were left decisively on the margins of the political process.

Julio-Claudian infighting continued through into Nero's reign; it was ultimately Nero's lack of an heir that brought it to an end and, as we shall see in a later chapter, opened the Principate up to new families and some new ideas. In Tiberius' reign (AD 14–37), the struggle was conducted with all the energy and potential for personal disaster that had characterised it in Augustus' days. Ironically, however, there is no indication that Tiberius tried, or even wished, to go back on the intentions that lay behind the Augustan 'package' of AD 4; he accepted that Germanicus Caesar would be his successor and provided for him the high profile that was consistent with such a future. A number of factors, however, disturbed this straightforward intention. First, Germanicus' family – in particular, his wife, Agrippina the Elder – clearly came to see themselves as 'the royal family', whose descent from Augustus gave them an especial claim on power. The idea emerged very clearly in the Principate of Agrippina's youngest son, Gaius (Caligula), although even before that there is evidence that Agrippina herself thought that she could and should inherit Germanicus' position when he died prematurely in AD 19. Although, on his deathbed, he warned her against setting herself up as a rival for Tiberius' power, it is clear from her claim to be the 'incarnation of his [Augustus'] divine blood' (Tacitus, *Annals* IV.53) that she did not heed the advice. Against such an attitude, Tiberius was viewed as at best a 'caretaker' and at worst a 'usurper'.

Secondly, the contrast of style between Tiberius and his family on the one hand and Germanicus and his on the other was not only sharp and obvious but was seized on (and exaggerated) by popular enthusiasm for the family of Germanicus; in this way, Germanicus was idealised as the hero figure opposing the 'villainous' Tiberius. A natural tension between the two men which derived from their differing characters and attitudes was thus built by popular opinion into something much larger and more sinister. Tiberius had never been totally happy at assuming the mantle of Augustus and was always an introspective and self-doubting man; his advancing years served to give him an air of isolation, and the constant and bitter disputes with the family of Germanicus simply emphasised this.

This isolation was a crucial ingredient in the rise to power of the Prefect of the Praetorian Guard, Lucius Aelius Sejanus; playing on and exacerbating Tiberius' acute sense of isolation, he set out to make himself the indispensable and apparently trustworthy agent of the *princeps*, the 'partner of his labours'. He convinced Tiberius of the danger threatening him from an ambitious and malevolent Agrippina, while at the same time convincing her of the danger to her and her family represented by Tiberius and his ageing mother. Although Sejanus orchestrated the 'plot' to destroy Agrippina – far easier to arrange once he had persuaded Tiberius in AD 26 to retire permanently to the island of Capreae – he ensured that the initiative for this should appear to have come from Tiberius; this guaranteed that the hostility between the *princeps* and Agrippina could only deepen. As a result of Sejanus' machinations, Agrippina and her elder sons, Nero and Drusus, were all removed between AD 29 and 33, although eventually Tiberius 'saw the light', had Sejanus executed and 'rescued' Agrippina's surviving son, Gaius Caligula, and three daughters (Agrippina, Drusilla and Julia). By the end of Tiberius' troubled reign, the Julian and Claudian families were each left with a single heir to Tiberius' power and position – respectively, Caligula and Tiberius' grandson, Tiberius Gemellus; Germanicus' brother, the future emperor, Claudius, was still regarded as half-witted and beneath consideration for a role within the power politics of the Principate.

Caligula's brief reign (AD 37–41) unsurprisingly saw the early demise of Tiberius Gemellus, whilst Caligula echoed and reinforced popular sentiment by stressing the unity and governing legitimacy of Augustus' Julian family. Germanicus, Agrippina the Elder, Nero and Drusus, and the Emperor's three sisters were all paraded on the coinage, alongside Caligula's 'natural' grandfather, Marcus Agrippa. Gemellus' death in 38 may have been the result of plotting that was centred around him as a reaction to this very public and excessive heroising of Germanicus' family. Of the Claudians, only Claudius himself remained, evidently the butt for his nephew's vicious humour, but perhaps 'hiding his light under a bushel'. Caligula's inability to maintain a good relationship with members of his own family and his growing unpopularity, particularly in senatorial circles, led to his removal by the Praetorian

Guard early in 41. It is not inconceivable, however, that, whoever were the agents of the assassination, the objective was to elevate Claudius, and that the well-known story of his 'accidental' promotion to the Principate was invented to exonerate him from accusations of complicity in his nephew's murder.

In AD 41, the principal 'survivors' of the Julio-Claudian blood-letting were Claudius himself, together with Caligula's sister, the younger Agrippina, and her son, Lucius Domitius Ahenobarbus (the future Emperor, Nero). Claudius was married to a noble-woman, Valeria Messalina, who bore him two children – a son (known as Britannicus) and a daughter (Octavia). Messalina is consistently portrayed as a vapid pleasure seeker, although the bitter dispute between her and Agrippina probably centred around the future positions of their children in the 'contest' to succeed Claudius. Messalina's ruin in AD 48 was encompassed through a bigamy scandal in which she 'married' a young *nobilis*, named Gaius Silius, whose father and mother had been close friends and confidants of Germanicus and the elder Agrippina. It is tempting to speculate that the 'marriage' and subsequent ruin of Messalina were intended to open a route to power for the younger Agrippina and her son. Certainly, the 'campaign' which persuaded Claudius, in the wake of Messalina's death, to marry his niece was conducted with great vigour, despite the fact that, in Rome, such a union was regarded as incestuous.

Agrippina had two immediate objectives: for herself, to achieve a position similar to that coveted by her mother by sharing power as Claudius' 'partner', and to secure the succession for her son. In both aims, she succeeded, legitimising her son's right to rule by securing his adoption as Claudius' son and his marriage to Claudius' daughter, Octavia; Britannicus was thus marginalised, although some – perhaps including his imperial father – thought that he would be safer that way. Whether or not Agrippina hastened her husband's death remains unclear, but, in AD 54, Nero came to power as the last of the descendants of Caesar and Augustus. Britannicus did not long survive Nero's accession, his end undoubtedly hastened by Agrippina's belief that she could exercise a stronger control over her wayward son by appearing to support a 'rival'. The unfortunate Octavia was removed in 62, soon after the death of her chief supporter, the Praetorian Prefect, Lucius Afranius Burrus.

Thus, rivalry within the dynasty had run its full course; Nero's conduct in his later years ensured that his critics and opponents derived from a wider field. Those who eventually contested his position had no thoughts of a return to the old Republic. In that sense, at least, the emperors of the Julio-Claudian dynasty had ensured the continuance and consolidation of the Augustan Principate.

The development of the Principate

Augustus was able to capitalise on the growing conviction of many in Rome's political community that the Republic required the guidance of a single individual and a centralised authority. Care, however, was needed because of the deeply held antagonism towards the notion of kingship and because many of those with whom Augustus had to deal had long family traditions of opposition to monarchy. Further, despite his obvious successes, some will have continued to reflect with apprehension on the fact that he was Caesar's heir. Augustus surmounted the difficulties, not only establishing his 'brand' of one-man rule but also securing it through a dynastic succession.

This success depended on the superficially co-operative nature of his formula for government – appearing to share power with senators as individuals and with the senate as a body. It also depended on his own success and wealth and the evident success of his scheme of government in restoring stability – in particular, his organisation of the Senatorial and Equestrian Orders into the administrative service that Rome and the empire had so obviously needed. Further, his insistence that the field of reform should extend from politics and government into such areas as society and religion brought the conviction that this deserved to be seen as a restoration of the *respublica*.

The old institutions functioned, and Augustus' wealth guaranteed support and work for those who came under their umbrella. He made himself the centre of Roman politics and society, and he made Rome and Italy the centre of a growing and thriving empire; he ensured, too, that in physical terms Rome was worthy of its central role in civilising the world. All of this was persuasively and elegantly communicated by the writers who, like Virgil, Horace and Livy, enjoyed his support and friendship; the organisation of this 'arm' of his government was in the hands of his friend, Gaius Maecenas. Augustus worked through various avenues to eulogise and retain the best of the traditions of the past and to strengthen these by his innovations – bringing a constant flow of new blood into the Senatorial and Equestrian Orders, making public service safe, rewarding and dependent on himself, patronising on a scale never before seen, and guaranteeing the stability of his new *respublica* through his re-organisation and control of the Roman army, which was ostensibly a vehicle to protect and develop the empire, although ultimately the means by which Augustus retained his position.

The historian, Tacitus, was in no doubt that this was a monarchy, in which all the state's functions depended on the *princeps*. However, it is also clear that the ability to achieve it arose from the circumstances of the times and the qualities of Augustus himself; nobody, wrote Tacitus, associated the Principate with anyone other than Augustus Caesar, who strengthened the image by the ever-youthful obverse portrait on his coinage. The idea of principate (*principatus*) was deeply embedded in Republican tradition and meant that it was something earned and enjoyed by Augustus himself, relating to his own achievements and qualities. He might (and indeed did) name a successor, but how could such a personalised role be transmitted to another man?

Immediately, this was a question to be faced by Tiberius Caesar, when he succeeded Augustus in 14, rapidly discovering that the

Plate 5.8 As of Tiberius, issued in AD 22–23, commemorating the virtue of Clementia (Clemency); the coin was probably an expression of the emperor's own view of his conduct in treason trials. © Copyright The British Museum.

Republic could not be restored all over again; it had to move on in credible directions. Tiberius' initial anxiety was how to establish the basis of his own *auctoritas* – difficult in view of the fact that some at least believed that his rise was the product of a senile adoption and feminine wiles and pressure. He had a problem of his own: although his own past achievements were worthy, even considerable, they were somewhat restricted in their application. Further, the new *princeps*, as a relatively unknown man, was rumoured to have character flaws, principally cruelty and a tendency towards dissimulation.

This was hardly an auspicious beginning, and it was made worse by the new Emperor's first tortuous steps along the corridors of power. Yet the difficulties masked a desire genuinely to follow in Augustus' footsteps and also to innovate with the organisation of the Principate. In the latter area, there was a difficulty, for, in order to succeed, the new *princeps* had to carry conviction and to be accepted as a man of *auctoritas*. It would be quite inappropriate to describe Tiberius as a 'republican', but he did hold views, particularly with regard to his relationship with the senatorial aristocracy, which were rather more traditionalist than many of those that had characterised the reign of Augustus.

On a superficial level, he was determined to show respect to senators and magistrates, as is clearly revealed in the anecdotal evidence of Suetonius, and which is shown in more detailed form in the episodic treatment of Tacitus. Tiberius would make way in the street for the consuls to pass; he objected strongly to being addressed as 'my lord' (*dominus*). He tried to restrict his contributions so as not to influence unduly the decisions of senators, and even on one occasion, quoting the words of the old *senatus consultum ultimum*, suggested that the consuls were the supreme guardians of the Republic. Such deference, however, put at risk a major principle of Augustus' policy, and one which was early on brought to the attention of the new *princeps*, that 'the accounts will balance only with a single auditor' (Tacitus, *Annals* I.6,6).

There were, in any case, substantial inconsistencies in Tiberius' behaviour, which stemmed from the fact that his 'senatorial policy' was an ideal, not one that he had subjected to practical scrutiny. Tacitus provides ample evidence of Tiberius' decisions to curtail debate because he wished to insist on its outcome, as in the matter of punishing those responsible for rowdyism in the theatre (*Annals* I.77), and when he wished to force the senate to a particular decision in a treason trial which involved a charge of disrespect shown to the memory of Augustus (*Annals* I.74). In the latter case, the viewpoint of the *princeps* seemed sharply in contrast with the attitude which he had expressed in the cases of other defendants (*Annals* I.73). Such inconsistencies led to what Tacitus calls the 'façade of liberty' (*simulacrum libertatis*); it is clear that the sense of deception implicit in a façade greatly undermined the senate's confidence in and ability to trust the new *princeps*. In their minds, it left them with one option only – to agree slavishly with whatever the *princeps* wanted or was thought to want. It is an irony that Tiberius consistently failed to appreciate how far it was he who was precipitating this 'crisis of confidence' which caused him so much frustration; 'men ready to play the slave', he was heard to mutter as he left the senate house.

However, an even bigger blow to his hopes of constructive co-operation with the senate sprang from the activities covered during his reign by the law of treason. Although Rome had had a treason law for centuries, activities in the early Principate were derived from a law passed in 103 BC by the tribune, Lucius Appuleius Saturninus (*Lex Appuleia*), and cases brought under it were handled in a 'dedicated' court (*quaestio*) presided over by a praetor. Embraced within the law were actions thought likely to have 'lessened the majesty of the Roman people' – hence the use of the Latin word, *maiestas*, in referring to the offence. The original law had received additions on a number of occasions in the later years of the Republic and perhaps revisions by Augustus in a *Lex Iulia*. Augustan reforms allowed competence to two courts: the senate was empowered to handle charges brought against its own members, while other accused persons were tried, as previously, by the praetor's *quaestio*.

Other significant changes during the Augustan period were the identification, in terms of the 'victims' of *maiestas*, of Rome's leading citizens (*principes viri*) with the *respublica* itself. Further, Augustus, angered at the publication of scurrilous verses, included written and spoken words in the law's application. Ironically, such 'sensitivity' on Augustus' part ran directly counter to advice that he gave to Tiberius that he should be concerned about hostile deeds, not hostile words. It appears that, when Augustus died, some doubt was left as to the continued enforcement of the law, although, when asked, Tiberius indicated that the law should be enforced. Nonetheless, it appears to have become customary for each imperial accession to precipitate at least a question regarding the law's continued operation. Most incoming Emperors were 'magnanimous' at first in seeking to restrain activities under the law, although many eventually revoked such decisions, despite the fact that it was relatively easy to deal effectively with offenders under other laws.

The *lex maiestatis* harmed Tiberius' attempts to conciliate the senate in a number of ways: indeed, Tacitus (*Annals* I.72) indicates that Tiberius' decision to maintain operations under the law was seen as totally at odds with his professed policies towards the senate. Fundamentally, it struck at the notion of partnership between *princeps* and senate by 'elevating' the *princeps* above the level of his 'fellow senators'; in practice, he was being afforded a special protection under this law.

Secondly, from the start, Tiberius' own stance with regard to operations under the law was, while undoubtedly well intentioned, completely arbitrary: sometimes he would quash cases before they came to court (as in two recorded by Tacitus under AD 15 – *Annals* I.73); on other occasions, however, if he felt personally angered (as was often the case when insults to *Divus Augustus* were involved), he would not only insist on a rigorous following of procedures but would even try to influence the senate or the praetor's court to his point of view. Again, he would on occasion let trials proceed to their ends, and then intervene with a pardon – an action which he commemorated on two coin issues of AD 21; these coins advertised the Emperor's 'clemency' and his 'moderation'. Such 'virtues' sound impressive, but in reality emphasised the dependence of all on the will of the *princeps*. Such an arbitrary procedure could never constitute justice and flew directly in the face of *libertas*, the 'virtue' which symbolised the character of the relationship which Tiberius, probably genuinely, wished to establish between himself and the senate.

Thirdly, such arbitrary behaviour inevitably created doubts in the minds of senators regarding their relationship with the *princeps* and, by its very inconsistency, provided fertile ground for the informers (*delatores*) and accusers who sought to make personal profit from the law. Lacking the types of enforcement agencies familiar in modern states, Rome relied on the activities of such private individuals who played on the sensitivities of the *princeps* to bring prosecutions from which they hoped to gain advancement and profit, winning one-quarter (or even one-half) of the confiscated property of convicted individuals. In this way, fear was sewn in the minds of senators that their own unguarded words might provide the basis of a prosecution, and inevitably (and indeed reasonably) they blamed Tiberius for this state of affairs. It was this, rather than the actual number of prosecutions and convictions, which caused what is often referred to as the 'Tiberian terror'; such was Tiberius' suspiciousness in his later years that informers could readily capitalise on it in the hope of making money and appearing as loyal supporters of the *princeps*.

Tacitus regarded the activities of these men as the real 'cancer' of Tiberius' reign; the *princeps*, as often misguided and unrealistic, refused to see these unscrupulous men as anything more dangerous and insidious than 'guardians of the law', obstinately setting his face against doing anything to restrain their activities. Such inevitably drove a further deep wedge between *princeps* and senate, particularly as, in the later years of the reign, the law operated without the amelioration of the presence of the 'merciful pardoner' and subject to the vested interests of more dangerous men, such as Sejanus and Macro (successive commanders of the Praetorian Guard).

Thus, Tiberius' 'experiment' with greater senatorial involvement in the government foundered, leaving the senate fearful and mistrustful and the *princeps* bitter, isolated and frustrated. Realisation of this failure played a large part in driving Tiberius into retirement on Capreae during his last decade of power. According to Tacitus, Sejanus capitalised on Tiberius' disillusionment to persuade him to retire from Rome, an absence which the historian perceptively described as *abscessus* ('a state of cringing withdrawal'), and from which Tiberius could never bring himself to return.

The absence created a crisis: an absentee Emperor ruling through agents and corresponding with the senate by letter. No longer could the *princeps* maintain the fiction that his chief practical legitimacy lay in his participatory membership of the senate. The chief issues of government – foreign and domestic – were not neglected, although the impression that they were itself proved dangerous, as when, from AD 35, Artabanus III of Parthia began threatening Roman regional interests in the expectation that the Emperor would fail to take notice.

Tiberius died in AD 37, his hopes for his Principate in tatters: with him, the notion of a genuine 'Republican Principate' was dead, too. Tiberius' reign had demonstrated the difficulty, if not the impossibility, of a meaningful partnership with the senate. With the idea of a structural link between Republic and Principate destroyed, future developments inevitably led in different directions.

Tiberius was succeeded by his great-nephew, Gaius Caligula; from his birth in AD 12, Caligula was idolised and, after the 'decimation' of his family during the reign of Tiberius, was looked on as filling the place originally 'reserved' by Augustus for his father, Germanicus. As we have seen, the evidence of Caligula's coinage indicates a strong emphasis placed on the young Emperor as part of a family which was not only large, but royal, too – a point 'confirmed' by Philo, who came to Rome to meet Caligula over the attacks made by Greeks on the Jewish community in Alexandria; Philo reported that Caligula admonished Sutorius Macro, his Praetorian Prefect, in a way that indicated his belief in his royal background and the right that this gave him to assume without question the role of an autocrat.

Caligula had witnessed directly the last troubled years of Tiberius on Capreae and will thus have understood well enough the cost to his great-uncle of his failed attempts to work with the senate. Caligula evidently did not intend to renew the experiment – even less so perhaps as he found himself the target of conspiracies involving senators. Like his father, Caligula was excitable and theatrical, although from his mother he appears to have inherited intolerance, obstinacy and an acerbic tongue. The characteristics of a *prima donna* hardly suited a man required to play a delicate balancing act. Obsessive suspiciousness may have been a characteristic learned on Capreae.

For Caligula, it was easier and more natural to rule Rome and the Empire as a monarch, surrounded by agents and acolytes who would do his bidding without question. In such a context, he may have encouraged worship of himself as a god, as is asserted in some classical sources, although the absence of supporting numismatic, epigraphic and architectural evidence from Rome itself leaves this somewhat in doubt. Such a rumour may, in fact, have been the result of a theatrical whim on Caligula's part, and a love of exotic dress – both characteristics detectable in his father – rather than a coherent policy deriving from a belief in his divinity. His alleged description of those who denied his divinity as 'fools' rather than 'criminals' seems to lend weight to this. However, we should not overlook the facts that his mother, the elder Agrippina, regarded her descent from the Deified Augustus as giving her 'sacred blood' and that, on his grandmother's side, he was descended from Marcus Antonius; all of this may serve to suggest the possibility that Caligula came to see himself as an Hellenistic 'god-monarch' rather than as a *princeps* in the Augustan mould.

Wayward, extravagant and unpredictable, Caligula rapidly earned the contempt of the senatorial class, who inevitably saw their own status as diminished in the face of his. The Emperor's removal offered the only viable course of action, although, of course, success in this enterprise required an acceptable alternative: for some this may have been a return to the old *respublica*; for most, however, it would have suggested an Emperor of a more traditional mind, and presumably more in tune with senatorial preoccupations. It is likely that Claudius (Caligula's uncle) was this choice, and that the bizarre story of his 'accidental' elevation was due to a desire to keep the new Emperor's image 'clean' and to explain why the new *princeps* at his accession needed to conciliate the Praetorian Guard. For the first time, in AD 41, the Praetorian Guard in a direct sense fulfilled its 'king-making' potential.

Claudius will not have been well known to many; although Augustus is said to have recognised positive qualities in him, Claudius' physical disabilities had left him on the margins of government, until elevated by Caligula to a consulship in AD 37. Quite simply, Claudius had been thought to lack the dignity of presence to be associated with the 'royal house'. He had spent the years of his marginalisation in study, particularly of Rome's past; while many thought that this had bred in him an irrelevant antiquarianism, events showed that the real product of his years of study was a re-assessment of where the Principate stood some seventy years after its inception.

It was natural, however, that at first at least Claudius should herald a return to sound traditionalism; that was required of a replacement for Caligula. Claudius' coinage indicates an attempt to portray himself as politically Augustus' heir; although the form of the Principate which he developed may have appeared to belie such a 'prospectus', in his readiness to innovate and experiment within a broad context of traditionalism Claudius was a worthy successor of Augustus Caesar.

Yet, he had to recognise the changes that had occurred: the senate was in neither spirit nor membership the body it had been in the aftermath of Actium; members of the Republic's governing families has dwindled in the face of the arrival of new members with a broader set of backgrounds and who recognised their debt to the patronage of the *princeps*. While Augustus' need in his own time to act conservatively in many respects is understandable, a precise continuation of that conservatism did not suit the condition of Rome and the empire in the middle of the first century AD. A better model for radical innovation was perhaps provided by Julius Caesar. Besides this, the reigns of Claudius' predecessors had all demonstrated in their different ways that the senate could not be involved in government as a partner; that body needed to continue down a path that would lead it to a recognition that it was, in fact, a part – albeit a vital part – of the administration by which the *princeps* ensured sound and effective government throughout the empire. Senators had to be brought to appreciate that their role was one of service, although not of servility – as indicated on more than one occasion by the historian, Tacitus, and laid out effectively in an oration put by Tacitus into the mouth of Nero's short-lived successor, Servius Galba (App. 1).

That Claudius saw himself as at the head of the empire's government and administration is not in doubt; that in the eyes of many, especially senators, this made him appear despotic is equally clear. Claudius' 'training' made him sensitive to tradition, while his inclination led him to look to the smooth running of the administration of Rome and the empire. His desire for efficiency led to his restructuring of the administration, which was done with characteristic directness.

The senate had, of course, been losing something of its special status ever since the Principate of Augustus; the first *princeps* had made it clear that senators should now see themselves as closely integrated with members of the Equestrian Order in the administration of the empire. Tiberius' failure to 'restore' the senate made the continuation of the Augustan tendency inevitable. Claudius effectively abolished the distinction between imperial and senatorial provinces in the sense that his *legati* now became legally the equals of senatorial proconsuls; the *princeps* was the ultimate authority for both, and both reported to him. This move firmly established the *princeps* at the apex of the system of provincial administration, reflecting that the dualism of the earlier practice could hardly be maintained in the face of the overwhelming *auctoritas* of the *princeps*.

At home, adjustments were made to the *cursus honorum*, so that in a number of cases new 'imperial' officials (of the Equestrian Order) were created alongside the older senatorial officials, many of whose positions probably became 'honorary'. Thus, in the administration of Ostia, Rome's port at the mouth of the Tiber, the *Quaestor Ostiensis* lost his real authority to an equestrian *Procurator Portus Ostiensis*, as did the *Praefecti* of corn distribution. The *Curator Aquarum* had to share his duties with an imperial official, while quaestors lost their responsibility for street maintenance, taking on instead the expensive task of organising gladiatorial games. Similarly, the old state treasury (*Aerarium Saturni*) lost its status as the central treasury to an enlarged *Fiscus* under imperial officials.

It was not, however, that Claudius wished to demean the senate; in enforcing attendance with fines for absence, he demonstrated the importance which he attached to its meetings and its functions, but he left it in no doubt that it now worked to an agenda prescribed by him. His assumption of the defunct office of censor in AD 47–48 shows this clearly, for this office was the vehicle for bringing in new members (notably, the chieftains of the Senonian Gauls), and removing those who were unworthy or who could no longer maintain the financial qualification. That Claudius continued to legislate by means of *senatus consulta*, however, shows the importance of the senate in the hierarchy of the *princeps*, but the senate had to get used to the fact that it now operated under the auspices of the *princeps*. Clearly, Claudius was moving the senate into a position in which it was less obsessed with its own principles, became more representative of a growing empire, and could therefore discuss more meaningfully a wide variety of issues, making a far more positive impact on government than it had allowed itself or been able to do in earlier reigns.

Such was the directness of Claudius' approach that the senate was hardly likely to view with equanimity what it must have regarded as an assault on its traditions. Tacitus, in reporting the senatorial discussion of Claudius' proposal to include wealthy Gauls in the Senatorial Order, shows how a number of senators protested at what they plainly regarded as an insult directed at themselves. Still less was the senate impressed with other aspects of the reforming Emperor's activities.

It is often suggested that Claudius deliberately marginalised the senate by the creation of 'departments of state' manned by his own nominees. It is true that these departments, overseeing official correspondence, finance, judicial petitions and literary matters, had existed since the time of Augustus, staffed by former slaves of the imperial household. In Claudius' case, these were Narcissus, Pallas, Callistus and Polybius. It is more reasonable to suppose that Claudius' contribution was not the creation of these departments; as Tacitus indicates, the senate's resentment sprang from the Emperor's failure to control these men, rather allowing them 'equality with himself and the law'. While Claudius probably felt confidence in men whose responsibility and loyalty were focused personally on him, for senators it seemed to demonstrate an emperor ready to diminish their privileges and to humiliate them, particularly when the freedmen amassed such wealth and influence in the court. Developments later in the first century, however, saw such jobs undertaken by members of the Equestrian Order rather than by former slaves.

Not surprisingly, the reforming *princeps* took an interest not just in making laws but also in 'monitoring' their effectiveness. This gave rise to the much-resented trials 'in the imperial bedroom' (*intra cubiculum*), in which Claudius was accused of giving himself over to the subversive influence of people who had no competence in the judicial procedure. It was said that large numbers of senators and equestrians perished as a result of such proceedings, which served only to heighten the sense of inferiority felt by the two orders in the face of those who were able to influence the *princeps*.

Equally disturbing to traditionalists was the degree of Claudius' perceived dependence on the imperial womenfolk. In all, Claudius was married four times – twice within the span of his Principate; his third wife was Valeria Messalina, who is usually depicted as empty headed and pleasure-seeking, while his fourth wife was his niece, Agrippina (the younger). This last union caused an outrage because of its incestuous status. The contrast between these two women was striking; both wanted influence, although Messalina probably entertained the 'normal' objective of ensuring the future of her children, Britannicus and Octavia. Agrippina, on the other hand, derived her objectives from those of her mother: to influence in the traditional manner – that is, from 'behind the scenes' – was not her aim. She wanted power, and from her marriage to Claudius she required a public partner-

Plate 5.9 Oplontis: rear façade and garden area of the villa which belonged probably to the family of Nero's second wife, Poppaea Sabina.

ship with her husband. Tacitus, again, no doubt, reflecting contemporary disquiet, calls Agrippina's role an 'almost-masculine despotism'. It was, however, a partnership which seems to have worked politically: domestically, the government of Claudius perhaps attained its best quality during these last few years, ironically because Agrippina may have managed to act as a check on some of her husband's reforming zeal.

Yet the period of Agrippina's ascendancy was also a bloody one; for alongside her 'modern' ambition she nurtured a traditional aim – that of securing a future in power for her son, Lucius Domitius Ahenobarbus (or Nero, as we know him). Rapidly, she succeeded in marginalising Britannicus and in persuading Claudius to adopt Domitius as his own son. Opinion has held – perhaps wrongly – that once this was achieved she murdered

Plate 5.10 Oplontis, Villa of Poppaea Sabina; atrium with central water tank. Note the perspective provided by the wall decoration.

Claudius, so that her son, by that time married to Claudius' daughter, Octavia, could succeed to power while he was still young enough to remain subject to his mother's influence. In this way, Agrippina's power could survive the death of her husband, although in a different setting.

On a cool estimate, Claudius' reign was a vital period for the development of the Principate; it succeeded in moving the Principate from the conservatism that had been vital in Augustus' reign and inevitable in Tiberius' and saving it from the autocratic despotism of Caligula's. That Claudius' reign itself had a despotic edge cannot be denied, but it was a despotism that served to ensure that the whole empire benefited from the government and that the vocal minority, the political descendants of those who had wrecked the old *respublica*, and who were demanding a continuation of their privileges, should yield to the needs of the majority. In the judgement of history, there has been little doubt that Claudius merited the 'accolade' of posthumous deification and a place of respectability alongside that of Augustus Caesar. As we shall see, the subjects of the empire at large recognised this more readily than did those in Rome.

Nero was only seventeen when he came to power in AD 54, evidently with little interest in the technicalities of government; the young *princeps* was more concerned with culture and pleasure. He had, however, three formidable advisers on hand – his mother, his chief tutor (the philosopher, Seneca) and the Prefect of the Praetorian Guard, Afranius Burrus. The 'prospectus' of the new government was early on made apparent in a speech to the senate, which Nero delivered, but which Seneca had composed, promising to 'roll back' some of what were regarded as Claudius' excesses and to return to a more 'Augustan' stance; the inclusion of descendants of the republican nobility in the consulates of the first eight years is evidence of this. Between them, Seneca and Burrus managed to minimise the influence of Agrippina, who naturally wished to see a continuation of policies in which she had been involved with her late husband, and to keep Nero's

Principate on lines which the members of the senate found less abrasive.

Nero's reign is often presented as consisting of two distinct parts – the first five years (*quinquennium Neronis*) and the remainder. In fact, the use of the term, *quinquennium*, appears to have been that of the later Emperor, Trajan, although he was evidently referring to the quality of building activity in Nero's final five years. Nevertheless, Tacitus appears to mark a change at the end of *Annals* XIII, which coincides with the end of the year, AD 58, and precedes the account of Nero's murder of his mother. It would be a mistake to overstress the turning point, although, of course, the murder of Agrippina was by any standards a heinous act: the earlier years were by no means free of controversy; Britannicus had been murdered in 55, and two men who were evidently seen by Nero as potential rivals – Rubellius Plautus and Faustus Sulla – were removed from Rome. These years also included the deterioration of Nero's relationship with his mother, and the beginning of that with Poppaea Sabina.

If there was a change, it is more likely that it should be placed in AD 62, the year of Burrus' death: this seems to have provided the key to the removal of Nero's wife, Octavia (who had been strongly supported by Burrus) and her replacement by Poppaea; Burrus evidently believed that Nero's marriage to the daughter of the late *princeps* provided the key to the legitimacy of Nero's succession. Although the character of the government may have changed from one that involved the senate to one that did not, it is less likely that this derived from a radical change of direction on Nero's part than from a realisation as he became older that he could order his life as he pleased. Indeed, the seeds of such a personal despotism were sown much earlier – for example, in the great interest which he evidently took as a boy in Greek culture – a leaning which he shared with others of his generation (for example, Tacitus' father-in-law, Agricola). Further, as his tutor, Seneca, tried to lead Nero into 'acceptable' ways, he produced for his education treatises such as *De Clementia* ('On Clemency') which may have advocated decent behaviour, although through the cultivation of qualities which were essentially despotic: as had been observed in the case of Julius Caesar, and was evident again in that of Tiberius, clemency may have produced some individually desirable outcomes; the problem with it, however, was that it was arbitrary, to be granted or withdrawn according to whim, that it was not based on an acknowledgement of the rights of others and that, by definition, it was not constrained within a legal framework.

Thus, while the early years of Nero's government displayed features which were pleasing to some groups (such as senators), there was no guarantee of the continuation of these. Claudius' reforms had made the Principate despotic; the fate of the Emperor's subjects thus depended on his character and behaviour. The change is thrown into high relief by the large amount of senatorial material in Tacitus' account of Tiberius' Principate and, by con-

trast, the virtual absence of such material from the historian's account of Nero's reign. The chief difference, therefore, between the two 'parts' of Nero's reign was the decline in the weight of government which he was prepared to delegate to others.

In his last few years, Nero's reign was despotic, but it was a despotism marked by his reliance then on more vicious characters, such as Poppaea herself and Tigellinus, the new Praetorian Prefect, and by the Emperor's growing megalomania. This megalomania is not simply a matter of allegation in potentially biased sources but is demonstrated independently by material for which Nero was himself responsible. The coinage, for example, associated him with deities, such as Apollo Citharoedus (the 'lyre player') – an issue sufficiently striking to merit a mention in Suetonius' biography of the Emperor. Also, a number of *denarii* show Nero, on the reverse side of the coin, wearing the radiate crown of Helios, the Sun-god; this association was paralleled by the allusion to Nero in AD 66 by the Parthian, Tiridates, as Mithras and by the erection at the entrance to Nero's new palace (*Domus Aurea*: the 'Golden House') of a 'colossal' statue of Nero–Helios–Apollo. The very extravagance of the Golden House, luridly described by Suetonius (see Appendix 3), points similarly to the Emperor's megalomania, which had been 'formalised' by some in the suggestion that Nero was seeking to change the Principate into a 'god monarchy' along Hellenistic lines.

Predictably, the acceleration of Nero's departure from Augustan principles precipitated opposition as exemplified by the conspiracies of Gaius Piso (AD 65) and of Annius Vinicianus (AD 66). Nero's escape from the former of these prompted his assertion that he had been under the especial protection of *Jupiter Custos* ('the Guardian') and the Sun-god. Further, the failure of these conspiracies led to increasing viciousness on Nero's part as he saw evidence of his subjects' lack of love for and gratitude to him; executions and banishments of suspects followed on both occasions. Similarly, the probably false accusations that Nero had set fire to

Plate 5.11 (opposite) Rome, Porta Maggiore: immediately inside the gateway is the tomb of Eurysaces the Baker, constructed in the form of bread ovens; at the upper level of the gate are the channels for aqueducts built by the emperors, Claudius and Nero.

Plate 5.12 *Paintings of extensive villas in the Bay of Naples with 'sun-courts' similar to that of Nero's Domus Aurea in Rome. Photo Scala, Florence.*

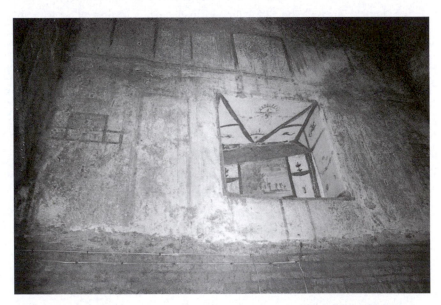

Plate 5.13 *Rome, Domus Aurea: detail of wall decoration with a 'false window' and 'external' view.*

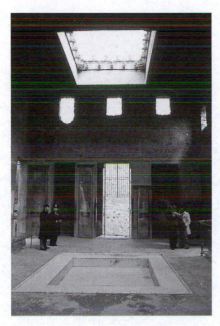

Plate 5.14 Pompeii, House of the Vettii: atrium.

Rome in AD 64 led to his need for scapegoats which prompted the vicious and counterproductive assault on the Christians. The 'evidence' of his subjects' ingratitude also set him on a course of escapism of which his popularity-seeking tour of Greece in 67 provides a prime example. Nero's behaviour was typical of him; in return for the Greeks' recognition of him as Nero–Zeus and Nero–Apollo and for their awarding to him of 1808 first prizes in artistic competitions, the *princeps* big-heartedly absolved Greece from the obligation to pay tribute to Rome – his 'Liberation of Hellas'.

Nero's despotism and megalomania were out of control; senators and other civilians showed themselves, however, incapable of conclusive action against him. In the end, the only effective 'tool' was the army which, ostensibly at least, had been 'made safe' by Augustus' reforms. To the re-emergence of the army in politics, and its role in the downfall of Nero in AD 68, we shall return in Chapter 7.

Roman society under the Julio-Claudian emperors

We have already seen that Augustus' perception of the *respublica* went beyond the narrowly governmental and political, and embraced a broad view of Roman society; senators, equestrians, urban plebs and provincials were drawn within the extensive 'umbrella' of his patronage, and he made himself responsible for their well-being. Augustus' quest to revive traditional values in public service, within the family and in religion derived from his

Plate 5.15 Pompeii, House of the Vettii: garden peristylium.

recognition that a society ordered along such simple and straight-forward lines would be more easily controlled and less likely to be tempted away by 'rival offers' of patronage. His propaganda machine, already well honed by its demolition of Marcus Antonius in the 30s, was put to good use in covering up the tensions within the immediate circle of the *princeps* and in demonstrating that the return to traditional values was vital as a guarantee of success for Rome, its ruler and its empire.

It was inevitable, however, that Rome's new form of government and its place within a growing empire would have their effects on society's expectations and indeed on the nature of that society. Although Juvenal, the satirist writing at the turn of the first and second centuries AD, may exaggerate, changes in society over the first century or two of the Principate become sharply evident in the poet's strictures: Rome became more cosmopolitan, and certainly more materialistic and competitive; the former 'underclass' – women, slaves, foreigners – sought to play more prominent roles.

Although denied access to supreme power by the dynastic arrangements of the Julio-Claudians and then of the Flavians (AD 69–96), senators were furnished by the patronage of Emperors with opportunities for good careers and the amassing of wealth; similar goals were presented to the restructured Equestrian Order. For both, as we shall see in Chapter 6, there were fruitful opportunities for investment as the development of empire accelerated the 'Romanisation' of provincial subjects. That lifestyles sharply improved for such people is plainly evident in the abundant remains that have been excavated in such areas as the Bay of Naples; evidence of a more negative kind is also to be seen in the onslaughts on luxurious living to be found in the writings of satirists and philosophers. The trade that resulted from an improved standard of living (for some, at least) is adequately demonstrated in the development of port sites, such as Ostia (at the mouth of the River Tiber), which clearly displays its prosperity in the early years of the Principate.

Augustus took care to ensure that for his ordinary subjects in Rome there was food, work and entertainment – 'bread and circuses', as Juvenal rather dismissively calls it. Although the favour of the urban mob might not be able to save an emperor when others wished to remove him, it did help to keep Rome in a stable condition and, when such people were recruited into the legions, to provide a reservoir of loyalty there, which showed itself on a number of occasions when recalcitrant senatorial officers failed to inspire their men to follow their rebellious lead. The importance of such loyalty is shown, for example, by Claudius' award of the titles, *Claudia Pia Fidelis*, to two legions (VII and XI) which refused to join an attempted rebellion in Pannonia in AD 42. However, the loss of popular political functions, a feature of the late Republic which was continued into the Principate, may well have contributed to the demoralisation of the urban plebs; the adverse effect of their dependence on imperial patronage is well highlighted by Tacitus, who shows how the urban plebs treated the street battles between Vitellians and Flavians late in AD 69 as if they were simply another arena-spectacle. Imperial building activity both provided work and enhanced facilities in Rome and in other towns and cities; an Emperor, such as Tiberius, who objected to bribing the masses through work and entertainment paid a heavy price in terms of personal popularity.

With regard to other sections of the 'underclass', although there was some prejudice against foreigners, particularly in Rome and Italy, many of them prospered and progressed in the empire at large. Further, those that found themselves caught up in slavery often found that their skills were much appreciated; for example, those who fought in the arenas or who drove chariots might well find themselves treated, temporarily at least, as popular idols. Roman society, of course, saw slaves as 'non-people' in a legal sense, as is demonstrated when they became enmeshed in the legal process; a slave was regarded as incapable of telling the truth, and so had to be examined under torture. Yet, there could be strong feelings when slaves were callously and gratuitously mal-treated, as when Augustus himself broke with a certain Vedius Pollio who used to throw clumsy slaves into his lamprey pool. Ultimately, freedom was the logical goal for many household slaves and, as freedmen (*liberti*), there was a range of jobs, some very powerful, open to them; many such people had acquired important administrative skills, particularly if placed in the households of significant men.

Some felt that the role of women had strayed a long way from tra-ditional expectations during the late Republic; certainly, many were left with major problems of 're-adjustment' as slaves took

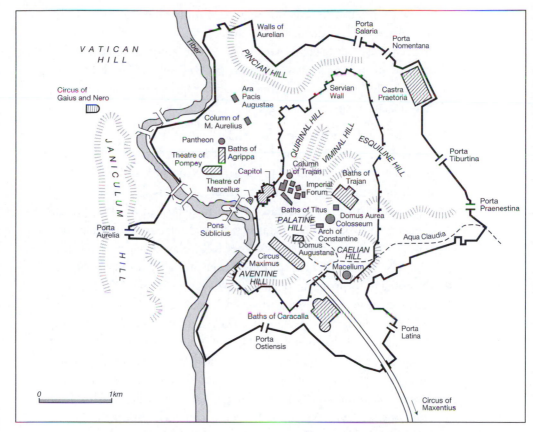

Figure 5.2 Rome in the imperial period. Source: After Swan's Hellenic Cruise Guide Book, © Swan Hellenic Cruises 2002.

over many of their functions in the previously self-sufficient family units. The public profile of some women had started to become more prominent, which caused considerable anxiety in the minds of traditionalists. Horace's writings praise traditional roles and modes of behaviour and warn against greater public prominence. The concept of the prominent woman of high profile is sharply contrasted with a traditional image of duty (*pietas*) in Aeneas' temptation by the Carthaginian queen, Dido, in the fourth book of Virgil's epic and his decision to abandon her in favour of the pursuit of his god-given mission.

A low public profile was not seen as diminishing the importance of women – or, indeed, respect for them. Horace recognises the respect owed to the senior womenfolk of a family, no matter what level of prominence was achieved by the men (*Odes* III.6), for such 'order' within the family unit represented an idealised microcosm of society at large.

Traditionally, Rome's prominent senators had looked to the advice (given, of course, in private) of mothers and wives; the significance in this respect of Cornelia (the mother of the Gracchus brothers) and of Aurelia (the mother of Julius Caesar) was well known and proper; both had a hand in determining the political allegiance of their sons. Augustus' wife, Livia, arguably the most influential of early imperial womenfolk, played her part without a high public profile, except in the use (probably) of her image on the coinage to promote personifications of essential 'virtues'. She received some public recognition in Augustus' will (in the form of her 'adopted name', Julia Augusta), although characteristically this was not welcomed by Tiberius. Livia could influence and orchestrate, but a public place in the power structure was not given – and, as far as we know, not requested; she was evidently content with her ability in a traditional way to influence her husband and her son. Whether she was ultimately responsible for all (or, indeed, any) of the dynastic machinations often ascribed to her is hardly material; her role was utterly traditional.

Agrippina, the wife of Livia's grandson, Germanicus, was, however, entirely different in her approach; she had ambitions for her husband and her sons, but – unusually – she had them for herself as well. She adopted highly public positions, as when she welcomed back the troops returning in AD 15 from across the Rhine; despite the fact that, four years later, her husband on his deathbed warned her against trying to rival those more powerful than herself – that is, Tiberius – she ignored his warning and evidently promoted her own image as the leader of a political faction (*partes Agrippinae*). The purpose of this faction was seen by her and by Tiberius as straightforward – to make Agrippina 'queen of Rome' on the basis of her claim to have been the 'true incarnation' of the blood of *Divus Augustus*. It was the divisiveness of this ambition which allowed Sejanus to wreak dynastic havoc in Tiberius' and her families. It is ironical, however, that the women who, over the years, had the greatest influence in constraining Sejanus were Livia and Agrippina's mother-in-law, Antonia, both of whom behaved totally in accordance with tradition.

Agrippina's 'modern' stance, however, left a clear legacy: her son, Caligula, based his despotism on his headship of a 'royal' family and, according to Philo of Alexandria, on the fact that he was fashioned as a 'king' within his mother's womb. This was a concept that raced far ahead of the traditional one adopted by Tiberius of acting in accordance with the political principles of Augustus. Agrippina's daughter, as we have seen, acted out her mother's ambitions by becoming Claudius' wife and partner in power. That Agrippina's 'modern' view of a woman's role struck a chord throughout society is seen in Juvenal's disparaging comments on women of his day who wished to appear in the arenas as wrestlers. The self-serving individualism which had proved so destructive an influence among men in the late Republic was now spreading through the whole of Roman society; it eventually saw its realisation in the third-century chaos when virtually anyone could hope for elevation to the imperial office.

Religion: the peace of the gods

Religion had always been a potent part of the nobility's political armoury and a cohesive factor in Roman society in the Republic. The fact that politicians doubled as priests meant that religious observance became an invaluable tool in the hands of the 'Establishment'. This was the principal reason why, in 186 BC, the senate had passed its uncompromising decree against Dionysiac worship – afraid of cults that were seen as politically and morally subversive in their ability to focus people's attention on different goals. That the influx of new ideas, mainly from the east, continued in the later Republic is not open to doubt; the growing uncertainties of life meant that people were more powerfully moved by gods who appeared to have a direct interest in their individual fates than by those who seemed indifferent. The traditional Roman gods presided over a materialism in which relatively few could participate; Cicero emphasised this when he cited Jupiter as the source of prosperity rather than of moral improvement.

Not only did the prosperity not touch everyone, of course, but increasingly the state of the Republic in the first century BC seemed to suggest that the gods had turned their backs on Rome – presumably because Romans had themselves lost sight of their collective destiny, or perhaps it was Romans who were ignoring their gods and thus incurring divine displeasure. Whichever it was, Horace (*Odes* III.6) was certain that it was an urgent duty incumbent on Augustus to initiate religious restoration in his 'restored Republic'. Not that Augustus required much persuasion; such a restoration would provide another important arm to his control and reinforce the conviction that normality and stability were returning. Besides this, his passage to power had been based in part on the criticism of wrongs done to the gods by the 'deviant' behaviour of Antonius in the east; further, Augustus' very success left him with debts to gods to repay. This was all encapsulated in the virtue of *pietas* (duty to gods and family) which, thanks to Virgil's publicity, was high on Augustus' agenda.

We have seen that action in this respect was vigorous – rebuilding, new building, revitalising in an attempt to make Romans aware of duty and tradition. Augustus did not, however, make the mistake of outlawing new (imported) cults, which were by now of considerable importance to many Romans. Rather, new cults could be 'sanitised' to rid them of undesirable elements; such happened to the cult of the eastern Earth-Mother, Cybele, whose worship had been brought to Rome in the troubled times of the late third century BC. Despite the wild rites that were associated with her 'at home' in Asia Minor (Catullus 64), under Augustus she could have her own temple on the Palatine Hill and take her place alongside gods of the Roman pantheon. In this policy of religious toleration, however, care was taken to ensure that foreign cults did not 'overstep the mark' or abuse Rome's hospitality. If this did happen, retribution could be swift and severe, as when Tiberius closed down Jewish and Egyptian cult centres in Rome in AD 19. Alternatively, attacks could be launched as 'diversionary tactics', as when Nero targeted the Christians in Rome after the 'Great Fire' of AD 64.

An important new element in the religious life of the Roman state under the Emperors was the introduction of the 'imperial cult' (or cult of Emperors). Ruler worship was an importation from the Hellenistic kingdoms of Asia Minor: as the successors to these rulers, Roman Emperors saw the political sense of allowing themselves to be worshipped as gods in such conquered lands, thus encouraging a sense of continuity with the past. Such a practice exemplified the generally observed Roman policy that people were happier if permitted to continue to seek support from traditional gods in a traditional way. Roman Emperors – even conservative ones – therefore had no difficulty in finding themselves worshipped as gods in such areas.

In the west, however, traditions were different: men were not identified with gods – and certainly not in Rome and Italy. Yet there was a profound sense of relief and gratitude to the man who had restored normality and to him and his successors when they initiated a benefaction to a local community. Thus, we commonly find requests from provincial communities for permission to erect temples to the Emperor. Most Emperors also understood that it was counterproductive to resist what were, after all, expressions of political enthusiasm.

In other words, in the west there was a tightrope to be negotiated: the 'answer' was the development of what we know as the 'imperial cult', sometimes expressed in the dual form, *Roma et*

Augustus ('Rome and Augustus'), where Rome was to be the principal focus of attention, and Augustus observed as the protector and saviour of Rome. In this form, the national and domestic families were treated as parallel: the Emperor was *pater patriae*, or protector of the 'national family', just as he, a father, linked gods and humans in the domestic context. Alternatively, the *numen* (or 'guardian spirit') of the Emperor was the object of attention. This was treated as a state cult, and its observance made obligatory, except where exemptions were made – as for the Jews, a practice which caused great difficulty in places where Jewish communities lived alongside other ethnic groups with no exemptions (as in Alexandria under Caligula and Claudius). The imperial cult was added to as some Emperors earned the honour of posthumous deification, and a calendar of birthdays and anniversaries was established on which ceremonial was obligatory. In the provinces, conducting and defraying the costs of such ceremonial was a useful way in which wealthy provincials could bring themselves to notice.

Few of the early Emperors believed that they were personally in any sense divine: indeed, Suetonius records Vespasian's dying words in AD 79, 'woe is me: I think that I am becoming a god'. Tiberius set his face strongly against any concession on this, even when it would not have been regarded as unacceptable; that Emperor is on record as saying that people's appreciation of his good administration would constitute 'his temples', and that he was content with honours appropriate to men. He could not, however, deny that Augustus' deification left him as 'son of God'. The most tantalising case among the earlier Emperors is plainly that of Caligula, who is stated to have encouraged a cult of himself in the west. Yet, there is no reference to it on his coinage nor on inscriptions; nor is there any sign anywhere in Rome of the site of a cult temple.

Some Emperors certainly publicly proclaimed the protection of certain gods, as Domitian did in the case of Minerva, and Nero of Apollo. Nor is the true intention behind such references always clear: for example, how were Romans expected to interpret Trajan's Column, which appeared on one of the Emperor's coins as the 'club of Hercules', or Commodus' statue depicting the Emperor clothed in Hercules' lionskin? Some references might, in fact, be little more than thank-offerings, as when Augustus coined in honour of *Jupiter Tonans* ('the Thunderer') to celebrate his escape from a lightning strike, or again when he dedicated the temple in his Forum (2 BC) to Mars the Avenger to thank the god for facilitating the deaths of Brutus and Cassius forty years before.

Thus, religion again became all-pervasive in the Republic, and the forms in which it appeared were designed to demonstrate that the gods presided over and guaranteed Rome's success: their willing-ness to do this on a continuous basis was in most cases portrayed as dependent on people's acknowledgement of their indebtedness to the gods' vice-gerents on earth – Augustus Caesar and his successors.

Appendix 1

Galba's oration to Piso on the latter's adoption as successor to the Principate (Tacitus, *Histories* I.15–16)

Tacitus provides what purports to be the text of a speech which Servius Galba made on 10 January AD 69 on the occasion of his adoption of Lucius Calpurnius Piso Frugi Licinianus as his son and successor. It is doubtful whether the text of such an oration survived for Tacitus to have consulted, although he probably could have gained an impression of it from people who did hear it. It is, however, more likely that, as with the speech of Claudius in AD 48 on the admission of Gallic aristocrats to senatorial membership, Tacitus has followed the maxim of the Athenian historian, Thucydides, in producing his own version of the speech, encapsulating 'sentiments proper to the occasion'.

The purpose of the oration in Tacitus' narrative has been much discussed, and by some it has been regarded as a Tacitean 'manual of statecraft', laying out the historian's own principles of government under the Principate. Because of this, it has been argued that the speech has less to do with events in the mid-first century AD than with Tacitus' own times – in particular, the confused and dangerous events of the Principate of the aged Nerva in AD 96–98, which culminated in that emperor's adoption of Trajan as his son and successor.

At the least, however, the 'dramatic date' of Galba's oration provides an opportunity for comment on the system of government under the Julio-Claudians – particularly with regard to the dynastic principle itself. It also offers in passing a senatorial view of the reign of Nero; however, as with other emperors – most notably, perhaps, Domitian (AD 81–96) – it is as well to remember that the senatorial viewpoint, because of the circumstances of the relationship between emperors and the senate, might present a set of opinions markedly different from those entertained by other sections of the community.

> 'If I were a private citizen, adopting you in the presence of the priests according to time-honoured formalities, I should content myself with dwelling on the great honour it does my family to bring into it a man who carries in his veins the blood of Gnaeus Pompeius and of Marcus Crassus; for your part, you would feel similarly gratified at the opportunity to link your own noble family with my roots in the families of the Sulpicii and the Lutatii. As it is, however, it is by unanimous consent of gods and men that I am emperor; thus it is your outstanding qualities of character and your patriotism that prompt me in a time of peace to offer you a Principate for which our ancestors – and indeed I myself – had to take up arms.
>
> I am conscious of the example of the Deified Augustus, who raised a series of men to a position of power second only to his own – first, his sister's son, Gaius Claudius Marcellus, then his son-in-law, Marcus Agrippa; later still, he promoted his grandsons, Gaius and Lucius Caesar, and finally his stepson, Tiberius Claudius Nero. Augustus confined his search for a successor to

his family, whilst I have extended mine to the whole state; this is not because I have no close relations or army-colleagues. My acceptance of the imperial power was not driven by my sense of ambition, and it would be taken as an indication that I have exercised my judgement that, in choosing you, I have passed over not just my relatives, but, yours too. You have a brother, as noble in birth as you, and older; he would be worthy of this honour, were you not the better choice.

You are old enough to have left youthful enthusiasm behind, and you have nothing in your past life which requires excuse. Until now, you have had only misfortunes to bear; success tests the human spirit more critically. This is because we bear misfortune, whilst success corrupts us. Loyalty, independence and friendship represent the outstanding qualities of the human character; you have maintained your grasp on these with great determination, and will continue to do so. Others, however, will seek to undermine them through their sycophancy. You will be assaulted by flattery, by specious arguments, and by individual self-interest, which inflict the greatest damage on sincere relationships. You and I to-day can talk straightforwardly to each other on a personal basis; others, however, will be more ready to treat us as emperors than as human beings. Advising an emperor on the right course of action is an act of real commitment, whilst agreeing with everything that an emperor says is accomplished with no real affection.

If this extensive empire of ours could remain stable without a ruler, I would consider it an achievement to be able to re-establish the old Republic. As it is, it long ago came to the point where, as I grow older, I cannot do the Roman people a better service than to give them a good successor, whilst your greatest gift to them in your youth will be to give them a good emperor. In the reigns of Tiberius, Gaius (Caligula) and Claudius, Rome was effectively the heirloom of a single family; thus my introduction of the principle of choice will represent a move towards liberty. Now that the Julian and Claudian dynasty has reached its end, the choice of the best emperor will be made by a process of adoption. To be born of emperors is a matter of pure chance, and is not valued more highly than that; the act of adoption implies an exercise of unimpeded judgement and, if one wishes, the choice is confirmed by public consensus.

Let Nero's example remain before your eyes; he vaunted himself as the last of a long line of Caesars. It was not Vindex with an unarmed province or I myself with a single legion that brought him down and freed the Roman people of the burden of him; it was his own excesses and luxurious wastefulness. Nor was there at that time any precedent for an emperor suffering such a condemnation. We won the power through arms and because we were thought right for the job; but no matter how outstanding our performance, we shall become the targets of envy. Do not feel threatened because two legions have not yet recovered their equilibrium after the greatest convulsion that the empire has seen; my accession was not untroubled, and once news of your adoption spreads I shall cease to seem old – which has been the only objection that could be levelled at me. Nero will always be missed by the worst elements of society; it is our job – yours and mine – to make sure that men of quality do not come to miss him too.

This is not the occasion for more extended advice; indeed, all necessary precautions are in place if I have done a good job in choosing you. The quickest and simplest test of right and wrong is for you to consider what actions you would approve or criticise if someone else were emperor. Rome is not like those countries which are ruled by kings, and in which everyone is a slave to the ruling house; you are about to become emperor amongst a people who can handle neither serfdom nor uncontrolled freedom.'

Appendix 2

Stemma of the Julian and Claudian families

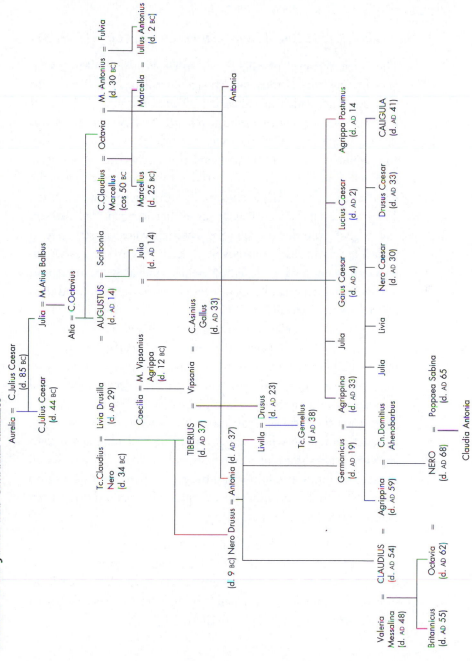

Source: D. Shotter, *Tiberius Caesar*, Lancaster Pamphlets (London: Routledge, 1992), p. 9.

Appendix 3

Suetonius' description of Nero's *Domus Aurea* (*Life of Nero* 31)

The most wasteful of all his activities was his building-programme: he built a house which stretched from the Palatine to the Esquiline, which he called the *Domus Transitoria*. When it was later burnt down, he rebuilt it with the new name, *Domus Aurea*. The following details will provide some idea of its size and opulence: at its entrance-way, there stood the *Colossus*, a statue of himself which stood 120 feet high; so spacious was the site that there was a triple colonnade running for a whole mile. There was a lake which was so large that it resembled the sea, and was surrounded by buildings which were constructed to look like whole cities; moreover, there were rustic areas which were landscaped with ploughed fields, vineyards, pastures and woods, in which great herds of every kind of domestic and wild animal roamed around.

In the house itself, all surfaces were covered with gold leaf, and encrusted with precious stones and pearls; the dining-rooms had fretted ceilings with panels of ivory which were movable and equipped with pipes so that flower-petals and perfumes could be showered on those below. The main dining-room took the form of a rotunda which revolved day and night in synchronisation with the heavens. The baths had a constant supply of sea-water and water from sulphurous springs. When the decoration of the house had been completed in this fashion Nero dedicated it, adding approvingly that he could now at last begin to live like a human being.

Tacitus (*Annals* XV.42) confirms that the designers/engineers, Severus and Celer, were masters of mechanical wizardry. For a description and plan, see A. Boethius and J. B. Ward-Perkins, *Etruscan and Roman Architecture* (London, 1970); also E. Segala and I. Sciortino, *Domus Aurea* (Milan, 1999).

Further reading

Balsdon J. P., *The Emperor Gaius (Caligula)* (Oxford, 1934).

Balsdon, J. P., *Life and Leisure in Ancient Rome* (London, 1974).

Barrett A. A., *Caligula: The Corruption of Power* (London, 1989).

Barrett A. A., *Agrippina: Mother of Nero* (London, 1996).

Bauman R. A., *Impietas In Principem* (Munich, 1974).

Brunt P. A. and Moore J. M., *Res Gestae Divi Augusti* (Oxford, 1988).

Campbell J. B., *The Emperor and the Roman Army* (New York, 1984).

Carson R. A. G. and Kraay C. M. (eds), *Scripta Nummaria Romana* (London, 1978).

Carter J. M., *The Battle of Actium* (London, 1970).

Chisholm K. and Ferguson J., *Rome: The Augustan Age* (Oxford, 1987).

Crook J., *Consilium Principis* (Cambridge, 1955).

D'Arms J. H., *Romans on the Bay of Naples* (Cambridge, MA, 1970).

Durry M., *Les Cohortes Prétoriennes* (Paris, 1968).

Earl D. C., *The Age of Augustus* (London, 1968).

Ferrill A., *Caligula: Emperor of Rome* (London, 1991).

Fishwick D., *The Imperial Cult in the Latin West* (Leiden, 1993).

Garzetti A., *From Tiberius to the Antonines* (London, 1960).

Gelzer M., *The Roman Nobility* (Oxford, 1969).

Grant M., *From Imperium to Auctoritas* (Cambridge, 1946).

Griffin M., *Nero: The End of a Dynasty* (New Haven, CT, 1984).

Hammond M., *The Augustan Principate* (Cambridge, MA, 1933).

Henderson B. W., *The Life and Principate of the Emperor Nero* (London, 1903).

Hooper F., *Roman Realities* (Detroit, MI, 1979).

Howgego C., *Ancient History from Coins* (London, 1995).

Jones A. H. M., *Augustus* (London, 1970).

Kuttner A. L., *Dynasty and Empire in the Age of Augustus* (Berkeley, CA, 1995).

Levick B., *Tiberius the Politician* (London, 1976).

Levick B., *Claudius* (London, 1990).

Maranon G., *Tiberius: A Study in Resentment* (London, 1956).

Marsh F. B., *The Founding of the Roman Empire* (Oxford, 1927).

Marsh F. B., *The Reign of Tiberius* (Oxford, 1931).

McKay A. G., *Houses, Villas and Palaces in the Roman World* (London, 1975).

Mellor R., *Tacitus* (New York, 1993).

Millar F. G. B., *The Emperor in the Roman World* (London, 1977).

Momigliano A., *Claudius: The Emperor and his Achievement* (Oxford, 1934).

Rodewald C., *Money in the Age of Tiberius* (Manchester, 1976).

Rogers R. S., *Criminal Trials and Criminal Legislation in the Reign of Tiberius* (Middletown, CT, 1935).

Rowell H. T., *Rome in the Augustan Age* (Norman, OK, 1962).

Rudich V., *Political Dissidence Under Nero: The Price of Dissimulation* (London, 1992).

Rudich V., *Dissidence and Literature Under Nero* (London, 1997).

Saller R. P., *Personal Patronage under the Early Caesars* (Cambridge, 1982).

Sandbach F. H., *The Stoics* (London, 1975).

Seager R., *Tiberius* (London, 1972).

Sear F., *Roman Architecture* (London, 1982).

Shotter D. C. A., *Augustus Caesar* (London, 1991).

Shotter D. C. A., *Tiberius Caesar* (London, 1992).

Shotter D. C. A., *Nero* (London, 1997).

Simon E., *Ara Pacis Augustae* (Tübingen, 1967).

Southern P., *Augustus* (London, 2001).

Sutherland C. H. V., *Coinage in Roman Imperial Policy* (London, 1951).

Sutherland C. H. V., *The Emperor and the Coinage: Julio-Claudian Studies* (London, 1976).

Syme R., *The Roman Revolution* (Oxford, 1939).

Syme R., *Tacitus* (Oxford, 1958).

Syme R., *History in Ovid* (Oxford, 1978).

Syme R., *The Augustan Aristocracy* (Oxford, 1986).

Talbert R. J. A., *The Senate of Imperial Rome* (Princeton, NJ, 1984).

Taylor L. R., *The Divinity of the Roman Emperor* (Middletown, CT, 1931).

Thornton M. K. and Thornton R. L., *Julio-Claudian Building Programmes* (Wauconda, IL, 1989).

Usher S., *The Historians of Greece and Rome* (London, 1969).

Veyne P., *Bread and Circuses* (London, 1992).

Wallace-Hadrill A., *Suetonius: The Scholar and his Caesars* (London, 1983).

Wallace-Hadrill A. (ed.), *Patronage in Ancient Society* (London, 1989).

Wallace-Hadrill A., *Augustan Rome* (Bristol, 1993).

Warmington B., *Nero: Reality and Legend* (London, 1969).

Weaver P. C., *Familia Caesaris: A Social Study of the Emperor's Freedmen and Slaves* (Cambridge, 1972).

Wells C., *The Roman Empire* (London, 1992).

White K. D., *Country Life in Classical Times* (London, 1978).

Wiedemann T., *Emperors and Gladiators* (London, 1992).

Woodman A. J. and West D. (eds), *Poetry and Politics in the Age of Augustus* (Cambridge, 1984).

Yavetz Z., *Plebs and Princeps* (Oxford, 1969).

Zanker P., *Forum Augustum* (Tübingen, n.d.).

Zanker P., *The Power of Images in the Age of Augustus* (Ann Arbor, MI, 1988).

Chapter 6

The *Pax Romana*: a new deal for the empire

The Principate and the Roman army

For the last century of the Republic, the Roman army had been a source of problems; the need to create the conditions of service and the flow of recruits necessary to protect the integrity of Rome's interests abroad led to the decision by Gaius Marius to open recruitment to all citizens, regardless of property levels. This change proved disastrous, because nothing was done to tie the army's loyalty to the Republic, which left it effectively within the patronage and thus under the influence of individual politicians/generals. The army needed these 'patrons' to lead it on lucrative campaigns and to arrange land settlements on demobilisation. The Republic was thus at the mercy of its armies, which inevitably, in their own interest, looked to the 'highest bidder'. As Cicero observed in 52 BC, the laws were powerless to protect the Republic from such armed pressure.

The final decades of the Republic witnessed a series of politicians who, to fulfil their ambitions, applied pressure to the Republic using armed force or, at the least, the threat of it; Sulla, Pompey, Caesar, Antonius and Octavian (Augustus) provide the best-known examples, although other, smaller, figures played a part also. Clearly, if Octavian and Agrippa were to capitalise on their success at Actium in 31, some means would have to be found to stabilise the army's sense of loyalty and to keep it out of the hands of adventurers and ambitious politicians. Otherwise, the Republic would continue to suffer these periodic armed threats.

Augustus himself was never a man of great military ability, although he did, of course, bear the name of Caesar and, as events on Sicily in 36 BC demonstrated, that could be a considerable asset in itself. The 'partnership' with Marcus Agrippa was vital to the achievement of military stability. As well as this, as we have seen, the capture of Egypt and its vast resources provided Augustus with the means to patronise on a scale never seen before.

The problem of stability was tackled in two ways – by revising the organisation of provincial government and by a wholesale revision of recruitment and service conditions for the army. The chief principle of the former was to ensure that those provinces which were likely to experience military problems should come under the control of the *princeps*. As we have seen, in the 'First Settlement' (27 BC) Augustus himself became the provincial governor of Gaul, Spain and Syria (the three military provinces shared between Pompey, Crassus and Caesar after the Lucca agreement of 56); the 'Second Settlement' (23 BC) gave the *princeps* an overriding proconsular power (*imperium proconsulare maius*), which enabled him, where necessary, to 'intervene' in the government of any province and provided him with the opportunity to redefine as his any provinces that required a military presence. Augustus was thus able to control the army.

Obviously, Augustus could not govern all of his provinces directly, so he relied on 'delegating' his authority to men of sufficient seniority whom he felt able to trust. These were the *Legati Augusti Pro Praetore*; the reference to 'praetorian' status was a fiction, for such men were always ex-consuls who accepted the lesser title in order visibly to subordinate them to the proconsular power which defined the *princeps* as the legal governor. However, the *legati* were the governors of such provinces *de facto* and the day-to-day commanders of the armies in them. Men lower in the senatorial hierarchy (ex-praetors) were entrusted with the command of individual legions in these provinces.

The reforms of the army structure itself were radical: during the Republic, armies were raised as campaign necessity dictated. Although they usually served for a number of years, they were at the end of a campaign brought back to Italy for demobilisation and settlement on smallholdings. As a result of the victory at Actium, Augustus had around seventy legions (approximately 380,000 men) under his command; such a number was far too high to be supported economically, and in any case might prove to be difficult to control and could have undermined Augustus' claim to be restoring the Republic to peace and normality. He thus demobilised all but twenty-eight of the legions, using his own resources. Since even the remainder would have given entirely the wrong impression if held in Italy, Augustus posted the great majority of them to the provinces for which he was responsible, thus creating the notion of a 'frontier army', which would be too far away from Rome for Augustus to be vulnerable to the accusation of operating a military despotism (see Appendix 1).

These legions received new service conditions, becoming permanent; individual soldiers served for twenty years, followed by a period in reserve. After this time, they would be discharged, receiving money or land (or both). Discharge thus became an ongoing process, bringing to an end the dangerous phenomenon of large bodies of troops arriving in Italy together for demobilisation. Indeed, Italy was now rarely used for legionary discharge; as the ethnic origins of the citizen body widened, so Italy became less relevant to many legionaries as a homeland. They might be discharged to their provinces of origin, or more likely they would receive land or an allotment in a *colonia* in the province in which they had served; thus veterans of the legions which had taken part in Claudius' invasion of Britain in AD 43, were settled in the new *colonia* established in AD 49 at Colchester (*Camulodunum*). In this way, legionary veterans provided an invaluable impetus to the process of Romanising the provinces, despite the fact that, at first, relations between the Trinovantes and the veterans were evidently not happy.

All of this was paid for by the *princeps*, initially from his own resources and, after AD 6, from a special treasury (*aerarium militare*), which was funded largely by receipts from the inheritance and sales taxes. In a real sense, therefore, the *princeps* was the army's patron and, in return, the soldiers swore an annually renewable oath of allegiance to him. Just as before, therefore, although the service conditions were more stable than during the Republic, this was the Republic's army in so far as it was under the day-to-day control of the Republic's magistrates. The 'improvement' lay simply in the fact that nobody enjoyed the level of standing and resources to match those of Augustus; in so far as he 'was' the Republic, Augustus had simply institutionalised the previous relationships between legions and generals. Events were to show, however, that the army's loyalty still had to be perceived by the soldiers as merited by the *princeps*.

The former allied contingents were also reformed: previously these had consisted largely of Italians, but under Augustus a wider collection of ethnic origins was to be found among the non-citizen troops who made up the *auxilia* (as they were now called). These consisted of small contingents of 480 or 960 infantry (*cohortes*) or cavalry (*alae*), who served for twenty-five years before receiving Roman citizenship and demobilisation onto a plot of land. During the Julio-Claudian period, the *auxilia* generally served under their own local commanders who, of course, were expected to have attained an advanced stage of Romanisation. However, after some unfortunate experiences over the loyalty of such officers, a decision was made by Vespasian (AD 69–79) to begin placing equestrian *praefecti* in command of auxiliary units, thus making a command of auxiliaries a step in the developing career structure for equestrians. The auxiliaries were maintained in total numbers approximately equivalent to the total of legionaries; under Augustus, this will have given a total army strength of around 310,000 men. The backing, therefore, which Augustus had at his disposal for protecting the integrity of the frontiers and (ultimately) for maintaining himself in power was considerable. Further, as we shall see, this army represented a significant force in the Romanising of the provinces – as an instrument for organisation, as a building workforce and as a well-paid 'market' for locally produced goods and services.

The purpose of empire

We have seen that the early centuries of imperial expansion were not marked by adherence to a coherent plan; land was acquired as a result of military conquest, when acquisition of that land had rarely provided the initial reason for the warfare. In time, a logic of a kind came to be recognised in the concept often referred to as 'defensive imperialism' – or the search for quiet neighbours, which had in a sense been a characteristic of the earliest expansion in Italy in the fifth and fourth centuries BC.

The advent in the first century BC of a larger body of military recruits, who had no property ties, allowed for more expansionist wars; in particular, soldiers looked to their commanders to lead them on lucrative campaigns, while commanders looked to high-profile conflicts which would enhance their reputations and provide them with funds and loyal followers for political battles in the future. In such a light we may view Caesar's activities in Gaul and Britain in the 50s BC.

Julius Caesar, however, was one of those relatively rare Roman politicians who thought beyond short-term advantage, although the political culture of the late Republic required him to take proper stock of the short-term considerations. His Gallic campaigns had in a dramatic fashion highlighted a problem for Rome in Europe – namely the population instability in central and eastern Europe which from time to time spilled over into the

Mediterranean area where, of course, Rome's interests were concentrated. This had posed a real threat in the last decade of the second century BC, when the Cimbri and Teutones had swept through Gaul and into Italy; there was a threat of it, too, in the 50s, when the German leader, Ariovistus, had come across the Rhine and was interfering with tribes on the west bank. Further south, the tribe of the Helvetii wished to pass through the province of *Gallia Transalpina* on their way from Switzerland in search of new homes in south-west France. To Caesar, the logical solution to such problems was to advance Roman territory to clear natural features, such as the River Rhine, where it could be properly defended.

In short, a philosophy of empire was taking shape: the 'central homeland' (Rome and Italy) was to be protected from the marauding enemies further afield by a buffer of Romanised territory held within defensible frontiers. To achieve this successfully required that Romanised territory be well defended and efficiently governed in a manner that gave an increasing amount of weight and responsibility to local people, who were prepared to act in Rome's – and their own – interests. The very variable – and often viciously self-interested – quality of provincial government had to be taken in hand, the assessment and collection of taxes regularised and programmes of Romanisation instituted with a view to making local people ready for grants of Roman citizenship. Further, Romans had to be prepared to understand that such advances in status carried considerable implications for the nature and level of participation to which the new citizens might eventually be able to aspire.

Writers of the Augustan age laid out – although not necessarily in coherent form – what the aims of empire should be; Horace, for example (*Odes* III.5), talks of the equation of territorial expansion with national honour, while Virgil (*Aeneid* VI.851–3) urged on Augustus a duty of civilising the world, first through force and then through the Romanisation of conquered peoples. It is evident from Dio Cassius' description of the German tribes in the

Augustan period who, he says, were 'becoming different without knowing it' (56.18,2) that there was a strong social and commercial thrust to this. Further, it can be recognised through Tacitus' description of Agricola's activities in Britain that the approach adumbrated by Virgil was accepted as the 'norm'.

Officially, therefore, Rome came to see a principal purpose of empire as providing a buffer of conquered territory between Rome and Italy on the one hand and the real enemies of order and civilisation beyond. This was achieved by Romanising the conquered territory and 'holding' it within defined frontiers, although views might from time to time differ on the questions of the location and nature of those frontiers. Order would ultimately be guaranteed by the presence of troops, particularly in sensitive provinces, but it was regarded as axiomatic that a high standard of government and the development of economic prosperity would bring provincials to the view that they had a positive stake in the running and development of their province. The rarity of genuine provincial uprisings – as distinct from rebellions within the Roman army – demonstrates the success of the policy. This, in essence, was the *Pax Romana* as settled by Augustus Caesar.

Wars and frontiers

The haphazard nature of imperial expansion during the Republic has been noted, as has the fact that, within western Europe, Julius Caesar pointed the way to an alternative model. Augustus built on these beginnings and, until expansion was brought to an abrupt halt by the Varus disaster in Germany in AD 9, spent his reign expanding towards definable frontiers. Previously, many provinces had ill-defined land frontiers, covered perhaps by a buffer of tribes with whom Rome established treaty relationships. This approach continued to play a part, as is seen by the temporary treaty that was struck up by Claudius with the tribe of the Brigantes of northern England to protect the northern flank of the fledgling province of *Britannia*. Generally, however, it was preferred to delimit territory by means of natural landscape features, usually supported by a system of linear defences – roads, palisades, ditches, forts, fortlets and watchtowers.

Horace urged on Augustus a high-profile military policy, although in the event Augustus did not find it necessary to do everything that the poet set out. Logic suggested that in Europe, with the chief enemies located to the east and the north, an acceptable and workable frontier system would be provided by a combination of rivers running from west to east and from south to north. The Danube obviously fitted the needs of the former, although there was a choice for the latter – the Elbe or the Rhine. During Augustus' reign, campaigning was virtually continuous in western and southern Europe – in Spain (where Augustus himself was a prominent presence in the mid-20s BC), and in Gaul, Germany and the middle-Danube regions, where, for a considerable period between 17 and 7 BC, Agrippa, Tiberius and his brother, Nero Drusus, worked in concert until the impetus was lost with the deaths of Agrippa (12 BC) and Nero Drusus (9 BC) and with the recall of Tiberius (7 BC). Flexibility of approach was demonstrated by the readiness to employ a combination of initiatives, using both provinces and kingdoms left under tutelage of 'client monarchs'. While most of this work was centred on the achievement of an Elbe/Danube frontier, events in the first decade of the Christian era showed the risks involved in overstretching resources – first, the Pannonian rebellion of AD 6–9 and then the traumatic loss of three legions in the Teutoburgerwald in AD 9 under Quinctilius Varus.

There were important lessons to be learned from these events: the potential unreliability of apparently Romanised local leaders was an obvious problem. Arminius, who brought Varus to destruction, was a Roman citizen, had commanded locally recruited auxiliary units and was regarded as reliable. It is evident, too, that the quality of Roman government was also an issue; the leaders of the Pannonian rebellion made a pointed reference to wolves who should have been sheep-dogs – an idea evidently picked up by Tiberius in his requirement that his provincial 'sheep should be sheared, not flayed'. Over-confidence on the Roman side was also an issue, as is seen in Augustus' appointment to Germany of Quinctilius Varus, a man who proved himself unequal to the difficulties of his command and on whom the classical sources heaped all the blame for the disaster (Velleius Paterculus II.117–8). However, the disaster demonstrated not only the commander's failings but also the difficulties of campaigning with legions in the types of terrain that characterised much of the land east of the Rhine. At any rate, this disaster saw the annihilation of three complete legions (XVII, XVIII and XIX); the effect on Augustus himself was considerable, as is shown by the fact that the three numbers in the legionary sequence were never replaced and by Augustus' decisions to settle finally for the Rhine frontier in the west and effectively to order that the 'empire should be kept within its existing frontiers'. The effects were thus long term, and the emergency recruitment programme necessary to bring the legions in Germany back to strength left that section of the army in a potentially unstable state – as was shown by the mutinies which broke out on Tiberius' accession in AD 14 among the legions of the Rhine and the Danube.

Tiberius evidently, as usual, took the Augustan advice to heart, although there was a temporary confusion at the beginning of his reign. Influenced by the serious mutiny among the Rhine legions which greeted his accession, he evidently went along with the plan of the local commander – his adopted son, Germanicus Caesar – to bring the recalcitrant mutineers to heel by letting them loose on a 'real enemy' across the Rhine. This mutiny was clearly made more serious by the deterioration in service conditions that had come about as a result of the Varus disaster and of the presence in the legions, owing to the need for rapid recruitment that was probably undertaken less critically than normal, of 'streetwise' men who in other circumstances would probably have been discarded as unsuitable. The situation was, for Tiberius, made more complex and worrying by the hint that the stability which Augustus had appeared to have achieved in the army showed signs of breaking down, as some of the mutineers offered to support Germanicus in a bid for power if he acceded to their demands. The episode thus provides an ominous portent of what was to happen in AD 68 (see Chapter 7).

Germanicus' troops in AD 14 achieved some easy success which seems to have convinced them and their commander that dreams of an enlarged *Germania* should not yet be abandoned. This, however, was not part of Tiberius' agenda, particularly after another near-disastrous encounter with Arminius in AD 15, and a near-catastrophe due to the weather in the following year. With difficulty, Tiberius managed to persuade Germanicus to desist, and the Rhine frontier was once again accepted. Through most of the Julio-Claudian period, seven or eight legions were deployed on the west bank of the Rhine in large fortresses, together with an equivalent force of auxiliaries; as elsewhere in the empire, the pur- chasing power and the needs of these troops proved a powerful force in bringing stability to the tribes in the region. Towns developed outside the military establishments and, in the territory of the Ubii, a *colonia* for veterans was founded at Cologne in the reign of Claudius.

The complex fortifications known as the *limes Germanicus* were thus begun, with especial care taken of the natural 'gap' which existed between the headwaters of the Rhine and the Danube. Roman territory was administered not as provinces: the 'two Germanies' (*Inferior* and *Superior*) were 'military districts', their civilian affairs being administered from Gaul; the 'Germanies' included what was effectively a 'buffer zone' on the east bank of the Rhine, which was used for such purposes as the corralling of horses.

After the difficulties experienced in the area in AD 68, the process of fortification was accelerated under the Flavians and later emperors. Roman fears of the destructive power of tribes east of the Rhine persisted, for the Varus disaster of AD 9 continued to rank among the great Roman catastrophes of all time. It is clear that it was rightly understood that this was one of the potential flashpoints in the empire's territorial integrity, and Tacitus' publication in AD 98 of his treatise on the German tribes (the *Germania*) was at least in part meant to bring the powerful forces represented by these tribes clearly into the view of a Roman audience.

Stability on the Danube had effectively been won by the time of Augustus' death; the southern bank of the Danube was guarded by a combination of heavily armed provinces and client monarchies. Although some changes in organisation and troop deployment occurred during the Julio-Claudian period, the only fresh territorial acquisition was the re-organisation into a province (by Claudius in AD 46) of the Balkan client kingdom of Thrace. Nonetheless, by the end of the Julio-Claudian period there were fresh signs of impending instability in this region: under Claudius, the relocation in the Roman provinces had been allowed of some 100,000 tribesmen from north of the river and, during the civil war of AD 69, the Danube frontier was breached by Sarmatians seeking new homes. From this, a major conflict developed in the later first and early second centuries, leading to the establishment by Trajan of the province of Dacia on the northern side of the river. It was clear, therefore, even at this stage that the population pressures on the two great European frontiers might eventually prove too powerful to resist.

The poet, Horace, had urged on Augustus the importance of following up Caesar's success by the annexation of Britain; Britain, in other words, was regarded as 'unfinished business'. The fact that Horace raised the subject may safely be taken as an indication that Augustus did entertain a plan for Britain; after all, the events of Caesar's proconsulship in the 50s BC demonstrated both the links between the Gallic and British tribes, and the difficulty of maintaining order in Gaul in the face of interference from Britain. This obviously became more crucial with the formal creation of the four provinces of Gaul – *Narbonensis* being joined by *Lugdunensis, Aquitania* and *Belgica* – and the need to secure settled conditions in them.

In the event, Augustus preferred to proceed through diplomatic channels, although, as usual in such circumstances, the threat of military intervention was a powerful feature of the diplomacy. Rivalries among and within the British tribes meant that, for the time being at least, 'divide and rule' was a feasible policy. A treaty was established with the pro-Roman Atrebates (who lived south of the River Thames), and this tribe opened itself in the early Julio-Claudian years to cultural and economic influences from the Mediterranean. North of the Thames lay the potentially more 'nationalistic' grouping of the Catuvellauni and Trinovantes who, despite Caesar's efforts to prevent it, had come together under Cunobelinus (Shakespeare's Cymbeline). This man clearly had statesmanlike inclinations for, despite his natural hostility to Rome, he, too, became a client monarch; indeed, it may even have been he who is said to have returned unharmed to Rome some legionary soldiers who had been swept across the North Sea by the great storm of AD 16.

Tiberius saw no reason to disturb the Augustan arrangements, even though the genuinely pro-Roman sentiments of some were beginning to lose out to those who were less enthusiastic. An indication of this was probably provided by a revolt in Gaul in AD 21–22, led by a Romanised Gaul, named Julius Sacrovir; this name, meaning 'holy man', strongly suggests the influence of Druids in the rebellion and possibly physical assistance from British Druids. After the suppression of the revolt, some of its participants were exiled, possibly to Britain; it would not be unreasonable to suggest that such frustrated Druids might have made common cause with the younger generation of British tribal leaders in questioning what probably seemed to them to be a rather spineless attitude to Rome on the part of many British tribal leaders. Here then were perhaps the ingredients to undo the diplomatic 'entente' that had for nearly a century made it unnecessary for Rome to invade Britain.

Plate 6.1 Britannia: Aureus of Claudius, showing a stylised version of a triumphal arch. © Copyright The British Museum.

The Augustan arrangements in Britain finally broke down with the death of Cunobelinus, either late in Tiberius' reign or early in that of Caligula; his place in control of his tribe was taken by his two elder sons, Caratacus and Togodumnus, who were strongly anti-Roman. It remains unclear whether Caligula tried (and failed) in AD 40 to mount an expedition to Britain, although it is on balance more likely that the presence of the *princeps* on the Gallic coast had more to do with a 'final' diplomatic effort centred around his formal acceptance of the submission of Cunobelinus' third son, Adminius (or Amminius), which was embroidered by hostile Roman sources into a farcical failure of an expedition. However, ultimately the treatment of the pro-Roman Verica (chief of the Atrebates) at the hands of Cunobelinus' anti-Roman sons made action by Rome inevitable; Verica was a client of Rome and, if he was not afforded proper protection, it might undermine a significant element of Rome's relations with foreign leaders across the empire.

It was thus left to Claudius to initiate the invasion of Britain in AD 43; as we have seen, the reasons were pressing enough, but since Claudius' elevation to the imperial power two years previously had involved the help of the Praetorian Guard, this may have provided a further reason stemming from a desire on Claudius' part to 'show himself' to his legions who were normally hostile in their attitude towards the praetorians. By the end of the Julio-Claudian period, the province of *Britannia* included the south and midlands, as well as south Wales. Claudius demonstrated the flexibility of his approach not only by initiating a treaty with the pro-Roman queen of the Brigantes (of northern England) in order to protect the northern flank of the new province but also by leaving two areas within the province, temporarily at least, under client rulers (the territories of the Atrebates and the Iceni); these two areas were probably brought into full administration under Nero. The conquest and initial consolidation were essentially smoothly run, probably because there was considerable willingness on the part of many British to comply; the only significant crisis was that caused by the rebellion of Boudica in 60, to which we shall return later.

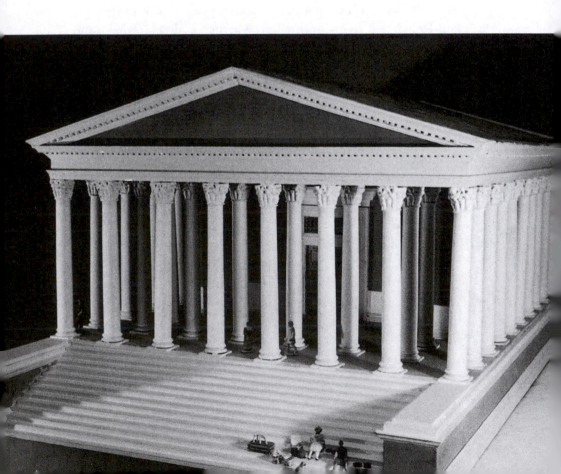

The eastern part of the empire posed problems rather different from those of the north and west: Greece itself, western Asia Minor and some of the coastal strip of north Africa had belonged to the empire for some considerable time; the holding of the fertile coastal land of north Africa was extended in the reigns of Caligula and Claudius by the addition of the two provinces of *Mauretania*, which had previously been client monarchies of Rome. In Asia Minor itself there were three provinces – *Asia*, *Bithynia with Pontus* and *Cilicia*; the rest of the area remained under monarchs of Hellenistic origin, some of whom were treated as client kings of Rome. Egypt and its vast resources were added to the empire by Augustus after the death of Cleopatra (30 BC), although the territory was administered as Augustus' personal property and was the source of much of the wealth that supported his patronage. Militarily, the 'nerve centre' of the region was the armed, imperial province of *Syria*.

Until the late 60s BC, Rome's chief adversary in the east had been Mithridates, the long-lived king of Pontus, in alliance with his son-in-law, Tigranes, the king of Armenia. To defeat Mithridates and Tigranes, Pompey had involved the Parthians in Rome's eastern affairs and rather unwisely had failed to deliver on promises made to them. From that point we can date the spasmodic hostilities between Rome and Parthia, which came to hinge largely on the status of Armenia – whether it should have politically an eastward or westward orientation.

In the last years of the Republic, two Roman armies came to grief in the area – under Marcus Crassus in 54 BC and under Antonius' general, Decidius Saxa, in 36 BC; on both occasions the disgrace was symbolised and compounded by the loss of legionary 'eagles'. For Augustus, the retrieval of these was a matter of honour and pride, vital both to Rome and to himself; it was achieved in 20 BC by himself and his young stepson, Tiberius Claudius Nero, by means of a combination of diplomacy and armed threat. The success was paraded on the coinage, and in contemporary literature (Virgil, *Aeneid* VII.606) and cited prominently in Augustus' *Res Gestae* (29,2).

Plate 6.2 (opposite) Britannia, Colchester (Camulodunum): reconstruction of the Temple of the Imperial Cult, built by Claudius. Source: Colchester Museums.

Augustus kept up the pressure on the Parthians: almost certainly, Tiberius would have been sent to the area in 6 BC, had he not decided to retire from public life to the island of Rhodes; Augustus' elder adopted son, Gaius Caesar, went to the east in AD 1. The problem of persuading the Parthians to a reasonable stance over Armenia was clearly regarded as requiring an imperial presence of high profile. When Tiberius succeeded Augustus, he found the area in turmoil once more and, in AD 17, he sent his heir, Germanicus, to resolve a number of problems. Germanicus succeeded by agreement in securing on the Armenian throne a king acceptable both to Rome and Parthia (Zeno/Artaxias), who remained in power until his death in AD 34. Germanicus also revoked a number of client monarchies and re-organised the territories concerned as provinces (*Cappadocia* and *Commagene*). This Tiberian settlement would probably have been hailed more enthusiastically, had the diplomatic achievement not been overshadowed by the death of Germanicus in the east and its complex and vicious dynastic ramifications.

By the time that Artaxias died, Tiberius was in his self-imposed seclusion on Capreae, and the Parthian king, Artabanus III, was convinced that he could operate with a free hand, installing his own nominee on the Armenian throne and threatening, like Mithridates before him, to drive the Roman presence out of Asia Minor. To his – and, no doubt, many other people's – surprise, Tiberius acted wisely and decisively, sending out Lucius Vitellius (father of the future emperor) to be governor of Syria. By the end of Tiberius' reign, the crisis was passed, and Artabanus had accepted the Roman will; ironically, it was at the time Caligula who won the plaudits for this rather than his predecessor.

Caligula's contribution to stability in the region was characteristically theatrical but broadly in line with the previous reliance on diplomacy. His construction of a 'Bridge of Boats' across the Bay of Naples, although regarded by some, in antiquity and since, as a sign of his insanity, seems to have been designed to convey a forceful message eastwards. We are told that he rode across this 'bridge', wearing the breastplate of Alexander the Great and accompanied by a young Parthian 'hostage', Dareus. The 'feat' itself was clearly designed to emulate that of the Persian king, Xerxes, in his attack on the Greeks in the fifth century BC. In all, it was a forceful and timely warning to Artabanus of the consequences of interfering with the recent treaty.

The last serious disturbance in this area came late in Claudius' reign, and the resolution of it was the responsibility of Nero, although it took most of his reign to achieve it. Nero's approach showed considerable flexibility, following the initial failure to come to an agreement with the Parthians. The threat of force in the region was constantly present in the person of the talented Domitius Corbulo; when the Parthians insisted on a king of Armenia of their choosing (Tiridates), Nero first of all imposed a Roman nominee and when that failed set out upon the annexation of Armenia as a province. In the end, a compromise was reached, with Rome accepting Tiridates but insisting that he come to Rome to receive his diadem personally from Nero. Amidst great pomp and circumstance, this happened in AD 66 with Tiridates saluting Nero as the god, Mithras, and Nero ceremonially closing the gates of the Temple of Janus to signify that the Roman world was entirely at peace.

An immediate dividend of the peace with the Parthians was Rome's ability in the last years of Nero's reign to turn its full attention to the mounting problems of Judaea, which broke into open warfare in AD 67. These problems, which came to a head in Nero's reign, were not new and do not offer a specific comment on the quality of provincial government in that period.

Essentially, the Jewish state and domination by Rome were incompatible ideas, since many Jews looked not just towards independence from Rome but to domination of the world by themselves. Judaea had been a province under an equestrian procurator since Augustus' time, with the exception of a brief return to a client monarchy under Claudius' friend, Herod Agrippa, between AD 41 and 44. The procurators tended to work through the Sadducees, although the feuding within this group made them rather ineffective. On the other hand, the Pharisees were more alive to the desired destiny of a Jewish state – particularly the most extreme of their group, the Zealots.

There is little indication that the standard of provincial government in Judaea had been particularly low, although Caligula's decision to have his statue erected in the temple at Jerusalem had caused a furore until it was rescinded. Tacitus alleges that Antonius Felix (procurator, AD 52–60) had behaved highhandedly, although this may reflect no more than the historian's antipathy towards a man whose brother was Claudius' freedman, Pallas. The immediate cause of the trouble in Nero's reign appears to have been a decision in AD 66 of the procurator, Gessius Florus, to infringe the temple sanctuary by taking from the treasury money which was 'due to Caesar'.

Riots broke out in Jerusalem, and a fortress at Masada was taken and its garrison annihilated; simultaneous disturbances broke out among Jews of the *Diaspora*, and in Egypt, the prefect, Tiberius Julius Alexander, used legionary troops to quell riots in Alexandria. If war was not already inevitable, it was made so when Cestius Gallus (governor of Syria), who had entered Judaea with legionary troops, was attacked. The death of Gallus during the winter of AD 66–67 enabled Nero to introduce revised arrangements in the area.

Licinius Mucianus was sent out as the new governor of Syria, and a new Judaean command established under the future emperor, Vespasian. He was given three legions; with them he worked systematically through Judaea, and was in a position to besiege Jerusalem by the summer of AD 68, when news came of Nero's death. This led to an interruption of operations, while Vespasian and Mucianus consulted on political matters leading to a decision in AD 69 by Vespasian to put himself forward as a candidate for imperial power.

Jerusalem eventually fell to Vespasian's son, Titus, in the summer of AD 70, though resistance continued in Judaea until the fall of

Plate 6.3 Gallia Narbonensis: Pont du Gard Aqueduct.
Source: photographed by J. Witherington

Masada in 73. The temple was destroyed in an effort to break the heart of Jewish nationhood. Although the payments which all Jews traditionally made to the temple were transferred to Jupiter Capitolinus in Rome, the basic privileges which the Romans had long accorded to the Jews remained: local freedom of worship, together with immunity from military service and from imperial cult worship. The Roman victory was celebrated in Rome, and scenes from the celebrations can be seen on the Arch of Titus,

Plate 6.4 Gallia Narbonensis: Nimes, Amphitheatre.
Source: photographed by J. Witherington

which was erected at the southern end of the *Via Sacra*, the road
leading out of the Forum.

Romanisation

Virgil's exhortations regarding the use of Rome's military might
were set into a broader context – that of a 'civilising mission'.
Indeed, military conquest was not, except perhaps in the minds

Plate 6.5 *Gallia Narbonensis: Nimes, Maison Carrée.*
Source: photographed by J. Witherington

Plate 6.6 *Gallia Lugdunensis: Vienne, Temple of Augustus and Livia (possibly 'modelled' on the Temple of Mars the Avenger in the Forum of Augustus at Rome).*
Source: photographed by J. Witherington

of a few 'traditionalists', an end in itself; its purpose was to establish the conditions in which a culture of Romanisation could flourish. Bringing together and fusing Roman and 'native' cultures was essential if the provinces were to accept the imposition of Roman taxes and, where relevant, successfully provide a buffer between Italy and Rome's more distant enemies. Only thus could prosperity be realised in the provinces, and with it internal security and the participation of wealthy locals in the administration of their own provinces and (eventually) the empire at large. Romanisation was, therefore, a crucial part of the process of empire building.

Of course, the forms which this might take were inevitably different in different parts of the empire, for a range of indigenous cultures and 'levels' of civilisation had to be taken into account. Urbanisation, for example, was clearly a different concept to Rome's subjects in Britain compared with those in the Greek east. Further, religious experiences and social and economic complexities varied across the empire, as well as the nature of government and administration.

As we have seen, during the Republic the pace of expansion and the quality of provincial administration were very varied; indeed, the latter was often extremely poor with little real opportunity for provincials to seek redress. Early in his *Annals*, however, Tacitus states unequivocally that the provinces gained substantially with the advent of the Augustan system; although obviously inefficiency and corruption were not banished overnight (as the rebellion of Boudica in Britain during Nero's reign shows), the introduction of salaries for officials and the emperor's ability to check and, if necessary, deploy sanctions against those who offended greatly improved the quality of provincial government: Tiberius' requirement that his 'sheep should be sheared, not flayed' was typical of the Julio-Claudians and most later emperors. There was a sound logic behind such attitudes: provincials would be more content with their status and those who were enterprising would prosper. This in its turn would provide them with greater scope in contributing to local administration, and

Plate 6.7 (opposite) Asia, Aspendus: exterior of the Theatre.

Rome's share of the prosperity (through taxation) would be enhanced. Further, it is stated by Tacitus (in an oration attributed to Vespasian's relation, Quintus Petillius Cerialis, – *Histories* IV.73–4) that the provinces enjoyed an even standard of government and did not suffer unduly from the activities of wayward emperors.

How, then, was the Romanisation of provinces managed? Romanisation was not a straitjacket, and changes were not introduced into provinces merely for the sake of change. Roman attitudes in such areas as local administration, religion and even taxation demonstrate that pre-Roman practices which worked were broadly retained with a minimum of modification. In many cases, this was relatively simple to achieve, as new provinces which bordered on older ones usually had pro-Roman groups who were already involved in the empire's economic network. Britain, added to the empire in AD 43, provides a clear example of this; indeed,

some local leaders may already have enjoyed formal political ties with the Roman government as client monarchs. In Britain, for example, it appears that Cogidubnus (a leader of the Atrebates of southern England) and Prasutagus (of the Iceni of East Anglia) both enjoyed a period after conquest in which effectively they acted as the emperor's governing agents in their tribal territories. Elsewhere, we may note the practice of taking to Rome young sons of ruling families to be educated in Roman ways and (probably) to act as 'hostages' against the good behaviour of their families. Thus, as we have seen, when Caligula mounted his 'Bridge of Boats' extravaganza across the Bay of Naples, he was accompanied by Dareus, a son of the king of Parthia. Such Romanised 'princes' might eventually be returned as client rulers of their ancestral kingdoms. Another method was to send teachers to new provinces; thus, Demetrius of Tarsus was in Britain during Agricola's governorship, although whether officially or on his own initiative is unclear.

One of the hallmarks of Romanisation was a local administration based on towns, with a high quality of services in these towns and good communication between them. Where necessary, the governor provided the impetus to set this in motion (Tacitus, *Life of Agricola* 21). In the east of the empire, such conditions were often already in place; in the west, more often than not some investment was required – either directly from the resources of local people or with money borrowed from Roman financiers (which had, of course, to be repaid with interest). In their keenness to participate, new provincials may on occasion have proved to be over-eager to take out loans, only to find themselves in difficulties later. Nero's tutor, the philosopher, Seneca, was just one financier who was prepared to lend money to provincials for such ventures. We know that Cornovian leaders at Wroxeter found themselves in financial difficulties as they accepted responsibility for the building of *Viroconium Cornoviorum* in the later first century AD, as apparently did their 'counterparts' on the other side of the empire in the province of Bithynia in Asia Minor in the early second century (Pliny, *Letters* X.39).

Britain shows us the processes of Romanisation and urbanisation in action: initially, much of the new province came under a direct military supervision; conquest and military consolidation led to the establishment of forts and a network of roads. Most of the forts, because they contained well-paid troops, rapidly attracted extramural civilians to provide for the troops' needs; such settlements were effectively urban. As the army moved on, forts were abandoned as military centres, and they, together with their adjacent civilian settlements, could be re-developed as towns for a population that was becoming Romanised; Cirencester provides a prime example of this process.

Romans visualised towns in a hierarchical structure, which had its origins centuries before in the process of Romanising Italy. At the top, there were *coloniae*, towns built as 'flagships' of the new order whose inhabitants were already Roman citizens – in most cases, especially later, retired legionaries. These men had land inside and

Plate 6.8 (opposite) Asia, Aspendus: interior of the Theatre.

outside the towns and encouraged Romanisation by marrying locally and by providing an economic and religious focus. In Britain, there were three of these before the end of the first century AD – at Colchester, Lincoln and Gloucester. Such towns may in time have proved to be rather elitist, as is demonstrated, for example, by the contrast between a rather static Gloucester and a far more vibrant 'native' town at Cirencester. On the other side of the country, however, the *colonia* of Colchester seems to have largely overshadowed the 'native' town of Chelmsford; similarly, in Gaul, we learn that the 'colonists' at *Lugdunum* (Lyons) looked down on the neighbouring 'native' town of *Vienna* (Vienne).

Second in the hierarchy was the *municipium*; the status of this town derived from a grant of Roman citizenship or 'Latin rights' made to an already-existing group of people. One such town in Britain was St Albans (*Verulamium*), where the grant of status presumably represented a recognition of an important group or was a reward for 'services rendered'. Roman *Verulamium* was not, however, built on a pre-Roman site; in terms of location and content, most of the pre-Roman centres (*oppida*) of the Catuvellauni would have been unsuitable for direct conversion into Romanised towns.

There has been considerable discussion over the significance of grants of 'Latin status' (*Latium*): a reading of the *Tabula Irnitana* (of the Flavian period; from Irni in *Hispania Baetica*) suggests that citizens of *municipia* with *Latium* enjoyed rights/privileges midway between those of full and non-citizens; in this way, communities were upgraded and those who lived in them drawn more fully into a Roman civil framework. Those who served as magistrates in these towns received citizenship at the end of their terms of office. There is uncertainty, however, about whether grants were made for individuals in the communities or for communities as a whole. At any rate, the grants encouraged communities to develop into regular urban entities. While the provisions of the *Tabula Irnitana* were initiated in the early 70s by Vespasian and

Titus, they did not reach their final form until the reign of Domitian.

Below the *municipia* came towns whose inhabitants did not enjoy Roman citizenship and which are known as *civitas* centres – that is, administrative centres for the Romanised tribes; these, too, like the *municipia*, were often constructed on new sites. Ultimately, the *municipia* and the *civitas* centres were dependent for their survival and development on administrative and economic success. As we have seen, this could vary a great deal from town to town and from type to type. Archaeological evidence has shown recently that a 'prestige' town, which was established in Hadrian's reign near the site of later Peterborough, was by the early third century experiencing widespread dereliction – perhaps the wrong town in the wrong place at the wrong time.

In Britain, of course, as in other central and western European provinces, Romanised towns were visually very different from their predecessors, even if functionally they may have had much in common. Technical help in such building projects was, however, closer to hand than financial help – in the form of the architects and engineers of the Roman army, who frequently took on such 'pioneer' roles; in Britain, for example, the close physical resemblances between the town-centre squares (*fora*) and military headquarters buildings (*principia*) and between the designs and execution of civilian and military bath-houses demonstrate clearly the military contribution. Similarly, the construction of civilian theatres and amphitheatres owed much to that of legionary amphitheatres (as at Caerleon in south Wales). Once constructed, the upkeep and development of such buildings became the responsibility of local leaders; it was thus imperative that their prosperity should continue and grow.

Here, again, appropriate policies from central government were vital, although the most important impetus came from conquest and occupation themselves. The well-paid soldiers in their fortresses and forts represented vibrant markets with their constant need of goods and services. People were attracted into the near vicinity of such establishments to satisfy these needs. The economic chain stretched into the wider hinterland, so that considerable sections of the population of any province stood to profit from the presence of the army. The evidence also shows that traders and craftsmen might be attracted over considerable distances, such as Barates, the sculptor from Palmyra (Syria), who worked at South Shields. The presence of such people, together with that of the multi-ethnic Roman army, points to the likelihood that the populations of most provinces of the Roman Empire must have become markedly cosmopolitan.

The means to prosper, therefore, clearly existed, and they would burgeon provided that taxation policies and tax collection did not prove to be an obstruction. The collection of direct taxes (on Roman citizens), of the grain tithe and of indirect taxes (on sales and inheritance) now came under the department of the procurator. Although private companies were still employed in this, they were not involved in the business of assessment, and it was up to the procurator and his officials to ensure that injustices either did not occur or were put right if they did. Boudica's rebellion in Britain shows what could happen with an inefficient or corrupt procurator, although we should remember that the procurator was appointed by the emperor, with responsibility directly to him; most emperors reacted promptly and toughly in cases of negligence or malpractice on the part of their officials. They recognised that discontent on the part of provincials was not in their interest nor in that of imperial security.

Trading and its success provided great momentum to the process of Romanisation, as the third-century historian, Dio Cassius, makes abundantly clear in his description of German tribesmen during the period of Augustus (56.18,2):

> The barbarians were adapting themselves to Roman ways, were becoming accustomed to hold markets, and were meeting in peaceful assemblages. They had not, however, forgotten their

ancestral habits, their old life of independence, or the power derived from arms. Hence, so long as they were unlearning these customs gradually and by the way, as one may say, under careful watching, they were not disturbed by the change in their manner of life, and were becoming different without knowing it.

Wealth was essential to progress in a Romanised environment, because, in the course of local administration, one had to be able personally to defray considerable expenses. Thus, it will have been common for wealthy provincial subjects to emulate Rome's own aristocracy by investing in land. Further, Nero is on record as attempting to increase individual wealth by taxation reforms which were designed to encourage increased trade.

If the possession of wealth opened up opportunities in local administration, wealth and Roman citizenship together enabled a man to go much further. From the time of Julius Caesar, Roman emperors consciously increased the citizen roll to reward and to encourage. Among the Julio-Claudians, Claudius was particularly active in this field; he is on record as having granted citizenship to a group of Alpine tribes who had usurped it, on the grounds that, in addition to the benefits, they had taken on the responsibilities of citizenship (*ILS* 206). Another document of the same reign (*ILS* 212) shows the emperor anxious to grant senatorial status to some former tribal leaders in Gaul – albeit in the face of Italian opposition – to draw them into the heart of administration and policy making. The effectiveness of this is dramatically demonstrated by the numbers of men of provincial origin who, by the end of the first century AD, were enjoying careers in the senatorial and equestrian branches of the emperors' service. While the process might have started relatively slowly under the early Julio-Claudians because of the sensitivity of those emperors over their relationship with a senate that was still traditionally inclined, it accelerated rapidly from the middle of the Julio-Claudian period, when the numbers of senators deriving from Republican nobility will have fallen away markedly. This social change encouraged the development of a new ethic in public service, as is shown clearly by the comments of Tacitus (*Life of Agricola* 42) on the qualities expected. In short, the social change in membership of Rome's 'upper classes' enhanced the importance of senators and equestrians as individuals, whilst reducing the significance of the bodies to which they belonged.

A powerful asset to the process of Romanisation was provided by religion, which in most parts of the empire was polytheistic in nature; the Roman pantheon could be set alongside such systems, particularly since the gods presided over designated functions. Apart from those cases where the Romans encountered monotheistic systems (for example, in Judaeism and Christianity), the official attitude was one of toleration based on the assumption that people would be stabilised more effectively and rapidly if allowed to continue to seek the protection of the gods that they regarded as traditional. These could themselves be 'Romanised' through the process known as *interpretatio Romana*, in which gods from different systems but with similar protective functions could be 'fused' into a single deity.

The practice of religion, therefore, was intended to produce a degree of homogeneity, but also to allow Romanisation to assume a local 'flavour'. Thus, with the exception of the Jewish people (in both Judaea and the *Diaspora*), the 'imperial cult' was introduced universally. It did not require provincials necessarily to believe that Roman emperors were gods, although many – particularly in the eastern provinces where ruler worship was long established – undoubtedly did. Officially, the object of attention was the *genius* or *numen* of the emperor, a kind of guardian spirit which existed within him and which he represented. Some emperors, notably Tiberius, set their faces strongly against any implication that they were themselves divine; Tiberius, for example, refused to allow worship of himself directly in Spain, although in common with most he went along with it in the east. The chief sites for the cult – for example, the temple at Colchester and the altars at Lyons and Cologne – effectively provided the focal point for the expression of the loyalty of a province to Rome and its emperor.

The Olympian deities, too, provided a Roman focus: Jupiter (the Greatest and Best) obviously represented Rome; we see, for example, a 'Jupiter column' in the forum at Cirencester, while at Dougga (in north Africa) the forum was dominated by a magnificent temple to the god. A local influence, however, may be seen at Sbeitla (in Tunisia) where the forum was headed by a triple-temple complex, which was Romanised as the Capitoline triad. Others of the Olympians, with their emphasis on functional protection, provided a link between Rome and its provincial subjects through their everyday activities. Britain gives ample evidence of these Romano-Celtic cults, in which the deities themselves were housed in so-called Romano-Celtic temples, which represented architecturally and structurally the Romanisation of the more ephemeral buildings that had existed in pre-Roman society. Some of these cults will have been helped in their diffusion by the presence of the army and the demobilisation of soldiers into the community. Mars and Hercules were particularly notable in this respect, the latter appropriately cultivated because of his natural appeal to many emperors. Vulcan, the 'smith-god', was popular among the artisans in civilian settlements, while Apollo may well have become widespread for his 'musical responsibility' and connection with military musicians, as did Mercury because of his 'involvement' with commerce.

The spread of communications within the empire also encouraged the movement of non-Roman cults, particularly those from the east. There had long been a natural antipathy in Rome towards many of these because, as we have seen, their often-exotic rituals were regarded as morally subversive, and political subversion was feared, too. In some cases, cults were curtailed (as happened to the cult of Dionysus in 186 BC) or subjected to disdain and contempt (as seen in Juvenal's withering attack on the Egyptian cults in *Satire* XV). The real basis of the fear is, however, seen in Tiberius' attack on Egyptian and Jewish cult groups in Rome in AD 19. In both cases, what worried the emperor was obviously the fear of the possible moral subversion, especially with Roman womanhood as its target.

However, despite individual fears, the practice of foreign cults increased; presumably, devotees were taken with the 'personal' relationship with a deity to them which contrasted favourably with the coldly national focus of Rome's state deities. The spread of such cults was enhanced, too, by the acceleration of travel in the empire, particularly in the service of trade and by the growingly cosmopolitan nature of Romanised society at all levels. It was only a matter of time before such eastern cults became parts of the way of life for people highly placed in Roman government – even the emperor himself and his family. As with the state cults, we find an imperial interest translated into a wider, although generally temporary, popular interest. Thus, the cult of Jupiter Dolichenus – from Doliche (Syria), the birthplace of Julia Domna, the consort of Septimius Severus – made an appearance in Britain, presumably in the time of the Severi; in the same way, the cult of the Egyptian god, Serapis, made a high-profile appearance at York, when the emperor and his entourage were using the fortress as their campaign base between AD 209 and 211. The most generally popular, however, were the cults of Sol (the Sun) and Mithras, both of whom evidently came to be thought of almost as elements of the Roman pantheon.

Such tolerance, however, was not generally afforded to the monotheistic religions. During the Julio-Claudian period, Christianity did not develop sufficiently for it to be recognised as a serious problem; Nero's attack on the sect in Rome, following the fire of AD 64, was little more than a piece of opportunism on his part. Christians were regarded as a splinter group of Judaism, and the recognition of specific doctrinal conflicts with Christians did not emerge until the reign of Trajan early in the second century AD.

With regard to the Jews, however, the potential for conflict had emerged early on, and the Romans put in place a policy designed to avoid it – by giving exemptions from military service and imperial cult observance. Rome clearly recognised the sensitivity of the Jewish people, but probably not the depth of it. Thus, for some Jewish leaders (the Zealots), the exemptions were virtually irrelevant, and what was at stake was effectively a refusal to co-operate on any terms with a policy of Romanisation.

In the main, however, Romanisation was a vital process, but one which was pursued with some care; education, inducement, physical aid, religious toleration and social, political and economic development all played their parts in persuading the 'vanquished' that co-operation was in their interests as much as Rome's. The 'programme' was aimed at local aristocracies, following the long-established Roman principle that, on grounds of birth, wealth and experience, these were the people with whom Rome could naturally do business; with their co-operation, the acquiescence of the rest would almost inevitably follow. Those that benefited would see the justice of Tacitus' assessment of Romanisation and would readily reject that critique of the policy put (by Tacitus) into the mouth of the Caledonian chieftain, Calgacus, before his battle with Agricola in AD 83 – 'They create a desolation and call it peace.' The *Pax Romana*, instituted by Caesar and Augustus and developed by their successors, was much more than that.

Appendix 1

The Distribution of the Legions during the Julio-Claudian Period

(a) At the time of Augustus' death (AD 14): 25 legions

Nearer Spain	IV *Macedonica*; VI *Victrix*; X *Gemina*	3
Upper Germany	II *Augusta*; XIII *Gemina*; XIV *Gemina Martia Victrix*; XVI *Gallica*	4
Lower Germany	I *Germanica*; V *Alaudae*; XX *Valeria Victrix*; XXI *Rapax*	4
Upper Illyria	VII *Macedonica*; XI *'Actiaca'*	2
Lower Illyria	VIII *Augusta*; IX *Hispana*; XV *Apollinaris*	3
Macedonia/Moesia	IV *Scythica*; V *Macedonica*	2
Syria	III *Gallica*, VI *Ferrata*; X *Fretensis*; XII *Fulminata*	4
Egypt	III *Cyrenaica*; XXII *Deiotariana*	2
Africa	III *Augusta*	1

(b) The reign of Claudius (*c.* AD 46): 27 legions

Nearer Spain	VI *Victrix*; X *Gemina*	2
Britain	II *Augusta*; IX *Hispana*; XIV *Gemina Martia Victrix*; XX *Valeria Victrix*	4
Upper Germany	IV *Macedonica*; XXI *Rapax*; XXII *Primigenia*	3
Lower Germany	I *Germanica*; V *Alaudae*; XV *Primigenia*; XVI *Gallica*	4
Dalmatia	VII *Claudia Pia Fidelis*; XI *Claudia Pia Fidelis* (formerly *Macedonica* and '*Actiaca*')	2
Pannonia	XIII *Gemina*; XV *Apollinaris*	2
Moesia	IV *Scythica*; V *Macedonica*; VII *Augusta*	3
Syria	III *Gallica*; VI *Ferrata*; X *Fretensis*; XII *Fulminata*	4
Egypt	III *Cyrenaica*; XXII *Deiotariana*	2
Africa	III *Augusta*	1

(c) The reign of Nero (*c.* AD 63): 27 legions

Nearer Spain	VI *Victrix*	1
Britain	II *Augusta*; IX *Hispana*; XIV *Gemina Martia Victrix*; XX *Valeria Victrix*	4
Upper Germany	IV *Macedonica*; XXI *Rapax*; XXII *Primigenia*	3
Lower Germany	I *Germanica*; V *Alaudae*; XV *Primigenia*; XVI *Gallica*	4
Dalmatia	XI *Claudia Pia Fidelis*	1
Pannonia	X *Gemina*; XIII *Gemina*	2
Moesia	VII *Claudia Pia Fidelis*; VIII *Augusta*	2
Syria/Armenia	III *Gallica*; IV *Scythica*; X *Fretensis*; XII *Fulminata*; V *Macedonica*; VI *Ferrata*; XV *Apollinaris*	7
Egypt	III *Cyrenaica*; XXII *Deiotariana*	2
Africa	III *Augusta*	1

(d) The Civil War (late in AD 68): 30 legions

Nearer Spain	VI *Victrix*; X *Gemina*	2
Britain	II *Augusta*; IX *Hispana*; XX *Valeria Victrix*	3
Upper Germany	IV *Macedonica*; XXI *Rapax*; XXII *Primigenia*	3
Lower Germany	I *Germanica*; V *Alaudae*; XV *Primigenia*; XVI *Gallica*	4
Gaul (Lugdunensis)	I *Italica*	1
Rome	I *Adiutrix*	1
Dalmatia	XI *Claudia Pia Fidelis*; XIV *Gemina Martia Victrix*	2
Pannonia	VII *Galbiana*; XIII *Gemina*	2
Moesia	III *Gallica*; VII *Claudia Pia Fidelis*; VIII *Augusta*	3
Syria	IV *Scythica*; VI *Ferrata*; XII *Fulminata*	3
Judaea	V *Macedonica*; X *Fretensis*; XV *Apollinaris*	3
Egypt	III *Cyrenaica*; XXII *Deiotariana*	2
Africa	III *Augusta*	1

Overall area distribution of legions

AD	14	46	63	68
Britain	–	4	4	3
Italy	–	–	–	1
Germany/the West	11	9	8	10
Central/Eastern Europe	7	7	5	7
The East	4	4	7	6
North Africa	3	3	3	3
Total	25	27	27	30

Appendix 2

Dates of acquisition of the provinces of the Roman Empire

BC	241	Sicily
	238	Sardinia; Corsica
	198	Hispania Tarraconensis and Baetica
	146	Africa; Macedonia
	133	Asia
	121	Gallia Transalpina (Narbonensis)
	100(?)	Cilicia
	89	Gallia Cisalpina (Northern Italy)
	74	Cyrene
	67	Crete
	63	Bithynia–Pontus; Syria
	58	Cyprus
	53(?)	Dalmatia
	51	Gallia Lugdunensis and Belgica

Battle of Actium

	30	Egypt
	27	Aquitania; Achaea
	25	Galatia
	16	Lusitania
	15	Raetia; Noricum
	14	Cottian Alps; Maritime Alps
AD	6	Moesia; Judaea
	10	Pannonia
	12	Germania Superior and Inferior
	17	Commagene; Cappadocia
	40	Mauretania Caesariensis and Tingitana
	43	Britain; Lycia
	46	Thrace
	106	Dacia; Arabia
	114	Armenia
	115	Mesopotamia; Assyria

Appendix 3

The status of the provinces in AD 14

In these lists, the provinces are given in two groups – imperial and senatorial; the status of each province is expressed in terms of the status of its governor: (a) ex-consul; (b) ex-praetor; (c) equestrian.

Imperial provinces

(a)	Dalmatia	2 legions
(c)	Egypt	2 legions
(b)	Galatia	
(b)	Gallia Aquitania	
(b)	Gallia Lugdunensis	
(b)	Gallia Belgica	
(a)	Germania Inferior	4 legions
(a)	Germania Superior	4 legions
(b)	Lusitania	
(a)	Hispania Tarraconensis	3 legions
(c)	Judaea	
(a)	Moesia	2 legions
(c)	Noricum	
(a)	Pannonia	3 legions
(c)	Raetia	
(c)	Sardinia–Corsica	
(a)	Syria	4 legions

Senatorial Provinces

(a)	Africa	1 legion
(a)	Asia	
(b)	Crete–Cyrene	
(b)	Cyprus	
(b)	Gallia Narbonensis	
(b)	Hispania Baetica	
(b)	Macedonia–Achaea	
(b)	Bithynia–Pontus	
(b)	Sicily	

Appendix 4

The Roman Empire in AD 14

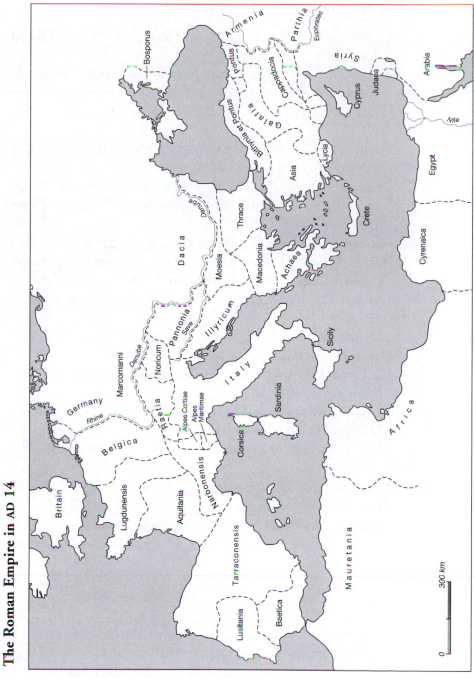

Source: D. Shotter, *The Fall of the Roman Republic*, Lancaster Pamphlets (London: Routledge, 1994). p. 40.

Further reading

Bowersock G. W., *Augustus and the Greek World* (Oxford, 1965).

Broughton T. R. S. *The Romanisation of Africa Proconsularis* (Baltimore, MD, 1929).

Cheeseman G. L., *The Auxilia of the Roman Imperial Army* (Oxford, 1914).

Cunliffe B. W., *Greeks, Romans and Barbarians* (London, 1988).

Drinkwater J. F., *Roman Gaul* (London, 1983).

Ferguson J., *The Religions of the Roman Empire* (London, 1970).

Garnsey P., *Social Status and Legal Privilege in the Roman Empire* (Oxford, 1970).

Garnsey P. and Saller R., *The Roman Empire* (London, 1987).

Jackson R. P. J. and Potter T. W., *Excavations at Stonea, Cambridgeshire, 1980–85* (London, 1996).

Kennedy D. and Riley D., *Rome's Desert Frontier from the Air* (London, 1990).

La Baume P., *The Romans on the Rhine* (Bonn, n.d.).

Lintott A., *Imperium Romanum* (London, 1993).

MacDonald W. L., *The Architecture of the Roman Empire* (New Haven, CT, 1982).

Magie D., *Roman Rule in Asia Minor* (Princeton, NJ, 1950).

Mattingly D., *Tripolitania* (London, 1995).

Millar F. G. B., *The Roman Empire and its Neighbours* (London, 1981).

Millett M., *The Romanisation of Britain* (Cambridge, 1990).

Parker H. M. D., *The Roman Legions* (Oxford, 1928).

Rivet A. L. F., *Gallia Narbonensis* (London, 1988).

Starr C. G., *The Roman Empire, 27 B.C.–A.D. 476* (Oxford, 1982).

Sutherland C. H. V., *The Romans in Spain, 217 B.C.–A.D. 117* (London, 1939).

Todd M., *The Northern Barbarians, 100 B.C–A.D. 300* (Oxford, 1987).

Todd M., *Roman Britain* (Oxford, 1999).

Webster G., *The Roman Imperial Army* (London, 1969).

Wells C. M., *The German Policy of Augustus* (Oxford, 1972).

Whittaker C. R., *The Frontiers of the Roman Empire* (London, 1994).

Wilkes J. J., *Dalmatia* (London, 1969).

Woolf G., *Becoming Roman* (Cambridge, 1998).

Chapter 7

The secret of empire

The Julio-Claudians and the Roman army

The Julio-Claudian dynasty, founded by Caesar and Augustus, collapsed with the military rebellion against and subsequent suicide of Nero in AD 68. Tacitus (*Hist.* I.8) recognised the significance of this: 'The secret of empire was out – that an emperor could be made elsewhere than at Rome'. In other words, just as in the late Republic, it was the pressure that could be exerted by the Roman army and its commanders that controlled events rather than political and dynastic arrangements conducted in Rome.

We have seen (in Chapter 5) that a major feature of the Augustan settlement consisted of reforms to the terms of service and the command structure of the Roman army, particularly of the legions. The effect of these changes, taken together with the fact that the army annually renewed an oath of allegiance to the *princeps*, was to make the position of Augustus dependent on the loyalty of legions and commanders. Such loyalty would presumably survive as long as commanders and men entertained sufficient respect for and fear of the power of the *princeps* over them. This 'military despotism' was less offensive to most than it might have been because of the fact that the armies were posted in the provinces and on the frontiers, and because the terms in place for demobilisation were structurally less disruptive than had been the case during the Republic. Augustus further minimised any potential danger to himself by posting his twenty-eight legions in relatively small groups. Even the 9000 strong Praetorian Guard was, until the middle years of Tiberius' reign, split into smaller units and barracked at a distance from Rome. The decision, however, evidently made in *c.* AD 21 at the urging of the prefect, Lucius Aelius Sejanus, to bring the guard under one 'roof' at Rome greatly emphasised the sensitivity and potential of their role.

Although none of Augustus' successors (prior to Nero) was seriously threatened with rebellion, each of them had reason to be aware of the need positively to keep the army and its commanders on side. Evidently, the danger was realised at the very moment of Augustus' death in AD 14; Tiberius was faced immediately with outbreaks of unrest among the legions of the Rhine and the Danube. Indeed, Tacitus records that the moment was deliberately chosen because the new *princeps* would be unsure of his position and would presumably for that reason be more ready to grant concessions over service conditions. Undoubtedly, the stability, particularly of the Rhine legions, had been upset by the need for a crash programme of recruitment to make good the losses of the Varus disaster of AD 9. Both armies plainly contained some men who might otherwise have been excluded as undesirable and who were articulate and thus charismatic in the eyes of their colleagues.

While a deterioration in service conditions clearly lay at the root of both of these outbreaks, and the granting or promise of concessions was helpful in the regaining of control, a hint of greater danger to imperial stability was provided by an approach made by some of the Rhine mutineers to their commander, Tiberius' adopted son and heir, Germanicus Caesar: they offered to support him in a bid for personal power (and the ousting of Tiberius), if he would guarantee to give in to their demands.

Germanicus' loyalty to Tiberius was steadfast, but Tiberius is said to have been worried by the implications of the episode; indeed, some of the new recruits may well have been aware of what common rumour in Rome made of the tense and suspicious relationship between Tiberius and Germanicus. It has to be said, too, that Germanicus' unguarded behaviour and what looked like the provocative conduct of his wife, Agrippina, served to exacerbate the tensions.

Both mutinies were eventually brought under control, and the potential threat to Tiberius' authority removed. However, much rested on the fact that on this occasion there was no hint of disloyalty on the part of the commanders. The episodes had, nonetheless, demonstrated that the potential for disruption had not been removed by the Augustan reforms.

Without doubt, the decision to bring the Praetorian Guard into Rome strengthened its political role and gave its commanders considerable leverage. Against a background of Tiberius' developing desire to detach himself from Rome, both Sejanus and his successor, Macro, wielded great power in the second half of the reign. Indeed, it is doubtful whether Tiberius could himself have managed the removal of Sejanus, had he not had Macro on hand to guarantee the Guard's quiescence. The Praetorian Guard and its commanders had become virtual kingmakers in Rome – a role that became clear in the removal of Caligula and the accession of Claudius in AD 41, and again in the accession of Nero in AD 54. Further, the Guard took a decisive role in the removal of Nero in 68 when its commander, Nymphidius Sabinus, accepted the promise of a bribe from Galba to change allegiance; the eventual non-payment of that bribe proved crucial to the Guard's decision in January AD 69 to withdraw its support from Galba and transfer it to Otho.

There were during the period a number of occasions when attempts were made to tamper with the allegiance of groups of legions: in AD 39, it was prompt action by Caligula which averted a rebellion engineered on the Rhine by Gnaeus Cornelius Lentulus Gaetulicus evidently in collaboration with Marcus Lepidus, the emperor's ambitious brother-in-law. It seems possible, in view of Caligula's decision suddenly to depose both of the consuls of AD 39, that support for this rebellion was widespread and that a considerable number of the senatorial aristocracy had become alert to their ability to manipulate sections of the army for their own ends. Yet, the army was no 'easy touch' for discontented members of the governing class; in AD 42, Furius Scribonianus tried to raise two of the Danubian legions against Claudius but failed because the legions (VII and XI) remained loyal to the *princeps*. Presumably, the fact that Claudius was the brother of the popular Germanicus was a decisive factor in this. Nero was to prove to be less fortunate when elements of the army started to turn against him in AD 68.

The largely static nature of the army began to be an influence in itself; it is clear that many of the legions were coming to feel comfortable in their postings. One of the factors which led to Gaetulicus' rebellion against Caligula was the low level of discipline which Gaetulicus had allowed to develop over a considerable period. It also showed the danger that might still be posed by aristocrats of old families and by keeping them in their commands for extended periods: Gaetulicus had been ten years on the Rhine. It was important to keep such men frequently on the move to prevent the development of dangerous liaisons – a lesson clearly learned by Vespasian during the civil war with Vitellius and put into practice when he became *princeps* at the end of AD 69. Towards the end of his reign, Nero appears to have tried to marginalise the older nobility, handing military commands to men such as Vespasian and Verginius Rufus, whose social backgrounds seemed to make them less dangerous as rivals.

Rivalry began to emerge between different parts of the army, undoubtedly enhanced by local recruiting; it was a clear phenomenon of AD 68–69 that rivalry between the principal groups of legions bred an *esprit de corps* which demonstrated itself in

Figure 7.1 The western provinces of the Roman Empire. Source: Peter Lee.

naming their own candidates for power against each other. There was some evidence, too, in Nero's last months of rivalry between legions and the auxiliary units alongside which they were stationed. Further, a powerful rivalry developed between the legions and the Praetorian Guard, the latter being regarded as over-privileged and overpaid. The consequences of this became strongly apparent when Vitellius (in April AD 69) yielded to his troops' demand, sacked Otho's Praetorian Guard and installed members of the Rhine legions in their place. Although such a move could have been justified as being in the interests of loyalty, it was undoubtedly the pressures of the men's envy that brought it about.

In all, therefore, by the end of the Julio-Claudian period, the changes instituted by Augustus were beginning to show that they were not foolproof. However, the real potential for damage and disruption was to become abundantly clear in the events of AD 68–9 – the 'Year of the Four Emperors', in which Nero, Galba, Otho and Vitellius were each removed by military insurrection stirred up by restless and ambitious commanders.

The fall of Nero

The precise sequence of events that brought about the fall of Nero has always been difficult to establish because of inconsistencies and contradictions in the surviving sources (principally Plutarch and Dio Cassius). The leaders of the rebellion were Gaius Julius Vindex (governor, probably, of *Gallia Lugdunensis*) and Servius Sulpicius Galba (governor of *Hispania Tarraconensis*); Vindex was of Gallic descent, while Galba hailed from a family of Republican nobility which had remained active in the early Principate. The chief issues which precipitated the rebellion were evidently Nero's murder of his mother some nine years previously and the degree to which he was perceived to have fallen short of the dignity due to his position; this again was in no way a new phenomenon. To this should probably be added restlessness over the perennial problem of taxation, which many will have found burdensome, particularly in areas settled relatively recently into Roman administration.

Later (in January 69) Galba is presented by Tacitus (*Hist.* I.15–16; see Chapter 5, Appendix 1) as making a lengthy oration, a good deal of which was concerned with the dangers of dynasticism; this, after all, represented a denial of the senior position in the *respublica* to all but a few men, and was thus a denial of *libertas*. Nor should we forget that, in AD 65 and 66, conspiracies mounted against Nero had failed and had themselves precipitated some vigorous reprisals on the emperor's part, which will have made life increasingly intolerable for members of the senatorial and equestrian orders, reminding them very sharply of their subordination to the *princeps*.

The opportunity to plan rebellion was undoubtedly provided by Nero's absence in Greece during AD 67, a venture which was undertaken probably to allow him to bask in a popularity which was not evident in Italy, and which Nero clearly needed; this absence was pretty clearly extended for a longer period than was wise. During it, Vindex appears to have taken the opportunity to sound out his colleagues among provincial governors regarding their likely attitude towards a movement aimed at removing Nero. It was, however, perhaps because of his own background that Vindex does not seem to have excited much enthusiasm; indeed, some governors are said to have reported Vindex to Nero.

Against such an unpromising background, we might ask why Vindex embarked on so perilous an enterprise with evidently very few troops committed to him and with his own principal town – the pro-Neronian *Lugdunum* – hostile. Nor at the moment of rebellion – perhaps on the Ides (15th) of March, if we interpret correctly the re-issue of the commemorative EID MAR ('Ides of March') coin type of Brutus and Cassius – had Galba even declared himself to be an ally of Vindex. Even after Galba had joined in (at the beginning of April), Vindex could count only on the troops which he could raise in Gaul, who will have been largely untrained, and on the two legions (VI *Victrix* and the newly raised VII *Galbiana*) from *Tarraconensis*. Vindex would have to expect to take on some or all of the legions of the Rhine, together with the forces which Nero was to put into the field in Italy to hold the line of the River Po.

To give himself a realistic chance, Vindex had to reduce this potentially daunting opposition. How far he succeeded is difficult to assess because of vagueness and inconsistencies in the sources. Further, Tacitus' statement that Nero was subsequently undone more by rumours than by force of arms suggests that there existed contradictory versions regarding the loyalties of the troops involved.

It is certain that Vindex had some support amongst the Gallic *civitates*: to these should be added some Germanic Batavians who were arrested by Fonteius Capito, the commander of *Germania Inferior*; that his stance and that of his army were hostile to Galba and Vindex seems certain from Galba's subsequent murder of him. Batavian support for Vindex may have been important, for some cohorts recruited from the tribe were stationed with legion XIV in the force which Nero later deployed in northern Italy; these cohorts boasted subsequently that they had put pressure on the legion and thus robbed Nero of Italy. Nero may at the time have believed this, but the signals were clearly mixed: Rubrius Gallus, one of the commanders of the Italian force, remained active during AD 68–69, and beyond. This would not suggest him to have been a Neronian loyalist, and in any case he appears to have been a man whose political sympathies were flexible. The other commander, Petronius Turpilianus, was subsequently put to death by Galba, a clear sign of the loyalty to Nero which Plutarch asserts.

It was crucial, however, to Vindex's cause that he should not have to fight Verginius Rufus and the legions of *Germania Superior*, and there is certainly evidence that can be interpreted as indicating that negotiations of some form were taking place between them. A number of factors lend weight to this proposition: first, the siege of *Lugdunum* by Vindex and the march to *Vesontio* (Besançon) by Verginius have the appearance of a 'cover' to allow negotiations to continue. Secondly, surviving accounts of the battle of *Vesontio* indicate that neither commander intended or wanted it; indeed, Vindex's strategy was probably dependent on *not* having to fight the legionaries. It seems clear that the battle was the result of a spontaneous upsurge of mutual hostility between the troops themselves. Thirdly, following the battle and Vindex's consequent suicide, Verginius appears to have 'retired' from the fray. Finally, Galba's subsequent treatment of Verginius – to sack him, but not to kill him – suggests that, in the upshot, Galba regarded him as neither a help nor a hindrance.

Almost certainly, however, Verginius contributed to the confusion which proved to be the undoing of Nero: after the battle of *Vesontio*, the German legions – oddly, it might seem, in view of their defeat of Nero's enemies – offered power to Verginius. The fact that he refused evidently made a smaller impact in the circulating rumours than the story that the offer had been made. Frustrated in their attempt to enthrone their candidate, the legions of Upper Germany did not join Galba – after all, they had just (as they thought) snuffed out his cause – but resumed what must have been an uneasy allegiance to Nero.

The power vacuum among the legions was filled by the action of the Praetorian Guard acting under the influence of one at least of their commanders, Nymphidius Sabinus, who for money, had espoused the cause of Galba; it is possible that the equally uncongenial Tigellinus, the other prefect, did too. It was they who precipitated Nero's final panic on 8 June and his death on the following day.

Thus, although the confusions in the accounts detract considerably from our understanding, there is no doubt that, in one way or another, substantial parts of the Roman army had had a decisive

Figure 7.2 Italy. Source: Peter Lee.

impact on the transfer of power from one *princeps* to another. The realisation of this could not, of course, be forgotten, and for the next eighteen months the army groups and their commanders – the former influenced by money and *esprit de corps*, the latter by personal ambition – continued to dictate political outcomes; the apparent stability induced by the Augustan reforms had, at its first real test, demonstrated its frailty.

The Principate of Servius Galba

Galba's principate lasted from 9 June in AD 68 until 15 January in the following year; the six-month reign is summed up by one of Tacitus' best-known aphorisms (*Hist.* I.49) – *omnium consensu capax imperii, nisi imperasset* ('everyone would have thought Galba capable of ruling, had he not tried it'). Galba was faced with an uphill task: could he, elderly and old-fashioned, display sufficient breadth of vision and elasticity to pull the warring elements together?

Galba's credentials were – or had the appearance of being – sound: he came from a distinguished family of Republican nobility which, thanks to the patronage of Augustus' wife, Livia, had continued to prosper under the Julio-Claudians. His own career had been distinguished; respect for his sense of discipline had led to his being picked by Caligula in AD 39 to restore order and pride to the German legions following Gaetulicus' conspiracy and the period of lax discipline that had preceded it.

By AD 68, his name evidently still counted for something: it had been sufficient to persuade Vindex to choose him as the figurehead for the anti-Nero movement. Galba's insistence on the senate's ultimate right to choose an emperor pointed both to traditionalism and a less consuming sense of ambition than was demonstrated by some. However, events were to show that his verve and vigour had gone, and his sense of discipline was inconsistently displayed, so that at times he could appear the martinet, while at others he would tolerate anything. This inconsistency (*mobilitas ingenii*) was to prove in major part to be his undoing.

Those who had opposed his rise to the Principate generally met with a bloody end, while his supporters could do as they pleased: the competing claims for rewards among them were a disastrous advertisement for Galba's Principate, as men such as Marcus Otho (the future *princeps*), Cornelius Laco (the prefect of the Praetorian Guard), Titus Vinius (consul for AD 69), Icelus (a freedman), Fabius Valens and Alienus Caecina (legionary *legati* in Germany) vied with each other for favours and rewards for services rendered. The obvious corruption among Galba's entourage sat ill with a *princeps* who promised bribes and then refused to pay them. Not only did Galba surround himself with this venal entourage but he also showed himself to be afraid of quality in his subordinate appointments. As we have seen, pro-Neronian officials were brusquely removed, only to be replaced by men whose main claim to fame was that Galba did not fear them as rivals. Thus, in the Germanies, Fonteius Capito was murdered on Galba's behalf but without his knowledge, and Verginius Rufus was dismissed; they were replaced by Aulus Vitellius, whose claim rested solely on the laurels of his distinguished father, and Hordeonius Flaccus, a man evidently prominent only as a sufferer from gout. It seems perverse that Galba should have entrusted such sensitive armies to men as weak and ineffectual as these.

There was little time for this Principate to settle down, although Galba is on record as having established a commission under Gnaeus Julius Agricola, the father-in-law of the historian, Tacitus, to claw back Nero's lavish personal expenditure. The dominant theme was, however, the vicious and destructive battle among Galba's chief subordinates either to win the accolade of nomination as his successor or to influence the decision.

In fact, Galba was overwhelmed by a combination of three independent forces, which crystallised in the rebellion on the Rhine, of which Aulus Vitellius was persuaded to become the figurehead. Beyond this, however, was the discontent of the Praetorian Guard at Galba's failure to pay the bribe which their erstwhile prefect, Nymphidius Sabinus, had promised in Galba's name in return for the guard's desertion of Nero; further, Marcus Otho who, as governor of *Lusitania*, had been one of Galba's principal supporters during the events of 68, came to feel that his earlier services were not sufficiently appreciated. For Galba, it was fatal that Otho and the Praetorian Guard combined their efforts, which by accident coincided with the raising of the rebellion on the Rhine.

Although Vitellius was the figurehead of the Rhine rebellion, the quarrel with Galba was in no real sense his: the troops, following their defeat of the Vindex–Galba coalition at *Vesontio*, had been understandably reluctant subsequently to embrace Galba's cause; they remained recalcitrant, not least because of the ways in which their previous commanders, Fonteius Capito and Verginius Rufus, had been treated. In particular – and ironically – Fabius Valens and Alienus Caecina, the two legionary commanders who had done most to persuade the German legions to accept Galba, felt that this important service to the new *princeps* had gone under-rewarded. The legions will have been confirmed in their desire for their own candidate once they appreciated the role of the hated Praetorian Guard in supporting Otho in Rome. Indeed, one of their requirements of Vitellius was that, when he became emperor, Otho's praetorian cohorts should be cashiered and replaced by themselves. The elderly Galba was simply not up to finding a path among these competing interests.

Galba thus faced two rivals, each with a major military group in support: not all legionary groups, however, were ready to become involved at this stage; the legions of the Danube provinces stayed out, significantly because they did not have a suitable candidate to advance, whilst those of the east were influenced by Vespasian (governor of Judaea) and Licinius Mucianus (governor of Syria), for the time being at least, to maintain their support for Galba. Such was the strength of the rival military *esprits de corps*.

Galba evidently failed to appreciate the nature of the forces working against him; Tacitus astutely observed that the emperor failed to reach an understanding because those close to him sought obsequiously to ingratiate themselves with him by confining their 'advice' to what they thought he wanted to hear – the very form of self-interest of which Galba spoke in his oration (*Hist.* I.15–16). For his part, Galba appears to have convinced himself that his real weakness in people's eyes was his lack of an obvious successor; for this reason, when it was already far too late, Galba adopted as his son and successor the blameless – but irrelevant – aristocrat, Piso Licinianus.

Physically, Galba was toppled by Otho and the Praetorian Guard; the German legions, despite playing their part in the destabilising of Galba, did not reach Italy and the line of the River Po in time materially to affect Galba's position one way or the other. While these legions were making their way to Italy in two separate battle groups, Otho staged his *coup d'état*, and the hapless Galba and Piso were assassinated in the streets of Rome.

The Principate of Otho

Otho's reputation, as a friend of Nero, was one of luxury and immorality: Tacitus, who saw him as responsible, through his attack on Galba, for the destruction of the fabric of loyalty within the Principate, regarded the new emperor as 'fatally flawed' by his part in the events of 15 January. Yet Otho had shown a better side: his governorship of *Lusitania* was generally regarded as equitable, and his own principate demonstrates his understanding of the problems associated with trying to weld together an administration out of both friends and enemies; in this sense, his attitude to an extent resembled those of Julius Caesar and Augustus.

However, the forces ranged against him were menacing and close to hand: the German legions did not bring their campaign to an end with the death of Galba. Instead, they regarded Otho as an opportunist and, for them, as legitimate a 'target' as they had believed Galba to have been.

Besides his greater youthfulness, Otho had one advantage over Galba: he was an effective manager of people, and possessed a strong personal magnetism. As the events surrounding his suicide in April 69 were to demonstrate, he showed care for the well-being of his supporters, who reciprocated with both loyalty and devotion. The legions of the Danube and of the eastern provinces declared their support for Otho, but were too far away to affect the imminent issue – that of repulsing Vitellius' army. There was another problem, too: while Otho's troops were personally devoted to him, they did not view with the same enthusiasm

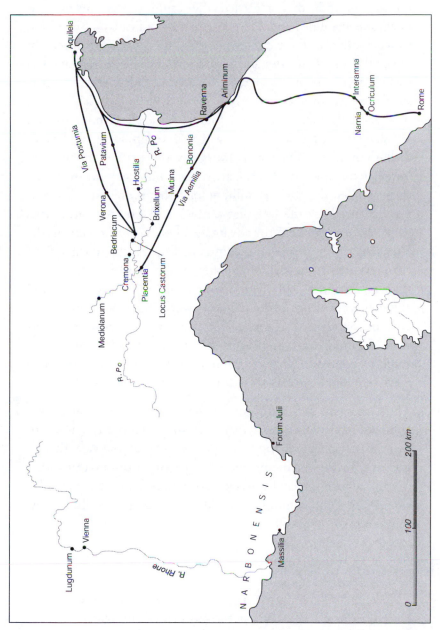

Figure 7.3 Northern Italy: the 'battle line' of AD 69. Source: Peter Lee.

those senior senators whom Otho appointed as his commanders on the ground; they regarded the caution of such men as Suetonius Paullinus and Marius Celsus as indicative of incipient treachery, and in these circumstances Otho's decision to remain in the rear (at *Brixellum*) and to mastermind the campaign from there has to be seen as a significant error of judgement. His personal magnetism could well have proved to be a decisive factor in the evenly balanced battle fought between Othonians and Vitellians at *Bedriacum*. There was also a significant (and fatal) dichotomy in the Othonian strategy: Otho's commanders were for delay to allow time for the arrival of reinforcements from further east. Yet, the obvious military logic that lay behind this view was 'balanced' by the fact that a quick strike by the Othonians would have given them the advantage of being able to take on the Vitellians before their two columns met up on the north side of the Po. Further, the lack of attachment felt by Otho's troops for their commanders led them to interpret their perfectly sound arguments for delay as the logic of treachery. As a result of this crisis of confidence, high morale, one of the most powerful assets of the Othonians, was dissipated; increasingly, they will have come to appreciate that, without the arrival of reinforcements, they were immeasurably weaker than their opponents.

The Othonians' best opportunity was, therefore, lost, and their failure to score a decisive victory at *Bedriacum* proved their undoing: morale collapsed, and Otho personally took the view that he was not, in these circumstances, prepared to do anything that would increase the civil carnage. To the profound distress of his supporters, Otho committed suicide, thus leaving Vitellius as the third emperor of AD 69.

The Principate of Vitellius

This reign, which lasted from April until near the end of December of 69, is usually portrayed as an unmitigated disaster, a period when all sense of decency and efficiency were abandoned. However, it is worth bearing in mind that, of all the emperors of this 'long year', Vitellius perhaps had the hardest lot with the sources. He was the son of a highly successful father and a well-respected mother (Sextilia), and he lived in the shadows of their reputations. His own reputation for lavish personal expenditure, heavy eating and drinking, and enjoyment of entertainment was undoubtedly deserved, although he was by no means the only Roman aristocrat of this period to have displayed such characteristics. He also had the 'misfortune' of raising the standard of rebellion against Galba and of precipitating the defeat of Otho, both of whom were supported, tacitly at least, by the Flavians; further, of course, he lost to the faction which ruled Rome for the ensuing quarter-century, in which time they had plenty of opportunity to 'manipulate the media'; it was not fashionable in Rome in the later first century to compose apologies for Aulus Vitellius.

There no doubt was much in the aftermath of the first battle of *Bedriacum* that was far from salutary; events at *Cremona* resembled the site of a defeated, foreign, city, and the sequel, as Vitellius and his troops proceeded southward to Rome, was at times explosive and dangerous. Vitellius himself is said to have been scathing in remarks which he made on visiting his predecessor's grave, but then it was important that he should 'establish credentials' for himself and his army; he could not allow himself to be seen as the man who had raised rebellion against Galba, only to be beaten to the 'finishing post' by Otho. Rather, he had to 'stand history on its head' and present himself as the avenger of Galba's murder; Otho, in other words, had to become the real villain in Vitellius' propaganda, and it was this, no doubt, that made Vitellius put to death in excess of one hundred and twenty men who, as he discovered in Otho's surviving papers, had sought rewards for their parts in the murders of Galba and Piso Licinianus. This might also be seen as a shrewd precaution against his own possible fate.

Full, as it was, of troops from all over the empire, Rome itself no doubt did resemble a conquered city; as the summer progressed, with open spaces taken up by encamped soldiers, disease must have become rife. Further, the physical appearance of many of these troops must have seemed to the city populace both bizarre and frightening. In such tense circumstances, incidents and skirmishes were inevitable, although it is worth noting that Vitellius evidently tried to prevent looting by his troops. Although in private Vitellius remained true to his lifestyle, his public demeanour appears in the few incidents to have been recorded to have been dignified and reasonable – as is to be seen in his treatment of the senate and of the magistracies. Although he had to keep his promise to replace Otho's praetorians with picked troops of his own, he was sensible with regard to the remainder of the consular year, retaining Othonians such as Marius Celsus. The state of the Treasury was undoubtedly poor after the years of Nero and subsequent warfare, but Vitellius seems to have tried to raise some money without causing too much dissatisfaction by levying a tax on the number of slaves held by freedmen, a class which remained deeply unpopular. Finally, although the upper classes of Roman society were no doubt unimpressed by Vitellius' personal habits or by his attempts to entertain on a Neronian scale – even to the point of honouring the memory of the last of the Julio-Claudians – the city populace will surely have relished this aspect of the new regime.

Thus, Vitellius' first few weeks and months in power should not have provoked undue opposition towards him: however, to many, his assurances that civil war was now at an end will have seemed decidedly hollow; there was too much dissatisfaction arising out of the recent warfare and too many scores to be settled for this to have seemed a realistic hope. Not least, there were the dismissed Othonian praetorians and those Othonian reinforcements who had arrived just too late for the battle, and who had subsequently been publicly humiliated and sent back whence they had come. The Othonian troops from the Danube provinces had no obvious imperial candidate whom they could put into the field, although there was plenty of vigour in their leadership, particularly the Gaul, Antonius Primus, *legatus* of VII *Galbiana* (now renamed *Gemina*). Lacking a realistic candidate of their own, the troops on the Danube looked east for salvation.

There was now more coherence in the east than had once been the case; Mucianus (governor of Syria) and Vespasian (governor of Judaea), once enemies, had been brought together through the agency of Vespasian's elder son, Titus. Their legions had taken no direct part in the earlier events of the civil war but had accepted both Galba and Otho in their turn. Their decision to raise the standard of rebellion in July may have been prompted by Vitellius' victory in April, or possibly by pressure to match the active involvement that had been a mark of other legionary groups since the previous summer; in view, however, of the short passage of time since Vitellius' accession, and the character of his early conduct, the decision of the eastern legions in July cannot reasonably have constituted a reaction to Vitellius' reign as emperor.

It was evidently arranged that the Flavian campaign would be raised by a declaration in Alexandria by the prefect of Egypt, Tiberius Julius Alexander, on 1 July. This was intended both to give a lead to the legions of Syria and Judaea and presumably, because of the potential economic consequences of the Flavian 'possession' of Egypt, to issue a clear threat to Vitellius. It is said that one of the arguments deployed by Mucianus was Vitellius' alleged threat to exchange the Syrian and Rhine legions; the prospect of service in north-west Europe did not appeal to the Syrian legions, and by the way indicates how important the local associations developed by the legions could become. The Flavian strategy thus became clear: to mount from Egypt a blockade of Italy – especially dangerous in view of the number of troops deployed there – and then to attack it across the line of the River Po.

Vespasian himself went to Egypt; his intention was two-fold – obviously to gather funds and support and also to enhance his reputation. As a first-generation senator, Vespasian could not in terms of family background match the Julio-Claudians – this, after all, had been a principal reason for Nero's appointment of him to Judaea – nor was he on a level socially even with men such as Otho and Vitellius. Egypt was an ideal location for the acquisition of *auctoritas*; surviving fragments of the declaration in his favour by Tiberius Alexander demonstrate the 'campaign' to enhance Vespasian's status, while Tacitus describes how Vespasian was associated with healing miracles in Egypt. All of this was in stark contrast to thinly disguised disdain to be shown later to Vespasian by some members of Rome's governing class.

The Flavian army would reach Italy in two stages – an advance force under Antonius Primus and the main thrust under Mucianus who, of course, laboured under the disadvantage of having a considerable distance to cover. It was evidently envisaged that these two arms would meet in northern Italy and together prepare themselves for an offensive in the spring of 70. Without doubt, Antonius Primus wished to upstage Mucianus and reach Rome before him, but there was also good sense on his side; the enthusiasm amongst the Danubian legions for the Flavian cause was great and, while there was a large number of troops in Italy, many of them were sick and demoralised. Further, the north of Italy was lightly held, and the chief Vitellian reinforcements in the western provinces would take time to arrive. However, to occupy the Rhine legions, Antonius Primus organised what was intended to be a diversion, in which the Romanised Batavians, Civilis and Classicus, would mount a 'mock' nationalist rebellion. Before long, however, this had become a serious and 'very real' rebellion, which the raw recruits amongst the Rhine legions were ill-equipped to handle. In these circumstances, Vitellius' judgement in allowing so many of his original German legionaries to join a reformed Praetorian Guard can be seen to have been seriously at fault. However, then, Antonius Primus' plan can be regarded as reckless in the extreme. Both decisions threw into high relief the real dangers posed as a result of civil war. In passing, it is worth noting that the overtly nationalistic Batavian uprising of 69 has prompted a number of historians to look (wrongly) for similar motivation in the uprising of Vindex in the previous year.

Although the Flavian leaders did not know it, there seems to have been no sense of urgency on the Vitellian side; in early September, Vitellius was busy celebrating his birthday in Neronian style, with no thought of preparations for a major campaign. The Flavian advantages, as Antonius Primus is represented by Tacitus as arguing, could easily have been wiped out by the winter and certainly by springtime. Thus, Antonius was for instant action – a policy which seemed even more sound when the state of the Vitellian 'high command' became clear.

Vitellius' two principal generals were still Fabius Valens and Alienus Caecina, who had masterminded his campaign against Galba/Otho, and who (as a reward) had been designated suffect consuls for September and October of AD 69. At the crucial moment, however, Valens was ill and unable to participate; the chief responsibility, therefore, fell to Caecina. According to Tacitus in a character sketch (*Hist.* II.101), which must have owed its origins to Flavian propaganda generated after Caecina had been put to death in 79 for conspiring against Vespasian, Caecina was a man to whom treachery came naturally. Also in negotiation with the Flavian side was the prefect of the Ravenna fleet, Lucilius Bassus. Defections such as these were fatal to Vitellius' cause even though 'loyalists', such as Fabius Fabullus (*legatus* of legion V *Alaudae*) and the now-recovered Valens, desperately tried to redress the balance. Antonius Primus was victorious in the second battle of the year between *Bedriacum* and *Cremona*, for which town those Othonians (now Flavians) who had been humiliated there earlier in the year had a terrible fate in store. However, before accusing Antonius Primus of lax leadership in 'allowing' the firing of Cremona, it would be as well to reflect on the hazards of command in civil war.

Vitellian troops that survived were sent back to their provinces, and although Antonius felt it prudent to leave some of his troops in the north to make sure that the Vitellians did indeed leave, Italy and Rome were now essentially his for the taking; indeed, Vitellius was by late autumn already in negotiation with Vespasian's brother, Flavius Sabinus, the Prefect of the City. Agreement had been reached to the extent that Vitellius would abdicate – a novel mode of bringing an emperor's reign to an end – and that Flavius Sabinus would administer to the former emperor's supporters the oath of loyalty to Vespasian.

The plan went awry to the extent that Vitellian supporters in Rome refused to allow the emperor to abdicate and, in the fighting and skirmishing that ensued, the temple of Jupiter on the Capitoline Hill was gutted by fire and Flavius Sabinus himself became a victim of lynch law. Vitellius could not reasonably be held directly responsible for either incident; the temple was not the target for fire but was the accidental victim of a fire which had been deliberately started in the tenement blocks at the foot of the *Capitolium*. Nor was it in these dying moments of Vitellius' reign in any sense in the emperor's interests to kill his successor's brother, particularly since Vitellius had consistently shown a very natural concern for the fate of his own family, should he lose. A further complication was the intervention of the festival of *Saturnalia*, which undoubtedly slowed down the Flavian advance and made them relax their drive when it was unwise to do so.

Vitellius' end was, however, inevitable; after trying to escape to link up with his brother at *Tarracina*, he was captured and, on 20 December, became a victim of the same lynch law that had so recently carried off Vespasian's brother. In Tacitus' eyes, the act reflected no real credit on anyone; as with the murder of Galba eleven months previously, the real victim of these events was the concept of loyalty, highlighted by Vitellius' own not undignified retort to a tribune who attacked him: 'And yet, I was your emperor'.

The next few days were spent in mopping up the remnants, a process in which Antonius, perhaps learning lessons from what had happened at Cremona, exercised considerable restraint. Vespasian was officially recognised as emperor on or about 21 December, with the passing of the still partly extant *Lex de Imperio Vespasiani*, one clause of which was clearly intended to cover the somewhat irregular situation that would obtain until Vespasian's own arrival in Rome. In the meantime, Mucianus, who reached Rome perhaps around 25 December, was Vespasian's acknowledged deputy and spokesman; even Antonius Primus, the hero of the Italian campaign, had to recognise that. However, in case he did not, an early start was made to the process of returning Flavian troops to their provinces of origin; this, although necessary in any case, would inevitably weaken Antonius' power base. Vespasian's younger son, Domitian, who was also in Rome was made a praetor with an *ad hoc* consular authority. As such, he was not sufficiently senior in the visible hierarchy to damage Mucianus but high enough to share in the burdens of reconstructing the government.

Thus, a new age, a new dynasty, and (evidently) new hope had dawned in Rome and the empire. To mark it, on 1 January 70, Vespasian took office as consul, with his elder son, Titus, as his colleague. Events which precipitated and followed the death of Nero had left the new dynasty with opportunities, but they had also left problems – the greatest perhaps summed up by Tacitus in his famous observation: 'the secret of empire was out, that an emperor could be made elsewhere than at Rome'.

The dissemination of information

Historical accounts of events such as those that took place in AD 68–69 are notoriously vulnerable to changing conceptions of who was 'right' and who was 'wrong'; sources writing close to such events may see them and the individual participants in a totally different light from those writing at a greater distance. On the other hand, the coinage of such a period must provide a clearer view of what the principal participants wanted people to think about them at the time. In this section, we shall attempt to piece together a collection of desired 'public images' from the coin evidence.

It has to be said that the considerable volume of coinage that was issued from a variety of mints during 68–69 has generated a very substantial amount of study; many issues remain unresolved regarding the origin and chronology of the coinage, let alone its meaning. A major matter of interest concerns the question for whom the 'messages' on this coinage were intended, particularly since there is evidence to show that, unsurprisingly, emperors or candidates for power were not generally able to coin in areas which they did not control. Thus, neither Galba, Otho nor Vitellius managed to mint (and thus issue) coinage very far to the east of Italy. So, to some extent, it might be said that this coinage was 'preaching to the converted' in an effort, presumably, to keep them loyal to the cause in trying times.

We can assume that in the towns most people were coin using; on the other hand, we have to remember that there was no way in practice that coinage issued by previous rulers could be quickly removed from circulation, so that, in addition to new coins that came on stream in 68–69, the populace will also have been using coinage of the Julio-Claudian period and of the Republic. This may well have helped to lend an especial poignancy to some of the new issues that were deliberately reminiscent. The coinage will, in the first instance, have been intended to pay the army, a vital activity particularly in civil war. In addition, Rome's middle and upper classes will have had frequent contact with coinage.

Obviously, a full analysis of all types would be far beyond the scope of the present context, so a selection of examples will be employed to highlight the stances of their issuers. In the major concordance (*The Roman Imperial Coinage*), the coins of AD 68–69 are arranged in groups – those issued by the renegade

Clodius Macer in Africa in AD 68, 'anonymous' civil war issues of 68–69 which originated in a number of different centres, those of Galba (from a variety of centres), those of Otho (from Rome only) and those of Vitellius (again from a variety of centres).

In the context of rebellion and civil war, the highlighted themes will be such matters as what the regime, if successful, claims that it will achieve, what its justification is and what elements of the past it takes as its models. The literary sources suggest the initial reluctance of Galba to assume imperial titles on his own or his associates' authority; the coinage of Macer does not generally give his portrait, but instead employs personifications of a type similar to those of the Republican coinage; the same is true of a number of 'anonymous' civil war types issued in Spain and Gaul either by or on behalf of Galba. Reverse types include such obvious allusions as Peace, the Rebirth of Rome, and a direct allusion to Augustus with the use of the oak-wreath ('for having saved the citizens'). There is also a series of restorations of coins of Augustus and Divus Augustus; the message of these is clear – that after the aberration of Nero, the Principate was being restored to its original model of the Augustan *respublica*. Not surprisingly, in this context, *Roma*, the senate, *libertas* and Jupiter figure strongly. There is also a considerable insistence on the notion of revenge; Mars, Hercules and Vulcan are all described as avengers, which may be seen specifically as indicating a primary purpose of punishing Nero for his departure from accepted norms.

Of course, vengeance was also inherent in the very name of Julius Vindex, the instigator of the rebellion against Nero, although the word, Vindex, never appears as such on the coinage. Another powerful and relevant type is that showing the cap of liberty (*pileus*) set between two daggers; this is a restoration of an issue of Brutus and Cassius in 44 BC, and may provide confirmation that Vindex chose the Ides of March (15th) as a symbolic date for the raising of his rebellion against the last of the Caesars. The appearance of 'health and well-being' (*salus*) is noteworthy for two reasons: a *salus* type had originally been issued by Augustus and the female personification has been taken to have been modelled on Augustus' wife, Livia; it will not have been forgotten that the connections between Livia and Galba had been very strong – Galba even changing his name to 'Lucius Livius Galba' at one stage.

Coins were issued in Galba's name from the time of his open entry into the fray on 2 April AD 68. The early coins were restrained in their use of titles, and not until his proclamation in June did Galba entitle himself *Augustus* and *Caesar*. The themes of the 'anonymous' coins were repeated, with the addition of a direct commemoration of Livia and references to Galba's victory. This was the 'new Augustus' intent on taking up the work of the old one. In addition, there were coins of reassurance – Liberty, Concord, Peace, Confidence and Equity; Equity (*Aequitas*) is probably a specific reference to the soundness of Galba's money. Galba is seen addressing his soldiers, showing his control of this most unpredictable of groups, while Vesta and Piety demonstrated that Romans could once more have confidence in the Republic, in the protection of the gods, in home and in family. The Republic was restored, and Providence suggested that Galba had the future assured as well. It was in all a strong and reassuring collection; too many, however, knew that the truth was very different and, as Tacitus put it, the gods that Galba was commemorating were presiding over an empire that was no longer his.

The coinage of Otho is far less plentiful, nor were any coins, of course, issued by him or on his behalf during the preparation of his rebellion, since he was in Rome during that time and the mints were in Galba's hands. Apart from the commemoration of his victory, Otho's emphasis was on things that will have mattered most to his supporters – peace, a good food supply, sound money and the safety of hearth and home. The output was entirely of silver and gold, suggesting that the immediate recipients of his propaganda were intended to be the praetorians and other soldiers who had brought him to power and who would spearhead his defence of Italy against Vitellius. The strength of his cause was, therefore, a principal theme – with Jupiter and thunderbolt, and Otho himself riding off as for battle.

Vitellius' coinage, like Galba's, originated from a number of different areas – Spain, Gaul and Rome. His coinage, too, offered standard reassurances regarding good order in government, money and food supply; Rome under Vitellius was re-uniting itself with traditional values and following the precedent of Augustus was the government's goal. Peace was guaranteed by Vitellius' victory over Otho and would be continued and strengthened by his forthcoming victory over Vespasian. Harmony (*Concordia*) had returned, not that those who witnessed the skirmishing between civilians and soldiers on the streets of Rome will have been too aware of it; *Concordia* also looks forward to the use of the 'virtue' as part of Vitellius' nomenclature at the end of his reign. The food supply might be regarded as especially sensitive in view of Vespasian's control of Egypt; Vitellius appears to hint at this added problem, as he issued not just a commemoration of Ceres but also an unusual type for Annona, who is depicted holding a victory figure, with a ship to her right. Nothing could indicate more directly that Vitellius was assured of the victory which would keep the food supplies to the capital in good order. This perhaps lends weight to the proposition that Vespasian's issue of *Victoria Navalis* was, in part at least, referring to *his* victory in this matter. A further reference to Vespasian is to be seen in Vitellius' *Victoria* coin, on which the 'goddess' is shown with a shield bearing the Augustan reference, 'for having saved the citizens', which she is attaching to a palm tree. The palm tree was synonymous with Judaea; Vespasian's generalship and victories in that province are thus proclaimed as being exercised under the auspices of Vitellius. It is as if, while Vespasian was attempting to enhance his *auctoritas* in the opening weeks and months after his proclamation, Vitellius was trying to demonstrate Vespasian's inferiority to himself.

Military themes are powerful, emphasising harmony among the armies and the loyalty of legions and praetorians to Vitellius;

the coins stress the special place of the German legions, which had brought Vitellius to power, and which subsequently made up his Praetorian Guard, in Victory, Peace and Reconciliation. It was perhaps this especial connection with the legions of the Rhine that prompted Vitellius to make so much of the title, *Germanicus*, in his own nomenclature. However, the title also stressed some past associations: Vitellius had an uncle who was close to Germanicus Caesar and the elder Agrippina while they were in the east (AD 17–19). The emperor's father had been an active courtier under Caligula and Claudius, both of whom used the title, which was originally inherited from Livia's son, Nero Drusus, the father of Claudius. Vitellius himself had associations with Caligula and Nero, both of whom used the title. Although such associations might not impress the more serious-minded, Vitellius' associating of himself with Nero's memory does appear to have been popular with the ordinary folk whom Vitellius wished to court. In uncertain times, therefore, the title, *Germanicus*, could suggest a lot of ideas which were sure of a broad welcome.

A further important departure from the coinage themes of Galba and Otho was the emphasis placed by Vitellius on the establishment of a new dynasty. His father, Lucius Vitellius, was commemorated with his Julio-Claudian links. So, too, were the emperor's children, reflecting also the family affection which appears to have been a feature of Vitellius' life and for which he is on record as showing great concern in the last days of his dying reign.

In all, therefore, the coinage of this uncertain and troubled period offers us an insight into truths, half-truths and downright lies that were the make-up of propaganda aimed at soldiers and civilians and into the hopes, fears and aspirations of men who sought to win power and stabilise it by continuing to keep a firm grasp on the support of men and gods alike.

Appendix 1

Timetable of events: January–June AD 68

Date	Gaul	Germany	Spain	Italy
March 11	Vindex declares revolt; blockades Lugdunum			
14/15		Verginius hears of revolt		
19+			Galba hears of revolt	Nero hears of revolt+
24/25				Nero writes to senate about Vindex
27+				Nero returns to Rome+
Late		Verginius mobilises		
April 2+			Galba declares support; recruits troops+	
16		Verginius reaches Vesontio		Nero hears of Galba; plans counters
18	Vindex hears from Vesontio; lifts blockade of Lugdunum			
25		Vindex reaches Vesontio		
26/27		Exchanges between Verginius and Vindex		
28		Battle of Vesontio; death of Vindex; Verginius returns to Moguntiacum		
May 6			Galba hears of Vesontio; writes to Verginius; retires to Clunia	Nero hears of Vesontio
				Nero's troops gathering in N. Italy Unrest among some of them; (revolt of Clodius Macer?)
June 8+				Nero gets report of Petronius' 'perfidy'+
9+				Death of Nero; proclamation of Galba+
16+		Verginius hears of Galba's proclamation; administers oath	Icelus reports to Galba+	
22/24			Galba hears from Verginius	

+ indicates a date exactly or approximately verified.
Source: *Historian*, Vol. XXIV, 1975 (Stuttgart: Franz Steiner Verlag), pp. 59–74.

Further reading

There is a large periodical bibliography on this subject, which is helpfully summarised in C. L. Murison, *Galba, Otho and Vitellius* (see below).

Bradley K. R., *Suetonius' Life of Nero: An Historical Commentary* (Brussels, 1978).

Chilver G. E. F., *A Historical Commentary on Tacitus' Histories I and II* (Oxford, 1979).

Henderson B. W., *Civil War and Rebellion in the Roman Empire* (London,1908).

Murison C. L., *Galba, Otho and Vitellius: Careers and Controversies* (Hildesheim, 1993).

Shotter D. C. A., *An Historical Commentary on Suetonius' Lives of Galba, Otho and Vitellius* (Warminster, 1994).

Wellesley K., *The Long Year, A.D. 69* (London, 1975).

Chapter 8

Emperors, dynasties, adoptions and a golden age

The Julio-Claudian dynasty had come to an end in circumstances similar to those that had characterised the end of the old Republic. In AD 69, as at Actium a century before, events produced a 'saviour'; just as in 31 BC, Augustus Caesar had emerged from the turmoil to restore and rebuild, so in 69, Vespasian, twice consul and governor of Judaea, found himself cast in a very similar role.

Reconstruction was clearly a priority, although it is possible to exaggerate the depth of the tumult that Rome and the empire had come through. While it is true that few provincial governors or their armies had been left untouched by the events of 68–69, it is doubtful whether the malaise, except in a few instances, had penetrated deeper into provincial communities. Indeed, Tacitus (*Hist.* IV.73–74) put into the mouth of Quintus Petillius Cerialis (possibly the son-in-law of the new emperor) an oration reflecting the general truth that provincials saw most of the benefits and few of the disadvantages of the imperial system. The idea was repeated in more general terms in the *Annals* (I.2), where Tacitus, writing of the Augustan period, stated that provincials were undoubtedly the beneficiaries of the change from Republic to Principate. Nonetheless, there were some problems in the provinces: obviously, events in Gaul and Germany in AD 69 had gone far beyond a straightforward strife between groups of legions. The Danube frontier had been penetrated by tribesmen from the north side who had, however, been unfortunate enough to have encountered Licinius Mucianus on his march to Rome in support of Vespasian's cause; this theatre continued to cause difficulty through the second century. In a general sense, legions distracted by internal rivalries will have given ideas to opportunists amongst Rome's enemies; the outbreak of trouble among the Brigantes in Britain in 69 highlights the reality of and dangers inherent in this.

The century-and-a-quarter which followed the wars of 68–69 was clearly a period of danger and opportunity; it was a period which was viewed in widely differing ways from different perspectives. For some, the Flavian emperors (69–96) were saviours who put a tottering fabric back on its feet; for others, they represented a descent into execrable tyranny. Yet these same senators and their descendants, who found so much tribulation in the Flavian dynasty, saw the century which followed it (in which emperors were 'chosen' and adopted by their predecessors) as a new 'golden age'. For them, it was an age in which 'principate' and 'liberty' were finally reconciled; this in practice meant that the post of *princeps* was at last open to senators who could, in a sense, pursue it as the summit of the *cursus honorum* and whose 'natural ambitions' were no longer curtailed by the operation of a dynastic principle. It was in part a reflection of their views which led Edward Gibbon to describe this as 'the most felicitous period in all human history'.

In other ways, the period sent out more disturbing signals; it was an age of inflation, coinage debasement, disease and military threat – in short, an age of anxiety. The traditional values and routes to prosperity seemed to be failing – and this was especially evident in Italy itself. It has been shown how people in the empire were looking for reassurance – popular philosophising, 'quack' oracles, dream interpretation and the like – as the traditional certainties wavered.

Economic signs had been causing concern since the middle of the first century: Nero's 'devaluation' of the precious metal currency was a sign that he was spending more – particularly after the fire of AD 64 – than could be afforded. Although there was some recovery of monetary standards under the Flavians, especially under Domitian, the trend from the end of the first century was for devaluation and debasement progressing inexorably until 'meltdown' was reached in the second half of the third century. The signs of inflation were also clear in the second century, with the progressive loss from circulation of the smaller denominations in the coin system, with the introduction of new coins of higher denomination – the double *denarius* (*antoninianus*) and the double *sestertius* – following in the third century. By the turn of the second and third centuries, silver provided less than fifty per cent of the metallic content of the *denarius* and sometimes was totally absent. This deterioration was probably symptomatic of two evidently opposed factors: the end of imperial expansion after Trajan's time effectively brought to an end the acquisition of new sources of wealth. On the other hand, the upkeep of an army sufficiently strong to defend the empire was becoming increasingly costly.

The introduction into the west of disease (specifically, plague) served to accentuate depopulation and to enhance anxiety and uncertainty. It is generally thought that plague was brought into the west by the armies of Marcus Aurelius returning from the east. Disease thereafter remained a problem in the west.

The problems of the empire's territorial integrity were not new but seemed to take on an added momentum in the mid-second century, with military action required during the reign of Marcus Aurelius on the Rhine and the Danube – to add to the eastern

Plate 8.1 Sestertius of Vespasian.

problems. To those with long memories, it must have seemed like a 'world away' from the 'glory days' of Trajan. In all, it does not seem at all surprising that the second century developed into an age of anxiety, in which the familiar certainties of life could no longer be taken for granted.

The Flavians and recovery

Although the civil war of 68–69 brought with it many uncertainties, the Flavian period dawned at the very end of 69 amid hope; Vespasian, by character and status, will have appeared very different from his Julio-Claudian predecessors, but he was a man with much practical experience through his passage along the senatorial *cursus honorum,* and he had defeated Vitellius and had almost brought the Jewish war to its conclusion. Such uncertainty as there was emanated from his status: as a first-generation senator he may have appealed to Nero precisely because of his lack of social standing, as the last of the Julio-Claudians in his later years bestowed more of his favour on men who, socially at least, seemed to offer him little competition.

Vespasian's practical good sense showed itself in his willingness to accede to the attempts made by his son, Titus, to heal the rift between his father and his colleague, Licinius Mucianus, the *legatus* of Syria. Although together they made a formidable fighting force, with evidently the ability to attract good subordinates to their cause, Vespasian was plainly aware that he lacked enough of two vital 'ingredients' for establishing himself in power – financial resources and *auctoritas,* that feature which had been so essential to the Augustan settlement after 31 BC. That Vespasian set out specifically to win these attributes seems plain from his decision in 69 to take the southern route to Rome through Egypt. This enabled him to pose the threat of interference with the grain supply to the capital as well as ensuring it for a 'future Rome' under his own control.

This episode was also used, as perhaps was intended, for the enhancement of Vespasian's 'image'. Although the new emperor had some impressive familial connections, he could hardly claim nobility; we have seen the weakness implied by his attractiveness to Nero as a first-generation senator. Indeed, Vespasian's brother, Flavius Sabinus, who was killed in the last days of Vitellius' reign, was evidently regarded with a greater measure of respect than was Vespasian himself. However, while Vespasian had worked for Nero, he had also managed to incur the displeasure of both Caligula and his sister, the younger Agrippina; this, to many, will have represented a positive recommendation.

It seems clear from Tacitus' account that Vespasian's time in Egypt was not intended to win him money and supporters alone; it also provided him with the equivalent of 'photo-opportunities' by which he could win and display an *auctoritas* which he did not naturally possess. The 'healing miracles' with which he was associated undoubtedly had this purpose. The importance of this is to be seen in the patronising way in which certain senators – notably, the Stoic, Helvidius Priscus – offered the new emperor advice with the obvious presumption that he was not 'up to the job'; indeed, tension was generated in the senate as such men were accused by partisans of the new regime of 'playing the schoolmaster' to Vespasian.

Plate 8.2 Sestertius of Vespasian, commemorating the capture of Judaea by depicting a 'dejected captive' sitting by a palm tree.

Yet, there can have been little stomach in Rome for further turmoil; to all but the most blinkered, the job of reconstruction overrode such carping which may in any case have been a product less of real disquiet over Vespasian as of competition between 'philosophical groups' for pride of place in the 'war of words' over principles. Nonetheless, recent events – both Nero's reign and the civil war that followed it – probably led to a sharpening of Stoic views on autocracy, and especially on the obsession with materialism which those recent events had seemed to emphasise; the conduct of the 'evangelising' Musonius Rufus and the reaction of the troops whom he attempted to influence pointed this up sharply (*Hist.* III.81). No longer did the Stoic agenda restrict itself to acts of civil disobedience undertaken to register protest at those actions of a *princeps* which seemed to be beyond the pale.

For most, however, Vespasian was not a threat of new dangers to come; rather, he was the best hope of renewal. As a man of simple tastes and known lack of extravagance he seemed ideally placed to be the restorer, the 'new Augustus'. The parallels between Vespasian's victory and that of Augustus at Actium could be played up: both were seeking to restore order from turmoil and could thus in a similar fashion present themselves as 'saviours'. Vespasian may not have enjoyed the services of a Virgil, a Livy or a Horace, but he did have at his disposal a coinage that could readily articulate the new opportunities.

The wide range of types on gold, silver and *aes* coinage from a variety of mints indicates the care taken by the new regime to boost confidence widely: there were Republican and suitable Julio-Claudian reminiscences; Peace, Security, Fortune and Victory are constantly commemorated, as well as the regime's one solid mili-

Plate 8.3 Rome, Arch of Titus.

tary success – the Jewish victory, which was also to feature on the Arch of Titus in Rome. Rome is at the centre of this output, with Vespasian's guardianship of the city and its people stressed; Rome is 'rising again', but she is also true to her traditions in a type depicting her sitting amidst the seven hills. Tradition, too, lies behind the frequent religious types: the Augustan connection emerges specifically in the *Libertas* type which shows the oak-leaf crown, while 'Naval Victory', as we have seen, may have been intended to show Vespasian as the architect of victory in his threat to the grain supply of Vitellius' Italy; perhaps this type was

also intended to 'downgrade' the victory which Antonius Primus
had won in Italy against the orders of both Mucianus and
Vespasian. It is likely, too, that exactly one hundred years on,
VICTORIA NAVALIS was meant to remind people of the naval
victory that had inaugurated the first Augustan age. The dynastic
references are powerfully produced to engender confidence in a
new and continuing stability: the dynasty is 'eternal' and, another
Augustan reference, the new Augustus had two *principes iuventutis* in the form of his sons, Titus and Domitian, who together
assured the future (PROVIDENTIA). Most importantly, the
Flavian army was successful, shown by recovered standards, and
supported the regime. In other words, the coinage, which was also
much better organised than previously, cleverly inspired confidence by showing that the 'new start' was totally sound and was
deeply related to the best of tradition both during and before the
Principate. Here, indeed, was the publicity of Vespasian which
paralleled that of Augustus in Horace's 'Roman Odes'.

The loss of Tacitus' account from early in *Hist.* V (AD 70) means that we lack a sound chronology for the remainder of the Flavian period; an assessment, therefore, has to be more thematic than chronological. The basis of the power and position of the new *princeps* was, as before, military – rather after the manner of Augustus' 'First Settlement' – although Vespasian understood the need to appear as a ruler with 'civilian' qualities (*civilis princeps*); thus far, his position might seem closely comparable with that of Augustus. However, the Julio-Claudian period and the civil war had taken their toll of *nobiles* of Republican origin: so Vespasian's relationship in government was with men who were essentially free of 'traditional baggage'; Vespasian did not have to make the seriously conscientious show of sharing power after the manner of Augustus and Tiberius. His 'civilian relationship' in government was thus far more patronal than collegial – a point emphasised by the rarity with which Flavian emperors shared ordinary consulships with men outside the family.

Among other things, the censorship of AD 73–74, shared with Titus, was an exercise of patronal power, creating new patricians such as Agricola and Trajan's father. The senate met frequently, was frequently attended by the *princeps* and asked for its advice; members of the senate continued to occupy the senior posts in the administration. Vespasian was generous in providing the subsidies necessary for many to retain their senatorial status. Although well received, this could only emphasise the reality of dependence, thus echoing the position established for himself by Claudius – outwardly deferential, but with an unswerving determination that power should be centrally concentrated. The importance of Claudius' development of the Principate can thus be fully appreciated.

Despite the concerns about the dynastic principle which Tacitus rehearsed in the oration of Servius Galba, an oration composed no doubt in the light of events in AD 97–98, Vespasian clearly did not share those concerns. From the outset, the basis of the Principate was now demonstrated to be strongly dynastic:

Plate 8.4 Rome, Arch of Titus: Detail of triumphal procession following the capture of Jerusalem in AD 70.

Plate 8.5 Rome, the Colosseum.

Vespasian no doubt expected that, by the involvement with him of his sons, the dynastic pitfalls of the Julio-Claudians would be avoided; 'training' and supervision would remove fear of a Caligula or a Nero. It is, therefore, ironic that when the new dynasty had run its course, Juvenal could refer to the last of the Flavians as the 'bald Nero' (*Satire* IV.38).

From the victory in December 69, power might temporarily be devolved to Licinius Mucianus, perhaps as a way of marginalising the precocious Antonius Primus, yet the dynastic presence was firmly marked by Caesar Domitianus, although only nineteen years of age. There were rumours regarding his ambitions, and it is suggested that Mucianus failed to take over command against the Gallo-German rising because it was felt necessary that he stay in Rome to keep his eye on the young Domitian. Despite, however, misgivings that might have been present, Vespasian's resolve was unshaken: 'either my sons will succeed me, or nobody will'. While Domitian was kept slightly more distant from the centre of power, Titus was right at the

Plate 8.6 Rome, the Colosseum: detail of exterior.

dynastic heart of it – *Caesar, princeps iuventutis, imperator,* prefect of the Praetorian Guard, seven times Vespasian's colleague in the consulship, sharing with his father the tribunician power and the censorship. Significantly, Mucianus is reported as having used of Titus a description which Tacitus was later to apply to Galba – and others: Titus was *capax imperii.*

For senators, the new dynasty promised work and honour, although not power: indeed, the Flavian philosophy was clearly that which Tacitus saw as the outstanding qualities of his father-in-law,

Agricola – active, involved, hard-working, respectful of the real authority and (importantly) not obfuscating the issue by attachment to anachronistic principles. On this basis, senators of high quality worked for Vespasian and were rewarded by him; they recognised increasingly that they were involved with others, such as equestrians and even freedmen, in an enterprise of administration of which Vespasian and his family were in firm control.

Because the 'lines' were so clearly drawn and pretence largely avoided, it was inevitable that some would object. On the whole, Vespasian remained cool in the face of stated opposition; it could not be disguised that the type of opposition which had concentrated previously largely on the unacceptable acts of particular emperors was now replaced by a small, but vocal, minority who espoused an outright opposition to the Principate. This was not, to Tacitus and the majority, pragmatic politics, but an unreasoning conviction – even obsession – that salvation for Rome had to rest in an abolition of the Principate and a return to the Republic.

Helvidius Priscus, son-in-law of the vocal Neronian Stoic, Thrasea Paetus, was the originator of a carping, derogatory and pointless opposition, tolerated by Vespasian for many years with his characteristic good humour; eventually, however, Helvidius became one of the few 'victims' of the wrath of the *princeps*. Helvidius' homonymous son prolonged this particular family tradition, revelling in the 'Caesar versus Cato' analogy, and perhaps by moving to an all-out and active opposition under Domitian in AD 93 brought down upon himself and his friends the implacable anger of Vespasian's younger son. Yet in reality this was not a hero's death, but one that was 'precipitate and of no value to the *respublica*'. Significantly, Tacitus specifically contrasted such behaviour with the far more constructive conduct of men like Agricola, the 'good men under bad emperors' who importantly were the ones who guaranteed the continuity of the Principate (*Life of Agricola* 42,5).

Under Vespasian, the only other known conspirators – with no known connection to Stoicism – were two less-than-salubrious survivors from earlier times, namely Eprius Marcellus, the prosecutor of Thrasea Paetus and antagonist of Helvidius Priscus, and Alienus Caecina, who already could boast treachery to Nero, Galba and Vitellius in his record; these men, although tolerated by Vespasian, were never likely to become the regime's leading lights. That Titus and Domitian were the objects of conspiracy is not in doubt, although little is known in Titus' case, while under Domitian the only well-known episode, other than that of the younger Helvidius, was the short-lived defection of Antonius Saturninus on the Rhine in AD 89. The names of others who were put to death are known; their offences in the main are not.

As we have seen, the principal tasks awaiting Vespasian on his arrival in Italy in AD 70 were those of reconstruction and reorganisation. Vespasian's family had a background in finance, and he had a personal reputation for parsimony, even avarice; after Nero's reign and nearly two years of civil war, the state's finances, although probably not completely wrecked, were in need of attention and restoration. Yet, there is no compelling evidence that Vespasian was extortionate, or even particularly harsh. It is true that some Neronian extravagances, such as the much-publicised 'Liberation of Hellas', were cancelled. Overall, however, Vespasian seems to have set himself two modest objectives – the receipt by the state of the revenue to which it was entitled and the control of expenditure. In the case of the former, it appears that overhauling the mechanisms of collection was the principal policy rather than the imposition of new taxes. Thus, few people throughout the empire would have had much ground to complain about new burdens imposed by a harsh and avaricious regime.

Expenditure arose from the predictable fields of activity – the army, food supplies, building work, entertainment and public munificence. In none of these is there any evidence of extravagance under Vespasian; rather, his attitude, where it is recorded – for example, in the restoration of the Capitoline Temple after the fire of AD 69 – was that the state should ensure good value, in terms of competence, for the money which it expended. The building programme was not inconsiderable, but it was not unnecessary or extravagant; it embraced the restoration work on the Capitoline (already cited), renovation of the infrastructure, and work connected with the public morale (which the Flavians saw as a priority). The programme also had political and patronal aspects, such as the Temple of Peace and the work on the site of the Colosseum (or 'Flavian Amphitheatre', as it was called), which was in part, at least, concerned with the obliteration of the signs of Nero's extravagant palace, the *Domus Aurea*, and especially the *Colossus* which stood outside it. Further, an inscription recently discovered in Rome indicates that the great amphitheatre was built from the spoils of the Jewish War. It should also be noted that Vespasian was acutely aware of a patronal aspect to all of the work, namely that programmes of public building provided work and thus the means of self-support to ordinary members of the population at home and abroad.

The attention given to the army was obviously of paramount importance and urgency; Vespasian had become emperor thanks to the efforts of parts of the army, and he needed to keep his control of those who had supported him, as well as winning over those who had not. There was work and campaigning to prevent the idleness that could prove dangerous; there were certainly infrastructural projects in the provinces – roads, urbanisation and (on the Rhine) the ongoing task of frontier construction, not to mention those cases (again on the Rhine) where recent events – that is, the Gallo-German rising – had left a need for substantial and urgent reconstruction. Major campaigns were fought in Britain, while recent events in other areas of the empire meant that good organisation and readiness to fight were essential. Discipline was emphasised by the disbanding and replacement of legions which had disgraced themselves in the fighting on the Rhine and by breaking up some of the groupings which were reminders of the depths plumbed in 68–69.

The Praetorian Guard required the most careful handling; this was partly because these cohorts represented almost the only part of the Roman army which continued to attract Italians and partly, too, because the Guard had undergone some traumatic reorganisations during the civil war. Vitellius had discharged Otho's praetorians and replaced them with men from the Rhine legions who were evidently anxious to win the better service conditions given to the praetorians. Vitellius had also raised the number of the cohorts from nine to sixteen. Vespasian was faced with requests to reinstate Othonian guardsmen, many of whom had fought on his side in 69, as well as retaining those recruited by Vitellius. He also needed, both for cost saving as well as for political pragmatism, to reduce the Guard to a size closer to its pre-Vitellian manning levels. How all of this was done is not clear, although it is known that, by the end of the Flavian period, the number of cohorts stood at ten. It is thought possible that some of the praetorians were sent for service in the provinces. However, the potential delicacy of the whole matter is perhaps demonstrated by the decision to entrust the command of the Guard to Titus.

We have seen that, like Claudius before him, Vespasian in AD 73–74 assumed the office of censor, with Titus as his colleague. Undoubtedly, and again like Claudius, he took the view that the directions which he wished to take were both significant and radical. Two principal examples of this, already cited, were the adlections to the senate and to the patriciate, and the financial reorganisations. An innovatory approach to the adlection of senators was to bring men into the *cursus honorum* at whatever level appeared appropriate to their age and standing. Thus, men of mature age were no longer necessarily required to compete for junior posts against young aristocrats who were perhaps no more than half their age. He also allowed more 'specialisation' in the *cursus*, which was obviously helpful to efficiency; thus men might proceed along a largely 'civilian' path. Two later emperors – Nerva and Antoninus Pius – can be cited as examples of this practice. Similarly, more attention might be paid to the military side: thus, Trajan undertook ten years' service as a military tribune, and Hadrian served three separate military tribunates.

Like Claudius, too, Vespasian wished to undertake radical activity with regard to provincial communities: grants of citizenship were made, and 'Latin rights' (or 'half-citizenship') were accorded to the whole of Spain. It also became customary to grant 'Latin rights' to non-citizens in the Roman army. Many *municipia* were founded, and a very fragmentary inscription from St Albans (Verulamium) commemorates Agricola's dedication of the *basilica* ('town-hall') there; in addition, there was a considerable programme of foundation (or re-foundation) of *coloniae* – in the empire to give a spur to Romanisation, and in Italy to provide incentive to certain towns and to arrest the increasing depopulation of certain areas.

Changes were made, too, to whole provinces, such as changes of status between 'imperial' and 'senatorial'; in some cases, boundaries were altered, and new 'administrative areas' formed. One of the principal changes was the creation of Cappadocia as an imperial province with legions; this appears to have been part of a reorganisation which must have arisen out of the new uncertainties that had been introduced into the region as a result of the wars of Nero's reign against the Parthians/Armenians and against the Jews. *Colonia* foundation was also a part of this process; undoubtedly, the successful conclusion of the conflicts was seen as an opportunity to breathe a new stability into this often-troubled region of the empire.

Vespasian died unexpectedly on 23 June AD 79; his contribution to stability and progress in Rome and the empire cannot be denied. Two sayings are attributed to his last moments which, although probably apocryphal, symbolise the perception of the man: 'Woe is me! I think I'm becoming a god', and he is said to have struggled to his feet saying that an emperor should die standing up. Perhaps the most appropriate 'epitaph' (and notable for its simplicity) is that provided by Tacitus: 'Alone of all the emperors who preceded him, he was changed for the better by his exercise of power'. Of the many sound things that he had done, he had, of course, ensured that there should be no uncertainty as to the future of the Principate; Titus was, after all, 'co-ruler' already; and Vespasian had become a god.

Titus was not an easy man to fathom, and the task is not made easier by the disparity of contemporary views concerning him. That his private life was wayward does not appear to be a matter of doubt; that he could be brutal seems clear from the account of the manner of his removal of Alienus Caecina in AD 79. Brought up alongside the courts of Claudius and Nero, he probably had a rather broader, if less salubrious, training than his father. That he was cultivated, but unpredictable, should perhaps, therefore, not surprise us.

It does appear clear that he preferred popular paths; this is shown by his building programme and by his generosity to communities in trouble (as at the time of the famous eruption of Vesuvius in AD 79). His generosity, however, was not outlandish and exhibited a sense of restraint which must have derived from his father. He strove for good relations with all, honouring his pledge not to execute senators, attempting to make peace with the philosophers, continuing his father's infrastructural work in the provinces. His re-introduction of *populi furor* – judgement by popular acclamation in the arena – as a form of justice perhaps betrays the cruel side of his nature as well as a desire to pander to the people.

It all reads like a quest for popularity, as if liberated from the tougher paths which he had trodden with his father. Yet his was a principate which, in its essentials, followed the lines initiated by Vespasian. No new powers were granted to Domitian, who remained *princeps iuventutis*, although there was never any doubt that Titus would be succeeded by his younger brother. His reign, in short, contained the virtues of Nero's, so that he could be seen as the 'darling of the whole world'; the more perceptive, however, who observed that he was fortunate in the shortness of his reign, could see that, as in Nero's case, there would in all probability have been a price to be paid.

Titus died on 13 September AD 81 from unknown causes, although there were those who were ready to accuse Domitian of a crime; certainly there was no love lost between the two brothers, and Domitian undoubtedly resented the special place which Titus had enjoyed in their father's affections. That the dynasty emerged from the reign of the second Flavian in as strong a shape as it had been in when Vespasian died is evident from the fact that no question was raised over Domitian's succession.

Domitian evidently had wished to be emperor in AD 69 and, despite the warnings of Mucianus, clearly thought himself capable of ruling. In his own eyes, he was *capax imperii*, though (as with Galba), Tacitus would have added *nisi imperasset*. That the Flavian principate was authoritarian, centralised and autocratic few could doubt; in this sense it followed a tradition inherited from Caligula. Domitian's character led him to believe, rather like Caligula, that he had no need to be over-indulgent with senators and that the Principate would be better run if people properly understood their roles. Like the third Julio-Claudian, the third Flavian evidently believed that his right to rule transcended constitutional forms. Although a comparison is made – and has been made right back to Domitian's own time – with Tiberius, it is both superficial and unhelpful. Tiberius' character and beliefs led him positively to want the co-operation of the senate; he failed because people neither understood his wishes nor trusted him. Certain similarities of character there may have been, but here the comparison ends; from the outset Domitian, because of his beliefs, wished to impose a personal monarchy on Rome. This is shown by his insistence that Domitia, like the younger Agrippina and Poppaea Sabina before, should be *Augusta*. Tiberius' hostility to such elevations for Livia and the elder Agrippina is well documented. Like Caligula, Domitian was the head of a 'royal' family (*domus regnatrix*), which ultimately was answerable to no-one. Many other things demonstrate that his manner was not simply a matter of gaucheness, but the very essence of the man's philosophy of ruling. In his lifetime,

Domitian was consul seventeen times; he started to use censorial power from 84 and became *censor perpetuus* in the following year. He adopted the *cognomen, Germanicus* – again reminiscent of Caligula – and renamed months of the year. He was addressed as *dominus et deus noster* ('our Master and our God'), and consecrated the house of his birth as a temple to the *Gens Flavia*. Further, he refused to give the undertaking, made by both his father and his brother, not to put senators to death.

All of this coheres into a philosophy of ruling; although senators were mindful of tradition, many of them were also well aware that they had changed in important ways since Actium. In other words, their expectations differed from those of early Julio-Claudian senators and, as we have seen from Tacitus' description of Agricola, many saw their role as one of 'service' rather than of governmental equality or partnership; the changing social backgrounds of senators had accelerated such realisations. As with Trajan later, so with Vespasian and Titus, senators would in the main accept reality in return for a 'face-saving' courtesy. Domitian was *dominus* and *deus* – a far cry from Tiberius' reaction to such appellations – and he required everyone, senators included, to behave accordingly. Objection to this 'new' style may have been the cause of the exiles and deaths among senators that are alleged by Dio Cassius to have occurred early in the reign.

The tradition regarding Domitian is, of course, essentially hostile because it was largely members of the senate who were responsible for it; the testimony of Tacitus and Pliny points up a hatred which bordered on the irrational and the obsessive. Yet, it is clear that such hostility was by no means universal: it was not to be found in the legionary army or in the praetorian cohorts who, after all, in 96 and 97, wanted Domitian's murderers apprehended and punished; nor was it to be found generally among members of the Equestrian Order or the ordinary people. All of these benefited from actions of the *princeps*; they could tolerate his personal autocracy, because they were enjoying the fruits of his patronage.

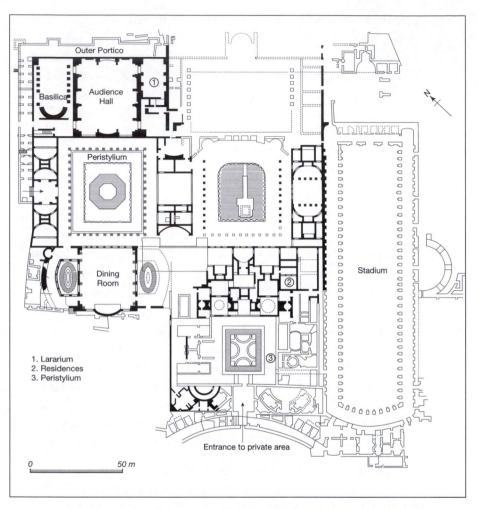

Figure 8.1 Rome, Palatine Hill: plan of the Domus Augustana. *Source: After A. Boethius and J. B. Ward-Perkins,* Etruscan and Early Roman Architecture *(London: Yale University Press, 1970), p. 231.*

It seems clear that everything that Domitian did – political, military or religious – was done, if not for the purpose of, at least with a view to enhancing his own *persona*. This is particularly true of his military campaigns; even though ancient sources are in all likelihood wrong to belittle them, Tacitus may be right in his obvious view that Agricola's victories in Britain did make the

Plate 8.7 Rome, Domus Augustana: peristylium *and entrance to imperial residences.*

Plate 8.8 Rome, Domus Augustana: peristylium *of the official section.*

princeps envious. Domitian's anger against those who, he felt, did not sufficiently honour him and the consequent resentment of the senatorial aristocracy at the emperor's overbearing, even tyrannical, behaviour were counterproductive in the matter of his relations with the senate. Similarly, new religious festivals, in concentrating attention on Domitian's 'favourite' deities (Jupiter and Minerva), seemed to be extolling him, just as the Secular Games of AD 88 appear to have been intended to identify Rome's well-being with those of Domitian and the Flavian dynasty.

Reaction was to be expected, since the senatorial aristocracy consistently objected to what it interpreted as its being belittled. There appears to have been a conspiracy in 87 involving one Civica Cerialis, and a potentially far more serious uprising threatened on the Rhine at the beginning of 89, when Antonius Saturninus was proclaimed emperor at Mainz (*Moguntiacum*); that Saturninus had sounded out others on his 'plan' seems likely from the death, probably at this time, of Sallustius Lucullus who may have been Agricola's successor in Britain. Two points may be made about this episode. First, it enhanced Domitian's suspicions with the result that, contrary to what was evidently his earlier policy, he began to encourage informers. Secondly, however, the fact that Saturninus' rebellion was short-lived may in part have been due to the vigilance of Domitian and his advisers, but the generally good relationship between the *princeps* and his legions was crucial to Saturninus' undoing.

It is clear that, in Tacitus' mind, the real danger of conspiracies rested in the effect which they had on the *princeps* if they failed; it was probably the last few years of Domitian's reign which alerted him to this outcome. The informers, of whom Juvenal provides a vivid and frightening picture, became active again, even though in his earlier years, in what appears to have been a reference to Tiberius' practice, Domitian criticised those who gave them free rein. It might be said, however, that such was the suspiciousness of Domitian's temperament in these later years that not even informers could feel safe, as the cases of Arrecinus

Clemens and Baebius Massa show. In short, it was all too easy to arouse the suspicions or bruise the sensibilities of the last of the Flavians. In the atmosphere that prevailed, it becomes less surprising that the treatment meted out to Agricola was so equivocal. It was easy to offend an emperor so preoccupied with his own sovereign power, and who could evidently be satisfied only by conduct and words as obsequious as those of the contemporary poet, Martial.

The last few years were marked by seemingly irrational deaths; not least among these were the leading Stoics of the day, of whom the younger Helvidius Priscus was a principal victim. Whether such men were attacked simply for their views and their writings is unclear; certainly, the 'majesty' of Domitian will have counted for little in their eyes, and the suspicious *princeps* affected to find offence in writings that went back some time. Alternatively, there may in AD 93 have been a real conspiracy, centred around these outspoken men with the object of eliminating the *princeps* in favour of a restoration of the Republic. Certainly, the Republic had for this generation of Stoics taken on a halo of glory (despite its obvious failings), and present conflicts were seen as extensions of the 'titanic clash' between Caesar and Cato in the 50s and 40s BC. The reign of Domitian thus drew to an end amidst suspicion and terror; although the final plot, which led to Domitian's death in 96, is often seen as 'domestic', it seems much more likely that a group of men plotted to replace Domitian with Nerva, and thus demonstrated the truth of the assertion that, no matter how powerless the senate might have become, few emperors crossed swords with it with ultimate impunity.

To Roman senators – or many of them – the days of Domitian were dark days: nonetheless, we should not lose sight of the fact that many senators not only survived but prospered in their careers; the historian, Tacitus, and the future emperor, Trajan, readily stand as two examples. Nor should we lose sight of the fact that, after the chaos of AD 68–69, the Flavians had restored stability, and that Domitian had contributed to that. Further, much of Domitian's legacy in the empire was of a positive nature: not only were frontiers positively safeguarded, but efforts were made to improve the social and economic life of the provinces; in this, Domitian was building on the work of his father and brother. The agricultural prosperity of the provinces was improved – Domitian's legislation on viticulture may have been intended to contribute to this – and town life was made more accessible with grants of citizenship, although, as always, a sense of civic responsibility was demanded of those so honoured, both administratively and financially. By contrast, Italy was in the doldrums; as a result, many more provincials than before with the 'qualifications' and the enthusiasm came forward to use their talents on a larger stage – much to the chagrin of 'xenophobes', such as the poet, Juvenal (*Satire* III). It is thus not at all surprising that these municipal and provincial aristocracies came to take many of the senatorial 'places' which had previously been filled by men from Italy: the 'special status' of Italy was thus fast disappearing.

It is when we take into account Domitian's continuing care for the provinces, for the armies, for the ordinary people who benefited from his lavish building programmes that we realise that he was essentially continuing in the modes of consolidation and development that had been initiated by his Flavian predecessors. What distinguished Domitian from them was his openly articulated insistence on his autocratic stance and the conflict with certain senators into which this brought him. 'Our master and our god' thus undermined one important feature of his father's position, and indeed of the whole Augustan system; this feature was *libertas*, which had been the cause of Nero's demise and which the Flavian victory had been won to secure. In such circumstances, it is not surprising that Domitian should fall to an assassin's knife; even less surprising that the conspiracy was centred around senators, of whom the future emperor, the elderly Marcus Cocceius Nerva, was one. Domitian had demonstrated the seriousness of the gulf that, at the end of the first century, separated *principatus* and *libertas*.

The Flavian period was one of responsible safeguarding of the empire's territorial integrity; as we have seen, Vespasian and his two sons took note of the chaos that had characterised the period of civil war and set out by reorganisation to remedy it. In truth, the situation on Rome's frontiers can, with the benefit of hindsight, be seen to have been moving towards the 'meltdown' which was to characterise the later part of the Antonine period. Vespasian's reorganisations were designed to ensure continued stability in the face of the Parthian threat in the east, while Domitian's much-derided personal military involvement sought to strengthen the European frontiers; his contribution to the development of the *limes Germanicus* and the *limes Raeticus* is now recognised.

Throughout the period, progress was made under a series of governors of high profile (Vettius Bolanus, Petillius Cerialis, Julius Frontinus and Julius Agricola) to advance the Roman control of Britain; Vespasian's extension of the *pomerium* (the sacred city limit of Rome) in AD 75 may have been intended to symbolise this. The province grew from an area encompassing the south and midlands of England and Wales to include the remainder of England and Wales, as well as the south and north-east of Scotland. The fact that, in the end, under Domitian Scotland had to be abandoned may have angered Tacitus who saw (or affected to see) it as a negation of traditional aspirations, but, viewed globally, it was a sensible balancing by Domitian of a range of imperatives across the empire for all of which he, as *princeps*, had to accept responsibility. In any case, although Vespasian's vision of an enlarged British province had had to be abandoned, Domitian had left Britain stable and with a traditional type of frontier (*limes*) – the 'Stanegate road' – which ran from Tyne to Solway and which was the precursor to Hadrian's Wall. Despite Domitian's unpopularity with some senators, a sense of responsibility was his inheritance from his father; it was also the feature that characterised his own reign.

Nerva and Trajan

The reigns of Nerva and Trajan are dramatically heralded by Tacitus in both his *Histories* and the *Life of Agricola*; in the latter, published in AD 98, Nerva is hailed as the emperor who reconciled *principatus* and *libertas,* two 'concepts previously regarded as irreconcilable'. Trajan, moreover, 'daily enhanced the happiness of the times'; for Tacitus, this was a 'most blessed age' (*beatissimum saeculum*). About five years later (in the *Histories*), Tacitus described the *principatus* of Nerva and the *imperium* of Trajan as a period of 'rare good fortune' (*rara temporum felicitas*), when 'a man can think as he wants, and speak as he thinks'. To men like Tacitus and his fellow senator, Pliny, and their friends this was a massive contrast with what had preceded these emperors. It is worth noting, however, that in his *Panegyric of Trajan* (published in AD 100), Pliny had to ensure that Nerva's reign, with all its upheavals, lay in the shadow of Trajan's, and was rescued from near-disaster by Trajan.

As we have seen, the idea that Domitian was the victim of a purely domestic plot is not acceptable; powerful forces were involved and their predetermined choice of successor was Marcus Cocceius Nerva. His family was distinguished for its legal expertise; Nerva himself, however, had not followed in the family tradition. Although he was well thought of in antiquity and has been in modern times also, his earlier career as a courtier of Nero (helping that emperor to uncover the Pisonian conspiracy of AD 65) and subsequently of the Flavians suggests that his influence was probably born of his connections and of the deviousness which allows a man to be courtier of many emperors; this was perhaps the less salubrious reality behind the Tacitean idea that there could be 'good men under bad emperors'.

There is no doubt that the specific direction of Tacitus' praise of Nerva in the *Life of Agricola* is significant in the historian's thinking; reconciling *principatus* and *libertas* was clearly important to the historian – and (in his view) a unique achievement. Its meaning appears to go beyond a better relationship between *princeps* and senate – although, following the grim years of Domitian, even this will have been welcome – to something far more fundamental. In the oration attributed by Tacitus to Galba in AD 69 (*Hist.* I.15–16; see Chapter 5, Appendix 1), Galba had spoken of choosing his successor from a broad senatorial constituency, arguing that the state could not live with *tota libertas* any more than it could with a dynastic imposition (*dominatio*). Nerva's choice of Trajan as his successor, whatever the real pressures which drove it, appeared to mark an important new departure; superficially, at least, the senate was encouraged to believe that it had a hand in the choice. Further, the relationship between Nerva and Trajan – or, more precisely, the lack of it – showed that for the first time senators could view the post of *princeps* as the potential summit of their own career structure. The fact also that Nerva was himself the choice for *princeps* of a group of senators (and others) appeared to make the same point. None of this had anything to do with the realities of power; in practice, no matter how strongly the *princeps* averred (as Trajan did) that he was subject to the laws of the *respublica,* his power and authority were effectively beyond challenge. It was considerations such as these, however, which persuaded senators that this at last was the 'golden age' (*beatissimum saeculum*), and it lasted until Marcus Aurelius inexplicably chose his wayward son, Commodus, to succeed him in AD 180.

When Nerva succeeded in September AD 96, it must have seemed like the dawn of a new era; but it had been said before that 'the best day after a bad emperor is the first one'. In Nerva's case, this turned out to be a reality: as we have seen, deep hatred of Domitian was evidently restricted to senators – and not all of them. Other groups had fared differently, and thus had different reactions to the assassination. The members of the Equestrian Order found their career prospects enhanced by the entrusting to them of the types of administrative posts close to the *princeps* that had under the Julio-Claudians been held by former slaves (*liberti*). The army saw an emperor who had shown interest in it and who had improved its pay and conditions; the legionary army had given its response to this in the short shrift which it afforded to Antonius Saturninus in AD 89. The Praetorian Guard was outspoken in its appreciation of Domitian through its demand that his assassins should be brought to justice. The ordinary people of

Rome had been fed, entertained and given work through a build-ing programme, which included a Circus (in the present Piazza Navona), the imperial palace (on the Palatine Hill; *Domus Augustana*) and the buildings which were later completed as the Forum of Nerva and the Markets of Trajan. 'Bread and circuses' represented an important reality, and if they were provided, the imperial patron stood to feel the benefit. People in the provinces had little ground to complain about a *princeps* who had safe-guarded the empire and the prosperity of its subjects.

Predictably, therefore, there were contrary currents abroad in Nerva's brief reign; the joy of some senators was soon tempered by attacks on 'collaborators'; after all, many (including such men as Trajan, Tacitus and Pliny) may have complained about Domitian, but their careers had prospered. Others must have wondered what such men had had to do to escape the attention of that most suspicious of emperors. Inevitably, there was a witch-hunt directed at Domitian's 'creatures', which was little short of anarchic; the *libertas* which Nerva's coinage proclaimed may to some have come to appear as a 'two-edged sword'. As Fronto, one of the consuls of 96, observed, 'it is dangerous to have a *princeps* under whom nobody may do anything, but even worse to have one under whom anybody might do anything'. To most, this was not utopia, and few probably would have honestly agreed with the poet, Martial, an adept at praising all emperors, when he announced that 'if Cato were alive today, he would be Caesar's supporter'.

In short, Nerva's reign exhibited anarchy and chaos, and the *prin-ceps* was exercising no sort of control. Indeed, in his *Panegyric of Trajan*, Pliny is frank about the depths of the discomfiture from which Trajan rescued the ageing Nerva; the true nature of Trajan's rise to power may have been uncomfortably reminiscent of the events of 68–69, for Trajan was *legatus* of Lower Germany through Nerva's reign. It is a moot point how explicit was Trajan's threat of force if Nerva chose not to be rescued by him. The realities of such coin legends as PROVIDENTIA (Foresight) and PAX (Peace) may be gleaned from the fact that they were accompanied by reverse designs showing a togate Nerva handing a globe to Trajan dressed in 'military uniform'. The political truth inherent in the rescue package was what it had been in 68–69, that 'an emperor could be made elsewhere than at Rome'. In this case, the reality was disguised by evident goodwill on both sides and a formal adoption of the type that Galba had attempted to use to secure the succession of Piso Licinianus.

Indeed, as Tacitus researched his *Histories* in the aftermath of these momentous events, one wonders how far he saw what happened in 97 as bearing an uncanny resemblance to the events of thirty years previously. The chief difference was that Trajan was a firmer and more determined figure than Piso, Otho or Vitellius. The 'deal' struck, Nerva was able to live out his last months in a manner more secure than that which had characterised the earlier years of his reign.

Trajan thus succeeded on Nerva's death in January 98; without doubt his intervention had headed off a crisis, and Rome and the empire were able to enjoy the security brought about by a man described simply and uniquely as 'the best of emperors' (*optimus princeps*). Trajan's name was to become a byword for imperial success, and he became himself the example in the light of which others were judged. Yet, it is clear from Pliny's *Panegyric of Trajan* that, 'spin' aside, this reign did not really represent a return of freedom; Pliny's proud announcement, 'You bid us to be free, so free we shall be', gives the lie to that. The real contrast with what had gone before did not lie in power levels but in the affability and easy charm of the new *princeps*, allowing people to believe that they had a real involvement. In fact, Trajan's control was in every way as complete as what had gone before; indeed, even *libertas* was now seen as a facet of the emperor's patronage.

Trajan was the soldier–emperor who respected the senate and sought to involve its members and those of the Equestrian Order in his administration. Both Pliny (in his *Panegyric of Trajan*) and

Dio Chrysostom (in his *Discourse on Royalty*) see Trajan as a model for government which was founded on principles which will have been eminently congenial to senators. It is, in fact, an adoption of a 'mild' version of what, during the first century, had been seen as the stance of the Stoic philosophers. Trajan was not *dominus et deus noster*, but he was the vice-gerent of Jupiter on earth; indeed, the Arch of Trajan at Beneventum depicts Trajan receiving a thunderbolt from Jupiter to mark a 'relationship' in which Trajan governed the world in Jupiter's name. It should not be forgotten that, in the most famous of the titles ascribed to Trajan *(Optimus Princeps),* the emperor shared the accolade, *optimus,* with the 'king of heaven'. Nor should we overlook Trajan's association with Hercules, which was not an elaboration of the imperial cult, in which Trajan's aspirations were modest and traditional. The connection with Hercules, demonstrated on a coin which portrayed Trajan's Column as Hercules' club, was rather more a method of expressing the ethic of hard work which benefited Rome and the empire, and which was a central feature of Trajan's administration.

More than ever before, Trajan was emperor of the whole empire, despite the traditionalist leaning to place much of the administration into the hands of senators and equestrians. It is, however, significant – and presumably indicates a concern for Italy's social and economic problems – that high-ranking officials (senators, in particular) were expected to have some of their land holding in Italy. Reforms were instituted to try to reverse Italy's decline, and Trajan made much more use of 'special commissioners' to address individual problems. Although imperial intervention in problem areas, as a principle, went back to the time of Augustus, the practice, introduced by Trajan all over the empire, effectively sent officials as *correctores* wherever a matter could benefit from such treatment. We know of many examples from inscriptions, although the best-known case was that of the younger Pliny in the province of Bithynia, which was suffering the effects of earlier maladministration. Pliny's handling of his commission, which is documented in Book X of his *Letters*, consisting of those which passed between Pliny and Trajan, bears witness to the level of detail that was involved: matters raised range from the handling of Christians in the province to Nicomedia's smelly drains. Like his predecessors, Trajan encouraged the spread of Roman citizenship and the growth of towns: some of the latter were spontaneous – a response to a developing market, as seen in the small towns outside forts in Britain – while some received, in the form of grants of colonial or municipal status, Trajan's own sponsorship.

One of Trajan's most celebrated innovations was the system of *alimenta*; the ultimate purpose of the system was to help poor families, and it appears to have operated principally in Italy. Documentation from Velleia and Beneventum shows that loans were paid out of official funds to people – mostly farmers – who required them; the interest that accrued from these loans was separately accounted for and paid out in monthly instalments to poor children who applied for them. It was of wide benefit, for not only did the ultimate beneficiaries gain, but so too did those who in the first place borrowed the money at the reasonable rates of interest that generated the funds for the poor. This was a striking example of the patronal role, prominently advertised on the coinage, which had always been a hallmark of the senatorial nobility, and which had grown in scope since the time of Augustus. It gave meaning to the protective element that was traditionally part of the tribune's relationship with the plebs. Another aspect of it was Trajan's concern for public safety by reinforcing the Neronian limits to the height to which tenement blocks (*insulae*) could be built.

In fact, Trajan needed to exercise considerable caution over the state finances; they had not been particularly strong in the later Flavian years and had been 'tested' further by Trajan's debt remission on his accession and repudiation of the 'accession gifts'. While it is true that the Dacian Wars brought in wealth and opened up new resources of gold and silver – no doubt, one of the

*Plate 8.9 Rome, the
Markets of Trajan.*

reasons why they had been undertaken – the wars themselves were expensive, as was the vigorous building programme which characterised Trajan's reign, and of which the most impressive 'symbol' was the completion of the complex consisting of the forum, the multi-level markets and, of course, the Column which crowned Trajan's mausoleum. To cope with this, there was some currency reform in the shape of a further (although small) devaluation of the silver coinage, which had to some extent recovered from the Neronian devaluation of AD 64. For the rest, more efficient organisation of tax collecting was instituted, which virtually saw the end of 'private enterprise' in this field through the old 'companies' (*societates publicanorum*) and their replacement by contractors (*conductores*), who possibly received a fixed sum for their efforts.

Although there was much in the field of civil administration which marked out the soundness of Trajan's reign and which persuaded members of the Senatorial Order that 'paradise' had come, Trajan's reign was also a period dominated by warfare – the two Dacian Wars (AD 101–102, 105–107) and the near-disastrous eastern wars at the end of the reign (AD 114–117), which also witnessed the emperor's death at the age of sixty-four.

There is no doubting the importance of the Dacian Wars, which led to the establishment on the north bank of the Danube of the new province of *Dacia*. These campaigns have their celebrated 'epitaph' in the form of the Column in Rome. Its spiral friezes tell of episodes of action in the wars and provide a backcloth for the depiction both of Trajan's relationship with his soldiers and of the success of the soldier emperor. Today, the Column has a further 'function' in providing for us the best documentation that we have of a range of activities in which the Roman army might typically be involved.

The 'Dacian problem' in various manifestations had been in existence for a long time, since Augustus had attempted to deal with a 'line' of tribes whose territories stretched along the north

Plate 8.10 (opposite) Rome, the Forum and Markets of Trajan.

Plate 8.11 Denarius of Trajan, commemorating victory in Dacia.

bank of the Danube from the headwaters of that river. While any of these tribes might have proved to be dangerous on its own, the Dacians (Daci), with their fighting traditions, probably rated as the most dangerous of Rome's opponents in the area; further, a very great danger would have been constituted in the event of an alliance among these tribes. Ultimately, Augustus' armies proved to be unequal to the task of incorporating this territory as far east as the River Elbe, or even the Vistula. Thus, the development of a frontier on the Rhine left all of these tribal areas unsupervised outside the empire.

Between the times of Augustus and Domitian, there had been no major Roman intervention, although Plautius Silvanus, governor of Moesia for much of Nero's reign, had defeated Dacians and others in battle and had resettled a considerable number of them south of the Danube. He also fostered the policy of 'divide and rule' by the creation of dependent 'kingdoms' north of the river. This had not brought peace, however, as in AD 69 Mucianus, on his way to Italy in support of the Flavian cause, ran into unauthorised Dacians south of the river. Domitian employed a combination of military force and diplomacy, and although the praetorian prefect, Cornelius Fuscus, was killed in 86 and a legionary eagle – probably of V *Alaudae* – lost, the Dacian leader, Decebalus, accepted a client kingship and a subsidy; these were (rather inconsistently) heavily criticised by Domitian's enemies in Rome, although fears that Decebalus was merely using this opportunity to strengthen his hand for future encounters would not have been groundless. Further warfare in 92–93 reduced the tribe of the Iazyges, but peace on the Danube remained tense and supported by strong new fortifications on the south bank.

Thus, the situation on the Danube when Trajan came to power was volatile – and probably deteriorating; Decebalus saw his 'arrangement' with Domitian as an opportunity to rebuild for

Plate 8.12 Rome, Trajan's Column.

another effort in the future. Not surprisingly, the Romans did not relax their preparations, and thus the early years of Trajan's reign represented an ominous build-up on both sides. In this situation, it is hardly surprising, therefore, that Pliny could say that Trajan was not seeking war, but did not fear it. The first Dacian War involved up to 80,000 Roman troops under the leadership (principally) of Tiberius Claudius Livianus (the praetorian prefect), Trajan's close friend, Licinius Sura, and the somewhat shadowy figure of the Moor, Lusius Quietus. Livianus was the first of a new type of praetorian prefect, who was a skilled administrator as well

Plate 8.13 Sestertius and as of Trajan, depicting respectively (left) the Column itself and (right) the Column as the Club of Hercules. © Copyright The British Museum.

as a military leader. This first war did not change the situation greatly: at the end of it, when Decebalus sued for peace, he remained a client king and was as determined as ever to use the peace to prepare yet another effort at empire-building.

The second war, however, had a different outcome; it was concluded by the suicide of Decebalus and the capture of his two sons. Many defeated Dacians no doubt fled, although most probably were allowed – even encouraged – to go back to their own homes, as Trajan's Column appears to indicate. There was some repopulation from provinces on the southern side of the Danube, including Dalmatians whose principal purpose was to work in the newly won gold mines. Dacia was turned into a province, a powerful protection to the north of the Danube, and effectively separating those tribal areas whose conjunction Rome feared.

There was not a great deal of town building, although by 110 the capital, Sarmizegethusa, had become a *colonia*; the principal building was to be seen in the older provinces on the south side of the river, with the establishment of *coloniae* and *municipia*. There is no sense that this was a conquest for the sake of empire building: the chief and immediate purpose was to resolve the problem that was of Decebalus' making. The war was followed by exploitation (of gold), and an attempt to stabilise this important (and dangerous) frontier zone by the existence of Dacia on the north bank of the Danube and by the rapid enhancement of the *pax Romana* on the southern side of the Danube. Megalomania is hardly adequate as a dismissal of all this, and if Trajan 'milked' the success by publicity on the coinage, in celebratory festivals and by the commissioning of the architect, Apollodorus of Damascus, to build the Column, this was no more than would have been done traditionally. Indeed, this was the opportunity to demonstrate that the days of Rome's military glory and supremacy were not over.

It is hardly surprising that Tacitus' publication in the first decade of the second century of his *Histories* will have offered a contrast by its highlighting of what the historian regarded as contemporary military 'failures' – a Germany that had been 'triumphed over rather than defeated' and a Britain that had been 'totally conquered and then allowed to slide'. However, with a massive commitment of troops to the Danube through much of the first decade of the second century AD, we are left to ponder on the effects on other military provinces. How far, for example, were troop deployments and secondments mentioned on the writing tablets from Vindolanda necessitated by troops that were being diverted from Britain to other, more pressing, theatres? Were such troop movements in any way responsible for the crisis in northern Britain with which Hadrian was evidently faced on his accession in AD 117?

These Trajanic conquests lent much weight to the notion of a 'golden age': certainly, the celebratory atmosphere in Rome and Italy must have helped to convince that this was indeed a return to the 'glory days' of Rome's past under a *princeps* who seemed deferential, generous and humane. Trade prospered within the empire as the infrastructure was enhanced to foster it. Indeed, while trade may not have been encouraged for economic reasons in isolation, it was obvious (as Claudius' speech to the Gallic aristocrats shows) that, with rising levels of wealth as a result of commerce, social (particularly urban) life could be enhanced, local people would have a better 'qualification' to become involved in local government, and this provided the most effective means for encouraging such people on to a wider administrative stage. Indeed, this appeared to be the spirit of an age dominated by a man who, although not a Spaniard as such, nonetheless came from Spain. If Pliny's *Letters* offer any guidance, this was also a period for Rome's upper classes that was characterised by culture and by material prosperity.

We might ask, therefore, why in the light of this Trajan again took the Roman world up to (and over) the brink of warfare – this time against the Parthians. Indeed, Trajan's ultimate failure in this war, precipitating as it did a new approach under Hadrian, seemed to mark the decisive line between unrivalled prosperity and the beginnings of decline.

The east had, of course, long been for various reasons a difficult area for Rome – dogged perhaps as they were by the long memory of the successes of Alexander the Great; not a few Roman leaders saw themselves as inheriting his mantle. Although Rome had faced many redoubtable leaders in the east – for example, Antiochus III of Syria and Mithridates of Pontus – it was with the Parthians that the longest-lasting problem rested.

In fact, Rome was drawn into the politics of Parthia and neighbouring Armenia as a result of her conflict in the first half of the first century BC with king Mithridates. The Pontic king allied himself with Tigranes, king of Armenia, and made him his son-in-law. Pompey, the last of many Romans to be sent into the field against him, drew the Parthians into his strategy in an attempt to neutralise the Armenians. The introduction of Parthia into

Rome's affairs was to cast a very long shadow: when Pompey in 63–62 BC completed a victorious war against Mithridates, he set about a settlement of the region of Asia Minor. Parthia was regarded as the chief regional enemy, and Asia Minor was organised into a 'circuit' of provinces around the coast, with the interior left in the hands of local monarchs who were given the status of client king; Armenia was one of these. The chief Roman military concentration was, after the establishment of the Principate, in the province of Syria, which was regarded as the 'senior' military (imperial) province.

Augustan policy in the area hinged on the 'orientation' of Armenia; while Rome and Parthia were supposed to agree on the occupant of the Armenian throne, the Romans for their part were insistent upon the king's western orientation – or, at least, his neutrality. From time to time, with the death of a king of Armenia, there was an embryonic crisis – twice in Tiberius' reign, and again in Nero's. Tiberius, as we saw, managed to restore stability, while Nero, after experimenting with the status of Armenia, allowed the king of Armenia to be a Parthian nominee (Tiridates), provided that he came to Rome to receive his diadem and, by so doing, acknowledged the overlordship of the Roman emperor. In the later first century, the chief changes concerned Roman and pro-Roman Asia Minor, with a more flexible deployment of legions – for example, in Cappadocia as well as in Syria – and a 'phasing out' of client kingdoms; one of the last to go was in AD 93.

The essence of the problem under Trajan was that Pacorus II, the Parthian king, had died in 110 and was succeeded not by one of his two sons but, perhaps reflecting the factional nature of Parthian politics, by his brother, Chosroes. Of Pacorus' two sons, Rome favoured the younger (Axidares) as king of Armenia, while Chosroes placed Axidares' elder brother (Parthamasiris) on the throne in contravention of the Neronian formula. Thus, the ostensible cause of the war from the Roman point of view was to secure the re-instatement of Axidares. However, other explanations have been advanced – a desire to exercise greater control over trade routes into and out of the east, a need to add new territory and thus exercise a greater measure of control over-all and finally a growing megalomania on Trajan's part. Whether Trajan in fact intended a large-scale addition of new territory to the empire is unclear; if he did, then he did not succeed in this intention. Indeed, it seems likely that, before his death, Trajan already appreciated the point and was in the process of bringing the campaigning to an end. The most obvious 'failure' of the episode was the refusal by the Parthians to accept as their king Parthamasiris, who was crowned by Trajan amidst great pub-licity, with REX PARTHIS DATVS proclaimed on the coinage. If this was Trajan's alternative to the annexation of Parthia as the province of Assyria, then his achievement did in the end fall well short of his hopes. On the other hand, the final solution – evi-dently Trajan's, but put into effect by Hadrian – was in essence an iteration of the long-held situation. In all, Trajan's plans look less like megalomania on his part than, as on the Danube, a vig-orous attempt to make the *status quo* sounder than it was before; criticism of the *princeps* has been generated by the fact that the seriousness of the Parthian/Armenian problem on this occasion hardly seemed to justify such an upheaval.

Trajan was already on his way back to Italy when he suffered on 9 August (117) what appears to have been a stroke, and he died a few days later. There is little doubt that Hadrian was his intended successor; although there appears to have been a spell in the middle of the reign when Trajan allied himself more closely with men who are not regarded as friends of Hadrian. Trajan's young kinsman (who was married in AD 100 to Vibia Sabina, the daughter of Trajan's niece) appears to have been firmly re-estab-lished in the favour of the *princeps* during the last years of the reign. It is unclear whether – as was put about by Trajan's wife (Plotina) and niece (Matidia) – Trajan did formally adopt Hadrian on his deathbed, or whether the imperial ladies put their own seal of approval on what the dying *princeps* was known to have intended. At any rate, whatever the truth, the opening of the new reign was inevitably blemished by suspicion of intrigue.

Hadrian: the new Augustus

It had long been common practice – we have seen it, for example, in the case of Vespasian – for an incoming *princeps* to enhance his stature as an embodiment of the true spirit of Augustus Caesar. For reasons that will emerge, Hadrian accomplished much in his reign that was deserving of that accolade. The new emperor was immediately offered – but refused – the title of *Pater Patriae* and the *cognomina* associated with his dead and deified 'father' (*Germanicus, Dacicus, Parthicus*). Yet, perhaps to dispel the rumours of intrigue which had surrounded his accession, he copied Trajan in including his predecessor's name in his own nomenclature – *Imperator Caesar Traianus Hadrianus Augustus*, the last of these names, as usual, abbreviated to AVG on the coinage. This form of the name was employed until AD 121, and then replaced by HADRIANVS AVGVSTVS; the intention is clear, for no predecessor had styled himself AVGVSTVS in full on the coinage. It heralded the 'true start' of a reign which was to witness the most thoroughgoing review of the whole administration so far; this was indeed the work of a 'new Augustus'.

Yet, the reign opened domestically on a discordant note from which it never fully recovered; the intrigue which was seen in the succession was linked in the minds of many to one of the more mysterious episodes in the reign – the murder of 'the four ex-consuls', C.Avidius Nigrinus, Lusius Quietus, A.Cornelius Palma and L.Publilius Celsus, all of them high in the esteem of the dead *princeps* and perhaps, in the minds of many, rivals for Hadrian's position.

Although Hadrian could never be regarded as 'soft' or sentimental over potential opponents and rivals, we must ask what benefit a man, generally so shrewd of political judgement, could have gained from such an act. Even if we allow that it freed him from

Plate 8.14 Rome, the Hadrianeum.

political rivals, it did so at an excessively heavy cost – a relationship with the senate which, despite all Hadrian's efforts at conciliation, was permanently damaged. In the face of this, and of Hadrian's constant denial of any involvement in an act that occurred before his own return to Rome in AD 118, it is probably more appropriate to seek the hand of another. The most likely perpetrator was, in fact, Hadrian's friend and praetorian prefect, Attianus; yet even the removal of Attianus brought no relief. The act was seen as devious and barbaric, lacking in judgement and a snub to the memory of the dead *princeps*. It seemed to symbolise the rejection by Hadrian of everything for which his predecessor had stood – and such an assessment was, in fact, very wide of the mark.

Like Trajan, Hadrian's concern for the security and prosperity of the empire was very considerable, and much of his reign was devoted to aspects of this concern. As we have seen, Hadrian's consolidation of the eastern frontier was not a negation of

Trajan's work, as shortly before his death Trajan had come to see the impossibility of imperial growth on the large scale and had turned to more conservative lines of approach. Further, although the methods of the two *principes* were different, their aims were much the same – to find adequate methods for dealing with enemies of the Roman order; Trajan sought initially to incorporate and police them, while Hadrian believed in strengthening the empire's territory within recognisable frontiers and using the frontier lines to control the activities of those beyond them, influencing them through such means as trade and commerce. This approach of supervision and the provision of commercial opportunities is clearly highlighted in the form taken by Hadrian's Wall in Britain.

Hadrian's care for the empire is demonstrated by, among other things, his ceaseless journeying around it – journeys which began very early in the reign, and which received strong publicity through the coinage. In common with Trajan, Hadrian evidently sought means to ensure that all parts of the empire were treated equally and that they had a stake in the common enterprise. As in Trajan's reign, Italy came to be treated in a manner increasingly similar to that experienced by other parts of the empire.

Like other emperors before him, Hadrian was accused of being excessively Hellenophile; the point appears to be substantiated by the effort and resources that were expended in what was effectively the rejuvenation of Athens. A closer examination may reveal a different motivation: for the west, Rome was the acknowledged focal point (rather than Rome and Italy); Hadrian's best architectural effort was put into the capital city. His magnificent reconstruction of Marcus Agrippa's Pantheon ('a temple to all the gods') symbolised this centrality of Rome in the western world. It was also, because of Agrippa's association with the building, a powerful reminder of the link between Augustus Caesar and Hadrianus Augustus.

In the east, the efforts of previous emperors had concentrated on 'neutralising' what was seen as the damaging and 'oriental' influence

Plate 8.15 Ephesus, the Temple of Hadrian.

of the Parthians, by ensuring the westward orientation of the client kingdom of Armenia. This had, in effect, been the 'solution' to which Trajan had eventually returned. The chief problem was that pro-Roman kings were not always popular in Armenia; Nero (and/or his advisers) had come up with the idea of accepting a Parthian preference on condition that he (and they) formally acknowledged the overlordship of the Roman emperor. This was what had lain behind the 'pomp and circumstance' that accompanied the crowning of Tiridates by Nero in Rome in AD 66 and behind the publicity devoted to the matter on Trajan's coinage.

Hadrian's scheme was larger – to give the east its own Romanised centre of gravity; it was not to be, as later, Byzantium (Constantinople) but a revived Athens, the traditional cultural centre of the eastern Mediterranean. No doubt it was felt that this was suitable and likely to be effective because of the Hellenistic origin of the ruling classes in many of Rome's eastern territories. It is probably in the same context that we should view Hadrian's

Plate 8.16 Rome, the Pantheon.

Plate 8.17 Rome, the Pantheon: detail of the interior and the Oculus.

interest in Greek religious cults. All of this certainly represented a bold advance in Roman thinking, for it was only a century previously that Tiberius' friend, Gnaeus Calpurnius Piso, had heavily criticised the delight of Germanicus Caesar at receiving Athenian citizenship. Piso observed that Athenian citizenship was 'cheap' and the ancient city peopled by the 'scum of the earth'; more recently than that, Juvenal's observations on Greeks and other easterners had been equally uncompromising. During his censorship in AD 47–48, Claudius had tried to correct what he saw as the excessive chauvinism and jingoism of Rome's governing class. Things had, however, undoubtedly moved on, and men with eastern origins, by Hadrian's time, found it much easier to 'rise to the top' in the administration of the empire.

Thus, Hadrian can be seen, not as the effete dilettante that some have over the years believed him to have been, but as a man with a seriousness of purpose, combined with an innovatory approach that was the very hallmark of Augustus Caesar. It is into this context that we should place Hadrian's dealings not only with Parthia/Armenia but also perhaps with the Jewish war (AD 132–135), which resulted in the emperor's decision to establish a *colonia* at Jerusalem; Judaism may have been seen as a 'centre of gravity' which threatened to rival the Graeco-Roman dominance; it was a threat that had to be demonstrably subordinated. Thus, at the end of the war, Judaea was given conventional provincial status, with no especial privileges.

Although frontier work can be detected in all parts of the empire – Europe, the east and Africa – the most celebrated manifestation is to be seen in Britain in the form of Hadrian's Wall; a study of this reveals much about the emperor's preoccupations and methods, although we are to an extent hampered by the poverty of our classical source material.

As we have seen, at the time of Hadrian's accession in AD 117, there was a major problem: 'the Britons could no longer be held under Roman control', we are informed by the emperor's biographer (in *Scriptores Historiae Augustae*), although without providing any clues regarding the nature, causes or location of the trouble. There is now evidence to suggest that the trouble was located at the western end of the frontier zone; that it had to be dealt with by warfare has long been appreciated because of the evidence of the contemporary victory coinage and has been recently confirmed by a fragmentary inscription from Vindolanda. In the aftermath, it is likely that orders were sent from Rome to construct a wall, which would presumably have been, as was normal, of turf and logically placed in the western sector. This seems to provide a more satisfactory explanation for the nature of the western part of Hadrian's Wall; that there was a shortage of other building materials seems decidedly 'lame' as an explanation.

In AD 122, Hadrian came to Britain himself; it is clear that the visit was intended to enjoy a high profile, for the *princeps* brought with him a new governor (his friend, Aulus Platorius Nepos) and a new legion (VI *Victrix*). This legion, which had been involved in frontier work on the Rhine, replaced IX *Hispana*, and was intended to act as a spearhead for Hadrian's enhanced policy in Britain. The immediate change was in the re-commencement of frontier construction in stone from the eastern end; the wall was to be ten feet thick and, probably, twelve to fifteen feet in height. It was to be fronted by a V-shaped ditch and to have fortlets (milecastles) at one-mile intervals (each housing between one dozen and two dozen men), with two watchtowers between each pair of milecastles. The main concentrations of troops which provided the small patrolling garrisons were to be held at the rear in the forts of the earlier Stanegate frontier.

This wall was a unique statement: built in stone and dominating by its hold on the most difficult terrain, it was clearly political in the sense of impressing on local groups, through its superior technology, the power of Rome and, particularly, of its emperor. As an architect of not inconsiderable talent, Hadrian fully understood the power of a building as a political statement. The wall was also intended, as Hadrian's biographer announces, to 'separate the

Romans from the barbarians'. It did not prevent movement, however, but rather allowed for its supervision. After all, each mile-castle was a fortified gateway, thus providing eighty gates through the wall, through which people might pass on legitimate business and, if involved in commerce, pay the appropriate taxes.

Hadrian's visit probably also gave a new impetus to Romanisation in Britain through the establishment of new *civitates* (Romanised tribal units) as organs of local government. The *princeps* may also have been involved in such major public works programmes as the draining of the East Anglian Fenlands. If the visit to Britain was typical of the imperial journeys, then we can readily appreciate the thrust which was lent by the encouragement of provincial security and the consequent local sense of responsibility. That the *princeps* left his mark on Britain can hardly be doubted.

Hadrian's Wall was probably completed by the end of the reign, but not before further changes of plan: for example, in *c.* AD 124–125, it was decided to add a series of large garrison forts to the wall and to close most of those on the Stanegate. The reason for this is nowhere stated, but probably had as much to do with convenience of deployment as anything else. At the same time, the linear earthwork, known as the *vallum*, was added to the southern side of the wall, perhaps to demarcate the southern extent of a military zone. Further, the *limes* was extended in the east to Wallsend and, in the west, by a series of forts, fortlets, watchtowers and linear features from Bowness-on-Solway to Maryport. The purpose of this extension appears to have been to outwit tax avoidance on the part of those who tried to outflank the wall and to offer to the evidently prospering rural economy of the Solway Plain protection from vandals and rustlers from Galloway (the tribe of the Novantae). It is likely that this rural economy will have represented a local input into the supplying of the wall garrisons.

The directness with which Hadrian 'intervened' in the administration of policy in Britain and elsewhere in the empire was

Plate 8.18 Britannia, Hadrian's Wall: Cawfields milecastle and the Vallum on the Great Whin Sill. Source: photographed by G. D. B. Jones.

typical of his style of government. This was partly due to his great interest in administrative detail (as is shown by the considerable volume of inscriptions from across the empire which provide information on such matters) and partly to his anxiety to be at one with and part of the senatorial aristocracy. In the tradition of the 'best' emperors, he attended the senate's meetings frequently, consulted the body and utilised it in the passage of his legislation. He was observant of its dignity – for example, not allowing appeal to himself from its judicial decisions, ensuring that senators were tried by senators only and helping deserving senators who had fallen on 'hard times', and who needed subvention either to remain in the senate or in seeking office. The apex of his administrative machine still remained senators in the emperor's service.

In other words, we can see Hadrian following in the best traditions and aspirations of emperors of the likes of Augustus, Tiberius, Vespasian or Trajan. It is possible, however, that the assiduity of his concern for partnership caused the same incredulity in some senators as it had in the days of Tiberius; after all, no matter how affable he might try to be, he was the 'master' of the governmental machine. To some senators, at least, his protestations (recorded by his biographer) that he was the 'state's servant, not its master' may have conveyed the same hollow ring as when such sentiments had been expressed a century previously. In view of this, it is particularly frustrating that we do not know for certain whether Tacitus lived into Hadrian's reign and had the opportunity to see this 'new Tiberius' in action.

Despite this, however, Hadrian never achieved accord with the senatorial aristocracy: there were probably many contributory causes. Specific events, such as the murder of the four *consulares*, left a 'bad taste', as did suspicions surrounding the legitimacy of Hadrian's accession and the fact that he could prove to be a martinet if crossed. No doubt, too, many felt that he was speciously offering a partnership which he could not (or would not) deliver. For many, he was the reverser of the expansionist policies of his popular predecessor which, of course, had provided seemingly limitless opportunities for senators to 'shine'. Further, there was his reputation for an obsession with all things Greek, even if the *Graeculus* (as he was pejoratively called) was exercising a clear imperial vision through his cultural interests. Nor should we forget the long periods of time which Hadrian spent away from Rome, which must have damaged the coherence of a relationship which he was evidently eager to establish. All such considerations contributed to a relationship which was ultimately so poor that senators hesitated to deify the dead emperor until forced to it by Antoninus, who thus won credit for his *pietas*.

Yet, despite an attachment on Hadrian's part to the Senatorial Order that was probably both sentimental and practical, an increasing burden of detailed administration fell on to members of the Equestrian Order and on people like them who were not formally part of that Order. The apex of the equestrian career remained the two posts of praetorian prefect, although for most of Hadrian's reign, after the dismissal of Suetonius' friend, Septicius Clarus, in AD 121/2, there was probably only one (Marcius Turbo). The praetorian prefects were senior members of the emperor's advisory group, the *consilium*, and from Hadrian's time tended to assume a different range of responsibilities; from being a predominantly military post, the prefecture took on wider administrative functions, particularly within the administration of justice and in the interpretation of law. In future, the praetorian prefecture was occupied by men who were seen as Rome's leading jurists.

The older prefectures – of Egypt, of the corn supply, of the fire brigade and of the fleets – remained equestrian preserves; these posts were enhanced by the appointment of *subpraefecti*, which had the effect of taking direct imperial interest and dominance further down the hierarchies of organisations to which they were appointed. Just as it had become possible for senators to pursue careers which were more exclusively civilian in character, so this became a feature of the equestrian *cursus* also. Typical of such posts were the *advocati* who, through legal expertise, concerned themselves in disputes between the treasury (*fiscus*) and private individuals, thus relieving procurators in the provinces of many of their burdens.

The procuratorial part of the administration also underwent review: ever since the time of Augustus, fiscal and other matters relating to the state's financial interests had been handled by *procuratores Augusti*, drawn from the Equestrian Order and responsible directly to the *princeps*. This created a duality of authority in a province which in certain circumstances – as in Britain in the events which led up to Boudica's rebellion – could cause a real and dangerous hiatus. Under Hadrian, the procuratorial offices were distinguished by salary levels: the most senior, *ducenarii*, were paid 200,000 *sestertii* per annum; beneath them were the *centenarii* (100,000) and the *sexagenarii* (60,000). The top grades included all the senior equestrian officials in the emperor's service – that is, those holding posts which, in the days of Claudius, had been occupied by ex-slaves – and equestrian procuratorial provincial governors; financial procurators in the provinces were usually *centenarii*, while procurators on their staffs who attended to specific activities were *sexagenarii*. It is reckoned that, in Hadrian's reign, according to our existing evidence, there were between thirty-five and forty men in each of the three grades. The introduction of extra procuratorial posts under Hadrian was particularly evident in the matters of census taking and tax collection.

Hadrian was in all things a man who paid great attention to detail; it is to be seen in domestic matters relating to marriage, inheritance and slavery, to taxes and exemptions, to matters concerned with decorum, fair-dealing, public safety and public utilities all over the empire. However, perhaps the outstanding example is to be seen in the codification of the 'praetor's edict'; this was a mammoth task to bring together enactments of the *praetor urbanus*, *praetor peregrinus* and the 'provincial edict' going back over hundreds of years and representing between them a compendium of enactments covering most aspects of life in

Rome, Italy and the empire. In all, therefore, we can argue that the great achievement of this reign was the establishment of codes of practice applicable across the empire and the creation of a bureaucracy of the size and status that could see to the proper practice of these codes.

Into all aspects of the life of Rome and the empire – governmental, financial, cultural, religious and architectural – Hadrian made it the purpose of his 'crusade' to bring integrity, efficiency and fairness of dealing. In everything he wanted his to be recognised as a new Augustan age; this was the goal and the achievement of Hadrianus Augustus.

As with so many before him, the one field in which it proved hardest to achieve such clarity and effectiveness was in that of the succession. Hadrian had no children of his own, but he does not appear to have given thought to the matter of succession until he started to become ill – evidently in AD 136. According to Dio Cassius, Hadrian had once said that, of all possible successors, only Lucius Julius Ursus Servianus, a relative of the *princeps* and a nonagenarian by the end of the reign, could be contemplated unequivocally. Yet Hadrian had never seriously advanced the cause of Servianus nor, more pertinently, that of Servianus' grandson, Gnaeus Pedanius Fuscus Salinator. Hadrian had never given undue preference to the advancement of members of his own family, but it remains a mystery why, in AD 136, he suddenly struck down both Servianus and Fuscus, an event magnified by the sources into a 'reign of terror' – possibly another 'Tiberian reminiscence'.

The sick emperor spent much of his last years at the extraordinary villa (Fig. 8.2) which he had constructed in the Apennine foothills at Tivoli (*Tibur*); like its architect, the villa was (and is) a restless place full of memories of foreign parts, which led one author to say of it that it 'fed the nostalgia of the ageing emperor'. Yet, it was no mere 'pleasuredrome', incorporating, as it did, accommodation suited to an emperor's continuing performance of his duties.

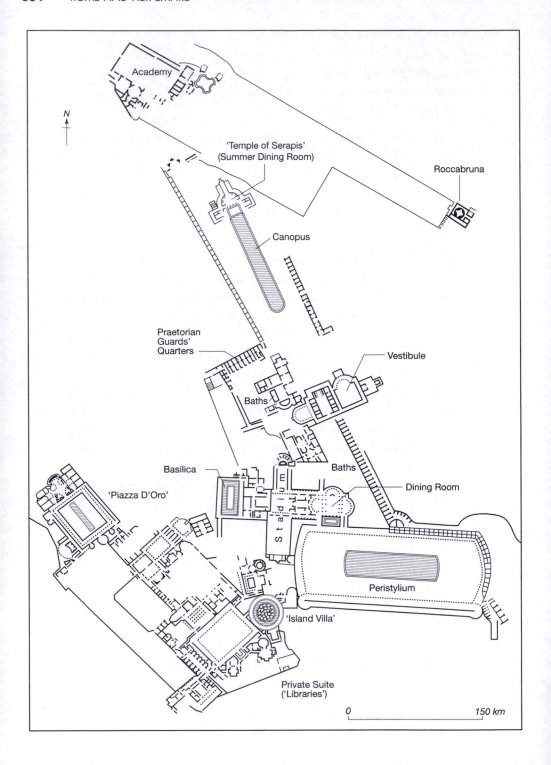

Academy

'Temple of Serapis'
(Summer Dining Room)

Roccabruna

Canopus

Praetorian
Guards'
Quarters

Vestibule

Baths

Baths

Basilica

Dining Room

'Piazza D'Oro'

Stadium

Peristylium

'Island Villa'

Private Suite
('Libraries')

0   150 km

Hadrian's first formal choice of successor was Lucius Ceionius Commodus, one of the consuls of 136, who was also the son-in-law of Avidius Nigrinus, one of the four *consulares* put to death at the opening of the reign. Commodus took the name, Lucius Aelius Caesar, after adoption and was given *tribunicia potestas* and *imperium proconsulare*. By the end of 137, however, Lucius Aelius was dead, prompting Hadrian to remark that he had 'leaned on a falling wall'. Hadrian then turned to Titus Aurelius Fulvus Boionius Arrius Antoninus, grandson of Nerva's partisan, Arrius Antoninus, and consul in 120. As far as we know, Antoninus had a blameless reputation but had never held a military post. He was married to Annia Faustina, the daughter of Marcus Annius Verus, the only man (other than Servianus) to have enjoyed the distinction of three consulships under Hadrian. Like Augustus before him, Hadrian went further than simply naming a successor, and put forward a 'succession package', as Augustus had done in AD 4. Antoninus was required himself to make a double adoption – Lucius Ceionius Commodus (son of the dead Lucius Aelius Caesar), now renamed Lucius Aelius Aurelius Commodus, and Marcus Annius Verus (grandson of the three-times consul, Annius Verus), now renamed Marcus Aelius Aurelius Verus, and in whom Hadrian had always shown especial interest. Hadrian expressed the wish that Lucius Aelius should marry Antoninus' daughter, Faustina (II), while Marcus Aurelius should marry Lucius Aelius' sister. In fact, Marcus Aurelius married Faustina, despite the fact that her mother, Faustina (I), was also his grand-mother. The result was that, with a fairly thin veneer of adoptive practices, the Principate was returning to dynasticism: Antoninus Pius was succeeded by Marcus Aurelius and Lucius Verus, while, on his death in AD 180, Marcus Aurelius passed power on to his own son, Commodus (see Appendix 3).

This was, in effect, the final act: Hadrian died at Baiae (on the Bay of Naples) on 10 July AD 138. The last two years had been happy for no-one and represented the peak of Hadrian's unpop-ularity with the senate, which as a consequence made no move to

Figure 8.2 (opposite) Tivoli: plan of Hadrian's Villa. Source: After A. Boethius and J. B. Ward-Perkins, Etruscan and Early Roman Architecture (London: Yale University Press, 1970), p. 329.

Plate 8.19 Tivoli, the Villa of Hadrian: the 'Canopus Canal'.

deify the dead *princeps*; that was left to his successor. Hadrian's true legacy, however, was a Principate, the organisation of which was stronger than it had ever been: Hadrian had proved himself a true Augustus.

The Antonines

In every way, Antoninus Pius is portrayed in antiquity as the perfect man and consummate ruler; no-one sums up better this view of the man than Marcus Aurelius, his son-in-law and successor (see Appendix 3).

Antoninus' reign marked little change from Hadrian's; *pietas* pervaded the style of government; this was a *princeps* who thrived on

Plate 8.20 Tivoli, the Villa of Hadrian: the 'Vale of Tempe'.

hard work, who involved himself in everything and who, though fair in his dealings with others, expected the same high standards of them as of himself. He showed conspicuous respect for the senate, kept his promise not to put a senator to death and allowed them to exercise jurisdiction over their own colleagues. As a consequence, this was a period of exceptional harmony with the senatorial aristocracy and with the Equestrian Order, too. Men of both Orders who performed their functions well were kept in post for long periods, especially at senior levels. Financial matters were conducted firmly, but fairly, and the essential criterion for expenditure was necessity. Antoninus' building programme shows this well, limited, as it was, to the completion of Hadrianic projects, such as the Temple of Venus and Rome and the harbour of Ostia at the mouth of the Tiber, together with required upgradings and repairs; coin evidence,

Plate 8.21 Ostia, household shrine to the Lares.

for example, indicates that Antoninus restored the Temple of Divus Augustus in Rome, perhaps indicating Antoninus' wish for association with the first *princeps*. One of the few new structures was a temple to his dead and deified wife, Diva Faustina, whose memory was kept alive by an extensive issue of coins after her death in AD 141. The temple, which was still unfinished at the time of Antoninus' own death in 161, was eventually dedicated to the Deified Antoninus as well. Similar criteria were applied to projects in the provinces.

Antoninus died on 7 March AD 161; according to the sources, his was virtually the first unquestionably peaceful death of a *princeps*

Plate 8.22 Ostia, the Capitolium.

Plate 8.23 Ostia, public lavatories.

in a century-and-a-half. As to the succession, there was no question; Marcus Aurelius had been associated with Antoninus since his formal adoption as heir (*Caesar*) in AD 145. Marcus was never co-emperor with Antoninus, but was associated closely in his rule; it was a collaboration based on a strong family bond. Marcus married Antoninus' daughter, Faustina, in 145, and she was styled *Augusta* after the birth of her first child two years later; she had a further eight children before AD 160. So strong was the dynastic appearance that Marcus' succession was never in doubt. His adoptive brother, Lucius Aelius (or Lucius Verus, as he became known), was advanced by Antoninus, but not at the rate of Marcus Aurelius, and certainly not with any hint of collaborative intention on Antoninus' part. Undoubtedly, the philosophical Marcus was more to Antoninus' taste than the more superficial, pleasure-loving, Lucius. It was thus a matter of surprise when, in 161, Marcus called on his 'brother' to be his co-emperor and betrothed his daughter, Lucilla, to Verus. Joint rule

Plate 8.24 Ostia, street with insulae.

lasted until Verus' death in 169, and was then 'resumed', this time with Marcus' son, Commodus, in AD 177.

Although Marcus had had all of the stages of education that were normal for young Romans, he had always been drawn to philosophy; unlike Agricola, he was not deterred by parental advice to be moderate in this respect, but was allowed to indulge himself. Thus, he was tutored in the rudiments of all the major Graeco-Roman philosophical systems but was increasingly drawn to Stoicism under the influence of Quintus Junius Rusticus, a descendant of one of Domitian's 'stoic martyrs'.

In no way, however, did the study of philosophy produce in Marcus the kind of extremism that had been common in the second half of the first century AD, but rather a man who was moderate, non-doctrinaire, humanitarian and practical. In other words, Stoicism brought Marcus Aurelius to what might be regarded as the ideal expression of the creed in the Roman world – a man who was good and principled, but who in no way shrank from the actions which he recognised as his duty. This was a *civilis princeps* with, perhaps, a nostalgic tinge of Republicanism in him, but again it was not of the doctrinaire type witnessed under the Flavians; rather, it was a reflection of the marriage of autocracy and a practical sense of tradition which had been a hallmark of the Principate since the time of Trajan. That this was to Stoics an acceptable 'compromise' is clear from the fact that the second century did not witness a return to the Stoic extremism which had so disfigured Domitian's reign.

Thus, like his immediate predecessors, Marcus made co-operation with the senate and honouring its traditions and current membership a key to his policy; he consulted it as a body, and its members as prestigious individuals, legislated through it, attended it assiduously and gave it the fiction of declarations of war and ratifications of peace. Its make-up, however, was changing during the second century; by the end of the century the senate contained Italians and provincials in approximately equal measure, while among the provincials those of eastern origin predominated. Despite the tendency in the second century for the bureaucracy to grow, room among the newly created posts was found for senators as well as equestrians. While, on a social level, distinctions between the classes were maintained, it was a sign of Marcus' practical application of his philosophy that he accommodated in both Orders 'outsiders' of merit; indeed, he chose husbands for a number of his daughters from such 'new men'. Also, Marcus was always ready to give practical expression to his belief in merit by the granting of citizenship and financial subsidies when these were needed to bring forward the 'right men'. However, by insisting on merit as an overwhelming criterion for advancement, his grants of citizenship still implied honour – in contrast to Caracalla's *Constitutio Antoniniana* of AD 212, by which citizenship was thrown open uncritically, largely for financial reasons.

Within Italy and the provinces, Marcus' rule was sound in its adherence to the principles laid down by his three predecessors; management, especially financial, was strict, although not excessively so. Although, like Antoninus Pius, Marcus made necessity the chief criterion of his expenditure, this was a period when 'necessity' covered a lot of eventualities – wars, disease, natural disasters; not unnaturally, the wars themselves gave rise to a certain amount of commemorative building, not least the great Column in Rome, imitating Trajan's, and celebrating the German and Sarmatian wars. This was started in *c.* AD 176 and was evidently still unfinished on the death of Commodus in 192. There was a certain amount of public utility building in the provinces – again largely in the form of necessary refurbishment, although a lot of this was financed locally. This was particularly true of Africa, which at this stage shows, through the magnificence of its buildings, the level of prosperity which it was now experiencing. Nevertheless, many parts of the empire found these straitened times, with drains on their populations because of the widespread plague and the burdens of military recruitment which Marcus' wars imposed. As a result of such pressures, the difference of status between Italy and the provinces, which had been narrowing through the second century, closed still further.

As a Stoic, Marcus Aurelius had a strong reverence for tradition and duty; it is not surprising, therefore, that in the matter of religion he turned first to traditional deities of the Roman state – Jupiter ('Preserver', 'Defender', 'Victor'), Mars, Minerva, *Roma Victrix, Fortuna.* These were deities who had a primary and obvious relevance to the troubled times in which Marcus reigned. Foreign cults were by this time practised in plenty; over the years, the number of such cults had grown, as people came to find the state's cults too impersonal to satisfy their own needs for salvation. Many now found succour in cults such as those of Isis and Cybele (the 'Earth-Mother'), as well as in Mithraism. Nor was the tolerant Marcus averse to many of these, believing perhaps that in such difficult times it was worth casting the net widely in search of relevant divine support.

Although it was still rare for an emperor to think of himself as a god, the tendency had grown for emperors to see themselves as the earthly vice-gerent of Jupiter; this was akin to the 'intermediary role' between gods and men which characterised the father's position in his household – a suitable analogy for the *Pater Patriae*. In Marcus' case, the Stoic belief in 'divine providence' (*providentia deorum*) perhaps helped to convince the *princeps* that he was a man with a special, divinely ordained, destiny – again, especially fitting in Marcus' time. Not only this, but the imperial cult had always been seen as the citizen's duty and, as a Stoic, Marcus naturally had a strongly developed sense of duty.

Yet, in his search for divine help, Marcus would not entertain the god of the burgeoning sect of Christianity; to him, it gave people a conflict of loyalties which detracted from a sense of duty, and (no doubt) the philosopher in him, as later with Julian, found the Christians' readiness to die irrational. The 'official line' remained that which was encapsulated in Trajan's reply to Pliny – that witch-hunts for Christians should not be encouraged, that attempts should be made to persuade them of the errors of their ways but that, at the end of the day, those who would not recant and do their civic duty were guilty of a criminal act. Although Marcus warned against the terrors inculcated by superstitions (and may have meant to include Christianity in this), he did not tighten the law, nor did he openly encourage, let alone order, persecution. On the other hand, he did nothing to check it when it appeared; nor can there be any question of ignorance on his part of what was going on – for example, in Lyons in AD 177–178 or in Rome in 167, when his tutor, Junius Rusticus was involved in the punishments as *praefectus urbi*. Indeed, it has been argued that Marcus may have facilitated the sale to the arena of prisoners condemned to death in Gaul.

For many, the coincidence of the growth of Christianity and the increase in disasters and difficulties could not be accidental; Rome's problems, as in the past, stemmed from the gods' anger at 'atheists', thus setting a trend which would provide convenient

Plate 8.25 Rome, Column of
Marcus Aurelius.

scapegoats through to the early years of the fourth century. Under the 'spiritual' leadership of Marcus Aurelius, the pagan opposition to Christianity became more articulate, which was to prove an important legacy through the next two centuries. Immediately, however, it served to intensify an atmosphere redolent with the spirit of opposition.

As already said, part of the accidental difficulty for Christians was the frequency of dangers and emergencies in Marcus' reign. In terms of military difficulties, the reigns of Antoninus and Marcus could not have been more different: Antoninus' reign was marked by relatively little military activity; as a pacific man, he certainly did not seek conflict. According to the traveller and geographer, Pausanias, he had, however, to face up to it in Britain. The true reasons for Antoninus' decision to abandon the recently completed Hadrian's Wall, to re-occupy southern Scotland and to build a new wall between the estuaries of the Rivers Forth and Clyde have been lost in the confused text of Pausanias, who appears to have mixed up the Swiss and British tribes, both called Brigantes. It has been suggested that Antoninus provoked a conflict in order to win a military reputation for himself, but it seems more likely that that portion of the Brigantes which was 'cut off' on the north side of Hadrian's Wall was having a disruptive effect on neighbouring tribes. To judge from the locations of new fortifications built at this time, their influence proved most dangerous with the Novantae of Dumfries and Galloway. Indeed, references on surviving inscriptions and in the texts of the historians suggest that the northern frontier zone in Britain may have continued to experience a degree of localised disruption until, in the first decade of the third century, Septimius Severus temporarily established the imperial court at York in order to campaign in the north. The ultimate and important 'casualty' of such tribal disruption may well have been the grain-producing tribes of eastern Scotland.

There is much that is unclear about the Antonine Wall; it seems, however, that this thirty-seven-mile long frontier underwent some changes of plan: it was evidently intended to build it in stone, yet in the event it was constructed of turf. It was probably initially planned after the manner of Hadrian's Wall, with forts, fortlets and watchtowers; yet, in the end, it was equipped with a closely set series of forts of varying size. Its construction also seems to have been temporarily abandoned in the mid-140s. Final abandonment came probably in the later-150s, and it was completed in the early years of Marcus' reign. On the basis of the evidence of coin hoards, these vicissitudes have been put down to trouble among the Brigantes, although it seems more likely that the hoarding, particularly of silver, had more to do with the deteriorating state of the coinage than with military threat. It may well be that, with growing trouble apparently north of the line of the Forth and the Clyde in the later second century, some of the forts of the Antonine Wall continued to be used for occasional patrolling into the reigns of Commodus and even of Septimius Severus.

The contrast between Antoninus' generally peaceful reign and that of Marcus could not be greater: three major theatres of warfare occupied almost the whole of Marcus' reign – in the east, on the Danube and against the German tribes. Indeed, it was probably this near-continuous warfare in major theatres that persuaded Marcus that the occupation of southern Scotland was too much of a luxury.

The problems of the east were no different in substance from what they had been for over a century. The timing of an offensive against the Romans was probably connected with the change of emperors, and the hope on the part of the Parthians that new rulers would be unsure of their ground. To an extent, this was good thinking: for Marcus did not wish to leave Lucius Verus alone in Rome, nor did he want both of them to be away together. This gave him no option but to entrust the eastern command to Verus who, apart from claiming credit for victories won, appears to have treated the episode like an extended holiday. There were three identifiable stages to the warfare – against Armenia (161–163), against Parthia (163–165) and against Media (165–166) – and operations were conducted by generals who either were of high calibre already or were to attain it in the future; overall, their 'roll call' makes as impressive a list of men as had been put into the field at any time since the reign of Augustus. By 166, victory was complete and terms agreed, the basis of which was, as always, the maintenance of the security of the eastern provinces. The emperors assumed an impressive array of titles – *Armeniacus, Parthicus, Medicus*. However, the real legacy of these campaigns was the plague which infected the Roman army and which was spread by them across the empire as they returned to their bases after the wars.

The European wars occupied a large portion of Marcus' reign – from the mid-160s to the mid-170s; for a substantial part of this period, Marcus did not return to Rome. The Rhine and Danube frontiers had not consisted of the rivers alone; not only were there the provinces on the 'Roman side' of these rivers, but a line of tribes along the east bank of the Rhine and the north bank of the Danube. Since Trajan's time, of course, part of this 'tribal line' – the Dacians – had been subsumed into the province of Dacia, the organisation of which had been tightened considerably since its annexation.

Whatever the temporary political sympathies of the tribes on the far banks, there were two interlinked considerations to exercise Roman anxieties. As had been the case while the Dacians remained a free people, there was the danger that the tribes might make common cause and come into an anti-Roman 'confederation'. This was the more likely when we appreciate the pressures that they themselves were under; faced by a 'buffer' consisting of rivers and Roman provinces, they were in great difficulty when pressure built up on them from behind. The causes of this were tribes whose names look forward to rather later events – Lombards, Alans, Goths, Vandals; these were trying to migrate southwards and westwards. The Roman frontiers thus became the 'points of explosion'. The depth of the danger was seen when, in AD 167, the Marcomanni and the Quadi broke across the Danube and penetrated Italy as far as Aquileia. This caused Marcus to raise two new legions (II and III *Italica*) which, for the first time for a century, were recruited from Roman citizens in Italy itself; it also caused the establishment of a new command, under an ex-consul, devoted to the protection of Italy and the Alps.

The details of this long period of campaigning are hazy; our sources and the coinage record Roman victories, although it seems that, often, no sooner had these been won but their effects were lost by fresh outbreaks of treachery on the tribal side. Nor should we overlook the fact that these wars were fought against the background of not only continuing plague but also the death of Verus in 169, leaving Marcus to shoulder the burden on his own. Marcus' preferred solution was, it seems, to follow Trajan's example and annex and organise into provinces (Marcomannia and Sarmatia) the tribes on the far bank of the Danube. In the event, this did not prove possible: so Marcus had to content himself with treaties which involved a certain amount of tribal resettlement within the empire – 5,500 Sarmatians, for example, were sent to Britain in AD 175 – and the clearance of *cordons sanitaires* on the north bank of the Danube which the tribes were not permitted to use; garrisons were also settled in tribal territories under the terms of the treaties.

Disharmony among the principal tribes – the Sarmatian Iazyges actually asked Marcus to annihilate the Marcomanni and the Quadi – left the Romans ultimately able to dictate solutions. It is likely that Marcus was on the point of initiating his preferred option of annexation when, in March AD 180, he died, possibly of the plague, but undoubtedly worn out by years of stress and hard work. His son and successor, Commodus, preferred the alternative solution of clientage; thus Marcus' new provinces never materialised. He had, however, brought to the European frontiers a security which at one time had hardly seemed possible and which was to last to be tested again in the third and fourth centuries.

A remarkable feature of the reign of this frail philosopher emperor, who spent so much time away from Rome, and in whose time the empire was plagued by so much difficulty and misfortune, is the lack of opposition to him. One major conspiracy is recorded – that of Avidius Cassius in the east in 175, the man who had been the chief architect of victory in the eastern wars at the beginning of the reign. Although attempts were made in some of the documentation to explain/excuse this disloyalty by claiming that Avidius Cassius believed that Marcus was already dead, and wished to avoid the calamity of civil war, it appears that his was the rebellion of a man who had been too powerful for too long. Avidius Cassius was by origin a Syrian, and his cause was taken up by cities in Syria and Egypt; against these, Marcus was severe. The legions, however, remained true to the *imperator* whom they had so often saluted; it was they who killed Avidius Cassius – a fact marked by the titles, *Certa Constans*, subsequently borne by Legion XII *Fulminata*. It was appropriate that the 'thunderbolt' legion should avenge the wrong done to Jupiter's vicegerent on earth. To Avidius Cassius' family and friends Marcus was just and fair; it was typical of this emperor that the moderation which had been his guiding principle as a ruler should be displayed in full measure in the event of a wrong done to him.

The epitaphs of the reign of Marcus Aurelius lay in the emperor's actions: he was a *princeps* who had done what to a Stoic stood first and foremost in the priorities – his duty.

Commodus: The last of the Antonines and the end of the Augustan Principate

It is an irony of history that Marcus Aurelius, a *princeps* with an elevated perception of duty and merit, should have broken with a system of succession which ostensibly recognised such matters and bequeathed power to a son who proved himself to be so unworthy of it.

When Marcus died on the Danube in 180, his son, Commodus, just nineteen years of age, was with him. Commodus' principal objective was to return to Rome to pursue a life of indolent luxury; thus, he disdained to pursue the now-realisable objective of territorial annexation on the far side of the Danube, preferring to make agreements with the tribes which, as we have seen, would leave them as clients of Rome. Not that the terms of agreement were lax: tribesmen were recruited into the Roman army, while others were resettled in the provinces south of the rivers – both developments which, as they accelerated, were to have major consequences over the next two centuries, when they would be seen as part of the process of 'barbarisation'. Garrisons were placed in the client territories and the *cordons sanitaires* were insisted on along the north bank of the Danube.

The dynastic principle once again produced, as in the cases of Caligula and Nero, a *princeps* convinced that he was 'born to be king'. However, since the pursuit of pleasures left little room for the affairs of state, the direction of government was largely in the hands of others – initially, the advisers of Marcus, such as Claudius Pompeianus, Aufidius Victorinus and the praetorian prefect, Tarutienus Paternus. This state of affairs was brought to an end by a plot which was evidently really concerned with the jealousy entertained by Lucilla (the sister of the *princeps* and unwilling wife of Claudius Pompeianus) for Crispina, the wife of Commodus. The plot itself, and 'sub-plots' that were interwoven with it, brought down Pompeianus (although he survived with his life) and Paternus (who did not), together with many aristocratic people; it was the type of 'blood-bath' that had not been seen in Rome since the first century.

Out of it came a new praetorian prefect, Perennis, who, between AD 182 and 185, was prepared to allow Commodus to indulge himself and effectively leave the conduct of affairs to him. Perennis may have been ambitious and may ultimately have looked to take over from Commodus, but his conduct of affairs was generally sound. The period of his ascendancy saw one of the most efficient governors of Britain, Marcus Ulpius Marcellus, who appears to have restored order in a frontier crisis which, although obscure, was evidently dangerous. Perennis' fall was brought about by a Phrygian ex-slave, M. Aurelius Cleander, who persuaded the *princeps* that Perennis was a threat.

Cleander's period of ascendancy (AD 185–189) was one in which the behaviour of the court sank to depths not seen in the second century, in which good men were removed and in which a cowed senate bestowed on the emperor the title of *pater senatus* ('Father of the senate'). Cleander, for his part, made a great deal of money from selling positions, offices and commands; this money he used to finance a life of luxury which was second only to that enjoyed by the *princeps* himself. Although there were some achievements on the frontiers during this period, Commodus preferred not to visit his armies, but to stay in isolation at Laurentum to avoid catching the plague, boasting of the *Roma Aeterna* that was his achievement. Cleander fell victim to a dispute with Dionysius, the prefect of the corn supply, who used the power of his office to make Cleander a hated and deeply unpopular figure. His murder was but a short step from there.

For the remaining years of his reign, Commodus had a plurality of advisers, which meant that no-one dominated after the manner of a Perennis or a Cleander. As a result, the last three years of the reign probably offer a better idea than the rest of Commodus' own view of his position.

In Rome, senators and many of the officers were treated to inanities, with which they put up, although, as we have seen, they could (and did on occasion) fall victim to the power struggles among Commodus' close advisers; they and other dignitaries in Rome and the provinces were expected to contribute to a special levy which supported Commodus' self-indulgences. On the other hand, it was not a period of extravagance with regard to building projects and military expenditure, the latter of which Commodus claimed as his own special achievement. Ordinary life in the provinces was, as Petillius Cerialis had said of a different time (Tacitus, *Hist.* IV. 73–74), not much affected by the crimes and caprices of the autocrat; indeed, there is evidence of some useful attention to detail on the government's part.

The overriding feature of the reign – increasingly as time went on – was the megalomania of the *princeps* which, as with others before him, expressed itself through religious outlets. It has been suggested that Commodus may have been attempting to produce a 'world religious order' with Jupiter at its head (*Juppiter Exsuperatorius*); all known religions would find a place within this. However, satisfying though it might be to find Commodus imbued with some of his father's thoughtfulness, the evidence appears to suggest that the interest in religions was based on his fascination with the exotic. Further, the 'superiority' of Jupiter was intended to provide a measure of his own earthly superiority as vice-gerent.

Commodus indulged in a variety of religious practices, including Mithraism and Isis worship, and the sources strongly suggest that it was a combination of mysticism, exoticism and sadism that drew him to them. These religions also gave him scope for the assertion of his own divinity, which became totally open in AD 192 when he declared himself *Hercules Romanus Augustus* and established a priesthood to this cult. On the coinage and in statuary, Commodus appeared as Hercules – a god who laboured for mankind; indeed, one statue was placed outside the senate house, with the Roman Hercules aiming an arrow towards the *patres*. In the arena, he indulged a Herculean passion for hunting, sometimes for days on end, with hundreds of animal victims. The egocentricity showed itself, too, in the attachment of his name to everything; even Rome itself was renamed *Colonia Lucia Aurelia Nova Commodiana.*

With the behaviour of the *princeps* developing along such lines as these – and at an alarming rate – it was only a question of time before something was done to bring the insanity to a close. His mad plans for the New Year celebrations of AD 193, which were to be marked by a procession of gladiators led by the emperor gladiator himself, brought matters to a head; he was murdered on the night of 31 December. Although people moved swiftly to annul his memory in all the usual ways, it is a mark of changing times that, within four years, all had changed and the memory of the Roman Hercules had been rehabilitated.

Commodus' reign effectively marks the end of the Augustan Principate and the inception of a new style of military monarchy. While his religious exoticism did not itself set a trend, it is perhaps significant that Jupiter and Hercules, the two gods whom Commodus favoured and with whom he identified, emerged again a century later as the high-profile protectors of Diocletian's reconstructed government. In the meantime, it was to be the empire's armies which demonstrated their power to make or break emperors. Inevitably, such power had to be recognised by more than deference and money: the outcome was the military monarchy of Lucius Septimius Severus, the 'African Emperor'.

Appendix I:

The dispositions of the Legions in the late First and Second Centuries AD

(a) Vespasian's reorganisation (c. AD 71)		30 legions
Spain	VII *Gemina* (formerly *Galbiana*)	1
Britain	II *Augusta*; IX *Hispana*; XX *Valeria Victrix*; II *Adiutrix*	4

Upper Germany	I *Adiutrix*; VIII *Augusta*; XI *Claudia Pia Fidelis*; XIV *Gemina Martia Victrix*	4
Lower Germany	II *Adiutrix*; VI *Victrix*; X *Gemina*; XXI *Rapax*	4
Pannonia	XIII *Gemina*; XV *Apollinaris*; XXII *Primigenia*	3
Moesia	I *Italica*; IV *Flavia*; V *Alaudae*; V *Macedonica*; VII *Claudia Pia Fidelis*	5
Syria	III *Gallica*; IV *Scythica*; VI *Ferrata*	3
Cappadocia	XII *Fulminata*; XVI *Flavia*	2
Judaea	X *Fretensis*	1
Egypt	III *Cyrenaica*; XXII *Deiotariana*;	2
Africa	III *Augusta*	1

(Note: I *Germanica*, IV *Macedonica*, XI *Primigenia* and XVI *Gallica* were disbanded by Vespasian after disgrace in the Batavian war; they were replaced by IV and XVI *Flavia*. II *Adiutrix* was recruited probably by Otho in AD 69, although some believe that it was formed from the Ravenna fleet after the defection to Vespasian in AD 69 (Tacitus, *Hist*. III.12).

(b) The reign of Vespasian (*c*. AD 75)		29 legions
Spain	VII *Gemina*	1
Britain	II *Adiutrix*; II *Augusta*; IX *Hispana*; XX *Valeria Victrix*	4
Upper Germany	I *Adiutrix*; VIII *Augusta*; XI *Claudia Pia Fidelis*; XIV *Gemina Martia Victrix*	4
Lower Germany	VI *Victrix*; X *Gemina*; XXI *Rapax*; XXII *Primigenia*	4
Dalmatia	IV *Flavia*	1
Pannonia	XIII *Gemina*; XV *Apollinaris*	2
Moesia	I *Italica*; V *Alaudae*; V *Macedonica*; VII *Claudia Pia Fidelis*	4
Cappadocia	XII *Fulminata*; XVI *Flavia*	2
Syria	III *Gallica*; IV *Scythica*; VI *Ferrata*	3
Judaea	X *Fretensis*	1
Egypt	III *Cyrenaica*; XXII *Deiotariana*	2
Africa	III *Augusta*	1

c) The reign of Trajan (*c*. AD 110)		30 legions
Spain	VII *Gemina*	1
Britain	II *Augusta*; IX *Hispana*; XX *Valeria Victrix*	3
Upper Germany	VIII *Augusta*; XXII *Primigenia*	2
Lower Germany	I *Minervia*; VI *Victrix*	2
Upper Pannonia	X *Gemina*; XIV *Gemina Martia Victrix*; XV *Apollinaris*	3
Lower Pannonia	II *Adiutrix Pia Fidelis*	1
Upper Moesia	IV *Flavia*; VII *Claudia Pia Fidelis*; XXX *Ulpia Victrix*; II *Traiana*	4
Lower Moesia	I *Italica*; V *Macedonica*; XI *Claudia Pia Fidelis*	3
Dacia	I *Adiutrix Pia Fidelis*; XIII *Gemina*	2
Cappadocia	XII *Fulminata*; XVI *Flavia*	2
Syria	III *Gallica*; IV *Scythica*; VI *Ferrata*	3

Judaea	X *Fretensis*	1
Egypt	III *Cyrenaica*; XXII *Deiotariana*	2
Africa	III *Augusta*	1

Note: during the Flavian/Trajanic periods, V *Alaudae* and XXI *Rapax* were replaced by I *Minervia*, II *Traiana* and XXX *Ulpia Victrix*.

(d) The death of Hadrian (AD 138)		28 legions
Spain	VII *Gemina*	1
Britain	II *Augusta*; VI *Victrix*; XX *Valeria Victrix*	3
Upper Germany	VIII *Augusta*; XXII *Primigenia*	2
Lower Germany	I *Minervia*; XXX *Ulpia Victrix*	2
Upper Pannonia	I *Adiutrix*; X *Gemina*;	
	XIV *Gemina Martia Victrix*	3
Lower Pannonia	II *Adiutrix*	1
Upper Moesia	IV *Flavia*; VII *Claudia Pia Fidelis*	2
Lower Moesia	I *Italica*	1
Dacia	V *Macedonica*; XI *Claudia Pia Fidelis*;	
	XIII *Gemina*	3
Cappadocia	XII *Fulminata*; XV *Apollinaris*	2
Syria	IV *Scythica*; XVI *Flavia*	2
Judaea	VI *Ferrata*; X *Fretensis*	2
Arabia	III *Cyrenaica*	1
Phoenicia	III *Gallica*	1
Egypt	II *Traiana*	1
Africa	III *Augusta*	1

Note: IX *Hispana* and XXII *Deiotariana* have disappeared from the list – both probably during the Jewish Rebellion of AD 132; IX *Hispana* was transferred from Britain in c. AD 122.

(e) The reign of Marcus Aurelius (c. AD 170)		30 legions
Spain	VII *Gemina*	1
Britain	II *Augusta*; VI *Victrix*; XX *Valeria Victrix*	3
Upper Germany	VIII *Augusta*; XXII *Primigenia*	2
Lower Germany	I *Minervia*; XXX *Ulpia Victrix*	2
Upper Pannonia	I *Adiutrix*; X *Gemina*;	
	XIV *Gemina Martia Victrix*	3
Lower Pannonia	II *Adiutrix Pia Fidelis*	1
Upper Moesia	IV *Flavia*; VII *Claudia Pia Fidelis*	2
Lower Moesia	I *Italica*; V *Macedonica*; XI *Claudia Pia Fidelis*	3
Dacia	XIII *Gemina*	1
Noricum	II *Italica*	1
Raetia	III *Italica*	1
Cappadocia	XII *Fulminata*; XV *Apollinaris*	2
Syria	III *Gallica*; IV *Scythica*; XVI *Flavia*	3
Judaea	VI *Ferrata*; X *Fretensis*	2
Arabia	III *Cyrenaica*	1
Egypt	II *Traiana*	1
Numidia	III *Augusta*	1

Note: II and III *Italica* were legions newly raised during Marcus Aurelius' German campaigns. Septimius Severus added three more legions, I, II and III *Parthica* – bringing the total to 33 legions. I and III *Parthica* were stationed in Mesopotamia, and II *Parthica* was stationed in Italy.

Area distribution

AD	71	75	110	138	170	200
Britain	4	4	3	3	3	3
Italy	–	–	–	–	–	1
Germany and the west	9	9	5	5	5	5
Central and eastern Europe	8	7	13	10	12	12
The east	6	6	6	7	8	10
North Africa	3	3	3	3	2	2
Total	30	29	30	28	30	33

Appendix 2

Marcus Aurelius on Antoninus Pius (*Meditations* VI.30)

Do all things as a disciple of Antoninus: imitate his keenness for logical action, his always equable temperament, his piety, the serenity of his features, his sweetness, his lack of vainglory, his ambition to understand affairs. He dismissed no course of action till he had fully examined and clearly grasped it. He endured those who unjustly blamed him without blaming them in return. He never rushed things. He did not listen to slander. He was an exact judge of character and actions, but he was not given to reproaches, not afraid of rumours, not suspicious, no sophist. He was satisfied with little in the way of a house, of bedcovers, of clothes, food, and servants. He was fond of work and energetic, able to remain at the same task till evening without even needing to relieve himself except at his usual hour, because of his scanty diet. His friendships were constant and unchanging. He tolerated outspoken opposition to his ideas and was glad if anyone showed him a better way. He was religious, but free from superstition. Be his disciple in all this, and may your last hour find you as much at ease with your conscience as he was with his.

From: *Marcus Aurelius, The Meditations,* trans G. M. A. Grube, Hackett Publishing Co., Indianapolis, 1983.

Appendix 3

Stemma of the Antonine emperors (simplified)

For full *stemmata* and discussions, see A. R. Birley, *Marcus Aurelius* (London, 1966), pp. 318–322.

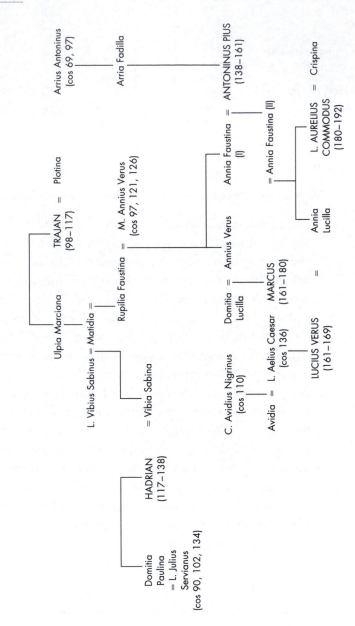

Further reading

Aurigemma S., *Villa Adriana* (Rome, 1961).

Balsdon J. P., *Roman Women* (London, 1969).

Bennett J., *Trajan: Optimus Princeps* (London, 1997).

Beschaouch A., Hanoune R. and Thébert Y., *Les Ruines de Bulla Regia* (Rome, 1977).

Birley A. R., *Marcus Aurelius* (London, 1966).

Birley A. R., *Hadrian: The Restless Emperor* (London, 1997).

Blake M. E., *Roman Construction in Italy from Tiberius through the Flavians* (Washington, DC, 1959).

Blake M. E. and Bishop D. T., *Roman Construction in Italy from Nerva through the Antonines* (Philadelphia, PA, 1973).

Boatwright M. T., *Hadrian and the City of Rome* (Princeton, NJ, 1987).

Breeze D. J. and Dobson B., *Hadrian's Wall*, 4th edition (London, 2000).

Buttrey T. V., *Documentary Evidence for the Chronology of the Flavian Titulature* (Meisenheim, 1980).

Carradice I. A., *Coinage and Finances in the Reign of Domitian, AD 81–96* (*BAR* International Series 178) (Oxford, 1983).

Champlin E., *Fronto and Antonine Rome* (Cambridge, MA, 1980).

Coarelli F., *La Colonna Traiana* (Rome, 1999).

Eck W., *Senatoren von Vespasian bis Hadrian* (Munich, 1970).

Gabucci A. (ed.), *The Colosseum* (New York, 2001).

Garzetti A., *Nerva* (Rome, 1950).

Grant M., *The Antonines* (London, 1994).

Hammond M., *The Antonine Monarchy* (Rome, 1959).

Henderson B. W., *The Life and Principate of the Emperor Hadrian* (London, 1923).

Henderson B. W., *Five Roman Emperors* (Cambridge, 1927).

Highet G., *Juvenal the Satirist* (Oxford, 1954).

Homo L., *Vespasian, L'empereur du bons sens* (Paris, 1949).

Howe L. L., *The Pretorian Prefect from Commodus to Diocletian* (Chicago, IL, 1942).

Jones B. W., *The Emperor Titus* (London, 1984).

Jones B. W., *The Emperor Domitian* (London, 1992).

Jones B. W. and Milns R., *Suetonius: The Flavian Emperors* (Bristol, 2002).

Jones C. P., *Plutarch and Rome* (Oxford, 1972).

Jones C. P., *The Roman World of Dio Chrysostom* (Cambridge, MA, 1978).

Levick B., *Vespasian* (London, 1999).

MacDonald W. L., *The Pantheon: Design, Meaning and Progeny* (Cambridge, MA, 1976).

MacMullen R., *Roman Social Relations, 50 BC–AD 284* (New Haven, CT, 1974).

Monti P. M., *La Colonna Traiana* (Rome, 1980).

Murison C. L., *Rebellion and Reconstruction, Galba to Domitian: An Historical Commentary on Cassius Dio's Roman History, Books 64–67* (Atlanta, GA, 1999).

Nicols J., *Vespasian and the Partes Flavianae* (Wiesbaden, 1978).

Oliva P., *Pannonia and the Onset of Crisis in the Roman Empire* (Prague, 1962).

Perowne S., *Hadrian* (London, 1960).

Pflaum H. G., *Les Procurateurs équestres sons le haut-empire Romain* (Paris, 1950).

Rajak T., *Josephus* (London, 1983).

Richmond I. A., *Trajan's Army on Trajan's Column* (London, 1982).

Rossi L., *Trajan's Column and the Dacian Wars* (London, 1971).

Scott K., *The Imperial Cult Under the Flavians* (Stuttgart, 1936).

Sherwin-White A. N., *The Letters of Pliny, an Historical and Social Commentary* (Oxford, 1966).

Sherwin-White A. N., *Racial Prejudice in Imperial Rome* (Cambridge, 1970).

Shotter D. C. A., *The Roman Frontier in Britain* (Preston, 1996).

Southern P., *Domitian: Tragic Tyrant* (London, 1997).

Speigl J., *Der romische Staat und die Christen: Staat und Kirche von Domitian bis Commodus* (Amsterdam, 1970).

Starr C. G., *The Roman Imperial Navy* (New York, 1954).

Turcan R., *The Cults of the Roman Empire* (Oxford, 1996).

Wardman A. E., *Religion and Statecraft among the Romans* (London, 1982).

Chapter 9

The military monarchy: dictatorship by the army

The death of Commodus at the end of AD 192 effectively marked the end of the Augustan Principate. Although it was followed by a period of civil war which bore apparent similarities with that which had followed the death of Nero in AD 68, the war produced as its final victor the African, Lucius Septimius Severus. During the civil war which, as before, involved the senate, legionaries and praetorians, Severus had uttered many of the customary platitudes regarding his respectful attitude towards the senate. However, after a victory, which had, of course, depended on legionary loyalty, Severus continued to base his future success on the loyalty of the legions, but in a way which made the army far more central to his government than had been the case with any of his predecessors. In short, the military monarchy represented a situation where promotion to most administrative ranks was achieved through the organisation of the army itself. Thus, it has been said that Severus' reign went beyond a dictatorship exercised through military backing to one which was effectively exercised by the army itself. This development realised its full danger in the chaos that marked the middle years of the third century, and from which the empire never really recovered.

The civil wars (AD 192–197)

The murder of Commodus at the end of 192 had been master-minded by Laetus, the praetorian prefect: it was in reaction to the increasing brutality, extravagance and exoticism of the emperor, which was due to reach a culmination on the first day of AD 193 with the emperor appearing simultaneously as consul and gladia-tor. Commodus' memory was condemned in the senate, his statues were pulled down and his name was erased from inscrip-tions. Laetus, however, with the permission of the new emperor, P. Helvius Pertinax, secured burial of the dead emperor in Hadrian's mausoleum in Rome (Castel St. Angelo); later, for reasons that will be discussed, Severus rehabilitated Commodus further by securing his apotheosis.

Pertinax, then sixty-six years old, had enjoyed a respectable career under the later Antonines but had a reputation in military circles as a strict disciplinarian. It was a sign of the times that he was presented first to the Praetorian Guard who accepted him after the promise of a large donative, though even then with some res-ervation because of his reputation; he was then taken to the senate, which was still the constitutional source of power, and accepted there with much more enthusiasm.

Although Pertinax indicated that he wanted to govern along Augustan lines, some of his actions, such as interference with the normal working of the *cursus honorum* and the sale of offices to try to repair the finances, were at variance with the 'model'. He lost popularity in the senate, and his standing with the praetori-ans, never good, was harmed by his failure to pay up the prom-ised donative in full. Opposition grew to conspiracy, and on 28 March Pertinax was murdered at the instigation of Laetus, who had originally been his 'sponsor'. The reminiscences of Servius

Galba are not inappropriate in the rise, rule and fall of Helvius Pertinax.

The army, in the shape of the praetorians, had played the decisive role, and it was not long before the legions, too, began to promote their candidates. In AD 193, the principal motivation on the part of the soldiers was financial; there were no points of principle involved. Indeed, this was demonstrated dramatically in the wake of the murder of Pertinax, when the praetorians, having no specific candidate in mind, offered the emperor's position to whoever would pay them most generously; the successful 'bidder' – for this was in reality an 'auction' – was a wealthy, sixty-year-old senator, named Didius Julianus. Neither senate nor people wanted the new emperor, which effectively opened the way to alternative 'claimants', this time with legionary backing.

Three names were canvassed – Pescennius Niger (the governor of Syria), Clodius Albinus (the governor of Britain) and L. Septimius Severus (the governor of Upper Pannonia). Of these, Severus' planning was the most impressive: he persuaded the legions of the Danube and the Rhine to make common cause behind him, he 'neutralised' Clodius Albinus – temporarily, at least – by adopting him as his intended successor (*Caesar*) and he presented the essence of his cause as the avenging of the murder of Pertinax, even assuming the name of the dead emperor into his own nomenclature. Above all, of the three 'candidates' Severus was closest to Italy and thus able to bring pressure most effectively on to Didius Julianus. Indeed, so comprehensive was Severus' 'strategy' that some have suggested that this was in reality the resuscitation of a plan originally formulated with a view to the removal of Commodus. Severus raised his rebellion on 9 April; by 1 June he was emperor and Julianus was dead.

Severus' first acts were studiedly aimed at restoring confidence, although his motive will have been solely to leave himself as free as possible of complications during the imminent wars with his 'rivals'. The praetorians, who had been responsible for Pertinax's death and the short, but deeply unpopular, reign of Julianus, were effectively disbanded and their place taken by a new type of imperial guard which was open to *any* legionary soldier. Severus' own arrival in Rome was made into a festive occasion evidently designed to allay fears that this would be a military dictatorship. Further, he made a gesture towards the senate which presumably he had no intention of honouring: he passed a law – not simply, as his predecessors had done, making a promise – to guarantee that no senator would be put to death without the agreement of his peers. The people were given money, games and a more stable food supply. This opening show of conciliation was completed with an extravagant ceremony to mark the official funeral of Pertinax. Having made all sections of the community feel secure and confident in their new emperor, Severus was now in a better position to prosecute his most pressing need – the elimination of his rivals; on 9 July he left Rome for the east to deal with Pescennius Niger.

According to Dio, Niger was a mediocre man and, after suffering a series of defeats, was dead before the end of 194. New arrangements were put in place for the governance of Syria, which was now split into two provinces (Syria-Phoenicia and -Coele), and towns in the new provinces were treated according to their allegiances in the recent war. With Niger removed, the empire was again under a unified control; new arrangements were put in place, with the addition of Osroene as a province, to strengthen the empire's eastern frontier.

Severus now started to create dynastic roots: during 195 he proclaimed himself the adopted son of the deified Marcus Aurelius and bestowed on his elder son by Julia Domna, hitherto called Bassianus (after Domna's father), the 'adoptive' names of Marcus Aurelius Antoninus. Caracalla, as he is better known to us, was also named as *Caesar*. In effect, Severus was broadening his appeal; of African origin himself, and a man of strong religious and cultural interests, he had in 187 married Julia Domna, one of the two daughters of Julius Bassianus, the High Priest of the Sun at Emesa (in the province which subsequently became Syria-Phoenicia). The eastern connection always remained powerful, and the influence of Domna and her family strong. His assumed connection with the Antonines will have brought him support in the west, particularly since he had been a supporter of Marcus Aurelius himself and had served in his campaigns. Indeed, Severus probably oversaw the completion of the Column of Marcus in Rome. Thus, the family and dynastic manoeuvres, combined with his own career, served to establish his credentials over most of the empire that he had, by his defeat of Niger, unified.

Of course, one person can be relied on to have greeted these new arrangements with less enthusiasm: since 193, Clodius Albinus (another African), who was governor of Britain, had enjoyed the title of *Caesar*. Severus' awarding of that title to Caracalla in 195 showed clearly that Albinus' usefulness was now at an end. Accordingly, he crossed to Gaul and made considerable inroads

Plate 9.1 (opposite) Rome, the Forum: the Arch of Septimius Severus.

into Severus' support there and in Spain. Indeed, the scale of Albinus' support becomes clear when we appreciate the level of deaths and confiscations which followed his suicide in 197 at Lyons after he had been militarily defeated by Severus. It used to be argued that Albinus' decision to fight Severus in western Europe led to the denuding of the northern frontier in Britain of troops and precipitated a massive attack from the north on Hadrian's Wall. Consequently, AD 197 became a 'major date' in Romano-British history; it is now thought that whatever happened in 197 was probably on a small scale and fitted into a pattern of localised raiding that had been characteristic of life in the frontier zone from the earlier second century and which was finally put to rest by Severus' campaigns in Britain between 209 and 211.

The character of Severus' reign (AD 197–211)

By 197, therefore, Severus had removed his rivals, established his power base with the army (particularly those parts of it that were stationed in central Europe), established complex dynastic arrangements which looked both backwards and forwards, established himself as a 'hard man' and immeasurably weakened the senate (in favour of the Equestrian Order) and the Praetorian Guard (in favour of the legionary army).

Whether or not Severus was a good campaign strategist is a matter of dispute, but he certainly afforded the empire's territorial integrity his attention. Very soon after his return to Rome following the defeat of Pescennius Niger, Severus set off eastwards again to deal with a threat posed by the Parthians who had invaded Mesopotamia. In reality, this was not a threat to match some of those that had previously arisen in this region; having inflicted defeats on the Parthians and having claimed the title, *Parthicus Maximus,* he simultaneously gave Caracalla the title of *Augustus* (or co-emperor with himself) and Geta (his younger son) that of *Caesar.* The most significant of Severus' re-arrangements in the region was the organisation of a new province of Mesopotamia which, in keeping with the emperor's unenthusiastic attitude to senators, was put in the charge of an equestrian *praefectus*.

Other areas of the empire were visited and, in some cases, administrative changes were put in place; however, the only other major episode of campaigning was that which took place in Britain in the last years of Severus' life (AD 209–211). The precise reasoning that lay behind this remains unclear; certainly, localised disturbances had continued to the north of Hadrian's Wall over a long period, and it may be that the major groupings north of the Wall – the *Caledonii* and the *Maeatae*, which had evidently been kept under control through the payment of subsidies, had become troublesome, perhaps to the point of interfering with friends of Rome, such as the Votadini whose land lay between the Tyne and the Forth. Alternatively, some have seen such things as a pretext, where the real point was the removal of his two 'warring' sons from Rome to give them a taste of military discipline. That he was contemplating a permanent expansion of territory in Britain seems unlikely, as he largely ignored the territory between Hadrian's Wall and the now long-defunct Antonine Wall to campaign in northern Scotland as far as the Moray Firth. It may be that his intention was in part a reiteration of Domitianic policy, namely to 'commit genocide' among the northern peoples and so buy time for the introduction of more coherent methods of control. Whether we can see in the payment of subsidies by Caracalla a fruition of Severus' intentions is hard to say, but despite the antagonism of classical authors (Herodian) towards the payment of subsidies, the result in this case appears to have been nearly a century of peace on Britain's northern frontier.

Septimius Severus died in York in AD 211; according to Dio Cassius (77.15), the advice which he passed to his sons was to 'live in harmony, keep the soldiers rich, and ignore everyone else'. Whilst Severus had not followed his own advice 'to the letter', it would be true to say that few (if any) of Severus' predecessors had paid so much attention to the welfare of the soldiers – particularly those in the legions. As we have seen, he not only disbanded the Praetorian Guard which had been disloyal to Pertinax but also destroyed its long-standing 'social élitism' by opening service in the praetorians to any legionary soldier. He increased military pay dramatically – the first emperor, since Domitian, to do so, although this move has, in part at least, to be seen against a background of growing inflation. The 'strain' of this measure is to be seen in the debasement of the *denarius*, to the point where it contained no more than 40–45% of silver. Although Severus' military changes were not entirely to blame for the financial deterioration, they certainly will not have helped.

Further, the army was itself enlarged – to thirty-three legions, the largest that it had been since Actium – with the addition of legions I, II and III *Parthica*. The new legions were all commanded by equestrian rather than senatorial officers, and one of them was permanently stationed in Italy – a further sign, perhaps, that Italy's status was coming increasingly to resemble that of an ordinary province and that its security was becoming more precarious. Another organisational device which, while not new, was used more widely in this period, was the taking of detachments (*vexillationes*) from legions to act, under equestrian officers (*duces/ praepositi*), as 'expeditionary forces' for particular campaigns. Here was a precursor of the 'mobile field army' that was to become so significant from Diocletian's time. The advantage of such a system was that it enhanced the stability of provincial garrisons by making them less vulnerable to sudden depletion in times of emergency. Severus also recruited many more auxiliary troops and structurally gave them a greater degree of independence from the legions.

Socially, Severan changes in army life were no less important: the long-standing embargo on marriage for serving soldiers was revoked, thus increasing the weight of military social influence in the communities that developed alongside forts. With this increasing 'militarisation' of civilian life it was hardly illogical or surprising that some of the 'grain grant' (*annona*) was made available to the army in the form of a new *annona militaris*. An emphasis on local recruitment strengthened the social and political coherence of provincial military groups; this and the tax immunities given to retired soldiers will have tended to make the extramural communities outside forts increasingly devoted to the emperor and his family as well as increasingly coherent and militaristic. This emerges clearly in a dedication from *Vindolanda* to the smith-god, Vulcan, by a group styling themselves the 'townspeople' (*vicani*) of *Vindolanda*; despite the dedication to Vulcan, the most prominent feature of the inscription is its opening invocation to the *Domus Divina* and the *Numina Augustorum*; there is barely sufficient room left to accommodate the remainder of the inscription (*RIB* 1700). Such provides a vivid demonstration of the new atmosphere created by Septimius Severus.

Equally, of fundamental importance was the opening up of promotions; it was far more normal for ordinary soldiers to aspire to the centurionate and, of vital importance, centurions were taken directly into the Equestrian Order. In view of Severus' favouring of the Equestrian over the Senatorial Order in the matter of senior administrative appointments, this meant that a growing number of administrators will have risen through an army that was closely involved with the emperor. The army was thus coming to dominate civilian life to the extent that Severus, as has been seen, initiated not a dictatorship exercised through the army, but one exercised *by* the army. This, then, was the character of Severus' 'military monarchy', of which the price was to be paid in the anarchic chaos that characterised the middle years of the third century.

In no sense, of course, did Severus intend anarchy to be the outcome of his reforms; his intention was a monarchy whose stability depended on the dominance of himself and his family and on its freedom from interference by other bodies, such as the senate and the army, a monarchy which was legitimised by his real (and assumed) connections and by his success, and which was guaranteed for the future by firm dynastic arrangements.

We have already seen Severus' own fictitious (and retroactive) 'adoption' by Marcus Aurelius and the assumption of the Antonine nomenclature for his family; indeed, Severus traced his 'new' links back as far as Nerva. These arrangements incidentally precipitated one notable incongruity: the once-execrable Commodus was now Severus' dead 'brother'; in 197, Commodus was duly deified; anything else would have been an unthinkable dishonour to the memory of the emperor's 'brother'. Caracalla and Geta had already been raised to the ranks of *Augustus* and *Caesar* respectively; in 209 Geta, too, became *Augustus*, thus giving a dynastic triumvirate of *Augusti*.

Throughout, an equally vital role was played politically and dynastically by Severus' wife, Julia Domna (*Julia Domna Augusta Pia Felix*); indeed, the dynasty which we call 'Severan' (down to AD 235) was in reality more that of Julia Domna than it was of Septimius Severus. The family was ever-present in the life of the empire; their portraits, individually or as a group, were everywhere to be seen, although subsequently Geta's were removed from many, following Caracalla's damnation of his brother's memory in 212. Julia Domna's name was used to link the family to all aspects of government and administration; she was 'mother' of the emperors, of the camp, of the senate, and she linked earth and heaven as a personification of *Juno Caelestis* and *Venus Victrix*, the latter, of course, serving to link this 'Syrian Julia' with another older, *gens Julia*. Severus practised nepotism with no compunction; considerable numbers of his relatives and connections reached high office, including notably the equestrian, C. Fulvius Plautianus, an African who was prefect of the Praetorian Guard from 197 to 205 and who acted as supreme commander of all troops in Italy, was awarded membership of the senate and consular insignia – and who became the father-in-law of Caracalla.

Severus was *dominus*; he was not literally a 'god upon earth', but connections were suggested with various gods, and his *domus* was *divina*. In the Septizonium (AD 203), the new entrance to the imperial residence on the Palatine, the emperor (as the sun-god) sat at the centre of the planetary system – and the building was pointedly orientated in the direction of Africa. In addition, the emperor had all his 'connections' with earlier emperors and dynasties. In other words, Severus was dominating in order to reconstruct the Roman world in a modern way, but aided in this by the best precedents of the past. Severus was the new, but 'updated', Augustus.

In such an arrangement as this, it is unsurprising that there was little role for the senate to perform: the social standing of its members was most of what it had left to it. Nothing shows this more clearly than the powers of the praetorian prefect in Italy and the fact that, in Severus' new legions and new provinces, the chief jobs went to equestrians rather than to senators. Despite the cynical law passed in 193 with its undertaking to respect the lives of senators, purges of members and confiscations of their property characterised this reign; membership of the senate was kept up by Severus largely through adlection to the body of African equestrian partisans of the emperor. It has been pointed out that the physical domination of the senate house (*curia*) by Severus' new arch in the Forum symbolically expresses the complete overawing of the 'fathers' by the new imperial *dominus*. Many times in the past the senate had 'lashed out' against such domination; on this occasion they found that they had lost the means to oppose, and they were becoming an anachronism in a political world that deliberately favoured those who were lower in the social order.

After two centuries of tension between legitimacy and reality, there was now, as the new century opened with its new dynasty, no doubt that 'what pleased the emperor had the value of law'; the emperor was above the laws of the *respublica*. The Principate of Augustus had become what it had long threatened to be – an absolute monarchy.

The reign of Caracalla

On his deathbed, Septimius Severus made his two sons his joint heirs, presumably under the supervision of their empress-mother; after a spell in the middle of Severus' reign when Julia Domna had given way in influence to the African praetorian prefect, Plautianus, the empress was restored to her full influence again during Severus' last years. Tradition shows Julia Domna as politically powerful, but also as highly cultivated; she is also said to have had a preference for her younger son, Geta, presumably because his quieter nature was more in tune with hers than was that of his elder brother.

Caracalla – the name derives from a Gallic military cloak which he habitually wore – is portrayed as boorish, cruel and vindictive. Apart from an obsessive interest in his own health, his chief enthusiasm was military life and a consequent devotion to the memory of Alexander the Great. In practice, this meant that he threw himself into the military actions of his reign, leaving civilian matters largely in the charge of his mother. Ironically, however, Caracalla's first act was to bring to an end fighting in Britain; it may, in any case, have been effectively complete, but in reality both brothers wished to return to Rome to gain an advantage over the other. The joint reign lasted a few days over a year, its chief event being the funeral and apotheosis of Septimius Severus, which was utilised for an utterly spurious display of Concord. Geta's murder – allegedly in his mother's arms – on 26 February 212 – not only left Caracalla in sole charge but was a signal for an explosion of executions, confiscations and bribery; according to Dio Cassius, twenty thousand people lost their lives in Caracalla's purges. The death of Geta was sealed with the Damnation of his memory.

Caracalla's chief interests throughout his reign were military affairs and, although Septimius Severus had left reasonably sound finances, his own military policies were expensive and those pursued by Caracalla (which *in nature* were not much different from those of his father) added considerably to the financial burden; according to Dio Cassius (78.10.4), Caracalla's extravagances were endless, incurring the criticism of his mother. Caracalla's reply – typically – was that he would not run out of money so long as he was in a position to kill people.

The chief drains on the finances – apart from Caracalla's personal extravagances and generosity to his favourites – arose out of his taking of his father's 'deathbed' advice regarding the army. Pay was raised, perhaps by as much as one-half, retirement gratuities were increased and gifts to groups of soldiers were frequent. This combined with increases in administrative costs, with large subsidies paid to foreign rulers, and with the building programme, such as the lavish Antonine Baths, rapidly led the finances into crisis. Taxes on inheritance and enfranchisement were doubled (from 5% to 10%), and Caracalla is said by Dio (78.9,2) to have 'milked' the practice of the payment of 'coronation gold' (*aurum coronarium*). He ensured a healthy 'take' from these taxes by his grant of 'Universal Citizenship' (the *Constitutio Antoniniana* of AD 212); Dio is in no doubt that the purpose of the measure was to catch many more people in the 'net' of taxation. Monetary measures were also introduced: the weight of the *aureus* was sharply reduced and it was re-tariffed at a value of fifty *denarii*. It has been suggested that the chief purpose of the *aureus* had become the payment of overseas subsidies. Dio also says that Caracalla was in the habit of issuing the *aureus* as a gold-plated copper coin. A new silver coin – which we term the *antoninianus* – was introduced; this portrayed the emperor wearing the radiate crown of the sun on the obverse and was intended to stand as a double *denarius*. In fact, it was one-and-a-half times the weight of the *denarius* and, although the silver content started, as with the current *denarius*, at approximately 50%, this fell to 5% by AD 219, when the minting of the coin was halted – although, as events were to show, only temporarily.

Caracalla was concerned almost constantly with campaigning, taking seriously his conviction that he should literally 'share' camp life with his soldiers. In his short reign, he fought on or visited the major frontier zones: AD 213 and 214 were spent on the Rhine and the Danube; although he won some success on the former, taking the title *Germanicus Maximus,* Caracalla's visit to the Danube was more by way of a 'pilgrimage' on which he could follow in the footsteps of his hero, Alexander. He even formed a sixteen-thousand-strong Macedonian phalanx and gave its commanders the names of Alexander's generals.

The eastern campaigns were hardly crowned with success: war against the Armenians ended in a Roman defeat in 215, while a campaign against Parthia had to be postponed so that Caracalla could go and deal harshly with a revolt in Alexandria, caused probably by tax rises. There is irony in the fact that this devotee of Alexander should have dealt so severely with the city that his hero had founded. The Parthian war commenced on the pretext that Artabanus, the king, refused to allow Caracalla to marry his

daughter. After some largely unopposed success, Caracalla withdrew to plan a fresh offensive for 217. It can be seen that the proposed marriage to Artabanus' daughter, together with the attention given to the status of towns in Syria and Osroëne, indicates firmly that the dynasty founded by the African emperor had now, under his son, become very obviously Syrian.

Caracalla was put to death on 8 April AD 217 at Carrhae; the originator of the plot, Opellius Macrinus, was prefect of the Praetorian Guard. His motive appears to have stemmed largely from the fear that Caracalla was about to put him to death. Macrinus did not declare his part in the plot; indeed, by taking the name Severus and by bestowing that of *Antoninus*, along with the title, *Caesar*, on his son, Diadumenian, he hoped to be able to profit in those areas in which the Severans had been popular. However, Macrinus showed little judgement: any hope that he might win senatorial support was lost by his assumption of imperial power without any acknowledgement of the protocols which traditionally involved the senate in the process. He also insisted on the deification of his predecessor with the name *Antoninus Magnus* (if indeed the relevant coins were issued by Macrinus).

Macrinus also forfeited the respect of the army: he lost out in the fighting/diplomacy that concluded Caracalla's eastern campaigns. Further – although, no doubt, for sound reasons – he attempted to reverse some of the very large expenditures on the army that had been incurred by Caracalla; he reduced pay for new recruits, and made the error of keeping in the east legions which had been brought from Europe for the campaigns. Thus, a combination of his own poor generalship and a rather importunate move towards financial control lost him the support of the military.

The rapid decline in such popularity that Macrinus may have had provided an opportunity for the Syrian side of Caracalla's family to reassert itself. Julia Domna had died (or had committed suicide) shortly after the death of her son. Her sister, Julia Maesa,

Plate 9.2 (opposite) Rome, the Baths of Caracalla: Frigidarium.

was dismissed from court by Macrinus but allowed to return to Emesa, her native town, which was also home to the great sun-cult of Elagabalus (Elah-Gabal). Julia Maesa had two daughters, Julia Sohaemias and Julia Mammaea, each of whom had sons, respectively Bassianus and Gessius Alexianus.

Bassianus was given the name Marcus Aurelius Antoninus and the story was put about that he was Caracalla's illegitimate son. Fourteen years old in AD 218, Bassianus inherited from his great-grandfather the role of the High Priest of the Sun and spent his days in religious ceremonial conducted in expensive and jewelled clothing and in a life of profligacy. He was declared emperor and legitimate successor of Caracalla on 16 May AD 218; the unmilitary Macrinus could not defeat the forces of Elagabalus (the god's name assumed, as was normal, by the High Priest), nor could he even hold on to what he had. Macrinus was defeated on 8 June, and he and Diadumenian were caught and put to death shortly afterwards. The reign of the Priest-Emperor had commenced; it is characterised in the following terms in the introduction by Mattingly, Sydenham and Sutherland to *The Roman Imperial Coinage*:

> The reign of Elagabalus is practically devoid of political interest. No event of importance is chronicled, no measures of national value were undertaken. Serious statesmanship and the machinery of government seem to have been suspended while the Roman world looked on, shamed and disgusted, at the exhibition of lust, cruelty and fanatical madness instigated by the priest-emperor.

Elagabalus and Severus Alexander: the Syrian Severi

The reign of Elagabalus (AD 218–222) was for the people of Rome, particularly the educated classes, a period of utter degradation, debauchery and religious fanaticism. When he came to power he had promised to adhere to the examples of Augustus and Marcus Aurelius; he assumed normal powers and titles, and styled himself 'son of Caracalla'. In reality, there was only one item on his agenda – his fanatical devotion to the god whose High Priest he was; indeed, his official titles faded before the one on the precedence of which he insisted – 'Priest of the Unconquered Sun-god Elagabalus'.

Abetted by his mother, Julia Sohaemias, he allowed himself every indulgence, undermining centuries of tradition. He married five times in three years; one of his brides was a serving Vestal Virgin, Acilia Severa. He appeared in public as a singer, dancer and charioteer, and distributed the great posts of state to former menial servants. Soldiers and people may have generally basked in the rewards which they received from their depraved emperor, although it is significant that the legions that had supported his bid for power and secured for him the destruction of Macrinus and Diadumenian within a few months were attempting to replace him with someone else.

The fanaticism of his religious practices did major violence to traditional religion: he constructed a new temple for his god on the Palatine Hill, near to the palace, and had all the sacred objects of Rome's traditional cults removed into it. This was not the 'ecumenism' which often in the empire effected the synthesis of Roman and foreign deities but an uncompromising assertion that *his* god was superior to all others. He even arranged a 'marriage' between his god and the African, Caelestis, symbolising the union of Sun and Moon, of Syria and Africa, recognising perhaps that in the early third century these were the empire's principal sources of wealth.

The only sound hand that remained was that of his grandmother, Julia Maesa who, along with her two daughters, had been (again in breach of tradition) made senators. There is no need to see in Maesa, however, selfless devotion to duty: her principal attribute was her common sense, which was deployed in the cause of retaining her ascendancy and that of her dynasty. She could see what the violent overthrow of Elagabalus might bring about. So, in concert with her other daughter, Mammaea, she sought to involve Mammaea's son, Alexianus, more closely in the government; she persuaded Elagabalus to adopt him as his son and heir in July of 221; the new *Caesar* took the names Marcus Aurelius Severus Alexander and became effectively Elagabalus' partner in power.

Alexander's disposition was very different; mild, affable and educated, he was well liked by soldiers and people. Elagabalus rapidly recognised danger in his young partner, and tried to humiliate – even assassinate – him. Mammaea was able to play on such incidents to persuade the Praetorian Guard to desert Elagabalus and his mother. On 6 March 222 they were put to death, along with their creatures. The tide of eastern fanaticism, for the moment at least, had turned.

Elagabalus was thus succeeded by his younger cousin, Severus Alexander, now seventeen years old; the young man was firmly under the guidance of his mother, Julia Mammaea, and (until her death in *c*. AD 226) of his grandmother, Julia Maesa. That the new reign reversed the fanatical excesses that were characteristic of Elagabalus is not to be doubted. It is, however, possible to exaggerate the significance and extent of this; certainly, to argue that Alexander's reign represented a full resuscitation of the senate's earlier role would be greatly to exaggerate. However, although a few of Elagabalus' nominees remained in their jobs, the general tendency of the reign was to relate more closely to that of Septimius Severus in bringing forward members of the Equestrian Order. Indeed, these continued to take over roles (particularly, provincial governorships) which had traditionally been the preserve of senators.

The principal 'advances' of the senatorial order were supposedly two-fold: first, a 'regency council' of sixteen senators was appointed to advise the young emperor during his minority. However, these sixteen appear to have been drawn from a full *consilium* of seventy *amici* who were neither exclusively senatorial nor, more importantly, chosen by the senate. Secondly, it is recorded that Severus Alexander gave senatorial standing to his praetorian prefects; the purpose of this appears to have been to make it possible for praetorian prefects to be members of the senate which, in its turn, allowed the prefects a jurisdiction over senators which would not otherwise have been compatible with the undertaking that senators could rely on being judged by their peers. In this sense, it could be argued that, while the move was an enhancement of senatorial *prestige*, it represented an actual diminution of their powers and privileges.

Other changes were probably of less consequence; the tribunate of the plebs and curule aedileship were removed from the *cursus honorum*. This was because their principal duties were now in other magisterial hands; in any case, 'fast-track' senators had been omitting one, and sometimes both, of these offices since the first century AD. Fourteen ex-consuls were formed into a 'board' to act as advisers to the *Praefectus Urbi* ('Prefect of the City') in administering Rome's regions. Beside all of this, Severus Alexander was always courteous to the senate, which will also have appreciated his care for Rome's cultural and religious traditions. Thus there was renewed dignity perhaps for the senate, while the real power in the state, under the emperor, belonged with the praetorian prefects and members of the Equestrian Order fulfilling functions in the imperial bureaucracy. Indeed, while tradition may have tried to paint Alexander's reign as resuscitating the senate, in reality the period represented its terminal decay. The *administration* was carried out by equestrians; real *power* remained where Septimius had placed it – with the army.

The real influence in the imperial court was that of Alexander's mother; she was responsible for the appointment of the jurist, Ulpian, as a praetorian prefect. His was a sound influence on government, although his strictness was resented by his troops, who first became restless and troublesome and then murdered Ulpian. Mammaea also both made Alexander's marriage to Sallustia Orbiana and then, from jealousy, 'unmade' it. The removal of

Alexander's wife ensured Mammaea's continued dominance of court and government, her hand strengthened by the deification of her mother and her own receipt of the title of *Augusta*.

Apart from the wars in the later years of the reign which led to the downfalls and deaths of both Alexander and his mother, this reign was a period of quiet consolidation: the finances recovered from Elagabalus' extravagances, and this was done largely by taxing luxury items. Indeed, the financial good sense of the regime enabled money to be spent on 'hand-outs' (*congiaria*) to the people and on building programmes which benefited both Rome and the empire and which greatly enhanced public services.

The major wars of the reign were in the east and in Germany. In the east, Rome faced a rather different situation from that which had broadly obtained since the mid-first century BC. The power of Parthia was now being challenged by a Persian dynasty which traced itself back to the great Persian kings of the sixth and fifth centuries BC, who now laid claim to all the territory that had then formed the 'Persian empire'; this meant nothing less than the removal of the Roman presence from Asia Minor and the Middle East. The situation was made more complicated and dangerous by trouble among some of the eastern legions. However, a campaign was mounted in 232; although Roman troops appear to have fared badly, the facts that Roman territory was recovered in Mesopotamia and that there was no further trouble for some four years suggest that the Persians must have fared even worse.

Alexander was able to leave his headquarters in Antioch to return to celebrate a triumph in Rome, although only a short time elapsed before he had to leave again – this time for the north. The trouble here was the crossing by tribesmen of both the Rhine and the Danube so that not only Roman provinces were threatened but even Italy, too. The removal of troops for the eastern campaign had undoubtedly helped to fuel this outbreak. The unwarlike Alexander was not held in high esteem by his European troops, the more so because of his attempts to buy peace and

Plate 9.3 (opposite) Africa, Sbeitla: forum with 'triple Capitolium'.

because of his own obvious predilection for troops who originated in the east and who provided a kind of bodyguard for the emperor. Further, Julia Mammaea was urging her son to return to the east where, presumably, she felt he could better withstand an attempt on his position. Smarting under such pressures, some of the European troops found an alternative leader in a Thracian named C. Julius Verus Maximinus. Offering him the throne, these troops murdered both Alexander and his mother in the fortress at Mainz (*Moguntiacum*).

The Severan period: a retrospect

The dynasty contained two very different strands due to the marriage of Septimius Severus to Julia Domna, which brought together a family from the growingly prosperous north African provinces with that of the High Priest of the Sun at Emesa in Syria. This, combined with the changes that took place or which

Plate 9.4 Africa, Dougga: the Temple of Jupiter.

were engineered during the period, affords the dynasty a sensitive place between what are generally known as the 'early empire' and the 'late empire'. Indeed, it is pertinent to wonder whether the Severan period represents 'the end of the beginning' or 'the beginning of the end'.

It is probably more appropriate to think of the period as a late (although not the latest) part of the early empire and keep the real division where it has been traditionally placed – with the accession of Diocletian in AD 284. Although much was changing – in politics and administration, in social, economic and intellectual life – the Severan period was still in essence a developmental stage of the Augustan Principate.

Nonetheless, the developments of the period were significant: the role of the senate and senators, already declining, was further subordinated to the relationship between the emperor and members of the Equestrian Order. They now generally expected to have responsibility for new posts which were created and also took over many previously senatorial roles, such as provincial governorships and legionary commands. Indeed, terms such as *praeses* (for provincial governor) and *praefectus* (for legionary commanders) became much more normal. We have noted that this is true not only of Severus and Caracalla but also of the so-called 'revisionist' emperor, Severus Alexander.

The legionary army and the Praetorian Guard had always exercised a crucial role in 'kingmaking'. This had been true in its way in the late Republic (after Gaius Marius), and had remained true after Actium in 31 BC; the real force in the Principate, when it came to a political crisis, was seen to be the army – in AD 68–69, in AD 192 and on numerous other occasions. However, a characteristic of this military power was that it was less in the hands of ordinary soldiers than in those of their largely senatorial commanders. In other words, although obviously an emperor needed to be able to guarantee his support among the ordinary soldiers, the armed force of which they were capable was essentially there to be deployed in the service of leaders whose social standing and political expectations were equivalent to those of the emperors whom they served. It was no accident that led Nero, in his later years, to prefer in senior commands men whose inferior social standing would, he hoped, discourage them from aspiring too high. Ironically, Vespasian was a product of that policy. After the Julio-Claudian period the threat posed by senators may have begun to diminish, replaced perhaps by a new threat from the soldiers themselves; Domitian's raising of military pay may have been a response to such a realisation.

The continued marginalising of senators during the second century had led by the end of that century to a rather different situation; soldiers were waiting to be empowered. Severus, by developing equestrian preferment over senators and by making military promotion the recognised route to membership of the Equestrian Order, left the army able to dictate terms to politicians in a new and dangerous way; Severus' frequent 'bribing' of the army with higher pay and donatives ensured that it became the dominant feature of government and contributed to the chaos that characterised the middle of the century. This was, in part, evident in the Severan period itself, as each of the emperors (except Severus himself) came and went by the sword; only Septimius Severus died a natural death.

As befitted an emperor who attained power by a series of civil wars, involving not inconsiderable treachery on Severus' own part, Severus was exceptionally conscious of the fragility of his own security. His attitude to senate and senators was but one sign of that; he also set in train provincial reforms which were far more concerned with imperial security than they were with raising the level of provincial prosperity and efficiency. The subdivision of provinces was intended – as was its further development by Diocletian at the end of the third century – to break down the coherence of military command structures in order to make it more difficult for individuals to be able to lay hold of sufficient power and resources to pose a threat to the centre. A policy was

Plate 9.5 Africa, El Djem: the amphitheatre.

Plate 9.6 Africa, Bulla Regia: lower (subterranean) level of the Maison de la Chasse.

also initiated of spreading troops more thinly; instead of the large concentrations in areas of particular sensitivity – a characteristic of early imperial dispositions – a *de facto* limit of two legions per province was imposed. A road-building programme in the provinces was intended to facilitate faster military movement in order to produce the necessary concentrations at crucial times and in crucial places, looking forward to the further reforms of the tetrarchic period. Of course, such a development had favourable effects on commerce – but probably fortuitously.

On the whole, although certain provinces, such as Africa and Syria (with their imperial connections), fared well, particularly town dwellers, the burdens imposed by civil and foreign wars and an army that was large and which was kept almost permanently bribed imposed burdens in terms of taxation and requisitions. The financial burdens of local administration became harder and, as a consequence, found fewer shoulders to bear them, a problem that was aggravated by the large number of exemptions that were granted – for example, to imperial officials, soldiers, imperial estate tenants, doctors and teachers. Against this, Caracalla's edict of 212 widened the number of those qualified, while his depreciation of the currency was designed to give an impression of greater affluence and thus ability to contribute. The government's policy during the Severan period created a great deal of hardship which might have been at that stage catastrophic had not a good deal of the money taken from provincials cycled back to them through the 'market economy' constituted by the now relatively wealthy military groups.

The chief exception to what is broadly a picture of decline and greater hardship is to be seen in a vibrant cultural and religious scene. The decline of Italy's superiority, which the Severan dynasty accelerated rather than initiated, continued. The ethnic orientation of the rulers and the policies which they espoused made the 'working manpower' of the empire far more cosmopolitan. A sign of this was the blending of classical and oriental cultures: although lip-service, at least, was still paid to the traditional deities, they were with increasing frequency paralleled with provincial alternatives. Indeed, there is a sense that *Sol Invictus*, as the third century wore on, began to 'take over' from Jupiter, being 'awarded' a role (*Propugnator*: 'Defender'/'Soldier') normally associated with Jupiter. Provincial cults were served by dedicated priesthoods and their ceremonies frequently attended by an exoticism and spirituality against which traditional religions and creeds could hardly compete in a world in which they were seen as much less relevant to man's needs.

At the heart of this religious and intellectual vibrancy stood the Syrian matriarchs of the dynasty, especially Julia Domna and Julia Mammaea. Under their influence there was an extraordinary outpouring of largely Greek writing – historians such as Dio Cassius and Herodian, philosophical writers of the stature of Philostratus, Diogenes Laertius, Sextus Empiricus (the sceptic), Plotinus (the neo-Platonist) and Origen (the Christian). Christianity itself, although subject to mainly local persecution under the Severi, shared in the intellectual renaissance to the point of producing theological writers of high stature – Irenaeus (bishop of Lyons), Hippolytus, Clement of Alexandria and Origen (an intellect of the very highest order). Further, under official prompting, Philostratus in his *Life of Apollonius of Tyana* produced what can only be described as a 'sanitisation' of Christianity, which was designed to bring it into conformity with the pagan world. Latin writing was much less formidable, although the African Christian apologist, Tertullian, deserves to be taken alongside the Greek writers. This impressive range of philosophical and religious thinkers highlights the degree to which the east now constituted the intellectual 'power house' of the Roman empire. Impressive, too, is the range of eastern religious cults – the worship of *Sol Invictus*, of Mithras, of Jupiter Dolichenus, of Juno Caelestis and others; many of these may not have had an empire-wide currency for long, but their existence is further testament to the religious and intellectual vitality of this age, and to the fact that this vitality did not have to descend into the absurd fanaticism evident in the reign of the priest/emperor, Elagabalus.

Appendix 1

Simplified stemma of the Severan dynasty

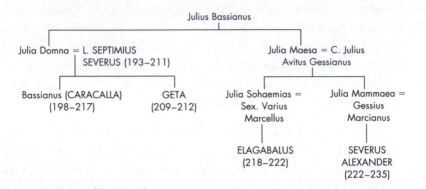

Further reading

Birley A. R., *Septimius Severus: The African Emperor* (London, 1971).

Grant M., *The Climax of Rome* (London, 1968).

Millar F. G. B., *A Study of Cassius Dio* (Oxford, 1964).

Platnauer M., *The Life and the Reign of the Emperor Lucius Septimius Severus* (Oxford, 1918).

Turton G., *The Syrian Princesses: The Women who ruled Rome, AD 193–235* (London, 1974).

Chapter 10

The third-century crises — and recovery

The middle years of the third century represented what appears to have been the lowest ebb of the Roman state: the frontiers in Europe and the east were under pressure and, in places, breached; the gulf between the eastern and western parts of the empire was widening; the Roman army was more concerned with king-making than with defending those frontiers. As a consequence, anarchy and, with it, economic chaos became apparently endemic. To all intents and purposes, it looked as if collapse was imminent. Yet, by the end of the third century, a recovery package had been put in place by Diocletian which seemed, against all the odds, to offer hope of survival.

East and west

An essential feature of the Diocletianic recovery was the appreciation that a single emperor ruling from Rome no longer had the ability to hold the whole of the empire together. Not only did the forces of disruption interfere with that greatest of imperial assets – communication – but the rivalry evident between different parts of the army ensured that different areas of the empire – not just east and west – had different expectations and ambitions.

Further, although the administrative and governmental machinery had undergone some changes over the years, it was still broadly as it had been put in place by Augustus, who was himself building on earlier (Republican) traditions.

Obviously, the cultural distinctions between the eastern and western halves of the empire were great: the east, largely steeped in Greek traditions, was urbanised and sophisticated both politically and economically. Much of the western empire had developed from hierarchical tribal societies which, although not as 'primitive' as once believed, were in many cases still not particularly sophisticated in a social and economic sense. Yet, for Rome, both traditions had advantages: in the east, they could deal with the Hellenistic monarchs and their dynasties and thus 'institutionalise' the long-standing dependence of *native* populations; in the west, the tribal dynasts provided the kind of oligarchic group with whom Rome was content to deal.

As we have seen, the Roman system of provincial management offered opportunities to local people to participate in their own administration and to entertain 'higher ambitions' in imperial administration. Thus, during the first century AD, an increasing number of administrators at all levels were being drawn from provincial aristocracies. Caesar and Augustus gave opportunities, particularly to westerners, for entry into the Senatorial and Equestrian Orders, and the ensuing harmonisation led by the late first and early second centuries to emperors from Spain (Trajan and Hadrian). The western provinces were drawn together into a virtually common political, social and economic system, linked together by the use of Roman coinage.

The eastern provinces made slower progress towards this kind of integration, because traditions allowed for a greater level of independence within the system; local administration was based on Hellenistic systems and local coinages continued to be produced. Here, then, there was the potential for separate development which might, in time, lead to the opening up of a gulf between east and west.

How early this was recognised as a problem is hard to say: although individual easterners prospered and much was left to local initiative *at a local level,* there was a residual distrust of the kind that had permitted Octavian, during his struggle with Marcus Antonius, to make propaganda advantage out of the 'conflict' between western (that is, Roman and Italian) traditions and 'oriental barbarism'. Much contempt has been poured on Nero's 'flirtation' with the east, although it may have been more than that – an attempt to draw east and west closer together. Hadrian, on the other hand, has received more credit, in his 'philhellenic tendencies', for an effort to seek out common ground between east and west. It would appear that he recognised the strength of the differences, but tried to bring the east closer to the west by providing, in his vision of Athens, a 'classical' focal point for the eastern provinces. Thus, the notion of a 'two-centred' empire, based on 'orientation' towards Rome or Athens, was born.

By the third century, however, new forces were at work: Italy itself, which had, since the earlier years of the second century, come to be seen increasingly as a province (rather than 'the homeland'), was suffering from depopulation, exacerbated by the periodic ravages of plague. While some western provinces continued to develop in prosperity (for example, the Spanish provinces, apart from Lusitania, and Gallia Narbonensis), others were static or even declining. In addition, across the frontiers new, and more cohesive, 'enemy groups' were appearing – such as the Alemanni, Goths and Franks, as well as Saxons crossing the North Sea, while older groups, such as the Sarmatians and the Quadi, continued to cause difficulties. The western provinces were clearly more vulnerable, and problems were experienced also over the Balkans and into Greece. Although the east was not without its threats – the Persians, for example, taking the place of the 'old enemy', Parthia – these provinces continued to grow in prosperity. The tangible result was the appearance in the later second and early third centuries of new ruling imperial dynasties from Syria and north Africa. Antioch had become one of the empire's most vibrant cities, while the quality of buildings in north African cities in the early third century provides an obvious testament to the prosperity of that region, which depended on grain growing, olive growing and viticulture.

It was perhaps a sign of change that, on his accession to imperial power in 244, Philip I (the 'Arab') appointed his brother to a newly created post of *rector Orientis* ('Director of the East'). The empire's centre of gravity was slipping inexorably towards the east, which was also increasingly the centre of the empire's intellectual and religious vibrancy.

Political and economic crisis

The Severan dynasties came to an end with the murder in 235 of Severus Alexander: throughout the Severan period, only one emperor, Septimius himself, had died a natural death. Not that imperial murders constituted a new phenomenon: political, social and economic problems had been developing for some time, but reforms of the Severan period ushered in an altogether more dangerous and lawless world. Alexander's death and his replacement by Maximinus ('the Thracian') represented a dramatic demonstration of the realities of the new political world.

Maximinus was a soldier – and a barbarian – a product of the process of barbarisation among the personnel of the Roman army that had accelerated during the Severan period. He had been promoted through the ranks of the Roman army and had achieved equestrian status: as a non-senator, he had no experience of civilian administration; he was, therefore, the first in a line of 'soldier emperors' who had 'reached the top' as a result of the support of fellow soldiers, and with no involvement – even nominally – of the traditional senatorial acceptance. In 235, the senate was simply informed of a *fait accompli*; in fairness, although during Alexander's reign the senate may have basked, as it had in the Antonine period a century earlier, in the studious traditionalism of its *princeps,* that had in the real world of the third century been shown for the irrelevant luxury that it really was. The Roman empire now needed an emperor who appreciated and could face life-threatening problems on a broad front – particularly with regard to a matter as basic as the empire's territorial integrity.

None of this is, of course, to argue that Maximinus represented the ideal alternative: although a man of considerable personal courage, he was also cruel and suspicious, especially of members of the Senatorial Order whom he (rightly) regarded as devoted to the memory of his predecessor. A process of distancing members of the senate from key posts had been in train for some time: for most of the Severan period, the Equestrian Order had moved towards becoming the natural source of administrators; the efficiency of its members pointed in the same direction as the political inclination of a succession of emperors. Under Maximinus, senators were displaced from senior military posts, replaced in the main by career soldiers; members of the senate were kept from 'meddling' (or worse) by a network of imperial agents/informers.

If the senate had been alone in its alienation, this might not have caused Maximinus too much anxiety; however, another major symptom of third-century problems spread the emperor's unpopularity far more widely. As a soldier–emperor, Maximinus was sharply aware of the basis of his power and spent money increasing the pay of the soldiers; not only this, but his necessary foreign wars were frequent and expensive. The acquisition from the empire's subjects of the money to pay for these spread the alienation still further. This and the cost of introducing physical defences to many of the towns meant that money came into shorter supply: nor could those, who normally had to pay such bills, be called on for ever without reaction – whether it be in the form of their alienation or in a reduction of the 'services' for which they normally paid. Some parts of the empire saw a reduction of services (particularly in towns) and a currency crisis, as money came to be 'printed' to pay the bills. The 240s saw the final disappearance, after nearly five centuries, of the *denarius* and its replacement by the debased and inflationary *antoninianus* (the 'double *denarius*' that had been the 'brainchild' of the uncongenial Caracalla).

Such burdens fell particularly heavily on the prosperous towns of north Africa; discontent there led to the octogenarian proconsul, Gordianus (Gordian I) of Thysdrus (El Djem), whose ancestry led back to Trajan and even the Gracchi, being persuaded to accept the call to rid the empire of the tyrannical rule of Maximinus. He associated in power with him his son (known to history as Gordian II) and demonstrated, from his appointment of a 'Commission of Twenty', that he appreciated the need for both reconstruction and reconciliation. Ironically, however, he and his son both fell victim to a personal feud with Capellianus, the governor of neighbouring Numidia: they had 'reigned' for barely three weeks.

The senate, with characteristic lack of foresight but with understandable enthusiasm, chose to replace the Gordians with two senators whom Gordian I had chosen for his Commission – Balbinus and Pupienus. Not surprisingly, this failed to impress either the people or the army who insisted that the two senators be joined by Gordian I's wealthy grandson (Marcus Antonius Gordianus, or Gordian III), who was then only thirteen years of age. Balbinus and Pupienus were then rapidly discarded, leaving Gordian III as sole *Augustus* in 238. Because of the young Gordian's age, the reins of power were held by others – principally his mother and the praetorian prefect, Timesitheus, who was also the young emperor's father-in-law. Gordian III's reign was dominated by foreign wars which, although costly, were conducted with success, so long as Timesitheus was alive; his death in 243, however, left the young emperor dangerously exposed and he was put to death early in 244 at the instigation of Julius Verus Philippus (Philip 'the Arab' or Philip I). Fittingly, his epitaph is given by the fourth-century historian, Ammianus Marcellinus: 'In honour of the Deified Gordian who repulsed sedition in Rome, defeated the Goths, Sarmatians and Germans, but who succumbed to Philip's men.'

Inauspicious his opening may have been, but Philip enjoyed a generally good reputation with the senate and with the ordinary people whom he kept well supplied with goods and services. His inclination for the future stability of the empire had a dynastic base, as can be seen from his association with him in the imperial power of his six-year-old son and by the appointment, already noted, of his brother to a new post of *rector Orientis*. As with Gordian's reign, Philip's too was expensive and burdensome because of the almost continuous warfare which characterised it. Yet, the emperor was not blind to Rome's and the empire's needs; his reign, seen by some as redolent of Stoic – or even (improbably) Christian – virtues, was characterised by what Cicero might have termed *cura reipublicae*.

There was no denying, however, that there were aspects of the 240s and 250s that might suggest that Rome and the empire were heading for 'meltdown'. The expense of the continuous warfare was creating havoc with the economy: Severus Alexander's brief revival, albeit in a heavily alloyed state, of the *denarius*, came to nothing; by the late 230s/early 240s it had disappeared from circulation to be replaced by the inflationary double *denarius* (or *antoninianus*) first introduced by Caracalla. Although the pretence was maintained into the 250s that this was a silver coin, its changing appearance to the often-small, roughly made, copper issues of the late 250s and beyond belied this pretence. The only feature that these 'barbarous radiates' (or 'radiate copies') had in common with the coins that were notionally their prototypes was the obverse head surmounted by the prominent radiate crown. The reverses of such coins commemorated an endless series of 'imperial virtues' which were much more a matter of hope than of reality, or even expectation.

Added to the 'double *denarius*', a radiate, and thus presumably double, *sestertius* appeared under Decius; although generally of decent artistic merit, the very existence of these coins indicates the degree to which inflation was developing, reaching its climax with the tens of thousands of locally produced pieces of execrable quality which were the sign of the hyper-inflation of the 260s and 270s, coins characterised by the variability of their flan size, by the unrecognisable nature of their imperial heads and by the absence or, at best, illiterate blundering of legends. Many ordinary traders must, in this situation, have been forced back into a barter system, and trade may, as a consequence, have become far more locally based – an indicator that the economic problems were leading to social and political fragmentation.

Warfare and the accompanying measures to improve security – for example, walling of towns – were, however, just one of the causes of economic difficulty; to this we have to add increased payments made to try to keep the army 'on side' as well as the bribes that will have been an essential part of the efforts deployed by emperors and 'would-be' candidates for power to gain and maintain support. The weakness in the army caused by methods of recruiting as well as by its frequent distraction by 'domestic politics' saw the frontier situation turn to disaster in the late 240s and early 250s; all frontiers came under pressure, and Goths penetrated Italy. Both Decius and Valerian were defeated at the heads of armies which could do nothing to save them. Decius, despite some initial success on the Danube, for which he took the title *restitutor Daciarum*, eventually died, although not without the aid of treachery on the part of Trebonianus Gallus who succeeded him. Valerian met a similarly desperate end in the east at the hands of the Persians in the late 250s, which was regarded by the fourth-century Christian writer, Lactantius, as an entirely justifiable fate for an 'enemy of Christ'.

Enemy action, combined with disease (plague) and internal dissension, served by the late 250s to reduce Rome to virtual bankruptcy and the empire to a mere 'rump' of its former self. It is hardly surprising that, in a situation so dire, attention should have turned to a search for scapegoats. As on previous occasions, the offence caused to the Gods of Rome by the apostasy represented by Christianity seemed a sure 'candidate'; more Christians did indeed seem to lead to more disasters. First, Decius and then, after a tolerant interval, Valerian, set about enforcing conformity. Decius, for example, established commissions in every town – itself a bureaucratic expense – to supervise a conforming religious act on the part of 'suspects'. Those who complied received a certificate to that effect while those who did not suffered in a variety of ways – although not usually by death. Decius' intention was genuinely to enhance the appearance of solidarity, not to damage it further by wild and gratuitously cruel spectacles. Valerian's persecution (from AD 257) started with a similarly 'constructive' aim; indeed, some freedom of worship was tolerated, as long as it was carried out *in private*. However, presumably the failure of this approach led Valerian to more extreme measures which resulted in excessive cruelty and to martyrdoms. It was this that earned for Valerian the hostility of Lactantius which has so coloured posterity's view of an emperor who might in other circumstances have earned a more favourable 'verdict'. The perceived uselessness of persecuting Christians, however, earned for the church a period of peace until the renewed hostility of Galerius and Diocletian some forty years later, and an 'Edict of Toleration' from Valerian's son, partner and eventual successor, Gallienus.

The crisis had now, by the late 250s, reached its depth: at the time of his succession as 'sole emperor', Gallienus was involved in an unsuccessful attempt to terminate an internal rebellion, in which one, Postumus, separated from the central government's jurisdiction the provinces in Germany, Gaul, Spain and Britain. The *Imperium Galliarum* ('Independent Empire of the Gauls'), as it was known, set itself completely apart with its own emperors and subordinate officials (including consuls) until it was finally defeated by Aurelian in AD 273. The Gallic breakaway will have been due partly to the almost endemic anarchy of these times, but perhaps also to a realisation at a local level that only a local effort was going to provide any chance of security from outside attack. This motive, for example, emerges very clearly in the later rebellion in Britain (AD 286–296) of Carausius who was evidently responsible for the planning and part-building of the coastal defence system known as 'The forts of the Saxon Shore'.

Plate 10.1 The rebel emperors of the Imperium Galliarum *(from left to right): top, Postumus, Laelianus, Marius; bottom, Victorinus, Tetricus I.*

Plate 10.2 'Wishful thinking': Antoninianus of Postumus, showing clasped hands with the legend, CONCORDIA MILITUM ('Concord of the Soldiers').

Such 'separatist' movements as that of Postumus constituted a new phenomenon: it was not a 'general rival' to Gallienus but was simply concerned to concentrate in its own hands the responsibility for the security of its own area. Thus, Postumus was not in the least concerned to challenge Gallienus for control of Rome, only to prevent Gallienus from retaking Postumus' western provinces; his movement may, however, have led to local confrontations between 'rebels' and 'loyalists' in the provinces concerned. Postumus' coinage, itself of a quality considerably superior to that of Gallienus, struck hopeful themes, such as SALUS PROVINCIARUM and RESTITUTOR ORBIS ('The Good Health of the Provinces' and 'Restorer of the World'). Like Galba's Gallic coinage of two centuries earlier, it was designed to highlight the failings of the 'legitimate emperor'. Eventually, Postumus' position was undermined by internal rivalry; he was overthrown in 268 by Laelian and Marius, and the internal coherence of the *Imperium Galliarum* was irretrievably weakened.

Gallienus also had a similar problem in the east: having an excess of problems in the west, he had allowed Septimius Odenathus, the Sassanid ruler of Palmyra who enjoyed a collection of imposing Roman titles, such as *clarissimus, consularis, dux* and eventually *imperator*, to act as 'Rome's agent' in trying to retrieve the losses of Valerian's Persian disaster. Some success on Odenathus' part was followed in AD 267 by his falling victim to an internal plot organised by his second wife, Zenobia. Although Gallienus tried to insist that her rule applied to Palmyra alone, he had no means to enforce this thus leaving the removal of this problem also to Aurelian.

Gallienus was undoubtedly one of the more cultivated of Rome's third-century emperors and is often compared in this with the Antonine rulers of the second century. However, the comparison should not be overstressed: although mild of disposition he was not of a mind to restore influence to the Senatorial Order. Indeed, Gallienus represents an important step in the opposite direction and, in this way, looks forward to the far more thoroughgoing reforms initiated in the 290s by Diocletian. The most significant pointer towards later changes was his enhancement of the military command potential of members of the Equestrian Order where senior commands, such as *praefectus legionis* (legionary commander) and *dux limitum* (frontier commander), were reserved for them. He also foreshadowed the later 'mobile field armies' by having *vexillationes* of cavalry stationed, for example, at Milan. Senators, by contrast, were now effectively removed from any contact with military command and left virtually as civilian administrators in the provinces. This should, however, be seen not so much as a 'disgracing' of senators, although many of them may, as is asserted by Aurelius Victor (*Caes.* 37.7), have been principally interested in an easy life. More constructively, it was probably a determination that, in the period of crisis, it was wiser to entrust senior military commands to men who had some experience of them.

In the final analysis, however, while the depth of the crisis at the time of Gallienus' murder in AD 268 cannot be denied, it should be said that it would be unreasonable to ascribe this situation to imperial dereliction: he accepted a tripartite empire because he had no practical means of reversing it. In any case, he worked hard to maintain a territorial integrity in that part of the empire in which his writ continued to run. He made administrative changes which were extended rather than reversed by his successors. As with so many of his third-century predecessors, in Gallienus can be recognised a victim rather than a perpetrator.

Although the 'great recovery' is rightly credited to Diocletian, it should also be observed that the foundations of this recovery were already being laid in the aftermath of Gallienus' murder.

Gallienus' assassins, in fact, had two candidates in mind from among the former emperor's leading generals; both of these were from Illyricum and had risen through the ranks of the army – Marcus Aurelius Claudius and Lucius Domitius Aurelianus. Claudius may well have been preferred because of Aurelian's reputation as a stern disciplinarian, not that this should imply weakness on Claudius' part. He deterred the senate from showing its pleasure at Gallienus' assassination, requiring the dead emperor's deification and the showing of proper respect to his family and supporters. He also approached his large problems in a logical fashion, putting a priority on freeing Italy from the Alemanni and the Balkans from the Goths. Indeed, his victory over the latter earned him his usual sobriquet of *Gothicus*. Time did not, however, allow him to turn his attention to the two major 'inherited' rebellions – in Gaul and in the east, although it would not be unreasonable to suppose that the *Imperium Galliarum*, since Postumus' death, was something of a spent force. It appears that the Spanish provinces returned to their allegiance to the central government during Claudius' reign, and numismatic evidence – and possibly inscriptions, too – suggests that there may well have been a growing tension between 'legitimist' and 'rebel' groups in Britain.

Although Claudius did not in any sense restore to the senate anything of what it had lost under Gallienus, he was nonetheless respected by the senate for his treatment of them and, on his death from plague in 270, was accorded a variety of honours, including posthumous deification. His immediate successor, his brother Quintillus, shared Claudius' mild manner but not his resolve; he committed suicide when challenged for power by Aurelian. Aurelian carries the credit for the end of the *Imperium Galliarum* and for the defeat of Zenobia (taking the title of *restitutor Orientis*). Indeed, the territorial integrity of the empire was probably more or less restored to the situation earlier in the century, apart from the final abandonment of Dacia across the Danube. To Aurelian also goes the credit for the building of a new wall circuit for Rome which, in large part, still survives, and for a first attempt at restoring the integrity of (and thus confidence in) the currency. The emperor was a devotee of *Sol Invictus*; this was not, however, the time for wild excesses such as those that had characterised the reign of Elagabalus. Aurelian seems to have had in mind a kind of monotheism, which perhaps brought closer an accommodation with Christianity, although it should be added that it was a monotheism which held *Sol* as a kind of 'updated Jupiter'. The virtue of such a move was clearly the cultural coherence which, it was hoped, might thus be achieved across the empire.

Even though Aurelian's successors (Claudius Tacitus, AD 275–276; Probus, AD 276–282; Carus, AD 282–283; Carinus, AD 283–285; Numerian, AD 283–284) were lacking in neither mental capacity nor courage, the long-established problems from across the European and eastern frontiers remained intransigent. It was another Illyrian of humble origin who put his very considerable personal courage and organisational talents to the twin tasks of rescue and restoration; this was Gaius Aurelius Valerius Diocletianus, an emperor who, with some justice, has been regarded as the greatest statesman of the Decline.

Recovery and reconstruction

As had so often happened in the past, a crisis in Rome's affairs evoked a hero, although first of all he had to fight against Carinus, brother of the late emperor, Numerian, for sole sovereignty in the empire. The new emperor appreciated that the principal task was to rein in anarchy: to achieve this the emperor had to be ubiquitous, rather than ensconced in Rome, which was, in any case, at a considerable distance from the real troublespots. Further, Diocletian knew that crises brought forth generals who were, in their turn, potential troublemakers.

Thus, he made the decision to abandon Rome as a static seat of government – indeed, he visited the city only once in his reign – and instituted instead the role of 'travelling emperor' with a mobile court (*comitatus*). Not surprisingly, this was too large a task for one man and, as he had no son with whom to share power, Diocletian in 285 nominated a junior partner (*Caesar*), Maximian who, like himself, was a career soldier from Illyricum.

Plate 10.3 Rome, the walls of Aurelian.

Plate 10.4 Coin of the British 'rebel'. Carausius; the legend, 'Carausius and His Brothers', indicates that Carausius was claiming equality with Diocletian and Maximian. © Copyright The British Museum.

In this partnership, Diocletian was the politician, Maximian the commander of armies. To inspire remoteness and awe, both *Augustus* (Diocletian) and *Caesar* (Maximian) took titles to indicate specific divine protection – respectively *Jovius* and his son, *Herculius*. As with the Romans of old, a divine ancestor added *auctoritas* to a man, whatever the reality of his background.

The initial task was to repair the effects of the civil war between Carinus and Diocletian: the western frontier was in a serious state, and it stands to Maximian's credit that he was able to restore order and – a novel experiment – installed a Frankish king (Gennobaudes) as a buffer between Romans and Germans. Recognition of Maximian's contribution came in 286 in the form of a 'promotion' to the title *Augustus*, although it was made clear that Diocletian still enjoyed seniority. Maximian's other military problem was piracy in the western seas, of which the leading figures were Franks and Saxons; Maximian bestowed this command on Carausius whose success was conspicuous.

Whether he thought he should be rewarded for this or believed that the principle of shared power should be taken further, Carausius styled himself *Augustus*, issuing coins proclaiming the rule of 'Carausius and his Brothers' (*Carausius et fratres sui*). Carausius' claim was never acknowledged; because, however, Diocletian and Maximian were unable to bring him to order, his position in Britain and coastal parts of Gaul became *ipso facto* rebellious. Thus the western empire was facing its second breakaway movement in the space of three decades. It was fortunate, however, that Carausius was talented and the period of his rebellion saw many improvements to the defences of Britain, most notably the inception of the 'Saxon shore defences', a series of 'castle-like' forts stretching from the Wash to Southampton Water. These forts stood in marked contrast to the 'police stations' which had previously housed units of the Roman army; the new forts often abandoned the quadrilateral shape and were distinguished by their high, thick walls and, in contrast to earlier forts, small numbers of small access points. The garrisons of these

Plate 10.5 (opposite) Venice, St Mark's Square: the tetrarchs.

forts are ill-understood and, judging from the lack of internal buildings (as at Portchester Castle, Hampshire), they were probably thinly manned. Some believe that the term, 'Saxon shore', as applied to this area of Britain's coastline, indicates that Saxons were bought off with land and perhaps helped to man the new forts. If so, the arrangements would have some similarity with Maximian's deal with the Franks.

The mounting difficulties showed Diocletian that the 'imperial presence' was still not sufficiently widespread: thus, in 293, a further adjustment was made; two junior figures (*Caesares*) – Galerius and Constantius Chlorus – were appointed; Galerius 'assisted' Diocletian in the east, while Constantius was attached to Maximian in the west. This imperial 'college' of four – or tetrarchy – was bound together in traditional fashion by marriage ties. The real qualities of the two new rulers are obfuscated by the propaganda that surrounded them at the time and later: Galerius,

seen as the mastermind behind the Christian persecutions from AD 303, was regarded by Christian writers as a monster of depravity, while Constantius partly because of his totally spurious claim to descent from Claudius II and partly because he was the father of the first Christian emperor was seen as the incarnation of every virtue. In reality, both Caesars were – and it presumably explained their promotion – tried and tested generals. Alongside the programme of reforms associated with the tetrarchic period, we should remember that all four rulers were engaged in military activity which restored a degree of territorial integrity to the empire. Constantius, for example (or perhaps, more justifiably, Asclepiodotus on his behalf), brought to an end the British rebellion which, in 293, had passed to the control of Allectus after the latter's murder of Carausius. The famous 'Arras medallion' depicts Constantius receiving the submission of a suppliant *Londinium* at the city gates. The legend ('Restorer of Eternal Light': RESTITUTOR LUCIS AETERNAE) carries overtones of the restoration of the empire's political integrity, as well as hinting, as Aurelian had done, at the importance of the sun-god in the Roman pantheon of the late-third century. Yet, for Diocletian, the tetrarchy was conspicuous for its *pietas*, or reverence for the traditional gods. Diocletian and his colleagues were not gods, but rather their representatives on earth. Like much of the spirit of the tetrarchy, Diocletian was clearly attempting in his religious attitudes to recapture the spirit of the Augustan revolution three centuries previously. His view of, and actions against, Christianity had much in common with those of earlier rulers, which was based on the indissoluble connection between political stability and the recognised place in the system of the traditional gods – as Horace had prescribed to Augustus.

The outward pretensions of the tetrarchic court, however, were (literally) derived from a different world from Augustus'. Although, as we have seen, there was no question of the tetrarchs claiming divinity for themselves, the orientalising of the court under Diocletian and Constantine struck a note that was at once exotic and remote; court practices were perhaps designed to heighten security through the sense of awe that was created around the imperial personages – jewel-bedecked robes and shoes, a diadem for a crown and such practices as self-prostration in the imperial presence and kissing the hem of his robe. Contemporary with this was the creation of the 'imperial bedroom' (*sacrum cubiculum*), presided over by a eunuch (*praepositus sacri cubiculi*); this was in future the heart of the court, doing a job somewhat similar to the advisers (*amici*) of earlier days.

Bureaucracy was a keynote of the new arrangements: it has been suggested that the ruling system itself was conceived in a bureaucratic fashion and that Diocletian had in mind a 'rolling system' for succession. The *Augusti*, it is suggested, would abdicate after twenty years, to be replaced by their *Caesares*; the four would at the same time agree on the creation of two new *Caesares*. It is hard to believe that a man of Diocletian's intelligence and practical aptitude would not have seen in this a fragility bordering on unworkability; if such was his intention, it faltered badly at the 'first test' in 305. It is more likely that this version has been built on the fact that Diocletian did abdicate after twenty years – although because of ill-health rather than previous intention – and seems to have wished an unwilling Maximian to do the same. The tetrarchic system broke down over this and because of Constantius' early death (soon after his elevation to Augustus); also, the rivalry over the replacement of the *Caesares* proved to be highly disruptive and was eventually resolved by Constantine I's military victory in AD 312 over Maximian's son, Maxentius, at the Milvian Bridge over the River Tiber. In the longer term, however, the 'vision' that Constantine allegedly witnessed before this battle, and which convinced him that the Christian God was 'on his side', had far greater implications for Rome and the empire.

There was virtually no part of the imperial machinery that did not feel the tetrarchs' reforming hand. As we have seen, the mid-third century had seen the economy and the coinage in chaos; the traditional denominations had all but disappeared and the system relied on a copper coin with a radiate crowned head on the obverse side, which was a complete debasement of the already-debased *antoninianus*. Such could not fail to destroy confidence; inflation soared and transactions were conducted through radiate copies produced locally on a gigantic scale and through a return to barter. Aurelian and his immediate successors attempted a modest reform by incorporating a small percentage of silver in the radiate and by striking on the reverse a 'value mark' indicating that the coin was meant to tariff as an *antoninianus* (or double *denarius*). It was a temporary solution only, and in any case could be sustained only if the drain on the empire's resources (through warfare) were reined in.

Diocletian's reform of the coinage, like so much of his work, had an 'Augustan ring' to it: he wished to re-establish a denominationally related set of gold, silver and copper coins; the first two were equivalent in many ways to the old *aureus* and *denarius*, while the new copper coin (which is now commonly called a *follis*) resembled, in size at least, the Augustan *as*. The concept was bold, although there were probably not sufficient resources of precious metals to sustain it. A problem which, as we have seen, developed during the third century had been the proliferation of local, unofficial, mints; the bulk of these were closed down, as were the 'independent coinages' of Greek city mints. Instead, the new *follis* was issued with a single legend (GENIO POPULI ROMANI) from (initially) fourteen licensed mints across the empire; for the first time, therefore, the whole empire was utilising a standard coinage marked with its mint of origin. It did not last, however; confidence did not return and inflation continued to grow.

Two significant events of 300–301 may be regarded as indicative of continuing difficulties: first, in 300, the *follis* was issued with a new legend (SACRA MONETA AUGG ET CAESS). The implication of declaring the sacredness of the coinage was that it was now incumbent on the state's gods to care for the integrity of a coinage which human agencies could no longer guarantee. In the

Plate 10.6 Africa, Sbeitla: the Arch of Diocletian.

Plate 10.7 Rome, Baths of Diocletian: Frigidarium *preserved as the Basilica of S. Maria degli Angeli.*

following year, clearly against a background of continuing price rises, Diocletian issued his famous Edict of Maximum Prices, in which a maximum price was fixed across the empire at which a range of goods could be sold. While this may well have been aimed at profiteering, its failure to take into account the rising costs of transportation will have rendered it difficult to enforce; it may well have had the effect of localising trade rather than bringing success and fairness to the concept of empire-wide markets.

The falling size of the copper coinage in the early decades of the fourth century is, however, indicative of continuing economic problems.

A major problem in this was that the empire's expenditure increased – on bureaucracy, warfare and expansive building projects – while resources did not keep pace, despite the availability of some new resources of precious metals and the product of confiscation of precious metals and recycling them. That this was not, however, sufficient is clear from the reform of the tax system that was necessary to bale out the state's finances; further, the new tetrarchic tax system was both complex and burdensome. Before Diocletian, the principal tax was the *annona* – a land and personal tax, which was collected partly in kind, although with a part (*annona militaris*) paid in cash for the army. The methods of assessment and payment were *iugatio* and *capitatio*, the former based on land, while the latter was either a personal tax or one based on the number of people working on an estate. Some

provinces paid by both schemes, others by one or the other. There were partial immunities, as for active and retired soldiers, while special taxes were levied besides from the richer members of society such as senators, municipal leaders and merchants.

So dependent was the state on these revenues that people were not permitted to leave their rank in society unless they first found a replacement. Needless to say, all of this required an ever-swelling bureaucracy to cope with the collection of taxes, which served only to aggravate the financial problems that taxation was intended to solve. Further, this growing burden on individuals lessened the money available for private investment, leaving some towns very short on care. This was also to be seen against a background of increased local expenditure on necessary defensive projects, such as town walls. These were not comfortable times, and it is predictable that some should have asked for ways of checking the tax burden by reviewing expenditure and reducing waste. It is equally predictable that such appeals fell on to deaf ears. It is ironical that, to avoid the stranglehold exerted by foreign enemies, the empire's population had to submit to a fiscal and economic stranglehold of its own making.

Obviously, in the drive for reform the most sensitive area consisted of armies and provinces: two principles prevailed – the separation of military and civilian powers and the subdivision of provinces into smaller units. Since the time of Gallienus, senators had been kept at a distance from military authority, such commands going to equestrians who, from Diocletian's time, generally went under the title of *duces*. The evidence for the subdivision of provinces, known to us through the 'Verona list', shows that the number of provinces was effectively doubled, reaching one hundred and twenty by the end of the fourth century. Italy was from now formally regarded as a province.

Needless to say, the senate as a body did not retain any formal role in the government of provinces; although the governors of Asia, Africa and Achaea continued to be styled *proconsuls,* they

Plate 10.8 (opposite) Split, Palace of Diocletian: the Peristylium.
Source: photographed by J. Thompson.

Plate 10.9 Rome, the Via Appia: Circus of Maxentius (showing the 'starting stalls' and 'judges' towers').

Plate 10.10 Rome, the Arch of Constantine, commemorating Constantine's victory in the civil war against Maxentius in AD 312.

Plate 10.11 Rome, Basilica of Maxentius and Constantine: surviving aisle of the building; the nave and nearer aisle are no longer extant.

were now responsible to the emperor. The remainder of provincial governors were called *consulares*, *correctores* or *praesides*, depending on rank; further, senators bore the title *viri clarissimi* and equestrians were styled *viri perfectissimi*. The provinces were grouped into twelve dioceses, each of which was under the control of an equestrian *vicarius*, who was responsible to one of four *praefecti praetorii* of equestrian standing, one of whom was attached to each tetrarch. Thus, Rome now saw the implementation of a principle which had excessively angered senators during the reign of Tiberius nearly three hundred years previously when they had objected to their effective subordination to the equestrian praetorian prefect, Sejanus. The reform also finally divorced the office of praetorian prefect from command of the imperial bodyguard.

Throughout the history of the Roman empire to the time of Diocletian, provinces and armies were thought of as parts of the

Plate 10.12 Trier, the Constantinian Baths.

Plate 10.13 Trier, the basilica.
Source: Photographed by J. Witherington.

same organisation, linked by the command structure. We have seen already the development during the third century of a more professional command structure for the army. It had also been the case that the army – legions and auxiliaries – was used as a garrison force in certain provinces: the problem with this arrangement was that garrison armies were inevitably weakened when other army groups required enhancement for the purpose of campaigning; the cost of this had been amply demonstrated during the third century in the form of weakened frontier defence.

The essence of the third and fourth century reforms was the division of the army into two distinct parts – frontier armies (*limitanei*) which on the frontier operated on the principle of defence in depth and mobile field armies (*comitatenses*) which consisted of the cream of cavalry and infantry. The field armies consisted of approximately 200,000 men divided into two equal parts in the east and the west. These troops were billeted away from the frontiers and close to the principal routes of communication, allowing ease of deployment.

The character of the army was thus altered, and the tendency was for the frontier groups (which consisted of *cunei equitum* (barbarian formations), *equites* (residue of older cavalry-units), legions, *alae* and *cohortes*) to become more akin to local militias. The legions, although still recruited from Roman citizens, lost their traditional superiority over the auxiliaries. The flower of the later Roman army was now seen as barbarian units, mostly German and Illyrian; it was a sign that the real vitality within the empire's population had slipped away from the Roman citizen body (burdened as it was by disease and taxation) to others who offered a better prospect for preserving the empire's integrity. The empire's defences at the turn of the third and fourth centuries looked in a better and more prepared shape than would have seemed possible a few decades earlier.

Thus, in the later years of the third century AD, an Illyrian soldier–emperor had achieved in different circumstances a stability that might be compared with that fashioned by the son of Julius Caesar at the end of the first century BC. The problems that had beset the empire during the third century had not vanished, although the empire was in an organisationally better position to handle them. The cost, in terms of burdens, was high; Diocletian had demonstrated the truth of the dying words attributed to Septimius Severus: 'Enrich the soldiers and despise the rest'.

Further reading

Arnheim M., *The Senatorial Aristocracy in the Late Roman Empire* (Oxford, 1972.)

Barnes T. D., *The New Empire of Diocletian and Constantine* (Cambridge, MA, 1982).

Casey P. J., *Carausius and Allectus: The British Usurpers* (London, 1994).

De Blois L., *The Policy of the Emperor Gallienus* (Rome, 1958).

Dietz K., *Senatus Contra Principem* (Munich, 1980).

Jones A. H. M., *The Later Roman Empire, 284–602* (Oxford, 1964).

MacMullen R., *Roman Government's Response to Crisis* (New Haven, CT, 1976).

Maxfield V. A. (ed.), *The Saxon Shore* (Exeter, 1989).

Nicolini R. (ed.), *La Residenza Imperiale di Massenzio* (Rome, 1980).

Syme R., *Emperors and Biography* (Oxford, 1971).

Wilkes J. J., *Diocletian's Palace, Split* (Sheffield, 1986).

Williams S., *Diocletian and the Roman Recovery* (London, 1985).

Chapter 11

The fourth century: change and decline

Church and state

The political, economic and military reforms of Diocletian and Constantine tackled most areas of government where weaknesses were apparent. A running sore, however, since the first century AD had been the intermittent conflict between the Roman state and the growing Christian Church. This came to its most violent head in the first decade of the fourth century, with the 'Great Persecution' which was authorised by Diocletian but which, according to Lactantius in *De Mortibus Persecutorum* ('On the Deaths of the Persecutors'), was principally orchestrated by Diocletian's *Caesar*, Galerius.

Nonetheless, it would be a mistake to see the Roman state locked into a constant battle with the Christian Church; hostility between the two was neither chronologically nor geographically consistent. Initial difficulties in essence sprang from Rome's relationship with various Jewish groups, for whom the preaching of Jesus Christ was undermining: those who were opposed to a Roman presence in Judaea saw Jesus' 'Messianic status' compromised in one crucial particular; the messages that 'people should love one another' and 'render unto Caesar the things that are

Caesar's' denied what was regarded as a principal Messianic aim – namely, that of ridding Judaea of Romans, by force if necessary. Even those who, like the Sadducees, were prepared to co-operate with Rome saw Christ's message as damaging to their own influence. It was not difficult for monotheistic Jews to find in the monotheistic Christianity items which Romans, always intensely suspicious of what really lay behind foreign cults, would find worrying. Thus, Rome, in the person of the procurator, Pontius Pilatus, was persuaded to act against Christ on the charge that he preached adherence to a 'rebel kingdom' which was opposed both to Rome and to Judaism. At this time, the emperor, Tiberius, was in retirement on the island of Capreae: whether a younger and less disillusioned Tiberius would have required his procurator to act differently can only be a matter of speculation.

Initially – and unsurprisingly – the Romans did not evidently mark a clear distinction between Jews and Christians; indeed, many early Christians will have been Jewish. This emerges from Suetonius' reference (*Life of the Deified Claudius* 25) to expulsions from Rome of Jews acting under the influence of *Chrestus* [*sic*]. Nor was the attack made on Christians during the reign of Nero 'doctrinal'; it was only Christians in Rome who were affected, and they were being accused less for their beliefs than for suspected incendiarism. The nature of the punishment of many of them – being covered in pitch and set alight – indicates this in a society which believed literally in making the punishment fit the crime. Nonetheless, there were misgivings and misunderstandings which opened Christians up to suspicion – not least concerning the Eucharist which it was easy, through malice or ignorance, to misinterpret as cannibalism. Something of the Roman readiness to 'expect the worst' of eastern cults and the reasons for this can be seen in the attitude of Tiberius Caesar, in AD 19, towards Judaism and the Egyptian cults. The overriding fear was of creeds or actions which threatened to undermine the carefully constructed stability of the Roman state, in which traditional religious observance was of primary importance.

It is with Trajan that we first encounter a clear statement of a legal/doctrinal nature in Rome's relations with the early Church: our information comes from the younger Pliny (*Letters* X.96–97) who, as governor of Bithynia (AD 111–113), had to deal with the growing 'problem' of Christians in his province and the 'crimes' associated with them; according to a surviving clause in the *Lex de Imperio Vespasiani*, the emperor's reply automatically carried the force of law, and indeed became the legal basis for Rome's dealings with the Church for the ensuing two centuries. As we have seen, Trajan's reply, which was intended to be humane, nonetheless established the illegality of refusal to acknowledge the gods of the Roman state, including the *numen Augusti*; invoking the gods of Rome would constitute a suitable recantation. Failure so to do constituted a crime which required punishment which, for the reasons that we have seen in the case of the Neronian attacks on Christians, were often of a horrendous nature. Ironically, few Roman emperors actually thought of themselves as gods; imperial cult observance was a political act. Nevertheless, the dressing of this political act in religious apparel, an essential feature of the traditional union of politics and religion in the Roman state, rendered it unacceptable to Christians. In practice, however, persecution was generally limited by the nature of the evidence and of its source and overall was much more restricted in time and location than is often supposed.

Yet, Christian communities tended not to be popular: they often frowned on the leisure activities of non-Christians, affecting to persuade people away from games and shows with the argument that even greater pleasure awaited those who so abstained – that of witnessing in the afterlife the spectacle of non-Christians 'roasting in perdition'. Their unpopularity, together with the myths which continued to circulate about them, made them targets whenever troublesome events occurred – whether it be military disasters or natural calamities such as poor harvests: 'more Christians means more disasters' seemed to open the gate to predictable apotropaic action in such circumstances. The official argument was totally consistent with centuries of tradition: the state's gods were angry because of the neglect which they had suffered and needed to be appeased. This was the essential cornerstone of the *pax deorum*, which Augustus Caesar had placed at the heart of the restored *respublica*.

The state's actions, however, seemed to be demonstrably counterproductive, Tertullian, the Christian apologist of the early third century, observing that 'the blood of the martyrs is the seed of the Church'; no doubt, many were impressed by the dignity and courage shown by Christians when facing deaths of indescribable horror, while others will have found their obstinacy irrational and disturbing. The Christians may have remained unpopular, yet the religion was spreading; by the mid-second century AD, it had reached the western provinces and, in Britain, a fragment of a cryptogram found at Manchester and dating to the Antonine period may provide the earliest evidence of Christianity in the province.

It is clear that the deteriorating condition of Rome and the empire in the later second century, which is evidenced not only by events themselves but also by a rise in such activities as 'street-corner philosophising' and dream interpretation, which are characteristics of an age of anxiety, led to frustrated attempts to apportion blame. These served only to heighten the sense of uncertainty: the state's gods, as in the late first century BC, were forsaking Rome because of the behaviour of the 'infidels'; but as the state sought to punish these law-breakers, so their numbers grew. It is little wonder that Marcus Aurelius, himself a man of humanitarian character but who saw in Christian martyrs an obstinate fanaticism of the most useless kind, had no taste for a confrontation with the Church.

It seems that the Severi had not either: although in AD 202 a ban had been placed on Jewish and Christian proselytism, the attitude of Septimius Severus appears to have exhibited little difference from those of his predecessors – that is, standing by the legislation framed under Trajan and Hadrian. There may have been local outbreaks of anti-Christian feeling, prompted perhaps by purely local circumstances – hostile mobs or an unsympathetic provincial governor – or perhaps a specific local antipathy towards a particular branch of Christianity; on the whole, however, the Christian Church probably benefited from the growth and spread of eastern religions during the Severan period and provides evidence in the form of art, buildings and an administrative hierarchical structure. In particular, we find Christian cemeteries appearing, and it may well have been at this stage that the graves and relics of martyrs became significant – as in the case of the tomb in the Vatican cemetery at Rome, which is believed to have held the remains of St Peter. It is evident from graffiti recovered from beneath the Church of S. Sebastiano on the Via Appia that the relics of Peter and Paul were taken there, probably during the persecutions of Decius and Valerian.

As we move into the third century, Rome itself, along with Carthage and Alexandria, began to emerge as the Church's principal centres in the Roman Empire. In such places, we also find during the Severan period the strongest evidence of a new and rigorous dimension to the intellectual expression of Christianity – from men such as Hippolytus, Origen, Clement and, of course, Tertullian himself.

In a more stable empire, the Christian Church might have fared better; but, as we have seen (in Chapter 10), beside the disasters of the mid-third century, those of earlier periods paled almost into insignificance. The troubled reigns of Decius and Valerian (AD 249–259) saw some of the bitterest attacks on Christians, especially in Rome, as the emperors struggled to restore stability by appeasing the traditional gods. Decius, for example, in AD 250–251, ordered that a general sacrifice be made to the pagan gods; many Christians could not endure the punishments for disobedience and forsook their faith. The tensions between those who had lapsed (*lapsi*) and those who had stood by their principles were great. Further such orders were given by Valerian in

257–258: the laws against Christians had apparently toughened or, at least, the old laws were being applied with extreme toughness. It is little wonder that Lactantius so relished the fate that the Persians had in store for the ill-starred Valerian in 259. Yet, the pointlessness of all this cruelty was obvious: in 260, Valerian's son, Gallienus, though not a Christian himself, issued an 'Edict of Toleration' which foreshadowed what Constantine was to do and which brought a peace to the Church for four decades.

The last great persecution of the Christian Church is always attributed to Diocletian, although its true authors were his fellow *Augustus*, Maximian, and particularly his *Caesar*, Galerius. Indeed, Diocletian needed to be persuaded to join in wholeheartedly by various acts of malicious sabotage in his capital at Nicomedia. A principal issue on this occasion appears to have been the feared effect of Christians 'lurking' in the administration and in the army, as is shown by the probably apocryphal anecdote concerning the onset of persecution. Anti-Christian activities began slowly, and were isolated, but in 303 began in earnest with decrees which insisted on the conduct of sacrifices by the army, confiscation of Christian literature, destruction of Church property, imprisonment or execution of Christian leaders – although, as in the 250s, balanced by freedom for those who recanted their beliefs. Not surprisingly, this period of persecution bore hardest on the eastern part of the empire; the extreme west, the part administered by Constantius Chlorus (the western *Caesar*), the father of Constantine, fared relatively better. The differing intensities of persecution led to differing attitudes among Christians as to what in their beliefs and activities was ultimately most important, and this played its part in the splits and arguments which were to disfigure the Church so often in the fourth century.

Diocletian and Maximian both abdicated in 305, and while Galerius, now the eastern *Augustus*, tried to cement together a new tetrarchy, competing claims led to a situation which was little short of anarchic. In the confusion that followed the natural death, in 306, of Constantius, western *Augustus* since Maximian's abdication, the troops in Britain proclaimed his son, Constantine, as *Augustus*. Over a period, Constantine eliminated rivals: his defeat of Maxentius at the Milvian Bridge at Rome in 312 left him as undisputed western *Augustus*; twelve years later, his victory over Licinius at Adrianople left him as emperor of a reunited empire.

In Constantine's reign, the position of the Church was, of course, to change completely: Galerius had issued an Edict of Toleration in 311, while in the following year his *Caesar*, Maximin Daia, renewed the persecution. The victories of Constantine and Licinius in 312, however, led to a general Edict of Toleration and the 'Peace of the Church'. This restored freedom of worship and the possessions which had been confiscated. The relationship between Church and State now changed fundamentally: instead of regarding Christians as marginal to itself, the government now felt Christianity to be so much a part of itself that it intervened in the Arles Council of 314 to secure the condemnation of Donatism and was instrumental in the declaration at the Council of Nicaea of 325 that Arianism was a heresy. The Church was now part of the Roman state; so too, significantly, were its differences.

The spur to Constantine's enthusiasm for the Church were the 'visions' – first of Apollo, which probably brought him to solar monotheism, and secondly the 'Christian vision' which preceded his victory over Maxentius at the Milvian Bridge; Constantine, it is said, saw a cross athwart the sun and the words *hoc signo victor eris* ('by this sign you will be victorious'). As a result, he instructed his troops to carry the *labarum*, a standard with the Greek letters X (*chi*) and P (*rho*), the beginning of the Greek word, 'Christos' ('the Anointed One'), embroidered upon it.

It may be asked whether Constantine was a Christian and what his view was on the relationship between Church and state: that Constantine was originally, like his father (see, for example, the Arras Medallion), a worshipper of the sun seems to be beyond

Plate 11.1 Coin of Constantine I (from AD 310), depicting the Sun-god, Sol.

dispute – as is demonstrated by his 'vision' of Apollo. Sun worship had developed in popularity since the times of the Severans, and one emperor, Aurelian (AD 70–275), had apparently sought to put Sol (sometimes identified with Mithras) at the head of the pantheon by investing the god, as we have seen, with certain of the attributes of Jupiter. At the same time, there was 'overlap' between sun worship and Christianity, as is demonstrated by such representations as the *Christos-Helios* figure in the so-called 'Tomb of St Peter' in the Vatican cemetery.

There is no doubting that Constantine took seriously his relationship with the Church: he involved himself, although

Plate 11.2 Rome, Church of S. Costanza: detail of mosaic ceiling of vault.

not necessarily knowledgeably in a theological sense, in the Councils called to resolve the doctrinal disputes of the day; and he was the sponsor of major Christian building projects, such as the Vatican and Lateran Basilicas in Rome. In the case of the former, the construction displays a good deal of knowledge of the history of the site: a building platform was created for the first Basilica of St Peter which respected the ground level of the tomb believed to be that of St Peter; the altar of the Constantinian Basilica was placed directly above the site of this tomb. In the context of the Church, as now visible, that 'holy spot' lies directly beneath the great cupola. The fact that Constantine was not baptised until late in life need occasion no misgiving, as this practice was not uncommon and was presumably intended to dedicate the body at a time when the potential for further sinning was chronologically limited; in the case of a Roman emperor this may have been no small consideration.

The Church was 'at peace' with Rome; but, although it enjoyed the emperor's support, it had not yet ousted pagan gods. In the decade which followed the Edict of Milan, traditional Roman gods, such as Jupiter, Mars, Hercules and Sol, continued to find a prominent place on the coinage of Constantine throughout the empire. By contrast, overtly Christian symbolism was absent or restricted in size and prominence by inclusion as part of some mint marks. Indeed, it was not until the rebellions of Magnentius and Vetranio in the early 350s that Christianity made an unequivocal appearance on the coinage – in the case of Magnentius by his representation of a prominent Christogram (*chi–rho*) as a reverse-type and of Vetranio, even more powerfully, by his becoming the only emperor (or candidate for the position) to provide a pictorial and verbal representation of Constantine's 'vision' at the Milvian Bridge. In view of the rebel status of both Magnentius and Vetranio, we may suspect that their motives were principally political and that they were attempting to win the support of the Church and to lay claim to a 'Constantinian' legitimacy which transcended that of Constantine's surviving son – the eminently uncongenial Constantius II (AD 337–361); political propaganda of this type will have been thoroughly 'at home' in a state whose earlier rulers had readily resorted to coin types which suggested that their political credentials associated them with Augustus Caesar.

Indeed, just as the behaviour of Magnentius and Vetranio was politically driven, we may reasonably suspect the same of Constantine himself; it is unlikely that he was motivated by an intellectual or spiritual affinity with the Church. As a politician, Constantine had seen all too clearly the effects of alienation and marginalisation; he appreciated the need for an embracing coherence. In this respect, he is strongly reminiscent of another who, much earlier, had helped Rome to 'snatch victory from the jaws of defeat' – Augustus Caesar.

Augustus had appreciated the strength of the part played by religion in the growth of the Roman *respublica* and its place in the

Plate 11.3 Rome, Church of S. Sabina on the Aventine (early fifth century AD), adopting the Roman basilican format.

'political armoury' available to him in his crusade to stabilise the Republic. Like Augustus, Constantine was trying to restore an equilibrium after a period of anarchy; like Augustus, too, Constantine appreciated this as a situation crying out for inclusiveness, and that it would, therefore, be seriously counterproductive gratuitously to alienate individuals and groups outside the Church. Many of such people were important for their continuing contribution to stable government; and just as Constantine was the Church's principal political agent and protector, so too for pagans he was still *Pontifex Maximus.*

The 'Peace of the Church' had much in common with *Pax Deorum* of earlier years: the Roman state of the fourth century required heavenly justification and sanction just as much as it had in the first century. As a politician, the architect of this fourth-century 'Peace' had clearly learned lessons from and shared a type of vision with his distinguished – and successful – predecessor,

Augustus. For both men, official religion was the 'cement' of the Roman state and a crucial element in the 'mechanics' which made it work. To this extent, Rome had in Constantine I a 'new Augustus', for whom keeping the Church united was far more important than keeping it united correctly.

Constantine died, a baptised Christian, in AD 337; yet his sons, who succeeded to his power, demonstrated the eclecticism of the times by securing for their father deification in the traditional pagan manner. The internal stability of the empire, which had been largely secured by Constantine, started to fall apart until Constantius II established himself in control by AD 353, supported by two *Caesares* – his cousins, Gallus and Julian. The character of politics, however, was changing: Constantius II, even allowing for propaganda that emanated from Julian, may be justly regarded as authoritarian and cruel; he dominated his court, and his reign, by that very authoritarianism, saw the undermining of the religious equilibrium which had been achieved by his father.

Already (in 331), perhaps as a contingency plan for paying for the new capital at Constantinople, Constantine I had required pagan temples to 'register their assets'. Almost as soon as Constantine was dead, various forms of attack on pagans were introduced and were to continue intermittently for the next century. Actions included bans on sacrifices, closing and destruction of pagan temples (thus 'liberating' their assets), bans on any form of pagan worship in public or in the home. Perhaps the most symbolic acts were the banning of all pagan rites in Rome (391), the destruction of the Temple of Serapis in Alexandria (391) and that of Juno Caelestis at Carthage (399), and the removal of the Altar of Victory from the senate house at Rome (after 382). The charged atmosphere introduced by such moves was heightened by the continuing disputes within the Church and the resumption of serious external warfare. It is surely significant that, a century after the 'Peace of the Church', the pagan gods still required the passing of legislation against them; the interlude of comparative calm under Constantine I, however, was now over.

The soundness of Constantine's judgement over the partial (and effective) toleration of paganism was amply demonstrated by the reaction to the excessive behaviour of his son, Constantius II. In 355, faced by internal rebellion and by external military threat, Constantius had sent Julian to Gaul as his *Caesar* to face what looked as if it might be an attack on the Rhine and the Danube by a combination of Rome's regional enemies. Required, even in this situation, to provide reinforcements for Constantius in the east, he refused, and was declared *Augustus* by his troops; opportunely, Constantius, at the prospect of further disaster, fell ill and died (361).

Julian's education had brought him a familiarity with traditional Roman – and Augustan – virtues, such as piety, justice and clemency, which were the product of the natural *humanitas* of this admirer of Marcus Aurelius. His experiences under the sons of Constantine, especially Constantius II, had turned him positively against the religion which he took to be the incentive to such behaviour. He attacked Christians through his writings, restored paganism by decree and banned Christians from a range of public activities. As with Marcus Aurelius, Julian's embracing of a philosophical paganism did not lead him to shy away from danger. His paganism was proudly proclaimed, as is shown by his famous coin issue with the bull of Apis dominating the reverse within the legend SECURITAS REIPUBLICAE, and by the fact that, inheriting the eastern war of Constantius against Sapor II, he faced the enemy in person and died of his wounds (363). Little credence should be attached to the demeaning Christian tale that, as he died, Julian effectively recanted his paganism with the words 'Galilean, you have won!' Julian's paganism and anti-Christian stance were, however, undone by his successor, Jovian, in the following year.

We should not imagine that paganism was completely cowed by the attacks launched against it: indeed, some were positive enough to preach the virtues of a kind of ecumenism. Britain, however, provides a specific and clear example of both the confidence and the wealth of pagans at this time through the extensive temple complex dedicated to Mars-Nodens at Lydney (on the estuary of the River Severn) and constructed entirely after AD 364. Late Roman art, in fact, provides countless examples of a surviving interest in the pagan cults, both traditional (western) and from the east. Indeed, we are alerted to the strength of paganism by the ferocity and the geographical and chronological extent of attacks made on it by a succession of emperors after 364. While some dissatisfaction with the times may have been channelled into the conflict between Christianity and paganism, some found its way into the continuing disputes about doctrine and conduct inside the Church itself.

Not that all of this was totally negative in effect: in Britain, in the late fourth century, Pelagius preached the denial of the 'act of Divine Grace', arguing that 'man was the master of his own salvation'. Translated into contemporary political and military attitudes in Britain, this appears to have produced a group of men in the province who took the view that, if Romano-British culture was to survive, then it would have to be as a result of their own efforts. This contrasted with the comparatively supine attitude of those who simply 'wrung their hands' at the current state of things and hoped that, somehow, Britain would be restored to its full place in the empire. Recent excavations at sites such as Birdoswald (on Hadrian's Wall) have provided positive evidence of warlords and their militias who may have given practical expression to the independent philosophy of 'self-help' espoused by Pelagianism.

Progressively, however, throughout a good deal of the empire – and certainly in the west – Christians, heretics of various kinds and pagans were, as Tacitus wrote of a much earlier crisis, 'praying to the gods of an empire that was no longer theirs'.

The fall of Rome

One might have been forgiven for thinking that, in the dark days of the third century, the demise of Rome could hardly be avoided;

however, the reforms initiated by Diocletian and Constantine belied the more pessimistic predictions. As we have seen, they affected virtually every aspect of the empire's life, benefiting from the good fortune of a period which, although it saw civil war, was relatively free of major external conflict.

Although the tetrarchy collapsed in confusion in 311–312, Constantine re-established a dual role with Licinius and then, on the defeat of Licinius in 324, brought the empire back under a single governance. To mark this, but also as a reflection of the fact that barbarian problems in the west were so serious, he initiated a new capital at Byzantium, with the name Constantinople. While this was in some ways seen as a parallel city to Rome, aspects of its government left it in some respects inferior to Rome, the city which remained the 'nostalgic' centre of the Roman Empire. Constantine attempted to make Constantinople an eastern city with a Latin character, recalling in some ways Hadrianic Athens, but the nature of the population ensured that its character and culture were essentially Greek.

During Constantine's later years, old problems began to resurface: although the messages proclaimed by the coinage were bold and confident enough, the very size and condition of the coins argued otherwise. The reformed tetrarchic coinage, impressive in its size, had been slipping relentlessly since the beginning of the fourth century; by AD 330, it was small, and genuine coins circulated alongside large numbers of copies of variable quality – a sure sign that inflationary pressures were again developing in the economy, perhaps as a result of military expenditure in connection with the expected campaigning in central Europe. If inflation were left unchecked, however, the damage to trade and, thus, to imperial coherence would be immeasurable. Further, it is clear that the tasks of local government, which fell on wealthy provincials, were becoming more burdensome, as was taxation, with the result that the lower age for qualification was reduced from twenty-five to eighteen, and new laws were required to prevent attempts to avoid such duties. Distress among the local-government class was bound to have an effect on rural prosperity; this, however, did not occur evenly, and there is evidence to suggest that, in Britain, some parts of the countryside were more prosperous than they had ever been – for example, the area of the Cotswold Hills, around Cirencester, which appears to have been one of Britain's most vibrant towns during the fourth century. The contemporary *Panegyrici Latini*, unless they were intended simply to boost a flagging morale, eulogised Britain's agricultural prosperity; it seems that the 'island status' did offer some degree of protection from current difficulties elsewhere.

Two areas of warfare were threatening in the later years of Constantine's reign – the tribes across the Rhine and the Danube, and Sapor II of Persia, with whom Rome's relations were deteriorating. Military campaigns in these areas were put under the control of Constantine's sons and nephews. At the end of the reign (in 337), the empire effectively consisted of five military districts: Constantine II controlled Gaul, Spain and Britain, Constantius II Egypt and the provinces of Asia, while Constans was responsible for Italy, Africa, Pannonia and Dacia. Of the nephews, Delmatius controlled the Balkans and Hannibalianus Armenia, Pontus and Cappadocia. It has to be borne in mind, however, that the character of the western provinces of the empire was changing: imperial territory was heavily settled by people with differing grades of rights, who had come across the frontiers. Certainly, this arrested depopulation in the west, but it was tending in the direction of settlement without Romanisation. Many provinces were becoming barbarised, and so too, therefore, were the workforces (including the army) which were recruited from them.

Despite this, however, there was development and prosperity to be found: while a very large proportion of the land and the workforce was devoted to the growing of wheat, viticulture was spreading northwards, whilst olive growing was making a great impact in Africa; indeed, the prosperity of Africa is obvious from the scale of its buildings and from the quality and the subject matter

Plate 11.4 'Morale-boosting' coins: top, GLORIA EXERCITUS (Constantine I); bottom (left to right), FEL TEMP REPARATIO (Constantius II), GLORIA ROMANORUM (Magnentius), FEL TEMP REPARATIO (Constantius II).

Plate 11.5 Gold solidus of Valentinian II, showing two emperors (Valentinian II and Theodosius) protected by Victoria. Photograph by Philip Cracknell.

of its mosaics. Evidence from the *Panegyrici Latini* further suggests that sheep farming experienced a boost in Britain in the fourth century, presumably as much for the wool as for the meat.

As we have seen, although Constantine ruled his empire with firmness and vision, there were at the time of his death five young men expectant of their inheritance; strife and intrigue had, by the early 350s, reduced this to one – Constantius II. This very intrigue, however, offered opportunity to external enemies whom Constantine had managed largely to keep at bay. The coin issue in celebration of Rome's eleven-hundredth anniversary (in AD 348) was striking for its quality, but illusory in its message: FEL TEMP REPARATIO (or 'Happy days are here again') hardly seems an adequate description – even for a 'soundbite' – of Rome in the middle of the fourth century. Although there were some military successes in these years, few would have seen much of a relationship between the propaganda and the reality of disasters of the like of those that hit the Rhine in 359 or Britain in 367. Yet, the coinage continued for the remainder of the fourth century with the same messages, repeatedly proclaiming glory, victory, security and good health, accompanied by reverse types highlighting Victory figures crowning Roman emperors and emperors dragging captives off to destruction. Yet, even these 'Victory figures' were themselves a pointer to cultural change: although the altar of *Victoria* had, as we have seen, finally been ejected from the senate house around AD 382, on the coinage the familiar figure of 'winged Victory' was evidently becoming the 'Angel of God'; her full Christianisation is achieved on a coin of Valentinian III (AD 417), on which she is depicted holding a prominent cross; the quality of the coin, however, is an equally powerful indicator of the true state of Rome and her empire.

From the middle of the fourth century, although there was some 'room' for social and religious policies, the emphasis was increasingly on warfare and the defence of the frontiers. The empire was now, in the aftermath of Julian's death, in the hands of the House of Valentinian: Valentinian I himself ruled the west (from

Milan), later sharing it with his son, Gratian (Trier); the east was entrusted to Valentinian's brother, Valens (Constantinople). As had happened so often before, external dangers did not bring unity, but opportunities for intrigue – based on such matters as religious division, burdensome taxation or simply ambition. Weak emperors and factious rivals gave external enemies the chances that they needed – indeed, precisely the same 'cocktail' that had caused so much difficulty during the third century.

Valens suffered a major defeat at Adrianople in 378 – a defeat which was probably exaggerated in its seriousness by the contemporary (western) historian, Ammianus Marcellinus; perhaps it was less serious because the east still retained the resilience and the resources of manpower to recover. The last great defender of the west was Rome's Vandal general, Stilicho, defeating the Visigoths (under Alaric) in 401 and the Ostrogoths (under Radagais) in 406. More of his wars, however, were of an internal nature and indicate that Rome and Constantinople, even in these circumstances, were expending precious energy in trying to undermine each other. Constantinople, however, was new and growing; Rome was declining, unable to organise herself in the manner that her enemies clearly could; she was burdened by bureaucracy, strangled by economic decline and shortage of currency. The truth could not be further from the URBS ROMA FELIX proclaimed by the coinage of the last years of the fourth century; the mistress of the world, as this coin issue depicted her, was, in short, a prey to her enemies.

In such circumstances, tensions and rivalries were to be expected both centrally and in individual provinces: in 408, Stilicho was executed; two years later, Rome was sacked and pillaged by Alaric and his Visigoths. Beyond this, the coinage tells its own story, in both style and content: Rome was now part of the barbarian west; her spirit lived on in Constantinople, but she, together with those who had for a millennium been her subjects, was once again in the process of 'becoming different without knowing it'.

Rome's physical remains are, however, evocative of her better times; and it is not difficult to imagine the ghosts of her heroes and villains still present in those gaunt ruins of the city whose civilisation came to shape the western world.

Further Reading

Alfoldi A., *The Conversion of Constantine and Pagan Rome* (Oxford, 1948).

Barnes T. D., *Constantine and Eusebius* (Cambridge, MA, 1981).

Bowden D., *The Age of Constantine and Julian* (London, 1978).

Bowersock G. W., *Julian the Apostate* (London, 1978).

Brown P., *The World of Late Antiquity* (London, 1971).

Brown P., *The Making of Late Antiquity* (Cambridge, MA, 1978).

Browning R., *The Emperor Julian* (London, 1975).

Burckhardt J., *The Age of Constantine the Great* (New York, 1956).

Chadwick H., *The Early Church* (London, 1967).

Christensen A. S., *Lactantius the Historian* (Copenhagen, 1980).

Dodds E. R., *Pagan and Christian in an Age of Anxiety* (Cambridge, 1965).

Esmonde Cleary A. S., *The Ending of Roman Britain* (London, 1989).

Ferrill A., *The Fall of the Roman Empire* (London, 1986).

Frend W. H. C., *The Rise of Christianity* (London, 1984).

Guterman S. L., *Religious Toleration and Persecution in Ancient Rome* (London, 1951).

Janes D., *Romans and Christians* (Stroud, 2002).

Johnson A. S., *Later Roman Britain* (London, 1980).

Jones A. H. M., *Constantine and the Conversion of Europe* (London, 1948).

Jones A. H. M., Martindale J. R. and Morris J., *The Prosopography of the Later Roman Empire, AD 260–395* (Cambridge, 1971).

King C. E. (ed.), *Imperial Revenues, Expenditure and Monetary Policy in the Fourth Century AD* (Oxford, 1980).

Krautheimer R., *Early Christian and Byzantine Architecture* (London, 1965).

Lane Fox R., *Pagans and Christians* (London, 1986).

MacMullen R., *Soldier and Civilian in the Late Roman Empire* (Cambridge, MA, 1963).

MacMullen R., *Enemies of the Roman Order* (Cambridge MA, 1967).

MacMullen R., *Christianising the Roman Empire (AD 100–400)* (New Haven, CT, 1984).

MacMullen R., *Constantine* (London, 1987).

MacMullen R., *Corruption and the Decline of Rome* (New Haven, CT, 1988).

Milburn R., *Early Christian Art and Architecture* (Berkeley, CA, 1988).

Pohlsander H., *The Emperor Constantine* (London, 1996).

Smith J. H., *Constantine the Great* (London, 1971).

Stevenson J., *The Catacombs* (London, 1978).

Syme R., *Ammianus and the Historia Augusta* (Oxford, 1968).

Thompson E. A., *Romans and Barbarians: The Decline of the Western Empire* (Madison, WI, 1982).

Toynbee J. M. C. and Ward-Perkins J. B., *The Shrine of St. Peter* (London, 1956).

Walbank F. W., *The Awful Revolution* (Liverpool, 1978).

Wilmott T., *Birdoswald Roman Fort* (Stroud, 2001).

Wilmott T. and Wilson P. (Eds), *The Late Roman Transition in the North* (*BAR* British Series 299) (Oxford 1999).

INDEX I:

Rome, subjects and locations

INDEX II:
The Empire, places and locations

INDEX III:
Personal and collective names

(Note: Romans will generally be listed under the names of their *gentes*; Emperors, however, will be found in capital letters under the names by which they are usually known.)